Demography and National Security

Demography and National Security

Edited by

Myron Weiner

and

Sharon Stanton Russell

Berghahn Books
NEW YORK • OXFORD

Published in 2001 by

Berghahn Books

www.berghahnbooks.com

© 2001 Myron Weiner and Sharon Stanton Russell

Library of Congress Cataloging-in-Publication Data

Demography and national security / edited by Myron Weiner and
Sharon Stanton Russell.
    p.   cm.
   Includes bibliographical references and index.
   ISBN 1-57181-262-8 (alk. paper)
    1. Population geography. 2. Demography. 3. Emigration and
immigration. 4. National security. I. Weiner, Myron. II. Russell, Sharon
Stanton, 1944–

HB1951 .D453 2001
304.6—dc21   2001025789

British Library Cataloguing in Publication Data

A catalogue record for this book is available from
the British Library.

Printed in the United States on acid-free paper

Contents

List of Illustrations

MAPS

Acknowledgments

This study was made possible by a grant from the Smith Richardson Foundation through the good offices of Nadia Schadlow. Earlier drafts of the chapters were presented at a conference on demography and security held at the Center for International Studies (CIS) of the Massachusetts Institute of Technology, 11–12 December 1998, organized by Myron Weiner under the auspices of the Inter-University Committee on International Migration, which he then chaired. The conference itself took place at a very poignant moment in time: five days earlier, on 7 December, Myron Weiner had been diagnosed with a malignant brain tumor which would lead to his death on 3 June 1999.

I am grateful to the authors and other conference participants who carried on as Myron would have wished, and especially to the Inter-University Committee's Steering Group members Nazli Choucri of MIT and John Harris of Boston University, to MIT colleagues Barry Posen, Lucian Pye, and Stephen Van Evera, and to Susan F. Martin of Georgetown University, all of whom chaired or served as discussants for individual sessions. Jessica Wattman helped to organize the conference and she and fellow MIT graduate students Kelly Greenhill and Sarah Lischer served as rapporteurs, while Alan Kuperman provided research assistance in preparation for the conference. Laurie Scheffler, Adminstrative Assistant at the Center for International Studies, helped to organize not only the conference but also Myron's papers and documents related to this book. She was aided in the latter task by his assistant in the Department of Political Science, Eva Nagy.

Myron's long-time former assistant, Lois Malone, who had served as his Administrative Assistant during his tenure as Director of CIS and later in the Department of Political Science, edited the chapters, produced the final manuscript, and kept this project moving forward. Our colleague Michael Teitelbaum, co-author with Myron Weiner of the related collection of essays entitled *Political Demography, Demographic Engineering* (Berghahn Books 2001), collaborated closely throughout. I am grateful to Myron's wife, Sheila Weiner, their son Saul Weiner, and their daughter Beth Datskovsky for their unflagging support during completion of this volume.

Sharon Stanton Russell

~

Notes on Contributors

T. Alexander Aleinikoff is a Professor of Law at the Georgetown University Law Center, where he teaches courses on immigration, citizenship, and refugee and constitutional law, subjects on which he has written widely. He is also a Senior Associate at the Carnegie Endowment for International Peace, where he serves as director of the Comparative Citizenship Project of the International Migration Policy Program.

Judith Banister is Professor of Demography in the Social Science Division of the Hong Kong University of Science & Technology. She previously headed the International Programs Center of the U.S. Census Bureau. Dr. Banister is author of *China's Changing Population* (Stanford University Press, 1987) and numerous articles and monographs on the demography of China and other Asian countries.

William J. Durch is a senior associate at the Henry L. Stimson Center in Washington, D.C. Prior to joining the Center, he was assistant director and research associate at the Defense and Arms Control Studies Program at MIT, a research fellow at the Harvard Center for Science and International Affairs, and a foreign affairs officer in the U.S. Arms Control and Disarmament Agency. He has taught at Georgetown University and Johns Hopkins SAIS, and both edited and contributed to *UN Peacekeeping, American Policy, and the Uncivil Wars of the 1990s* (St. Martin's Press, 1996) and *The Evolution of UN Peacekeeping: Case Studies and Comparative Analysis* (St. Martin's Press, 1993). He holds a doctorate in international politics and defense studies from MIT.

Jack A. Goldstone is Professor of Sociology and International Relations at the University of California, Davis. He has written and edited numerous books and essays on population, revolution, and social change, including *Revolution and Rebellion in the Early Modern World*, *Revolutions of the Late Twentieth Century*, and *The Encyclopedia of Political Revolutions*. He is a member of the advisory committee of the Woodrow Wilson Center Environment and Security Project.

Sanjoy Hazarika is a former South Asia correspondent for *The New York Times;* he is a Senior Fellow at the Centre for Policy Research, New Delhi; a columnist, documentary film maker and author of *Bhopal: Lessons of a Tragedy; Strangers of the Mist, Tales of War and Peace from India's North East.*

Douglas Klusmeyer is an Associate in the International Migration Policy Program of the Carnegie Endowment for International Peace. He holds both a Ph.D. and a JD from Stanford University. His forthcoming book, edited with T. Alexander Aleinikoff, is *From Migrants to Citizens: Membership in a Changing World.*

Ronald R. Krebs is a doctoral candidate in the Department of Political Science, Columbia University. He has published articles on international relations in such journals as *International Organization* and *Security Studies*, as well as in edited volumes, and is also the author of *Dueling Visions: U.S. Strategy Toward Eastern Europe Under Eisenhower* (2001). He is currently working on his dissertation, which examines the relationship between the structure and policies of military institutions and patterns of effective citizenship. His research has been supported by fellowships from, among others, the John M. Olin Institute for Strategic Studies at Harvard University, the United States Institute of Peace, and the Institute for the Study of World Politics.

Jack S. Levy is Board of Governors' Professor of Political Science at Rutgers University. He has also taught at Tulane, Texas, Stanford, Minnesota, Harvard, Yale, Columbia, and New York University. His research interests concern the causes of war and foreign policy decision-making, and his current research projects include economic interdependence and war, the militarization of commercial rivalries, diversionary theory and politically motivated opposition to war, the conditions under which democracies fight "preventive wars," the conditions under which states engage in balancing behavior, applications of prospect theory to foreign policy and international relations, and the criteria for evaluating successful scientific research programs.

Susan Martin is director of the Institute for the Study of International Migration in the School of Foreign Service at Georgetown University. She has served as the Executive Director of the U.S. Commission on Immigration Reform, and was also the U.S. coordinator for the Binational Study on Migration between Mexico and the United States, a joint study with the Mexican government. Prior to joining the Commission staff, Dr. Martin was the Director of Research and Programs at the Refugee Policy Group. She earned her doctorate in American Studies from the University of Pennsylvania. She served as the managing editor of the *World Migration Report 2000,* published jointly by the International Organization for Migration and the United Nations, and is the author of *Refugee Women* and numerous monographs and articles on immigration and refugee policy.

Terry Martin is an Associate Professor of Russian History at Harvard University. He is the author of *An Affirmative Action Empire: Nations and Nationalism in the Soviet Union, 1923–1939* (Cornell University Press, 2001).

He is currently researching a book on the politics and sociology of information in the Soviet Union under Stalin.

Sharon Stanton Russell is a political scientist and Research Scholar at the Center for International Studies, MIT, where she chairs the Steering Group of the Inter-University Committee on International Migration and directs the Mellon-MIT Inter-University Program on Non-Governmental Organizations and Forced Migration. Her research focuses on global migration trends and policies, the relationship of migration to development, and forced migration. Her publications include, "International Migration: Global Trends and National Responses"; "Migration Patterns of U.S. Foreign Policy Interest"; "Migrant Remittances and Development"; *International Migration and International Trade*; and *International Migration and Development in Sub-Saharan Africa*. Dr. Russell has served as a member of two United Nations Expert Groups on international migration and has consulted extensively on migration policy issues with private foundations and UN organizations. She has been a member of the Expert Panel on Global Population Projections (1998–2000) and of the Roundtable on the Demography of Forced Migration (1999–2001), both convened by the Committee on Population of the U.S. National Academy of Science, and serves on the Academic Advisory Board of the International Organization for Migration.

Michael S. Teitelbaum is a foundation executive at the Alfred P. Sloan Foundation, New York. By background he is a demographer, educated at Reed College and at Oxford University, where he was a Rhodes Scholar. He has served previously on the faculties of Oxford University and Princeton University; as Staff Director of the Select Committee on Population, U.S. House of Representatives; and on the professional staffs of the Ford Foundation and the Carnegie Endowment for International Peace. From 1988 to 1990 he served as a Commissioner of the U.S. Commission for the Study of International Migration and Cooperative Economic Development, and from 1991 to 1997 as a Commissioner and Vice Chair of the U.S. Commission on Immigration Reform. He has been elected to numerous honorific positions, including First Vice President of the Population Association of America and Fellow of the American Association for the Advancement of Science. He is the author of many scientific articles, and has written or edited six books on demography and international migration.

Riwanto Tirtosudarmo is a social demographer and senior researcher at the Indonesian Institute of Sciences, where he is also director of the Centre for Social and Cultural Studies. He publishes extensively in scientific and popular journals on the politics of population mobility in Indonesia and Southeast Asia, and is the author of *The Political Demography of Development in Indonesia: From Riau to East Timor*. A Visiting Fulbright Fellow at the Department of Sociology, Brown University (1996–97), and

Fellow-in-Residence 2000–2001 at the Netherlands Institute for Advanced Study in Humanities and Social Sciences (NIAS), he is conducting research on the political demography of ethnicity in Indonesia and preparing a book, *From Colonization to National-State: The Political Demography of Indonesia.*

Myron Weiner was Professor of Political Science at the Massachusetts Institute of Technology, former Director of MIT's Center for International Studies, and Chair of the External Research Advisory Committee of the United Nations High Commissioner for Refugees. He was the author or editor of numerous books and articles in the field of development, on South Asian politics, and on international migration, including *Temporary Workers or Future Citizens? Japanese and U.S. Migration Policies* (1998), *Migrants, Refugees, and Foreign Policy: U.S. and German Policies toward Countries of Origin* (1997), *The Global Migration Crisis: Challenge to States and to Human Rights* (1995); *Threatened Peoples, Threatened Borders: World Migration and U.S. Policy* (1995); *International Migration and Security* (1993); and *The Child and the State in India: Child Labor and Education Policy in Comparative Perspective* (1991). Professor Weiner taught or held research appointments at Princeton University, the University of Chicago, Harvard University, Delhi University, Hebrew University, the University of Paris, and Balliol College, Oxford. He was a member of the American Academy of Arts and Sciences, chaired the MIT-based Inter-University Committee on International Migration, and for 35 years co-chaired the joint Harvard-MIT Seminar on Political Development. Myron Weiner died at his home in Vermont in June 1999.

≈

Introduction

Myron Weiner and
Sharon Stanton Russell

As some global threats to security have receded with the end of the cold war and the breakup of the Soviet Union, others have emerged to take their place. Among the newly salient perceived threats to the security of peoples and their states are the rapid world population growth that has taken place since the Second World War and its long-term sequelae, great disparities in population growth within and between developed and developing countries, and increasingly large-scale movements of people within states and across international boundaries.

Demographic variables—fertility, mortality, migration, and the growth or decline of populations—have been variously characterized as important determinants of violent conflict and political instability, national power, imperial expansion, ethnic conflict, radicalism, terrorism, religious fundamentalism, environmental degradation, and economic growth and stagnation. Some observers contend that population density and rapid population growth will lead to the breakdown of regimes, or, alternatively, that they will lead countries to become militarily expansionist in the quest for more territory; others argue that international migration, whether or not it contributes to economic growth, could erode national identity, national sovereignty, and stability.

Political Demography Revisited

This volume addresses the ways in which demographic factors, alone or in conjunction with other variables, affect the stability and security of states and societies. Its three parts deal with three sets of questions about the relationship between demography and security.

The first set of questions deals with what we actually know and do not know about how changes in demographic variables—population size, growth, distribution, and composition—influence a country's political stability and real or perceived threats to its security. An example is whether illegal migration across international borders is in part the combined result of high population growth rates in developing countries and stagnant or declining population in developed countries; another is whether and how changes in population variables are associated with environmental degradation, increased risks of internal conflict, and international wars. A related question is how population size and growth affect military power, economic development, national power, and international conflict. Part I of this volume undertakes a critical examination of theories about the links between demography and security, what they purport to explain, the weight they assign to demographic variables as determinants of security outcomes, their predictive and prescriptive values, and the empirical evidence upon which each of these theories rests.

The second set of questions pertains to how governments respond to demographic trends, or what may be called "population-responsive policies." What policies do governments adopt to deal with the consequences of population changes, and how do these policies in turn affect political stability and security? How, for example, do governments respond to an influx of illegal migrants across their borders? Do they interdict boats at sea? Do they use their armed forces to prevent entry? How do governments respond to having significant portions of their populations abroad or significant numbers of foreign nationals in their midst? Under what circumstances do they opt for plural citizenship, and what are the implications of that choice? What foreign policy initiatives do governments adopt to manage international migration and mitigate its security consequences? Part II considers how states have responded to these questions in the context of demographic change.

The third set of questions concerns how governments attempt to change demographic variables in an effort to enhance national security. For example, when and how do governments engage in "demographic engineering" by promoting the movement of people within their territories or across international borders in order to achieve security objectives? Part III of this volume examines empirical cases in which states have sought proactively to "engineer" the composition, status, and location of population groups for security purposes.

A brief discussion is in order about what we mean by "national security." Threats to security have traditionally been seen as highly specific: "Country X is an enemy, and possesses the following military capabilities that we must confront." Now the threats are understood to be far more diffuse. For example, they emanate not only from governments, but from small groups of terrorists, or ethnic groups that seek power or separation in ways that challenge existing regimes and may produce large and destabilizing numbers of internally displaced persons or the flight of refugees across the border. Alternatively, the threats or perceived threats may be from large numbers of individuals who want to cross borders in search of jobs or a better life. In addition, security threats are now also seen to include environmental factors.

As Jack Goldstone observes in this volume, "a more realistic definition of security today would include any action or event that can create
outcomes deemed harmful or undesirable by nations and that require
mitigating diplomatic or military action." In keeping with such a
post–cold war conception of security, the term "national security" as used
in this volume pertains to non-military as well as military threats, and to
threats that may arise from domestic, internal sources of instability as
well as those arising from external, international sources.

Where does demography fit into this picture? In a 1971 essay, Myron
Weiner provided the following answer:

> Political demography is the study of the size, composition, and distribution of
> population in relation to both government and politics. It is concerned with
> the political consequences of population change, especially the effects of pop-
> ulation change on the demands made upon governments, on the performance
> of governments, and on the distribution of political power. It also considers
> the political determinants of population change, especially the political causes
> of the movement of people, the relationship of various population configura-
> tions to the structures and functions of government, and the public policy
> directed at affecting the size, composition, and distribution of populations.
> Finally, in the study of political demography it is not enough to know the facts
> and figures of populations—that is the fertility, mortality, and migration rates;
> it is also necessary to consider the knowledge and attitudes that people have
> toward population issues. (Weiner 1971: 567)

In the years since this definition of political demography was articulated, a substantial body of literature has developed on how rapid population growth generates political conflict within states. Although much of
this literature provides a nightmarish, apocalyptic vision, more thought-
ful studies note that the effects of rapid population growth are condi-
tional upon the presence or absence of intervening variables. In a society
with a low rate of economic growth and rising unemployment, for example, a rapidly increasing population has different consequences for young
people than in a society with rapid economic growth and an expanding
demand for labor. Similarly, a growing population increases the demand
for education, food, health services, transportation, water, and land; but
societies have very different political, financial, and administrative capacities to respond to these demands.

To the question, then, of whether rapid population growth can constitute a threat to the stability of a government, the security of a regime,
and the security of its citizens, the answer is yes, but only under certain
conditions. Scholars and policy makers, therefore, have given attention
not only to attenuating the rate of population growth, but also to formulating measures that respond to the fact of growing population size and
to the institutional structures that facilitate or impede these policy
responses. Conjectures about the international—as distinct from domestic—consequences of rapid population growth are in large part derived

from this prior analysis. If such growth contributes to environmental degradation and scarcity within a country (a shortage of water, for example), the result may be conflict with a neighboring country. If rapid population growth is a factor in the escalation of violent conflict within a country, for example as a consequence of the emergence of a large unemployed youth cohort, there may be international security effects, such as the flight of refugees. Some argue that population growth enhances national power and that the growing share of world population found in developing regions may constitute a potential security threat to countries of the more slowly growing developed regions. Others hold that rapid population growth makes a country less stable and slows its rate of economic growth, and that changes in military technology have made population size a less significant factor in national power.

In recent years, scholars have pointed to other international consequences of population change. Some have hypothesized that low rates of population growth and aging populations in developed countries, coincident with high population growth rates and young populations in low-income countries, may result in large-scale population movements. Studies conducted under the auspices of the International Organization for Migration and UNFPA (Appleyard 1999), for example, postulate that demographic and economic disparities have created a high potential for world-wide migration that is likely to persist throughout the twenty-first century.

Others have hypothesized that there is a relationship between population growth, environmental degradation, and the availability of both renewable and non-renewable resources. The most sophisticated political analysis along these lines, the Project on Environmental Scarcities, State Capacity, and Civil Violence, sponsored by the University of Toronto and the American Academy of Arts and Sciences and directed by Thomas Homer-Dixon (popularized by Robert Kaplan in his 1994 article in *The Atlantic Monthly*), focuses on how environmental scarcities may undermine state capacity. Scarcities of renewable resources, it is argued, may contribute significantly to ethnic conflicts, population flight, and elite struggles over resources (Homer-Dixon 1991, 1994; Homer-Dixon, Boutwell, and Rathjens, 1993).

This body of literature and the theories it propounds are in need of critical review. Professional demographers have largely ignored the topic of political demography, or have been critical of what they see as exaggerated claims about the consequences of population growth. On the other hand, some have incorporated demographic analysis into areas of scholarship and public policy, such as the future of national health care and social security systems, education and housing policies, and urban and regional planning. There is now also a large body of work on national and international migration and on the causes and consequences of refugee flows, but much of it emanates from disciplines other than demography.

Similarly, political scientists and international relations scholars have seldom incorporated demographic considerations into their analyses of conflicts between states, or into analyses of how developments within states shape international conflict—the latest of their concerns. To the "realist" school of international relations scholars, the questions posed by those who use demographic data have seemed too remote. Many political scientists consider the work of demographers to be technical and dull, focussed on data-gathering and number-crunching, and concerned with narrow aspects of fertility, mortality, and migration, rather than with matters of political import. Perhaps, as some ecologists argue, the world's ecosystems (or at least some countries') have a limited carrying capacity; but even if that were true, what could it mean for national security strategies? Moreover, it is often difficult to ascertain when a demographic variable is a determinant of a security threat or simply one possible contributing factor.

While many scholars have eschewed examining the relationship between demography and security, practitioners have come to pay greater attention to these connections. Militaries use demographic analysis to assess the future availability of military manpower, while security agencies track the likely loci of global humanitarian emergencies that might evoke a military response. Foreign policy analysts now recognize that forced movements of populations are not simply a consequence of repression and civil war, but can also be a factor in generating conflict between states and in the use of force by others—witness the U.S. intervention in Haiti, undertaken in part to end the influx of Haitian migrants to Florida in small boats; the foreign policy issues posed by people fleeing Castro's Cuba; the U.S. decision to create a "safe area" for the Kurds in northern Iraq to prevent them from fleeing to Turkey; and the NATO intervention in and around Kosovo.

Still, we have only begun to identify the important issues in the relationship between demography and national security and to find empirical ways to examine it. This volume, and the project on which it is based, seeks to advance the intellectual frontiers of both theory and evidence about demography and security.

Patterns of Demographic Change

Government officials, politicians, journalists, and scholars have delineated at least three major regional or global demographic changes that may be expected to have a significant impact on security by generating conflicts within and between states. First among these demographic phenomena is the changing size and the global distribution of the natural increase in the world's population, which, between 1950 and 2000, more than doubled—from 2.5 to 6 billion. During the 1980s and 1990s, world population increased by a billion people every 12 or 13 years, with almost all that growth occurring in low-income countries. In 1950, the share of the world's population living in industrial regions was 32 percent; by 1998, that share was down to 20 percent (United Nations 1998a: xviii, Table 3). Rates of global population growth slowed to 1.33 percent per year between 1995 and 2000 (from a peak growth rate of 2.04 in 1965–1970), and, in the UN's "medium fertility variant," are projected to decline further, to 0.34 percent per year in 2045–2050.

However, even as fertility rates decline in many developing countries, population momentum resulting from the large numbers of young women already born ensures continued substantial population growth for several generations. In a number of developing countries, HIV/AIDS has significantly increased mortality and decreased fertility, but even in those most affected, HIV/AIDS is not projected to result in a decline in absolute population size, because fertility rates remain high (United Nations 1998b: 58, 63). As a result, the population of developing regions, estimated at 4.7 billion in 1998, is projected to increase by 64 percent to 7.8 billion by 2050 (United Nations 1998a: xvii).

In contrast, the population of the more developed regions is projected to decline slightly (by 2 percent) by 2050. The German-speaking area of Europe—Germany, Austria, Switzerland, Luxembourg—was the first major cultural area to fall below replacement. Now China, Japan, and virtually every European country (including Italy and Spain—high-growth countries only a generation ago) are experiencing below-replacement fertility, that is, fewer than two children per couple. Indeed, the countries of Europe and Japan are projected to decrease in population size by 2050 (United Nations 2000: 6, Table I.1). What will be the effects of these marked differentials in population growth rates between developed and developing regions, upon the balance of military and economic power?

This leads us to international migration, the second significant element of global demographic change. In countries with low or negative rates of natural population increase, migration looms large as a determinant of population growth. In the United States one-third of population growth between 1990 and 1995 was the result of migration; in Germany, Italy, the Russian Federation, and Ukraine, net migration accounted for all population growth in this period (United Nations 1998b: 53, Table 27). Migrants and their children are more visible—in schools, in the work force, in neighborhoods, and in their claims on social services—than ever before, not necessarily because their numbers are increasing any more rapidly than previously, but because the numbers of natives are increasing more slowly.

The United Nations (1998c: 4) estimates that the world's stock of foreign-born or foreign nationals grew from 75 million in 1965 to 120 million in 1990, the last year for which census data are available. Although, as a percentage of the world's population, the international migrant stock has varied little—only 2.3 percent in both 1965 and 1990—in some countries the percentage of foreign-born in 1990 was significantly higher: over 90 percent of the population in the United Arab Emirates, 72 percent in Kuwait, 31 percent in Israel, 23 percent in Australia, 16 percent in Switzerland, 15 percent in Canada, and from 6 to 10 percent in the United States, Germany, France, and Belgium (United Nations 1998c). However, a relatively low percentage of migrants in a country's total population is no guarantee that migration will not become a salient political issue, as it has done in Austria and Spain, where the foreign-born constitute less than six percent and two percent of the population, respectively.

Countries of origin and destination have changed significantly. Migration is no longer from Europe outward (as it was for a century before 1950), but from Asia and Latin America to the United States, Canada, Australia, and Europe, from Asia and the former Soviet Union to the Middle East, from one developing country to another, and including large refugee movements within Africa, parts of Asia, and Southeastern Europe.

One feature of these movements is their consequences for the unmixing and mixing of peoples. In some countries or territories, wars, civil conflict, and ethnic cleansing have led to the unmixing of peoples, as newly formed countries engaged in their own form of nation-building or as long-standing ethnic rivalries flared. Bosnia, Rwanda, and Kosovo are but a few examples. Other migration processes have led to *greater* ethnic diversity within countries—as people in one country seek higher wages, jobs, and land, as well as protection, by crossing international borders to another country. International migrants are now more likely than before to retain ties to their countries of origin, and a few migrant-receiving countries have redefined themselves as multicultural. Islam is now the second largest religion in Europe; Hispanics will soon outnumber African-Americans in the United States; Asia is now the principal source of migration flows into Australia; in Israel, Jews and their children from the former Soviet Union may soon be more numerous than those who migrated from the Middle East. The new diasporas may prove more durable than older ones. The declining costs of telecommunications and increasing access to the Internet enables migrants and their children to maintain ties with a homeland and to sustain their own distinctive cultural boundaries.

The third notable global demographic trend is the changing age distribution. In one respect the trend is hardly new. The size of the youth cohort increased with population growth, first in Western Europe in the nineteenth century, then in Eastern Europe in the first quarter of the twentieth century, then in Asia, Africa, and Latin America from the middle of the twentieth century onward. There appeared to be a noticeable relationship between the "youth bulge," youth protest movements against all forms of authority, and attempts to bring down governments. In Paris in 1968, Dacca in 1971, Tehran in the late 1970s, Manila in 1986, in Tiananmen Square in 1989, and in Jakarta in 1998, youth and student protests have challenged regimes.

How countries use their youth cohort has significant political consequences. With the introduction of compulsory military service in most of

Europe in the nineteenth century, many young men of violent disposition were removed from civil society; young men were sent abroad, to fight, to administer, and to colonize, all alternatives to crime and protest at home. There was also virtually free world-wide migration for young people in Europe to North and South America, Australia, and to colonies in Africa and Asia.

The situation for young people is markedly different today in many developing countries, where unemployment rates are high as a result of the youth bulge. In many cases where central authority has eroded, as it has in much of Africa, young men are the backbone of mercenary forces in the service of political freebooters—warlords, religious fundamentalists, ethnic leaders—and of all varieties of protest movements aiming to acquire control over state resources and the production and sale of oil, minerals, and drugs. These activities are facilitated by the increased availability of arms on the global market, and the ease with which grenades, Kalashnikovs, Stinger missiles, and even nuclear materials can be moved across national boundaries at remarkably low prices, payable by trafficking in drugs and in illegal migrants, and through remittances from overseas ethnics.

The future may be very different: the projected changes in fertility and mortality noted earlier will also bring changes in the age compositions of both developed and developing regions. In the former, the percentage of the population below age 15 is projected to decline from around 20 percent in 1995 to 15 percent of total population in 2050, while the percentage aged 60 and over is projected to rise from 18 to nearly 33 percent over the same time period. In the developing regions, similar— but even more dramatic—patterns of change are expected to emerge: Those under age 15 are projected to decline from 34 to 20 percent of total population, while those age 60 and over are expected to increase from 7 percent in 1995 to over 20 percent of total population in 2050 (United Nations 1998a: 4–6, Table A.1). If, as these projections suggest, the youth bulge declines in many countries over the next half century, as it already has in Eastern Europe and Russia, should we anticipate a decline in protest movements, less radicalism, less violence, less crime?

The aging of populations in Europe and Japan, together with projected declines in absolute population size, may also have implications for the future of international migration. For example, even assuming some in-migration, Italy's total population is projected to decrease from 57 million in 2000 to 41 million by 2050, while the working-age population is projected to decrease from 39 million to 22 million in the same period. To maintain its current population size to 2050, Italy would need to take in an average of 235,000 migrants annually; to maintain its ratio of working-age (15–64 years) to retirement age (65+ years) population would require millions of immigrants (United Nations 2000: 1; 45; 114, Table A.6). We cannot predict how countries with aging populations will respond, but these changing demographic conditions will present serious challenges to countries already ambivalent about their immigrant populations.

Population Dynamics and National Security: Theories and Evidence

The demographic changes outlined above form the backdrop for this volume, Part I of which considers the broad theoretical and empirical links between demography and security and how changes in demographic variables influence political stability and real or perceived threats to security. Michael Teitelbaum begins this inquiry by assessing the extent to which major demographic, economic, and other social science theories have contributed to our understanding of why international migration occurs. He concludes that no single body of theory suffices to explain international population movements. Each has useful insights to offer, but a synthetic approach offers better understanding. Moreover, extant theories largely neglect the role of the state in initiating, regulating, and controlling international migration. A balanced appraisal would include not only the importance of controls used by individual states to manage migration, but also the effects on population movements of international and regional agreements and of opposition to both immigration controls and international intervention.

In considering the likely future of migration, Teitelbaum argues that policies of receiving governments will be affected by cultural and historical factors, the structure of political institutions and norms of political debate, and public perceptions of the effects of migration. He concludes that a predictive theory of migration is elusive, as it would require "predicting the unknowable": how people and their governments will respond to future experiences with international migration.

Jack Goldstone turns our attention to the links among demography, environment, and security, distinguishing security problems characterized by violent armed conflicts from those that, while non-violent in nature, pose challenges for diplomacy and hence become issues of national and international security. Is environmental change or scarcity a major cause of violent conflicts? Goldstone and others he cites find little evidence to support this contention. International environmental conflicts are generally settled without resort to arms; in the domestic political arena, conflicts over environmental issues (where they exist) tend to be confined to elite factions. On the other hand, short-term natural and man-made disasters have resulted in more widespread unrest, notably when the state is seen to be responsible for causing or failing to respond adequately to these events.

While overall population growth or increases in density generally do not lead to violent conflict, Goldstone notes that a number of analysts have found the presence of a youth bulge to be a major factor in political conflicts, especially when those youths are relatively highly educated and urbanized, with low employment prospects. Specific demographic variables (youth bulge, urbanization/development ratio, life expectancy, and adult and infant mortality) are useful predictors of political violence, but it is also the case that violent conflicts can have large and long-lasting effects on demography—creating shifts in age and gender composition, marriage and birth rates, and population distribution that increase the potential for renewed conflict in the future.

Non-violent security issues, such as production of ozone-depleting gases, climate change (global warming), the generation of toxic wastes, and threats to species diversity constitute a new security arena in which the condition of the environment itself is the security threat. Goldstone concludes that such issues cannot be dealt with effectively by deployment of armed force; rather, it will require sustained international negotiations and new cooperative arrangements to ameliorate their threats.

In their chapter, Ronald Krebs and Jack Levy systematically consider the conditions under which demographic changes may pose security threats. They conclude that neither population growth nor size translates smoothly into military power and effectiveness; rather these connections are mediated by factors such as "resolve" and technological capability. Considering in turn the relationships between (1) population growth and economic development (as the latter relates to national power); (2) national power and international conflict; and (3) population growth and international conflict as mediated by resource scarcity, the authors find linkages between these variables to be indeterminate outside specific societal and institutional contexts. They posit three causal mechanisms leading from population factors to resource scarcity to international conflict: the use of military force to eliminate scarcity; the provocation of external conflict to divert domestic opposition; and "opportunistic" military intervention in cases of resource scarcity combined with political weakness.

Krebs and Levy further assess the hypothesis that differential population growth rates among ethnic groups change the distribution of power and lead to ethnic tension and conflict. Although some empirical cases (Russia, Lebanon) seem to support this contention, the authors find that the hypothesis lacks firm theoretical grounding and fails to recognize "identity" as a variable. They argue for more attention to elucidating conditions under which ethnicity becomes salient and suggest several causal mechanisms that may link ethnic tensions to international conflict. Similarly, they identify pathways by which international migration and international conflict may be linked. Of the various relationships considered, the authors find the most promising area for future research to be in the domain of migration and ethnic conflict.

State Responses to Demographic Trends

How do states respond to demographic changes in their midst? Part II considers three types of response: the use of militaries to control borders, the character of citizenship laws, and efforts to manage the security implications of migration through foreign policy discussions.

Defending territorial borders against "unwanted entry" is one of the oldest roles of military institutions, although, as William Durch reminds us, regular militaries have not only protected borders but also helped to produce mass exodus. He suggests that the greater the levels of political hostility within origin countries or between origin and destination countries, and the greater the economic disparities between them, the more likely is a militarized response. Collaboration among police, paramilitary, and regular military forces in the control of entry is a feature in virtually all the cases Durch examines—the United States, Russia, the European Union, Turkey, India, and South Africa.

Durch concludes that militarized border controls are costly and difficult to apply (especially in cases of mass exodus), and their efficacy varies widely: Altering "push factors" in countries of origin and "pull factors" in countries of destination may prove to be more effective medium-term strategies. He cautions however that, with the involvement of organized crime in human smuggling, distinctions between illegal migrants and bona fide asylum seekers are becoming blurred, a circumstance that poses serious threats to the international refugee regime.

A second arena in which governments have been challenged to respond to demographic changes is citizenship law. Douglas Klusmeyer and Alexander Aleinikoff outline the issues posed by the increasing incidence of plural nationality. They first consider the concept of nationality under domestic and international law. Although nationality policy is traditionally the purview of sovereign states, international legal norms have qualified this authority. The chapter reviews the principal means by which nationality may be acquired and lost, as well as the complexities that arise when multiple states are involved in these processes.

Klusmeyer and Aleinikoff attribute the rising incidence of plural nationality to a number of factors: most importantly, the lack of agreement among states over rules governing acquisition and loss of nationality, but also the extant conflicting combinations of *jus soli* and *jus sanguinis*; changes in how gender factors into nationality policies; and the globalization of travel and commerce. They see little likelihood that states will agree on an enforceable set of uniform standards for the acquisition and loss of nationality, given the wide divergence of interests among states. Migrant-receiving states are traditionally more concerned with allegiance, while states of origin are more concerned with protecting their nationals abroad and encouraging ties with the home country. Despite historic objections to plural nationality and the existence of several potential points of tension (voting and office holding by plural nationals; perceived "unfair advantages" of plural nationals; and divisibility of loyalty and community building), Klusmeyer and Aleinikoff conclude that the increasing incidence of plural nationality has not been and is not likely to become a major source of conflicts between states, nor to subvert the international order.

The security aspects of international migration have become increasingly prominent issues on foreign policy agendas, notably in the context of regional economic and political integration. Multilateral regional approaches to addressing the security dimensions of migration started in Europe with development of the European Union and the collapse of the Soviet Union; they have evolved as well in the Asia-Pacific region and the CIS. More recently, the economic and security implications of migration have prompted bilateral, regional, and hemispheric initiatives in the Americas. The latter are the focus of Susan Martin's chapter, which examines four arenas: the North American Free Trade Agreement (NAFTA); the U.S.-Mexico Binational Commission; the Puebla Process; and the Summit of the Americas.

Martin argues that discussions of migration and security surrounding NAFTA created a new, more cooperative phase in U.S.-Mexican relations by fostering a bilateral approach to easing migration pressures and managing migration, in contrast to earlier unilateral approaches. As a byproduct of the NAFTA process, other bilateral mechanisms have been strengthened. In addition to these national-level efforts, a number of state and local government initiatives, as well as private forums, have emerged. However, Martin cautions that responses to immigration still tend to be episodic: negative in times of economic stress and less intense when economic conditions improve.

International migration has also become more prominent in multilateral relations within the Americas, as the so-called Puebla Process illustrates. While this regional process is not without its weaknesses, Martin contends that its potential as a forum for resolution of divisive issues represents an important contribution to cooperation on migration matters and to the reduction of potential sources of domestic instability and international conflict. At the hemispheric level, discussions of migration are in their infancy, but have been a subject at the Summits of the Americas.

The growth of bilateral, regional, and hemispheric approaches signals a fundamental shift in perspective. Long viewed as a matter of purely national sovereignty meriting only unilateral policies to address national security concerns arising from population movements, migration has come to be recognized as a matter of collective international interest and a salient topic on governments' foreign policy agendas. This is not to say that traditional unilateral security and economic concerns will not assert themselves, but the "habit of cooperation" being developed through these mechanisms may lead to new breakthroughs in cooperative action for more effective management of international migration and its security implications.

Demographic Engineering for National Security Objectives

Part III of this volume turns to a subject that has been relatively neglected in the theoretical academic literature, concerning which empirical case studies are only beginning to appear: When and how do states proactively engage in efforts to enhance their stability and security by "engineering" the composition, status, and geographical distribution of their populations? The four case studies presented here address this question and begin to provide empirical, comparative data on which theory may be built.

In the first case study of "demographic engineering," Riwanto Tirtosudarmo traces the evolution of Indonesia's population relocation (known as "transmigration") policies, beginning with the Dutch colonial period in the mid-nineteenth century and continuing through the late twentieth century. Indonesia's transmigration policies involve government-organized efforts to move populations from densely populated Java to previously uncultivated, or sporadically or illegally cultivated, lands in the other islands. While the general process of transmigration has remained relatively unchanged over the years, the stated objectives of these policies have varied considerably. In addition to the demographic aims of reducing population growth in Java and promoting a more balanced population distribution, social, political, economic, and—most importantly for this volume—security objectives have been invoked at various times, depending upon the changing influence of various political actors. These objectives have included improving conditions of the indigenous population, promoting national unity and national integration, providing cheap labor for plantations in sparsely populated areas, promoting industrialization, and integrating Indonesia into the regional and global economies. Transmigration policies have also been undertaken for explicit security reasons: to mitigate social and political unrest and to strengthen national defense.

Tirtosudarmo concludes that Indonesia's transmigration policies have had little effect on reducing population growth in Java or on population distribution in the archipelago, although they have had great demographic impact on the receiving areas. The pursuit of transmigration policies clearly illustrates the power of the central government over affairs in the country's regions, but the changing goals of the policies, along with frequent changes in the government agencies implementing them, also reflect the rivalries among economist-technocrats, government bureaucrats, and the military, as a result of which the program has never been carefully monitored or evaluated. From the mid-1980s onward, he argues, implementation of transmigration policy foundered for internal management and budgetary reasons and because of mounting international criticism.

The main legacy of transmigration policy, Tirtosudarmo concludes, has been to provide the ruling elites with a tool for defending their political and economic interests, and for subjugating rebellious indigenous groups perceived as threats to the regime. Given its instrumental value, transmigration is likely to continue on Indonesia's policy agenda.

Sanjoy Hazarika examines three cases of demographic engineering: Bangladesh, Myanmar, and Bhutan. Although these countries have dissimilar political systems, all three share a history of ethnic conflicts, and all three have played a role in creating conditions of internal instability that have uprooted entire communities and generated flows of refugees to neighboring countries. Hazarika reviews the policies adopted by each state toward its ethnic minorities, the instruments used to effect the removal of these minorities, and the factors that have conditioned the resolution or persistence of these conflicts.

Despite significant differences among them, all three cases involve a religious and linguistic majority pitted against a smaller religious and linguistic minority that, to varying degrees, has resorted to violence to assert its identity. All three states have used similar tools of demographic engineering in attempts to cope with the perceived security threats posed by minority groups, including denial of citizenship rights, intimidation, forced displacement, and resettlement of "friendly" groups on vacated lands. Illustrating the point that demographic engineering has international as well as domestic dimensions, each situation has also involved an outside actor or "meddling neighbor": India in the case of the Chakmas in Bangladesh, Bangladesh in the case of the Rohingyas in Myanmar, and Nepal in the case of the Lhotsampas in Bhutan. International organizations have had only a limited role in these confrontations, and only one situation—that of the Chakmas in Bangladesh—has reached a settlement, albeit an uneasy one. Hazarika concludes that only cessation of provocative interference by neighboring states, more sensitive and steady involvement of regional bodies and international organizations such as UNHCR, and the firm establishment of democracy will help to defuse these complex conflicts and ensure genuine national security for the countries in question.

For at least three millennia, government-sponsored migrations in China have been undertaken to secure state borders, to further policies of political and social integration and economic development, to mitigate the effects of natural disasters, and as a means to exert government control over the rich and powerful. Judith Banister's chapter focuses on the goals and results of government-directed migration to three of the most potentially explosive border regions of the People's Republic of China: the Muslim-populated and Russian-influenced province of Xinjiang; the Inner Mongolia Autonomous Region (IMAR); and the Tibet Autonomous Region (TAR).

Migration policies and their outcomes have differed in these three areas. In Xinjiang, the policy first aimed to increase the proportion of Han Chinese (who constituted 94 percent of total Mainland China's population in 1949, but only 7 percent of Xinjiang's population), and then—in the face of higher rates of natural increase among the province's minorities—to maintain the Han proportion through continued positive net Han migration. In Inner Mongolia, Han control was assured before 1949 through migration and, while there was some directed Han migration to the province during the Great Leap Forward, this subsequently ceased, as it was not needed for economic and political control. In Tibet, Banister argues that there has been no policy to promote massive permanent migration of Han; rather, maintenance of security has been sought through a strong military and police presence and through small numbers of cadres.

On balance, Banister concludes that the PRC has consolidated its control over these three border provinces, partly through Han in-migration and partly through a strong and visible Han military presence. Economic opportunities for minorities have increased and health conditions and educational attainment have generally improved, although economic development has been uneven. On the other hand, Han in-migration, along with increased ethnic consciousness, has also brought resentment, cultural clashes, and increased instability within the three regions and heightened tensions with some neighboring countries. The long-term security consequences of China's demographic engineering may well depend upon the extent to which minorities benefit from future development of their provinces.

Although other states have forcibly relocated more people than did the Soviet Union under Stalin, the Stalinist state was unique in the complexity of its forced relocation policies, the variety of political goals pursued, the diversity of population categories deported, and the frequency of mass deportations. Terry Martin traces the patterns, causes, and consequences of this grim exercise in demographic engineering, drawing upon archives that became available only after the fall of the Soviet Union.

Stalinist mass deportation was "categoric," focussing on stigmatized population categories, and "prophylactic," removing individuals not for what they had done, but for the threats to security they might pose. Martin distinguishes two major types of deportation: "sovietization deportations" to establish the Communist Party's rule, and "security deportations," aimed at potentially disloyal population groups. He also identifies four minor types of deportation undertaken to remove "harmful social elements"; to further ethnic homogeneity; to remove ethnic minorities and promote russification; and to exact retribution.

Martin argues that while the long-term consequences of Stalinist forced relocations for countries of the former Soviet Union are not negligible, they are also not as significant as often asserted. One notable exception is Chechnya, although causes of conflict there are multiple. Perhaps the most important long-term consequence is the contribution of the deportations to the perception of the Soviet Union as an empire, a perception crucial to its collapse.

Martin concludes from the Stalinist case that internal forced relocation is not especially robust in the long term; most of those displaced have been allowed to return. Diaspora nationalities are an exception: The territorial claims of "indigenous" nationalities were given precedence over those of groups (such as the Volga Germans) with "homelands" outside the former Soviet Union. In contrast, international forced relocations, such as those of

Poles and Ukrainians, have been more permanent. Martin argues that voluntary migration in a multiethnic state is potentially more consequential than forced migration. He contends that the outflow of Russians to non-Russian republics had little to do with forced relocation policies, but was rather the combined result of a high degree of social mobilization among the Russian population, its large size, the tendency of many non-Russians to russify, and the decision to forbid the republics to control migration.

Conclusion

Comprehensive, generalizable theories remain elusive that can explain the linkages between demography and security and predict their implications. Inevitably, many variables intervene between causes and consequences, outcomes are highly contextual, and data limitations confound empirical analyses. Nonetheless, this volume suggests that careful efforts to chart the pathways linking population growth, composition, and distribution to security can deepen our understanding of how demographic factors affect the potential for conflict—or its mitigation. With or without robust social science theories, states continue to respond to changes in demography by controlling their borders, adjusting their citizenship laws, and finding new ways to address the security implications of population movements through foreign policy channels. States also continue to engage in proactive policies to engineer the composition and distribution of their populations for security purposes.

Further efforts to elucidate the relationships between demography and national security are critical for several policy applications. Government policy makers and scholars alike have reason to be concerned with understanding the extent to which demographic factors do—or do not—contribute to generating violent conflicts within and between states. Demographic trends and the policy options to affect them can and do have relevance for security, whether states choose to intervene or not. Consider, for example, the question of whether or how to prepare troops for deployment in international humanitarian crises. Many of the links between demography and security are present, and often salient, in countries' foreign policy challenges. In the cases of Bosnia, Rwanda, Israel, and elsewhere, states have been faced with policy decisions about responses to the internal and international relocation of populations, including issues of settlement, repatriation, and population exchanges. Demography and national security also intersect at and have a direct bearing on domestic policy issues, particularly the questions of border controls, interdictions, labor market controls, plural citizenship, and plural nationality. Given present fertility, mortality, and migration trends in both developed and developing countries, and the persistent efforts of states to mix or unmix populations, we can expect demographic developments to play an increasingly important role in international politics.

References

Appleyard, Reginald. 1999. *Analysis of Present and Future Emigration Dynamics in Developing Countries, Vols. I–IV*. Abingdon, England: Ashgate Publishing Ltd.

Homer-Dixon, Thomas F. 1991. "On the Threshold: Environmental Changes as Causes of Acute Conflict." *International Security* 16 (2) (Fall): 76–116.

———. 1994. "Environmental Scarcities and Violent Conflict: Evidence from Cases." *International Security* 19 (1) (Summer): 5–40.

Homer-Dixon, Thomas F., Jeffrey H. Boutwell, and George W. Rathjens. 1993. "Environmental Change and Violent Conflict." *Scientific American* (February): 38–45.

Kaplan, Robert. 1994. "The Coming Anarchy." *The Atlantic Monthly* (February): 44–76.

United Nations. 1998a. *World Population Prospects: The 1998 Revision. Vol. I, Comprehensive Tables*. New York: United Nations Secretariat, Department of Economic and Social Affairs, Population Division, ESA/P/WP.150.

———. 1998b. *World Population Prospects: The 1996 Revision*. New York: United Nations Secretariat, Department of Economic and Social Affairs, Population Division, ESA/P/WP.138.

———. 1998c. *Trends in Total Migrant Stock by Sex: Diskette Documentation 1998*. New York: United Nations, Department of Economic and Social Affairs, Population Division, POP/1B/DB/98/4.

———. 2000. "Replacement Migration: Is it a Solution to Declining and Ageing Populations?" New York: United Nations, Department of Economic and Social Affairs, Population Division, ESA/P/WP.160.

Weiner, Myron. 1971. "Political Demography: An Inquiry into the Political Consequences of Population Change." In *Rapid Population Growth: Consequences and Policy Implications*. Compiled by the National Academy of Sciences. Baltimore, MD: Johns Hopkins University Press.

PART ONE

Population Dynamics and
National Security:
Theories and Evidence

CHAPTER 1

International Migration: Predicting the Unknowable

Michael S. Teitelbaum

This chapter addresses the extent to which the theoretical perspectives and empirical analyses produced by several social science disciplines have contributed to our understanding of the causes that underlie international migration. In American academic circles, the subject has been addressed most prominently by demographers, economists, sociologists, and political scientists, with all four drawing upon historical evidence. Elsewhere other academic disciplines such as geography have been prominent as well.

Demographic Theory

If the truth be told, demography has not produced a coherent and convincing theory of international migration. However, a number of demographic forces are often described as important elements underlying the initiation of international movements.

High Fertility and Rapid Population Growth

Many commentators have suggested that the very rapid demographic growth experienced in the developing world over the past three decades (due to rapid mortality declines accompanied by sustained high fertility rates) leads to a kind of demographic "overspill": Rapid natural increase in regions or countries with populations already large relative to available resources impel some residents to seek better opportunities elsewhere. They argue not that this is the sole cause of international migration, but rather that it is important among other contributing factors. A related point is that high rates of natural increase produce, with roughly a two-decade lag, rapid growth in the numbers of young adults, empirically shown to have the highest migration propensities. Internal and international migratory movements are often linked, with many rural young adults moving first to urban areas seeking better economic opportunity, and then abroad when these urban labor markets become saturated.

Low Fertility

Some believe that the low fertility rates that now generally characterize industrialized countries lead, over time, to rising demand among employers for imported workers. Other things being equal, labor markets in such settings become tighter (again with a two-decade lag), producing pressures for higher wages and in some cases labor market bottlenecks. Meanwhile, low fertility rates imply a demographic age structure characterized by rapid increases in the proportion of those beyond retirement age and rising tax burdens on the working-age population to support public pension systems financed by taxation on a pay-as-you-go basis. In this analysis, then, imported workers serve the interests of employers (by holding down wage inflation) and of governments and older native populations (by slightly reducing the average population age and by increasing the number of workers contributing to financially unstable pay-as-you-go pension systems).

Some analyses also allude to indirect effects or intermediary elements through which demographic forces operate. These include not only the impacts of high or low fertility upon age composition, as noted above, but also the effects of rising agrarian population densities upon overgrazing and related environmental pressures that eventually stimulate outmigration. Similarly, large cohorts of young adults concentrating in urban areas with high unemployment rates may produce political and social instabilities (for example, higher crime rates), which in turn may result in substantial movements of people.

Some analysts seem confident that such demographic arguments can suffice to explain trends and patterns in international migration. Unfortunately, while these do offer valuable insights, they are but partial ones: the realities are far messier than any simple demographically based theory would imply. For example, the bulk of international migration takes place within the developing world, between countries with similarly high fertility rates and youthful age structures. Moreover, the substantial migrations that have occurred in recent decades from very low-fertility Eastern Europe to moderately low-fertility Western Europe and North America can hardly be explained by fertility or population growth differentials, as the relationships run in the opposite direction from that implied by purely demographic explanations.

Economic Theory

As in demography, the truth is that there is no single coherent economic theory capable of providing a convincing explanation of trends and patterns of international migration. Numerous economic explanations of international migration have been proposed. Publications emanating from a recent Committee on South-North Migration established by the International Union for the Scientific Study of Population (IUSSP)[1] have provided a useful and well-informed review of the economics literature, grouping current theories into five categories. The following section summarizes these review papers in very brief form.

Neoclassical Macroeconomic

Migration flows are said to arise as a kind of international labor market arbitrage between countries and regions with differing labor supply and demand situations. These labor market differentials are seen as the primary forces that initiate international migration movements; government policies affect such movements only by affecting the underlying labor market. Under this framework, international migration movements would not be expected to begin without labor market differentials, and should end when such differentials decline to insignificant levels.

Neoclassical Microeconomic

This framework views international migration as driven by decisions made by rational utility-maximizing individuals who perceive positive net returns from international movement, taking into account both its benefits and its costs. Hence if certain human capital attributes increase potential returns to migration while its costs are reduced by social, political or technological developments, the volume of such migration will increase. As in the Neoclassical Macroeconomic framework above, labor market differentials in supply and demand, operating through differentials in potential earnings and employment, are said to drive the process. Hence government policies can affect migration patterns only by reducing such earnings/employment differentials, or by increasing the real cost of migration.

The "New Economics of Migration" (Group/Family Theories)

Here the decision-making unit is broader, the social group or family unit rather than the individual, which (again in a rational utility-maximizing format) decides whether or not one or more of its members should migrate internationally in the service of the economic interests of the group. The goals are to diversify the origins of total group/family income so as to minimize its exposure to non-diversified risks such as crop failure, local economic or political crises, and so forth, and to gain access for the group/family to capital and credit not available locally. In this framework, then, labor market differentials are not necessary factors underlying international migration; instead, the driving forces are access to insurance, capital, and credit. Hence, government measures aimed at creation of more effective capital, insurance, and futures markets may be expected to affect group/family decisions about international migration of their members.

"Dual Labor Market" (Recruitment) Theories

In this framework, the critical factor initiating international migration is the international recruitment of low-wage workers by employers and governments in higher-wage economies. Such workers are described as necessary to restrain otherwise inflationary forces in their labor markets, and to provide a contingent labor force that can be expanded or contracted in response to varying demand. Hence international migration is argued to be inherent in the economic structure of recruiting economies, and can be affected only minimally by direct policies intended to affect migration.

"World Systems" Theories

As in Dual Labor Market theories, international migration is an inherent element of economic structures, but in this case the focus is less on national economies and more on world markets. The driving forces are those embodied in the penetration by "capitalist economic relations into peripheral, noncapitalist societies," driven by multinational firms, neo-colonialism, and the actions of national elites in peripheral societies. As in Dual Labor Market theories, the key policy decisions are those affecting the international flow of capital and goods rather than migration policies per se.

As is also true for demographically based theoretical perspectives, some proponents put forward one or another of these economics-based approaches as sufficient explanations of migration behavior, in either theoretical or empirical terms. Such claims are unconvincing. None passes muster on its own, notwithstanding the grandiosity of some of the titles chosen. Yet while all have their deficiencies, each offers some important insights into key forces that may underlie international migration.

Other Theoretical Perspectives

Demographic and economic perspectives focus sharply upon factors affecting the potential for international migratory movements, but offer only limited attention to the actualization of such potential or to their persistence. Factors that contribute to the actualization of potential appear to be heavily in the realm of policy, and are discussed in some detail below. Before considering these, we turn briefly to the common observation of the persistence of international migration—the fact that migration flows often continue long after the economic and demographic circumstances that underlie them have changed.

Casual newspaper reading makes it readily apparent that international migration movements are associated with the development of dense social networks across borders, and with the emergence of profitable networks of intermediaries providing assistance (both legal and illegal) to would-be migrants. These phenomena have been addressed by two social science frameworks, emanating from outside of demography and economics:

Network Theories

Network theories are not in conflict with economic theories, but emphasize that the factors perpetuating international migration may be different in character from those initiating it. In particular, the transnational social networks which develop between migrants and their kin and neighbors in the origin country serve as the "social infrastructure" of international migration—social connections that make further international movements less risky and lower in cost, and thereby have the effect of perpetuating and perhaps increasing international migration flows even when the initiating forces have waned. Policies that favor family unification of migrants facilitate the effects of such networks.

Institutional Theories

These theories point to the roles played by intermediaries that typically develop to serve the needs of migrants and would-be migrants. These institutions cover a wide range: from the prosperous immigration bar (recently one of the most rapidly growing sectors of the U.S. legal profession); to lawful nonprofit religious and/or humanitarian organizations that see themselves as serving the needs of vulnerable migrants; to clearly illegal, profit-driven, and sometimes predatory organizations of "people-smugglers" who extract substantial fees to facilitate the unlawful entry and employment of migrants.[2, 3]

In between are twilight institutions such as so-called "immigration consultants" (some of them both competent and law-abiding, some not) and farm labor contractors—legally constituted firms providing contract workers to farmers with often less-than-careful scrutiny of their workers' legal status. Like social networks, such institutions serve to perpetuate and sometimes to increase migration movements long after the initiating forces have waned, and present significant challenges to many governments seeking to regulate their activities.

Some syntheses of these various perspectives may prove useful, drawing eclectically from diverse perspectives that appear to be supported by empirical test. One worthwhile example of such theoretical eclecticism, undergirded by empirical sophistication, is recent work by scholars seeking to assess the relative importance of demographic and economic differentials and other forces in the enormous wave of migration from Europe during the nineteenth and early twentieth centuries. In brief, their findings to date indicate that:

> ... rates of natural increase at home and income gaps between home and overseas destinations were both important, while industrialization (independent of its influence on real wages) made a moderate contribution. Our results also support the arguments of those who stress the influence of "friends and relatives" among previous emigrants abroad. Our results suggest that these latter effects were strong, creating persistence and path dependence in emigration flows. (Hatton and Williamson 1994: 557)

In short, their findings suggest that demographic differentials, economic differentials, and network factors may all have played important roles in explaining the trajectories and pace of this movement of more than 50 million persons out of Europe.

The Actualization of International Migration Potential: The Roles of States

However, even a combination of demographic and economic theories with network and institutional elements provides an inadequate explanation of international migration. As noted earlier, such a hybrid theory would provide useful insights into the potential for and persistence of international movements, but would have little to offer about the actualization of such potential. Yet it is actual, not potential, migration for which an explanation is sought, and the actualization of potential depends heavily upon factors arising in many other domains of human life.

It is precisely at the boundary between the potential and the actual that the state plays such a central role.[4] The most striking weakness in migration theories drawn from the social sciences is their failure to deal in a serious way with government action in initiating, selecting, restraining, and ending international migration movements. Zolberg (1999: 71), for example, notes that "it is remarkable that the role of states in shaping international migration has been largely ignored by immigration theorists."

Whether or not academic and political commentators consider state action, they often see international migration as driven by economic, demographic, and social forces so powerful as to overwhelm any efforts by governments to affect them—a kind of human tectonics.[5] This may be a legitimate perspective in theoretical terms, but it is not one that fits the facts very well.

First, there are numerous cases in which government policies—whether formal or informal, explicit or implicit—serve to promote the export of migrant labor. This point is so obvious as to not require detailed elaboration; one need only refer to the actions of governments such as those of the Philippines, Mexico, the Dominican Republic, Bangladesh, India, Turkey, Morocco, Tunisia, El Salvador, Guatemala, Nicaragua, Vietnam, Barbados, and many others.

Second, there are all too many examples of governmental action (or inaction) that results in mass emigrations due to war, violence, persecution, human rights abuse, mass starvation, and/or ethnic tensions. Here again, one need only provide a partial list of recent examples: Kosovo, Bosnia, Rwanda, Burundi, Zaire, Mozambique, Sudan, Somalia, Myanmar, Afghanistan, Nicaragua, Guatemala, El Salvador, Cuba, Haiti, Turkey, Iraq, and so on.

Finally, all governments adopt policies and actions designed to limit inflow or outflow of international migrants, either directly via border and interior controls, or indirectly via diplomatic, economic, or military actions. No government has ever renounced its right, under the global system of states, to control the entry of non-nationals across its borders, other than in the context of specific bilateral or multilateral treaties such as those underlying the European Union.

Two caveats must immediately be noted: that of the United Nations Convention and Protocol (1951, 1967) regarding refugees, which constrain state actions in returning refugees in their territories to persecution in the refugees' own homelands; and the self-evident fact that the effectiveness with which states have exercised their right to control entry has varied greatly over time and place.

Even with these caveats, the array of instruments deployed for the purpose of control is impressive. These include both direct controls to prevent unwanted entry, and indirect or remote controls to affect behavior well beyond national borders. The following instruments are typical:

Direct Controls at Borders

The most visible and near-ubiquitous form of state control over entry is that exercised by immigration authorities at land borders, ports, and airports. Such activities are often exercised by specialized police forces (for example, the U.S. Border Patrol; the German Bundesgrenzschutz). In addition, governments concerned about potential mass movements across their borders sometimes mobilize regular and reserve military forces (as in Austria) and coast guards (as in the United States and Italy) for border activities.

Indirect or "Remote Controls" Beyond Borders

Passports and Visas: Zolberg (1999: 73) suggests that during the last "world immigration crisis" around the turn of the twentieth century, the

United States and other Western countries developed then-novel "remote control" mechanisms such as passports and visas to regulate immigration. These devices are now such conventional requirements for international movement that it is hard to recall that they were once striking innovations. Previously, entry of immigrants had been regulated post hoc, only after the would-be immigrants had arrived. (The purpose of Ellis Island in New York harbor was to screen immigrants who had already crossed the Atlantic, so as to prevent the entry of "undesirables.")

Mandated Sanctions on Carriers

A related form of remote control places upon the carrier (airline, shipping line, etc.) the burden of validating that each of its passengers has the passport and visa needed to enter the country to which he or she is traveling. If arriving passengers are found to lack the necessary documents, governments may impose monetary fines on the carriers, and/or require them to transport such passengers back to their points of origin at no cost.

Intelligence

A less conventional form of remote control involves the collection of overseas intelligence about the backgrounds and activities of individuals and organizations facilitating the fraudulent movement of migrants. This has been a relatively weak part of state efforts to regulate international migration, but cooperation among national police agencies has been increasing in recent years.

Externalization of Asylum and Refugee Claims

Rising numbers of asylum claims, many of them based upon unlawful entry and/or fraudulent documents, have led many industrial countries to elaborate a further set of measures and proposals aimed at expediting review of claims at borders and ports of entry, and/or forcing such asylum claims into venues external to the territory of the destination state. Such measures fall into several categories:

Expedited asylum procedures: efforts aimed at initial screening of asylum claimants at airports and other entry points so as expeditiously to examine and potentially to exclude those that are "frivolous" or "manifestly unfounded."

External or offshore screening: efforts intended to limit access to in-country asylum adjudications, via initial screening in another country— in the asylum claimant's own country, in a third country, or in some cases on the high seas (as in the U.S. policy toward Haitians being transported in boats).

Safe country lists: Some countries (for example Germany) have developed formal lists of "safe countries," including both those found to involve little or no risk of persecution and "third countries" across which asylum claimants have transited and in which they could have claimed asylum had they so wished. Asylum claimants in these categories can be provided with "fast-track" examinations of their claims.

In sum, it is fair to conclude that control by states over entry by non-nationals is normal, and substantial. All governments consider it to be among the most fundamental elements of their sovereignty. No government has renounced the right to exercise such control. Nor has any government admitted publicly that it has lost control over such entry, presumably because public perceptions that such control is not being exercised can be politically explosive.

Although such controls have many deficiencies in practice, they are far from ineffectual. Consider that among the countries of large-scale emigration, there are very few indeed from which more than ten percent of the population has emigrated: Haiti, Afghanistan, Cuba, Rwanda, and not many others. Even Mexico, a country well known for the large and sustained volume of emigration by its citizens, reports that less than ten percent of Mexican-born persons reside outside of Mexico (most in the United States). In most countries, no matter how poor they may be, the overwhelming majority of people do not leave. In part this results from inertia, lack of information, and the importance of familial and related ties; but governmental policies limiting access to desirable destinations are also significant factors.

The case of migration from the Commonwealth of Puerto Rico to the U.S. mainland provides a valuable quasi-natural experiment as to what levels of migration might be expected in the absence of state regulation. Puerto Rico has long experienced considerably lower income than the mainland United States, but Puerto Ricans are U.S. citizens by birth, hence there are no legal restrictions of any kind upon their migration to the mainland. As early as 1950, nine percent of Puerto Ricans were already living on the mainland, and in the ensuing two decades this percentage rose rapidly, reaching 23 percent by 1970 (Massey et al. 1994: 703). During the mid-1970s, legal changes required that the island's minimum wage rates be the same as those on the mainland, thereby reducing the economic incentives for lower-income Puerto Ricans to migrate. Still, emigration to the mainland continued, although its rate slowed and migration selectivity shifted toward the unemployed and most poorly educated groups on the island.[6]

The case of Puerto Rico offers but one especially clear case from among mountains of evidence for the centrality of the state in international migration movements. It seems quite likely that, even in the absence of state controls over entry, only a minority of the populations of poor countries would migrate to rich countries, but the numbers who would do so would nonetheless be far larger than at present. While the capacity and willingness of states to exercise highly effective control over entry do vary a great deal, and in some cases may have decreased in recent years, it is important to emphasize that international migration is neither uncontrollable, nor is it uncontrolled.

International and Regional Agreements

Beyond their own unilateral policy measures, many industrialized countries have sought to engage multilateral cooperation on migration issues. Some have even entered into international agreements embodying such mechanisms. Examples include the 1990–1991 Dublin Convention;[7] the 1990 Schengen Agreement;[8] and the 1992 Edinburgh Declaration. There are also bilateral agreements, including "readmission agreements" between the United States and Haiti for return of Haitian nationals, and agreements between Germany and its eastern neighbors that embody the "safe third country" concept.

Preexisting regional security agreements have also been used to minimize migrations perceived to be destabilizing. In substantial part for such reasons, Costa Rica and Mexico led regional efforts to end the civil wars in Central America. The United States, driven largely by concerns about uncontrolled migrations (*Washington Post*, 1994), sought to engage the Organization of American States, and failing that, sub-regional Caribbean organizations, in support of its diplomatic and ultimately military efforts to reestablish the elected government of Jean-Bertrand Aristide in Haiti. Many states have sought to mobilize the Organisation of African Unity to support military action in Somalia, Rwanda, and Zaire/Congo, with concerns about the humanitarian and security implications of mass migrations never far from the surface. NATO and the Organization for Security and Cooperation in Europe (OSCE) have been deeply engaged since 1992 in the political and security implications of asylum, refugee, and migration issues (Russell 1993: 23, 81). Military initiatives by NATO in Bosnia and Kosovo have been motivated to a substantial degree by threats perceived by NATO member states, both indirectly from the feared consequences of a Yugoslavia fractionating along ethnic lines, and directly as consequences of the mass migrations unleashed by violence in these areas.[9]

As may be seen from the above examples, some efforts to involve regional organizations and security agreements have met with considerable success, while others may be judged failures. Whether successful or not, all illustrate the growing intersection between migration and security concerns.

Opposition

To be sure, many efforts by states to exercise control (whether unilateral, bilateral, or multilateral) have attracted controversy and criticism. Expedited processing, for example, has been criticized as an unwarranted limitation upon due process obligations to would-be asylees; critics note in particular that genuine asylum-seekers often arrive without adequate documentation of persecution, or with documents that are fraudulently obtained because the persecuting authorities refuse to provide *bona fide* documents (Moussalli, cited in Russell, Keely, and Christian 2000: 30).

Similarly, external or offshore screening is criticized on grounds that it limits the legal rights of asylum-claimants under international law, and may impose an unjustified burden upon such persecuted people. The basic idea of safe countries is criticized by some as a potentially serious infringement on the rights of refugees, and the particular lists of safe countries have themselves been challenged.

Much of such criticism is based upon principled opposition to any limitations upon the rights of individuals to claim asylum, as a matter of basic human rights. Other critics act for a variety of less principled motives: ethnic solidarity with those claiming asylum; political use of asylum as a foreign policy tool to embarrass the governments of source countries; and the more mercenary interests of those who, for a fee, advise their clients to file dubious asylum claims as a means of gaining long-term and perhaps permanent residence.

There has also been considerable opposition to proposals for humanitarian military interventions such as those in Somalia, Haiti, Bosnia, and Kosovo. For some opponents, such interventions smack of colonialism or neocolonialism; others oppose military intervention on principle; others believe that the circumstances of such cases do not warrant the costs in casualties and expenditures resulting from such intervention.[10]

Likely Futures

In Dante's *Inferno*, there is a special place in Purgatory reserved for "prognosticators." With this imagery held firmly in mind, what can available theory, assessed in the light of recent experience, tell us about likely futures?

If migration patterns are determined by demography and economics, recent world trends would suggest increasing international migration movements in the coming decades. Fertility rates in many industrialized countries are already very low, and where they are not, they are tending toward decline. Meanwhile, in many developing regions fertility rates are far higher, although commonly also tending toward decline. No matter what happens to fertility rates over the next few decades, the powerful and long-lived momentum of rapid population growth implies with considerable certainty that we will see even larger growth in the labor forces of the developing world.

In the economic domain, the trends we can see are toward increasing extension of international market forces to more and more of the world (that is, more "capitalist penetration"), globalization of production, and so forth. In addition, in recent years we have seen widening differentials in economic prosperity, with incomes and wealth rising in Western industrial countries and falling in the former Soviet Union, in the formerly rapidly growing "Tigers" of East Asia, and in much of Africa and Latin America. Given such demographic and economic trends, many of the theoretical propositions summarized earlier would lead to expectations of substantial increases in the potential for international migration.

Are these demographic, social, and economic propensities, all seeming to favor increasing potentials for international movement of people, so powerful that states can have only an insignificant degree of control?

No, not really. In fact, very substantial state control is in evidence. We can surely acknowledge that a good deal of present-day migration is unwanted by the governments of receiving states, and often in violation of their laws. Still, there is far less international migration occurring than would be the case if states were not regulating entry (as in the Puerto Rican case described earlier). Theoretical propositions that fail to reflect this set of powerful forces thereby diminish their own credibility.

The forces that affect state policy stances vary widely, even among prosperous liberal democracies. The power of such variables is illustrated very well in a recent study by a leading French analyst, Patrick Weil, who compares the policy behaviors of Germany, France, the United Kingdom, and the United States in light of their differences along such dimensions:

> The recent evolution of immigration policies demonstrates the adaptability of the democratic developed states. In reaction to increased migration pressure and the extension of rights for migrants, states have answered by mobilizing more legal, financial and bureaucratic means. Therefore the transformation of migration into a worldwide phenomenon has not automatically involved an increase in immigration flows: when this has happened, it was due primarily to legal windows still open to entry. The closure of these windows has demonstrated that regulation is possible for a democratic state. When the level of uncontrolled flows is still high, as in the United States, it depends more on cultural and historical than on economic or demographic factors. (Weil 1998: 18)

Among the "cultural and historical" factors that Weil sees as dominant, differences in political ideologies and processes should not be minimized. Europeans of the Left and the Right are often astonished to learn that one thread of American conservative thought includes the so-called "libertarian" ideology that argues for borders wholly open to unlimited international migration or, in more muted form, for increased levels of legal immigration and minimal efforts to restrain illegal entry (Teitelbaum 1992). This perspective is most visibly represented by the editorial board of the Right-libertarian newspaper *Wall Street Journal*, which has on more than one occasion editorialized for adoption of a five-word Constitutional amendment on immigration: "There shall be open borders" (*Wall Street*

Journal 1990). These elements of the political Right form common cause with those of the Left who are committed to mass immigration for reasons of human rights, civil rights, multiculturalism, ethnic politics, or the likelihood that new immigrants of low income levels are likely to support liberal political and economic policies. In no other country can such an odd coalition of right-wing and left-wing advocates be found.[11]

The structure of political institutions and the norms of political debate will also affect public responses. A parliamentary system dominated by two parties can be expected to react differently from one based on unstable and shifting coalitions, and both will differ from the behavior of the congressional system of the United States. Voting systems based on proportional representation or transferable ballots have different implications from the first-past-the-post constituency systems of the United States, the United Kingdom, and Canada. The importance of interest group politics and of access to campaign finance varies as well, and can be expected to affect the behavior of states.

In the United States, the twin facts that interest groups have long dominated U.S. congressional politics and that immigration policies have traditionally been controlled by the Congress rather than the Executive means that the policies that emerge typically reflect the strongly held views of certain well-organized and deeply interested groups: some employers (California agribusiness traditionally; the information technology sector more recently), immigration lawyers, and ethnic organizations. The further facts that the United States is characterized by high levels of residential segregation (Massey and Denton 1994), and that most immigrants settle in a few states and metropolitan areas, combine to magnify the significance of immigration policies for these few geographic areas, while making these policies less relevant for most of the rest of the country.

As to the future, if levels of international migration were to stay high or increase in future years, should we anticipate that such movements will likely produce significant threats to the internal coherence and stability of receiving states, as the compositions of their populations are rapidly transformed?

Again, not really. Instead, we should expect a wide range of consequences, depending heavily upon a host of other factors in the spheres of demography, economics, social structure, and politics, all of which are themselves affected by differences in history, values, and cultures. Not only do factors vary widely from country to country, but in most cases their evolution is almost impossible to predict.

In demographic terms, the pace of change (national and local) resulting from both migration and fertility rates can be an important factor affecting political and other responses. Yet much about such long-term outcomes cannot be predicted: To what extent will the preferred destinations remain constant or change over time? What will fertility trends be among natives and migrants? To what extent will there be substantial intermarriage between resident and migrant groups? How will expressions of ethnic identity evolve over the long term? One of the best treatments of this set of uncertainties has been developed by a committee of the National Research Council (Smith and Edmonston 1997).

Moreover, in the real world what matters is change *as perceived by the public*. While public policy experts properly pay careful attention to quantitative data, it is visible changes "on the ground" that seem to matter most to broader publics: language changes on local business signs; types of restaurants and bars; characteristics of elementary school classes; and so on. If immigrant groups choose to cluster heavily in a few locations, only those already living in these places are likely to perceive the demographic changes underway, and in these locations the pace of such change will be magnified by its concentration.

Rates of fertility and natural increase are also relevant for affecting perceptions about the pace of change. If the society into which migration is occurring is itself experiencing rapid demographic growth due to high rates of natural increase (the difference between births and deaths), the *perceived* demographic impact of migration may be less than from similar volumes of migration into a society experiencing slow indigenous demographic growth.

Characteristics of migrants, defined in social and cultural terms, are also of relevance to public perceptions. If new migrants are perceived as similar to or ethnically connected to the resident population (for example, *aussiedler* moving to Germany from Russia, *nisei* from Brazil and Peru to Japan, or Bangladeshis to the Indian state of West Bengal), demographic change may be perceived as smaller than if comparable numbers of migrants are seen as ethnically, racially, or linguistically distant from the receiving population.

There are also uncertainties about whether or not relevant publics will perceive migration trends as threats to their "national identity." Both the elites and the masses of most societies see important value in their distinctive national cultures—language, history, political systems, the arts, and so forth. For many societies, the arrival of large numbers of foreign migrants (or of other foreign cultural elements such as films and television programs) can be seen as a threat to the cohesiveness and integration of the society. Such perceptions can be especially strong if such foreign influences are perceived to be increasing rapidly, are concentrated as to locale, or attract the rhetorical attention of visible political groups.

Among liberal democracies, the most energetic debates of this type have appeared in France, Germany, and the Canadian province of Quebec. In all three, political parties committed to "protecting our national identity against foreigners" emerged during the 1980s—the National Front in France, the *Republikaners* and similar groups in Germany, the *Parti Quebecois* in Quebec. Initially such groups were ignored or dismissed as trivial by the political establishment, but over time they have proved to attract significant numbers of political supporters. Ultimately, center-right establishment parties in France[12] and Germany came to embrace some of the rhetoric of the National Front and *Republikaners*.

Meanwhile, in other countries such as Australia, Canada, the Netherlands, and the United States, there is a countervailing stream of political thought described generally as "multiculturalism." Its supporters see a multicultural society as richer than a culturally homogeneous one, benefiting from diversity in values, religions, languages, worldviews, cuisines; hence immigration from culturally distinct societies is a virtue rather than a threat. Both Canada and Australia have established national government agencies and funding directed toward goals of multiculturalism, while in the United States such support is more at the level of rhetoric accompanied by legal requirements for bilingual education and multilingual ballots.

Much will also depend upon economic trends, and these too are quite unpredictable over the longer term. Will there be growing prosperity, or rising privation? Will labor markets be tight or loose; will unemployment be low or high? As correctly noted by many advocates favoring high levels of immigration, public opposition to such policies is at its strongest during recessions and economic crises (in the language used in such discussions, immigrants are "scapegoated" for high levels of unemployment, inflation, or other economic problems.) Based on this kind of analysis, the long-term strategy is that of the "ratchet," with tactics determined by short-term economic circumstances: During periods of economic stress, the goal is to prevent the adoption of any legislative or enforcement changes; during periods of prosperity, the focus turns toward adoption of expansionary measures.

Based on the above discussion, one conclusion seems inescapable—although some will find it esthetically unappealing. A genuine theory of migration, that is, a set of predictive hypotheses that can be tested empirically, may well be a mirage. Since the role of states is an essential feature affecting the scale and character of migration, a predictive theory would require us to know the unknowable: how people of diverse countries, and their governments, will respond to future experiences with international migration.

Notes

1. The analyses of this committee have been presented in a series of journal articles, including Massey et al. (1993: 431–466; 1994, 699–751). For a lucid summary, see Sharon Stanton Russell, 1995.
2. These range from the inexpensive smuggling services along the Mexico-U.S. border to the $30,000–40,000 per person services provided to Mainland Chinese by the organized crime syndicates known as Triads.

3. Personal interviews by the author with government officials and researchers in Xiamen (Fujian Province), Guangzhou (Guandong Province), and Hong Kong, 3–10 January 1994.
4. This section draws upon Russell and Teitelbaum (1992: 6–7).
5. See, for example, Cornelius, Martin, and Hollifield (1994).
6. See Ortiz (1986), Castillo-Freeman and Freeman (1992), and Ramos (1992), as cited in Massey et al. (1994: 705).
7. The Dublin Convention is known more formally as the "Convention Determining the State Responsible for Examining Applications for Asylum Lodged on One of the Member States of the European Communities." It was signed by the twelve Member States in 1990 and 1991. For a fuller discussion, see Hovy and Zlotnik (1994), and Russell, Keely, and Christian (2000).
8. The Schengen Agreement is among Belgium, France, Germany, Luxembourg, Netherlands, Italy, Spain, and Portugal.
9. The argument is that the West has a strong security interest in what happens in these regions of the former Yugoslavia, given the deeply cultural, ethnic, and religious origins of the war among Serbs, Croats, Bosnian Muslims, and Kosovo Albanians. As but one example, consider the following commentary from *The New Yorker* in 1994:

> Forgetfulness [about Bosnia] would be catastrophic, since Bosnia really does matter to the security of Europe, and the security of Europe, for all the Clinton Administration's efforts to place stronger emphasis on other parts of the world, really does matter to the United States. If the war spills over the borders of Bosnia, Europeans had better learn to duck. But, even if NATO now succeeds in containing the war, the stakes are very high. Bosnia is more than simply another state, internationally recognized in the usual ways. It is a secular state and a democratic one, and it is multicultural, multi-ethnic, and multi-confessional on a continent that, thanks to patterns of migration, is increasingly all those things. If Bosnia's dismemberment is tolerated, nationalist demagogues, in Europe and elsewhere, will take note. (*The New Yorker* 1994: 6)

10. The *Washington Post* invoked all these arguments in a June 1994 editorial opposing military intervention in Haiti.
11. For a discussion of these ideological perspectives and the odd alliances among them, see Teitelbaum (1992).
12. Stanley Hoffmann summarized the French politics as of 1994 as follows:

> [Premier Edouard Balladur] knows that the National Front's progress, both in percentage of the electorate (12.5 percent in 1993 as against 8.5 in 1988) and in all the traditionally conservative sectors in French society—particularly the rural districts and in the urban lower middle and even upper-middle classes—is a major threat to his own moderate right constituency. With the enthusiastic help of Interior Minister Pasqua, he has proceeded to appease right-wing voters and inpatient deputies with tougher laws on immigration and on the requirements for French nationality.
> ... As a clever Machiavellian, Balladur, without making any fundamental changes in French practice, may have pacified the fears of the voters who supported him that French national identity is being eroded. (Hoffmann 1994: 14)

References

Cornelius, Wayne A., Philip L. Martin, and James F. Hollifield, eds. 1994. *Controlling Immigration: A Global Perspective*. Stanford: Stanford University Press.

Hatton, Timothy J., and Jeffrey G. Williamson. 1994. "What drove the mass migrations from Europe?" *Population and Development Review* 20: 557.

Hoffmann, Stanley. 1994. "France: Keeping the Demons at Bay." *New York Review of Books* XLI, no. 5: 14.

Hovy, Bela, and Hania Zlotnik. 1994. "Europe without internal frontiers and international migration." *Population Bulletin of the United Nations,* No. 36.

Massey, Douglas S., and Nancy Denton. 1994. *American Apartheid: Segregation and the Making of the Underclass.* Cambridge MA: Harvard University Press.

Massey, Douglas S., et al. 1993. "Theories of International Migration: A Review and Appraisal." *Population and Development Review* 19: 431–466.

———. 1994. "International Migration Theory: The North American Case." *Population and Development Review* 20: 699–751.

Moussalli, Michel. Cited in Russell, Keely, and Christian (2000).

New Yorker, The. 1994. "This is War." 21 February, 6.

Russell, Sharon Stanton. 1993. *International Migration in North America, Europe, Central Asia, the Middle East and North Africa: Research and Research-related Activities*. Geneva: Economic Commission for Europe and the World Bank.

———. 1995. *International Migration: Implications for the World Bank, Human Resources Development and Operations Policy*. Working Paper Number 54. Washington: The World Bank, May 1995.

Russell, Sharon Stanton, Charles B. Keely, and Bryan P. Christian. 2000. "Multilateral Diplomacy to Harmonize Asylum Policy in Europe: 1984–1993." Washington, D.C.: Georgetown University, Institute for the Study of International Migration.

Russell, Sharon Stanton, and Michael S. Teitelbaum. 1992. *International Migration and International Trade*. World Bank Discussion Paper No. 160. Washington, D.C.: The World Bank.

Smith, James P., and Barry Edmonston, eds. 1997. *The New Americans: Economic, Demographic, and Fiscal Effects of Immigration*. Washington, D.C.: National Academy Press.

Teitelbaum, Michael S. 1992. "Advocacy, Ambivalence, Ambiguity: Immigration Policy and Prospects in the United States," *Proceedings of the American Philosophical Society*, 136: 208–225.

Wall Street Journal. 1990. "The Rekindled Flame," 3 July, A10.

Washington Post. 1994. "Invade Haiti?" 8 June, A22.

Weil, Patrick. 1998. "The State Matters: Immigration Control in Developed Countries," preliminary unedited version prepared for Population Division, Department of Economic and Social Affairs, United Nations, ESA/P/WP/146. New York: United Nations.

Zolberg, Aristide R. 1999. "Matters of State: Theorizing Immigration Policy." In *The Handbook of International Migration: The American Experience*, edited by Charles Hirschman, Philip Kasinitz, and Joseph DeWind. New York: Russell Sage Foundation.

꙳

CHAPTER 2

Demography, Environment, and Security: An Overview

Jack A. Goldstone

In the last few years an enormous literature has sprung up addressing the connections among demography, the environment, and security; a recent bibliography, the *Environmental Change and Security Project Report* (Woodrow Wilson Center 1998), lists over 1,100 items. Nonetheless, the expansion of this literature has not improved its coherence. Contributors include authors seeking to redefine "security" (Matthews 1989; Rothschild 1995); those seeking to "securitize" environmental issues (Myers 1993), those seeking to link demographic changes to security concerns (de Sherbinen 1995), and those seeking to link environmental change (or environmental resources more generally) to violent conflict (Homer-Dixon 1991, 1994). This chapter seeks to clarify the major security implications of demographic and environmental change, and to point out those particular changes and regions most likely to pose significant security issues in the coming decades.

Security Issues: Violent and Non-violent

Let us begin by noting that demographic and environmental change can produce security problems of two distinctly different kinds. We need to differentiate clearly between them, because they have entirely different processes and outcomes, and generate rather different sorts of concerns and remedies.

This chapter will use the term "violent" environmental/demographic security issues (VEDS issues) to denote the impact of demographic and environmental changes on traditional security concerns—that is, ways that demographic and/or environmental changes increase the risk of violent international or domestic conflicts. To foresee and effectively intervene in those situations, we need to understand the specific pathways by which demographic and environmental factors can lead to political crises.

This chapter will then use the term "non-violent" environmental/demographic security issues (NEDS issues) to denote changes in population or in the environment that have consequences across international borders and that in and of themselves produce undesirable outcomes, thus becoming issues of international security even if they are unlikely to produce armed violence. These include emissions that damage the ozone layer or contribute to global warming; logging, damming, or other development that reduces biodiversity or depletes watersheds by diverting water or increasing erosion and silting across international borders downstream; acid rain or particulate pollution that travels across borders; overfishing oceans or estuaries which depletes global stocks; generation of nuclear wastes or toxic wastes and their transport in international waters or across national borders; environmental damage due to military operations, whether collateral damage from conflicts or incidental damage from the operation of bases and routine missions; the spread of harmful biological agents, such as pathogens or perhaps undesirable genetic elements from genetically modified biota; and environmental damage to agrarian regions or other population/resource imbalances that lead to large and unexpected international migrations. In all of these cases, events or decisions in one nation can pose a threat to the quality of life in another nation even if these do not result in armed violence, posing problems for diplomacy and negotiation, and thus falling into the general realm of international political/security concerns.

While considering both violent and non-violent environmental and demographic security issues expands the traditional notion of "security," this expansion is no longer simply a matter of academic debate; rather it is an accepted fact of modern military and diplomatic life.[1] The traditional notion of security has centered on threats projected by armed force, including threats of war, terrorism, and guerrilla activity. Yet that is not the military's sole, or even most active, mission today; humanitarian relief, intervention in ethnic conflicts, and drug interdiction are undertaken in response to other kinds of threats. A more realistic definition of security issues today would include any action or event that can create outcomes deemed harmful or undesirable by nations and that require mitigating diplomatic or military action. U.S. military and diplomatic resources are being deployed in an effort to find the best strategy for negotiating global accords on the production of carbon dioxide gases. In recent years, NATO and UN forces have frequently been called on to intervene in ethnic conflicts. A possible oil cut-off is a national security issue; so too would be damage to our atmosphere's ability to block dangerous ultra-violet radiation, or a sharp reduction in the atmosphere's ability to transmit Earth's excess heat back into space.

The operating definition of security has thus already changed. Still, while security may be more broadly defined, we need to be very clear in defining (1) the processes that lie behind *violent* security threats from demographic or environmental changes that increase the risks of war, terrorism, or revolution and (2) what processes lie behind *non-violent* threats from demographic and environmental changes that in themselves pose threats to the quality of life in multiple nations. Having made this distinction, we can better clarify the role of population and environmental change with regard to security issues.[2]

Demography, Environment, and Security: Key Findings

After nearly three decades of debate and analysis, stemming from Myron Weiner's ground-breaking NSF study (1971: 567–617), scholars are beginning to develop much clearer answers to the complex questions regarding how environmental and population changes affect security concerns. Those answers can be summarized briefly in the following propositions, each of which we shall treat in greater detail below:

- Long-term environmental degradation is not a major or pervasive cause of international wars, ethnic wars, or revolutionary conflicts. Such degradation often brings misery, and can exacerbate local tensions and conflicts in a society, yet such misery does not generally trigger the elite alienation and opposition necessary for large-scale violence to occur. Short-term disasters, however—floods, hurricanes, droughts, earthquakes, and major accidents—can contribute to major political conflicts if elites and popular groups blame the regime for causing them, or for a particularly poor or corrupt response.
- While overall population growth and population density do not generally predict political risks, a number of distinct kinds of demographic changes *do* increase the risks of violent internal political and ethnic conflicts. These generally involve changes in the *balance* between population change and the absorptive capacity of the economy. Such changes include particularly rapid growth in the labor force relative to the growth of the economy, unequal population growth rates between different ethnic groups, urbanization that exceeds employment growth, migrations that change the local balance among major ethnic groups, shifts in age distribution that create relatively large youth cohorts, and a rapid increase in higher-education graduates relative to the growth in elite positions.
- Population changes do not directly increase the risks of international wars between domestically stable states; however, because many international wars have their origins in domestic conflicts (for example, the Iran/Iraq war growing out of Iran's revolution; international wars in West and Central Africa growing out of the collapses of Liberia, Sierra Leone, and Congo/Zaire), in those contexts

where population changes produce domestic political crises, the risk of international war is also increased.
- Certain demographic changes, such as a rise in infant mortality, aside from whatever role they may have as causes, can be powerful indicators of coming political violence.
- Rapid and large-scale demographic changes, such as a rise in mortality or a sharp rise in migration, can arise as an *outcome* of violent conflicts.
- In many states, a combination of population and environmental changes produces environmental changes having a global impact; in countries with large populations and large or rapidly increasing levels of per capita environmental impact (that is, carbon dioxide output, forest reduction, natural habitat destruction, and colonization), environmental changes carry implications for global security.

The Environment as a Cause of Violent Conflicts

Thomas Homer-Dixon of the University of Toronto aroused a great deal of controversy and concern with his claim that we are "on the threshold" of an era in which traditional security concerns such as armed conflicts will come frequently, if not primarily, as a result of environmental change (Homer-Dixon 1991, 1994). However, in the eight years since his warning, the search for evidence behind this claim has provided little support. As Paul Diehl (1998: 275–276) has remarked, the "many publications from the [Toronto] project have produced largely abstract conceptions of the environment-conflict nexus, with actual cases presented only as anecdotal evidence or as illustrative examples." After nearly a decade of research, it now seems clear that long-term environmental degradation of the kind that often accompanies development (soil erosion, deforestation, air and water pollution, to name a few) has little or no significant role in generating traditional security concerns (Deudney 1990; Levy 1995). Detailed cross-national studies have found only very weak relations between environmental degradation and either international or domestic armed conflict (Gleditsch 1998).

Hauge and Ellingsen (1998), in the most comprehensive global test of the hypothesis that environmental scarcity leads to violence, presented recent data (1980–1992) showing that while deforestation, land degradation, and freshwater availability were positively correlated with the incidence of civil war and armed conflict, the *magnitude* of their effects was tiny, raising the probability of civil war by only one-half to under one-and-a-half percent (Hauge and Ellingsen 1998: 311, Table II). These factors did have a slightly higher effect on the probability of lesser kinds of armed conflict (causing increases in the chances of such conflict by from four to eight percent), but their influence paled compared to that of such traditional risk factors as poverty, regime type, and current and prior political instability.

Indeed, in their historical data, depending on the type of conflict, the combination of high income inequality, poverty, regime type, and current political instability created a probability of conflict ranging from 18 to 64 percent. In their conclusion, they note that "Environmental factors emerge as less important in determining the incidence of civil conflict than economic and political factors" (Hauge and Ellingsen 1998: 314).

A second thorough and extensive study of the relationships between environmental change and violent conflict (Baechler 1998) found that while conflicts over resources, in some sense, could be generated by environmental degradation, most such conflicts were local and peacefully resolved by government regulation or negotiations. Whether or not such conflicts produced violent struggles did "not [depend] on the degree of environmental degradation as such," but on sociopolitical factors unrelated to the environment (Baechler 1998: 32).

A third extensive study, undertaken by an academic Task Force on State Failure sponsored by the U.S. government (Esty et al. 1995, 1998), deliberately sought environmental causes for a wide range of violent conflict events, including authoritarian coups, revolutionary wars, ethnic wars, and genocides. However, even after adjusting for the impact of living standards, regime type, and involvement in international trade, no direct impact of environmental variables could be found. If environmental change had a causal relationship to political violence, the authors of this study suggest, it would have to be indirectly, through influencing overall living standards or trade. In other words, only environmental change that was so drastic and far-reaching as significantly to reduce lifespans, or substantially to impair international trade in a major commodity, would be likely to increase the risks of violent struggle.

It must be admitted that the range and quality of data on environmental change leave much to be desired, and the poverty of such data may be one reason for these negative findings. Still, if environmental change were truly a major and pervasive cause of violent conflicts, it seems likely that some large cross-national studies of recent political violence would show more positive findings.

Should we therefore dismiss the environment and environmental resources as a cause of conflict? Not entirely, although it appears that environmental decay is unlikely to unleash wars and revolutions across the globe. Rather, research has shown that, although environmental issues do cause international and domestic conflicts, they are of the kind that are generally settled by negotiation and compromise, and not by taking up arms.

The reason for this is straightforward. Where the dispute between two groups, or two nations, is over the degradation or depletion of an environmental resource, war neither solves the problem (it cannot make more of the resource), nor is it an economically efficient way to redistribute the resource (the costs of war almost invariably far outweigh the cost of gaining alternative resources or paying more for a share of the resource). For example, if two nations have a conflict over sharing river water—such as India and

Bangladesh over the Ganges (Hill, Ganguli, and Naylor 1998: 127–176), Israel and Jordan over the Jordan River (Lowi 1993), or Hungary and Slovakia over the Danube (Lipschutz 1997)—they may threaten violence, but are in fact most likely to produce non-violent resolution through negotiation or arbitration (indeed, all of the above conflicts led to treaties and/or international arbitration [Gleick 1998]). The reason is that for one party to insist on *all* the water would in fact be a casus belli, and to risk a war simply to increase one's access to water is economically foolhardy. Throughout the world, the main use of freshwater (over three-quarters) is for irrigation to produce food. A reduction in water can be compensated for either by adopting more efficient means of irrigation (drip rather than ditch); by switching to less water-intensive crops (dry grains rather than rice; tree crops rather than grains); or by importing food rather than producing it. All of these steps, though costly, are vastly less costly than armed conflict. Thus both for the country able to take a greater share of a river, and for the country dependent on downstream flows, the issue will be how most efficiently to use and negotiate use of the resource; resort to war would inevitably be more costly than any possible gains from increased access to the resource or the expenses of compensation for partial reductions. No nations have ever gone to war strictly over access to water; nor are any likely to do so in the future.[3]

The issue of access to water is therefore not truly a VEDS (violent environmental/demographic security) issue; rather, it is a new type of issue in which nations face conflicts of interest that, although potentially costly depending on the degree of resource depletion, must be settled by negotiation or arbitration, what we shall call a NEDS (non-violent environmental/demographic security) issue, in which the condition and/or depletion of the environmental resource are themselves the main problems to be addressed, not any armed conflicts that may result.

Many other environmental issues take a similar form. Whether it is deforestation, or land degradation by overgrazing or erosion, or local atmospheric pollution, violent conflict involving nations—or even large sub-national groups—is simply not a viable way of resolving the problem. Most environmental degradation is a local and long-term process, in which local residents fully participate. Local residents who have burned forests, overgrazed land, or created pollution generally see these effects as side-issues in their own efforts at economic gains, and do not blame their government or others for these environmental changes.

In some cases, as when logging concessions are granted to elites who then rapidly cut forests without regard to the effects of run-off or flooding on farmers in surrounding lowlands, or when exclusive land-use privileges are granted to elites, leading to the exclusion of indigenous farmers, violent conflicts may indeed arise. However, the conflict is generally aimed at ending the unjust concessionary rights granted to government cronies, rather than at stopping the land-use itself. Indeed, if granted the rights to fell forests or farm land, indigenous people will do so with much the same enthusiasm as privileged elites (Terborgh 1999).

Elites and Violent Conflict

Much of the literature on environmental scarcity and violent conflict has erred in predicting violence because of a fundamental misunderstanding regarding the causes of political crises. It is a profound and repeated finding that the mere existence of poverty, inequality, or even increases in these sad conditions, are not sufficient causes for political or ethnic violence (Gurr 1980; Goldstone 1998a). In order for popular discontent or distress to create large-scale conflicts, there must be some elite leadership to mobilize popular groups and to create linkages between them. There must also be some vulnerability of the state, in the form of internal divisions and economic or political reverses. Otherwise, popular discontent is unvoiced, and popular opposition is simply suppressed. The general assumption that environmental change, because it is so sweeping, *must* lead to large-scale and violent conflicts, is somewhat like a revival of the now-discredited modernization theory, in which political theorists argued that modernization itself was so traumatic that it would inevitably lead to widespread violence and rebellion in countries undergoing industrial change (Feierabend, Feierabend, and Nesvold 1969; Huntington 1968; Tilly 1973).

Political analysts of violent conflict now recognize that the essence of political stability or instability lies in a set of reciprocal relationships: among states in the international system, between states and their societies' elites, among elite factions, and between both states and elites and popular groups. When states are fiscally sound, free of severe international threats, and supported by their elites, they are enormously resistant to popular discontent. It is only when states become financially unsound or subject to international pressure and are deserted by their elites, that popular distress furnishes raw material for mobilizing forces for conflict (Foran 1997; Goldstone 1998a).

Oddly, although the environment conflict literature has conceded that environmental impacts on violence depend on interactions with political and economic structures, this literature has not closely examined the impact of environmental change on states and elites. In fact, most environmental degradation (deforestation, soil erosion, water depletion) takes place precisely in ways that strengthen states, elites, or the ties between them. Thus deforestation often occurs because elites gain concessionary rights from states for timbering; soil erosion and water depletion often involve large-scale agricultural and irrigation projects that benefit states or elites through involvement with international funding agencies or land reclamation. Although exhausting firewood and degrading land often have an adverse impact on popular groups, such changes have little impact on state finances or elite loyalty; they thus have little or no impact on political stability.

In those cases where struggles over land or other resources have played a role in regional and ethnic conflict—in South Africa or Kenya, for example (Percival and Homer-Dixon 1998; Kahl 1998)—the essence of the conflict has been the struggle among elite factions for control of political power, with control of land simply representing one of the prizes that go to the winning faction. Without political struggles that turn elites against the state, or that turn elite factions against each other, large-scale political conflicts are unlikely to arise. While control of land—like that of mineral or other resources—may figure in such struggles, the degradation or exploitation of the environment generally is not significant enough to cause major conflicts.

Long-term environmental degradation, whatever popular misery may follow from it, generally does not erode the loyalty of elites to governments, and indeed more often provides opportunities for states and elites both to profit; it does not generally lead to violent conflict.

Disasters—Natural and Man-Made

While long-term environmental degradation has not been proven an important determinant of violent conflict, this is not true of short-term and large-scale disasters, such as hurricanes, droughts, floods, earthquakes, and industrial accidents that affect the environment (such as the Chernobyl nuclear power plant accident in the former Soviet Union). A number of studies (Albala-Bertrand 1993; Drury and Olson 1998; Shefner 1999) have shown how political mobilization and unrest are often sharply increased following a disaster. The 1972 Nicaragua earthquake, the 1988 Armenia earthquake, Hurricane Hazel in 1954 in Haiti, and the 1970 typhoon in then-East Pakistan, were followed by violent changes of regime. The 1976 Guatemala earthquake and the 1985 Mexico City earthquake were both followed by massive political mobilization. The 1986 Chernobyl disaster, and the secrecy and inadequate protective measures that followed it, are widely credited with undermining elite support for the Soviet government (Haynes and Bojcun 1990). Of course, not all such disasters have this effect. The 1995 Kobe earthquake in Japan, and the devastation of Hurricane Mitch in 1998 in Central America, did not produce such unrest. While Drury and Olson (1998) have shown that, all other things being equal, the larger the disaster the greater the degree of subsequent political unrest, "all other things" are not generally equal: The context of the disaster matters a great deal.

The key in turning natural or man-made disasters into political turmoil is the responsibility placed on the regime, whether for pre-disaster causation or post-disaster mitigation. In Mexico and Armenia, the central governments of course bore no responsibility for the earth-shaking itself; they drew popular ire for the collapse of poorly built government-constructed apartment blocks, which caused the bulk of the fatalities. In Nicaragua, the Somoza regime alienated business elites as well as ordinary urban dwellers by treating the international aid that flowed to Nicaragua in the wake of the earthquake as an opportunity for graft rather than a resource for reconstruction. In East Pakistan, the population turned against the political regime in West Pakistan in response to the perceived indifference of and inadequate succor given them by that regime.

An interesting example of the divergent political potentials in natural disasters lies in the 1998 floods in China. The unusual magnitude of the floods was due to the extensive logging that had been supported by the communist regime. The regime could have taken a great deal of blame for this event, however it responded to the flooding with spectacularly publicized intervention by the army in public relief efforts. These efforts, treating flood mitigation as a patriotic enterprise, actually gained popular support for the regime.

In short, natural disasters provide an opportunity for the regime to display its flaws or to demonstrate its competence. Where the latter is shown, natural disasters can be a cause of increased support for the government; but where the flaws come to the fore, political unrest and violence is a widely observed response.

Population Change as a Cause of Violent Conflicts

While an enormous literature has developed regarding the potential for environmental change to bring about violent conflict, as noted above it is largely much ado about nothing. With the exception of devastating natural disasters occurring under regimes that display a corrupt or incompetent response, environmental change generally leads to non-violent conflicts that are resolved by negotiation.

A somewhat separate judgment, however, must be made for population changes. It is true that overall population growth, or increases in overall population density, do *not* generally lead to violent conflict. But research has shown a variety of instances in which *particular kinds of population changes* are strongly associated with political instability (de Sherbinen 1995).

For example, if a rapidly growing agrarian population needing more land finds that adjacent land is owned, and even being expanded, for the exclusive use of large landowners, conflict is likely and indeed nearly inevitable. Throughout history, confrontations over land between growing populations of peasants and large landholders have prompted rural rebellions in China, Latin America, and Europe. In most such cases, there is no environmental degradation—the land is often being improved by peasants and landowners alike. However, population growth leads to the cultivation of more marginal lands and to incursions by land-hungry peasants into areas also sought by profit-hungry landlords. The result is a combination of pressure on peasant incomes and heightened conflicts with local elites. Conflict of this sort has arisen most recently in Chiapas in Mexico (Whitmeyer and Hopcroft 1996), but is typical of peasant/landlord relations throughout history, appearing in the French Revolution of 1789, the German Revolution of 1848, the Mexican Revolution of 1910, the

Russian Revolution of 1917, and the Chinese Revolution of 1949 (Skocpol 1979; Wolf 1973).

Such rural conflict can be avoided if the urban and industrial economy can absorb an expanding population. However, studies have shown that where urban growth is not matched by an increase in economic growth, risks of political turbulence increase (Brennan 1999). The most recent State Failure Task Force study of political crises in sub-Saharan Africa from 1955 to 1995 found that the risk of crises, other things equal, *doubled* in countries with above-average levels of urbanization but below-average levels of GDP/capita (Esty et al. 1998: 15).

The problem of over-urbanization relative to incomes is just one aspect of a more general principle relating population changes to political instability, namely that problems arise when there is a persistent mismatch between employment prospects and the size and nature of the labor force. Thus not only over-urbanization, but also over-education relative to the caliber of available jobs, can create political discontent. In revolutionary situations ranging from Tudor England to Enlightenment France, from late Tokugawa Japan to modern Iran and the Soviet Union, political upheaval has been preceded by a surge in the number of youths with advanced education in the context of a relatively limited, semi-closed structure of elite positions (Doyle 1984; O'Boyle 1970; Remington 1990). The central authorities, who guarded the gates of social and economic advancement, drew elite discontent for a situation in which social mobility was increasingly sought but the paths of mobility were increasingly clogged.

Even without increases in higher education, the rapid growth of the number of youths can undermine existing political coalitions, creating instability. Large youth cohorts are often drawn to new ideas and heterodox religions, challenging older forms of authority. In addition, because most young people have fewer responsibilities for families and careers, they are relatively easily mobilized for social or political conflicts. Youth has played a prominent role in political violence throughout recorded history; the existence of a "youth bulge" (an unusually high proportion of youths 15–25 relative to the total population) has historically been associated with times of political crisis (Esler 1971, Moller 1974). In the State Failure Task Force study, the presence of a youth bulge was found to be a major predisposing factor in ethnic conflicts throughout the post–World War II world (Esty et al. 1995); absent such a youth bulge, major ethnic conflicts rarely occurred.

Population movement across, or even within, political borders can also lead to violence. The U.S. Indian Wars of the eighteenth and nineteenth centuries were caused by the expansion of the United States into already-settled Native American territories. The state-assisted migration of Han Chinese into the mainly Uighur-settled region of Xinjiang and into Tibet has led to violent episodes of rebellion in both the latter regions, as their inhabitants struggled to maintain their distinctive identities and control over their territories (see the chapter by Judith Banister in this volume).

The Bantu migrations into southern Africa led to wars throughout the continent, while the movement of peoples, both forced and by choice, across ethnic borders within the former Soviet Union left a legacy of ethnic and separatist conflicts.

The crucial element here is not migration per se; economic migration often leads to substantial benefits for both migrants and the destination country. What appears to matter for conflict are those cases wherein migration leads to clashes of national identity (Teitelbaum and Winters 1998), that is, where one ethnic group migrates into an area that is considered "homeland" by another ethnic group, and challenges the dominance of the latter. If such a conflict escalates into a contest for political control of the region, then ethnic war and even genocide often results.

To sum up, a number of specific population changes are strongly associated with increased risks of political violence:

- an expanding agrarian population denied access to land that is controlled or being expanded for exclusive use of large landlords;
- an expanding urban population in an economy that is not providing commensurate economic growth;
- an expanding population of higher-educated youth facing limited opportunities to obtain elite political and economic positions;
- a large "youth bulge," that is, an expansion of the 15–25 age cohort relative to the overall population of a society;
- the migration of populations into regions already settled by a population with a distinct ethnic or political identity.

Clearly, none of these conditions arises solely from population growth, or even from specific population changes. The conditions that lead to violent conflicts involve population changes in specific contexts in which the desires or needs of an expanding population are blocked. Thus, if we wish to know in what regions of the globe we are most likely to see population-induced political conflicts, we need to examine both expected population changes and the contexts in which they will occur.

Population Changes and Risks of Violent Conflict

As we cross into the new millennium, the world seems finally to have turned the corner on population growth. A combination of increased education for women, national and international support for policies of population planning, and the spread of economic development and its accompanying movement along the demographic transition frontier has led to falling population growth rates around the world. Whether among the behemoths—China and India—or among the smaller but rapidly growing nations—such as Saudi Arabia, Kenya, and Malawi—population growth rates have dropped dramatically in the last decade (U.S. Bureau of the Census 1999: 11).

Yet while population growth rates have dropped around the world, they remain high in some areas. Many nations in sub-Saharan Africa and the Middle East, and several countries in Latin America and Southeast Asia, are still growing at nearly three percent per year, a growth rate that, if sustained, will lead to a doubling of population in approximately twenty-five years. Moreover, although in most countries the rate of population growth has slowed, the absolute number of people being added to the world's population has not; the large number of women of childbearing age in the developing world, carrying the momentum of past population growth, ensures that even as growth rates fall as a percentage of the existing population, the number of new births each year continues to rise. For example, although China's growth rate has fallen to 1.0 percent per year, China will still grow by 10 to 11 million people per year for the next fifteen years. The world as a whole will add roughly 80 million people per year, or another 960 million (that is, another India) in the next dozen years (U.S. Bureau of the Census 1999: 12).

Agrarian conflicts thus still arise, particularly in areas that pit growing rural populations against private landlords seeking exclusive rights to large holdings. Where land reform has not corrected the imbalance between large populations holding a minority of the land and small elites holding a majority of the land (or of the best land), population growth exacerbates this imbalance and fuels rural conflict. For example, in Zimbabwe and Kenya, conflict recurs over access to the best farmland, historically farmed by whites and now increasingly controlled by government-sponsored cronies; in Brazil's northeast, violence repeatedly flares between organizations of the landless and large landowners; and throughout Central America and the Andean region of South America, guerrillas (including the Sandinistas in Nicaragua, the Shining Path movement in Peru, and the FARC in Colombia) have engaged in warfare due to conflicts between marginalized indigenous farmers and state-supported commercial landlords. In sum, we would expect rural conflicts of this sort to arise wherever the population seeking a living in agriculture is growing rapidly, but most land (or most of the best land) is controlled by a relatively small and privileged elite.

Moreover, because it is not the absolute rate of population growth, but the imbalance between growth in specific sectors of the population and growth of the economy that is crucial to the creation of conflicts, even countries with relatively low growth rates may encounter situations in which population changes contribute to political violence. For example, from 1970 to 1991 in the former USSR, when economic growth slowed almost to zero, population growth was also minimal. However, the Soviet Union still encountered four of the five demographic "risk conditions" noted above: an urban population that continued to grow despite minimal economic growth; an over-expansion of young men with a technical higher education, most of whom were relegated to blue-collar jobs due to party restrictions on entry to the managerial and political elites and a stagnant economy; a large youth bulge in the Central Asian republics; and large-scale migration of Russians into many non-Russian ethnic Soviet republics. All of these factors, plus the environmental disasters of the Chernobyl explosion and the Armenia earthquake, became important in mobilizing the urban and nationalist oppositions whose union produced the collapse of the Communist regime (Urban, Igrunov, and Mitrokhin 1997; Lane 1996; Goldstone 1998b: 95–124).

It is precisely because of the importance of such imbalances that countries such as Saudi Arabia and China bear watching for political unrest, despite their success in reducing their rate of population growth. Although Saudi Arabia has dramatically decreased its population growth rate from 5.2 percent per year in the 1980s to 3.2 percent per year in the 1990s (World Bank 1998), that rate of population growth will double the population in less than twenty-five years. It has produced a large youth cohort, combined with rapid expansion of the labor force and rapid urbanization (an annual urban growth rate of 7 percent in the 1980s and 4 percent in the 1990s [World Bank 1998]). The slowdown of the Saudi economy with the decline in world oil prices portends problems in absorbing this large number of urban youth into the economy.

China has succeeded in cutting both its overall population growth and labor force growth to less than one percent per year, but because of its enormous size, this still means finding new jobs for roughly 13 million people per year. Far more important, however, is the shift in China's population from the countryside to the city. Because of the saturation of the agricultural sector, the population has been shifting to cities; virtually all of these new job-seekers, plus many older agricultural workers, have been seeking urban employment. In an odd anomaly, despite very low overall population growth, China has one of the world's highest annual rates of urbanization, at nearly 5 percent in the 1980s and 4 percent in the 1990s. These rates, combined with China's size, mean that in each decade, approximately *150 million* people have been added to the population of China's cities, and are dependent on urban jobs. Until recently, China's enormous rate of annual economic growth, averaging nearly 10 percent, has allowed its economy to absorb these job-seekers. Yet in 1998, China's economic growth rate dropped as the economy tipped toward deflation. A sustained collision between diminished economic growth and the tens of millions moving to cities in search of work every year bodes ill for social and political stability.

Therefore, while the marked decrease in population growth in many countries and regions is good news for those concerned about global population, it offers no clear relief for concerns about the security implications of population change. Despite slowdowns in growth, many countries may well experience collisions that inflame ethnic and regional tensions: between their agrarian populations and access to land, between the expansion of their labor force, educated aspiring elites, urban population, and youth cohorts and the absorption rate of their economies; and as detailed in other papers in this volume, between migrants and resident populations.

For a quick overview of regions where such imbalances are most likely to arise, consider that one of the regions with the most rapid population growth in recent years has also been the region with the worst record of economic development: sub-Saharan Africa. The two areas with the highest anticipated annual rates of population growth in the next decade are the Middle East (2.4 percent) and sub-Saharan Africa (2.3 percent) (U.S. Bureau of the Census 1999: A-4). While such growth is not itself the crucial issue, it invariably brings rapid labor force growth and increasingly large youth cohorts, and is often linked to rapid urbanization. In fact, urbanization is extraordinarily rapid in sub-Saharan Africa, reaching annual rates in excess of 5 percent in many countries. What is truly cause for concern is that these anticipated trends of rapid labor force growth, youth bulges, and dramatic urbanization are combined with the world's lowest rates of economic growth. In 1990–1995, average annual growth in *total* (not per capita) GDP in sub-Saharan Africa was 1.4 percent per year, down from an average of 1.7 percent in 1980–1990; on a per capita basis, real income has been in decline for over a decade. It is economic contraction combined with several specific, volatility-inducing population changes that has helped make Africa a continuing caldron of political and ethnic conflicts.

Looking outside of Africa, urbanization has been slower in most parts of the Middle East, although high annual rates (4 percent or more) persist in Turkey, Saudi Arabia, Syria, and Iran. If we look to South Asia, we find a large difference between Pakistan and India. India appears likely to face far fewer population/conflict challenges from urban and labor force growth (respectively 2.9 and 1.9 percent per year in the mid-1990s), while conditions in Pakistan raise concerns (urban and labor force growth of 4.7 percent and 3.1 percent per year, respectively). However, economic growth has so far been robust in all of these nations (World Bank 1998). The only areas outside of Africa that currently combine high demographic risk factors and low economic growth are Central America and the Caribbean (including Haiti, Nicaragua, and even Mexico); the former states of the Soviet Union in Central Asia; and the Palestinian territories of the Gaza Strip and the West Bank.

While these population changes are most directly linked to domestic political conflicts, these conditions are also relevant to the international problems posed by genocides and international wars. One major finding of recent genocide studies is that these grisly episodes almost always take place in the context of existing domestic or international violent conflicts (Gurr and Harff 1994). A second concern is that most international wars in sub-Saharan Africa have arisen as a result of domestic conflicts. Thus the Eritrea-Ethiopia conflict is a legacy of the upheaval that felled the imperial regime in Ethiopia; the Central African conflict involving several nations is a result of the collapse of the Mobutu regime in Congo-Zaire and the internal ethnic turmoil in Rwanda and Burundi; and the West African conflicts that called for a Nigerian-led international expeditionary force arose from internal rebellions in Liberia and Sierra Leone. Other conflicts in Angola and Sudan have sparked more sporadic cross-national intervention. Thus the demographic changes that raise the risks for domestic conflicts simultaneously pose heightened risks of international wars in the region.

To sum up, while most scholarly attention has focused recently on the environment as a source of violent conflict, it appears that the more fundamental threat to international security in the area of violent environmental/demographic security issues (VEDS) lies in a set of specific population changes occurring in the context of limited economic growth. Substantially increased risks of violent political conflict are found when imbalances arise between population changes and the absorptive capacity of societies.

Demographic Changes as Indicators and Outcomes of Violent Political Conflicts

Unfortunately, there are literally dozens of nations in sub-Saharan Africa, Latin America (especially Haiti), the Middle East, South Asia, and East Asia (especially North Korea) in which past demographic momentum and current population movements are set to produce sustained increases in the labor force, urban populations, educated aspiring elites, or bulging youth cohorts while their economies are threatened with slow growth, setting the stage for political crises. How can we foretell which countries are most likely actually to fall into violent political conflicts?

Part of the answer, of course, may be found by tracking economic and political indicators. However, demographic factors have also proven highly useful in models for forecasting political risks. In the work of the State Failure Task Force (Esty et al. 1995; 1998), probably the most comprehensive modeling of risks of a variety of kinds of violent political conflicts in the years since the Second World War, several demographic variables (including youth bulge, urbanization/development ratio, life expectancy, and adult and infant mortality levels) were found to be useful predictors of political violence, even after allowing for the impact of regime type and such economic factors as international trade relations. In particular, the rate of infant mortality was found to be an important predictor of risk in almost all models. This is not because infant mortality itself directly affects political processes; rather, it appears that infant mortality is the best single tool for assessing the wide variety of factors (average income, income distribution, provision of health care, nutrition) that affect the overall quality of life for individuals in a society. High levels of infant mortality, relative to world averages, indicate higher risks of political crises. Nick Eberstadt (1988, 1993) has further argued that in communist countries in particular, a rise in infant mortality—something hardly ever seen, even in the Third World—is a powerful portent of coming upheaval. Such a rise occurred in the Soviet Union prior to its collapse, and now appears to be occurring in North Korea. These demographic changes may serve as a useful "early alert" of coming security problems.

Finally, it should also be remembered that the relationship between population changes and violent conflicts is not unidirectional. Violent conflicts can also have large and long-lasting impacts on demography. Revolutions frequently bring marked shifts in marriage and birth rates (depending on whether the post-revolutionary period is one of rampant optimism or pessimism), in urbanization (if the new regime sponsors urban development), in education (if the new regime dramatically expands enrollments), and in migration (as the new regime and the violence associated with it may either attract migrants from abroad, or send them across borders seeking escape from violence or persecution). Violent conflicts rarely end conclusively; a more common pattern is that cycles of violence succeed one another. Part of the reason for this is that violent conflicts often produce population changes that, in the next generation if not earlier, feed back into the creation of renewed political risks.

For example, in Palestine the preservation of stateless Arabs in refugee camps following the 1967 Israeli-Arab war led, twenty years later, to the growth in the occupied territories of a vast, aggrieved youth cohort with limited economic prospects. It was this cohort that played a crucial role in the *intifada* uprisings in Gaza and the West Bank. In Central Africa, the movement of Tutsi and Hutu groups across borders as a result of internal conflicts in Rwanda and Burundi led to destabilizing ethnic conflicts in Congo-Zaire, and to renewed and intensified conflicts when new cohorts of formerly exiled Hutus and Tutsis returned to their countries.

Unless measures are taken to provide a semblance of economic hope to the populations of present-day Kosovo, Bosnia, Serbia, and Albania, it is likely that the population displacements that have occurred in the recent Balkan conflicts, and the weak economic conditions that will face the next cohorts of young men growing up in those regions, will produce not a lasting peace, but a renewal of ethnic conflicts. It thus appears that a focus on demographic changes can be helpful both in alerting us to coming security problems, and in helping us foresee how these might fuel further problems in the future.

Population Change, Global Environmental Impacts, and International Security

In contrast to violent conflicts, there are other security issues that cannot be dealt with effectively by the deployment of armed force. These are situations in which resources vital to life—such as the atmosphere and freshwater flows—are degraded by actions taken in other nations. We have already mentioned possible conflicts over water supplies from rivers that run through two or more countries as issues that require international diplomatic negotiation. However, as the world's population grows, and that increased population engages in more activities that generate environmental impacts, the total scale of such environmental degradation can threaten the health of ecosystems that sustain life across the globe. Thus, with increasing population and development, this class of security issues is growing. For these non-violent environmental/demographic security issues (NEDS issues), both population growth and environmental degradation play critical, interrelated roles.

Water issues are generally bilateral or regional; for these, relatively straightforward negotiations or arbitration are generally able to produce progress toward a settlement. However, a few key issues today are not simply bilateral, or even simply multi-lateral, but are truly global in scope. For these issues, the actions of a small number of countries pose security threats to every other country in the world, regardless of size or income level. These are truly novel issues, which pose challenges in the new area of non-violent global security.

At least three such issues are already evident. One has been the subject of successful global negotiations; one is in the midst of difficult and often deadlocked global negotiations; one has yet to produce any such negotiations, except on a very limited scale.

The first is the production of ozone-depleting gases. Once it was discovered that the gaping holes in the ozone shield protecting the earth from solar ultra-violet radiation were being caused by human activity, it was fairly clear that action to halt that activity was imperative. If no action were taken, population growth and economic development around the world would soon produce an exponential increase in the use of ozone-depleting substances (mainly freon in cooling systems, but also various solvents and other industrial chemicals) that would expose most of the temperate zones to cancer-inducing radiation. The major producing and consuming nations of ozone-depleting substances thus came together and produced an international agreement—the Montreal Protocol of 1987—which called for a fairly rapid phase-out of those substances. These swift and successful negotiations were greatly helped by the fact that the major companies producing ozone-depleting substances were able to produce safer substitutes that they could continue to sell at a profit. Nor did any nation stand to benefit substantially from violating the Protocol. The Montreal Protocol stands as a model of a globally negotiated solution to a global environmental threat.

The second such issue is the threat posed by climate change, most likely global warming. As with ozone, it has become clear that human activity is altering the atmosphere. The burning of fossil fuels releases gases (mainly carbon dioxide, or CO_2) that increase the earth's absorption of solar heat energy. If unchecked, these changes could lead to substantial warming of the planet, with unpredictable effects on weather, crop production, sea levels, and the spread of disease vectors and pests (Brown 1989; Gleick 1989; Soroos 1997). These effects are no longer speculative: Global temperatures have increased markedly in the last two decades;

extreme weather events of all sorts (hurricanes, tornadoes, droughts, storms, freezes, floods, El Niño) have become more frequent and severe; the Arctic, Antarctic, and Greenland ice-packs have lost tens of square miles to melting, as have glaciers around the world; and plants and animals (from insects to otters) have extended their winter ranges farther toward the poles. Recent studies of Greenland ice-core samples suggest that global temperatures can shift suddenly and dramatically over the course of a few decades as tipping points are reached. While we are not certain how much of the current climate change could be reduced or halted by stopping the man-made production of CO_2 contributing to it, it seems certain that a further exponential increase in CO_2 production can only accelerate climate change. Stabilizing CO_2 production, and eventually reducing it, is the goal of the current global climate negotiations now being conducted by most nations of the world. The most recent accord reached in these negotiations, the Kyoto Protocol of 1997, calls for substantial reductions in CO_2 production by rich countries, although it leaves open the actions expected of developing nations.

However, these negotiations have been constantly threatened with derailment over the issue of how developing nations will participate in the accords. Population changes and development make this a vexing issue. At the present, the largest producer of CO_2 gases in the world is the United States, which in the early 1990s produced more CO_2 each year than China and India combined. Yet current projections of population growth and economic development in the latter countries suggest a huge increase in their future CO_2 output; by 2010 China and India will be producing fifty percent more CO_2 than the United States (Goldstone 1999: 255). What then should be the path for CO_2 reductions? Clearly, current reductions are not credible unless they begin with the largest producer, the United States. However, unless China and India bind themselves to a development path that will greatly curtail their burning of fossil fuels, then any reduction achieved by the United States will go for naught, as in a few years the larger countries' emissions will continue to escalate global warming. How can India and China—with large populations demanding economic development, which on today's known pathways entails massive increases in energy consumption—bind themselves to constraints on their development? Although one can hope for a minor miracle—for example, a cheap way for India and China to produce the energy they need from wind power and solar cells, thus obviating the need for vast increases in coal or oil consumption—these negotiations still are looking for a breakthrough that will solve this problem.

A final issue that likely will demand global attention is the preservation of species diversity (Terborgh 1999). It is already well-known that simplified ecosystems—such as parks, gardens, and agricultural fields—are enormously more susceptible to infection, parasites, and catastrophic species extinctions than are the more varied natural ecosystems. In addition, complex ecosystems harbor millions of species whose role in sustaining the global ecology, or providing specific useful substances, is yet unknown. Thus many scientists suspect that deforestation, particularly in rainforests, or ocean pollution that kills plankton species, may not only drastically affect the ability of the earth to recycle CO_2, but may have unknown effects up or down the ecological scale that would change the balance of species around the world. European nations are also deeply concerned about the potential impact of genetically modified crops and animals upon the quality and diversity of the global gene pool. No global negotiations are yet bent on scaling back activities that reduce the diversity of species, although there have been limited moves in this direction. Controls on genetically modified crops are a subject of discussion in the recent round of World Trade Organization agreements. International action has been taken to protect certain "charismatic" fauna, such as elephants, rhinos, dolphins, and whales, and the United States and many European nations have strict laws aimed at protecting any and all endangered species in their territory. But that is the rub: The majority of the world's species diversity is contained not in the rich societies in temperate climates, but in the poorer societies of the tropics. Their development seems to demand environmental and species destruction, which they are in fact carrying on at a rapid rate. Whether it is a lack of urgency regarding this issue, or a sense that there is no straightforward solution to trading off development in semi-tropical and tropical nations versus species preservation, it may be some time before coordinated international action is taken on this issue; by then it will be too late for many species. However, as with ozone and CO_2, the key to solving the problem is the impact of population movements and growth: The most rapid adverse changes are taking place among countries with the largest populations, and are in response to government efforts to settle those populations in more extensive areas and provide them with agricultural incomes.

Conclusion: From VEDS to NEDS—Facing up to Real Population and Environmental Security Issues

Discussions of environmental security have been muddied by the confusing multitude of ways in which population, the environment, and security have been combined. In fact, environmental issues appear to have very little impact on traditional security concerns, those focusing on armed conflict within and between nations. Population changes, historically and in some regions (mainly Africa) today, have in fact posed such security concerns. Where demands for access to land and/or employment, for political participation, and for ethnic or regional political power have been intensified by shifts in the size and distribution of populations; where urbanization, the emergence of new aspiring elites, and growing youth cohorts have undermined existing political and economic regimes, civil violence has become dramatically more likely.

In addition there is a substantial set of serious future security threats stemming from what I have labeled NEDS issues—issues in which the condition of the environment itself is the security threat. Several such issues—shared freshwater resources, ozone depletion, global warming, and concerns over species preservation and the global gene pool—have already become evident. The first of these has been the source of numerous bilateral conflicts and treaties, while the others have to varying degrees become the focus of extended global negotiations aimed at creating treaty regimes. In all these cases, population growth and economic development combine to place the environmental risk on an exponential growth track unless global actions are taken to halt or reverse the trend. Unfortunately, these negotiations often pit the interests of the wealthy developed nations against those of the poorer, but far more numerous, peoples of developing nations.

To return to the main focus of this volume, it appears that we are on the threshold of a new era in security, but it is not an era in which environmental changes become new sources of traditional security concerns. Homer-Dixon and his colleagues, who have emphasized the role of environmental change in bringing about violent and acute conflicts, provided a valuable service in stimulating debate on the relationships among environment, population, and security. However, the initial specification of environmental degradation as a major new threat to stability and a cause of violence now appears to be mistaken.

Rather, this is an era in which several specific aspects of population change—rapid increases in labor force, youth cohorts, urban population, elite training, or migration that produces a collision of ethnic groups—promise to spread recurring political crises when they occur in countries with struggling economies and inflexible or transitional political systems.[4] Indeed, a major reason to fear that such VEDS issues will grow more important in the future is that the vast majority of the world's expected growth in all the aforementioned aspects of population change will take place in precisely those countries and regions that have either struggling economies, or inflexible or transitional regimes, namely Africa; the Middle East; the Andean region of South America; Central America/Mexico/the Caribbean; Russia and the former Soviet Republics; China; and South and Southeast Asia.

In addition, there are countries whose regimes are actively involved in worsening the effects of natural disasters—whether by taking actions that increase their likelihood or their toll, or by making a corrupt or ineffective response; here political upheavals are likely to follow. Population changes and natural disasters, in vulnerable economic and political settings, are thus likely to provide the major VEDS issues for the foreseeable future.

Where long-term environmental degradation emerges as a major security issue is not in war-prevention and managing internal domestic conflicts, but in a new security arena, that of transnational and global threats to the environment itself. Such NEDS issues have already provoked confrontations and international negotiations in regard to water use, ozone depletion, CO_2 production, the preservation of certain species, and controls on genetically modified crops. Such fundamental environmental security issues will take us to new frontiers in science to understand their nature, and—we must hope—to new frontiers in international negotiations and security arrangements to deter and ameliorate their threats.

Notes

1. This formulation owes much to Nazli Choucri's three-fold definition of security as embracing military security, regime security, and structural security, the latter including all threats to "life-supporting properties—as well as prevailing sources of livelihood" (Choucri 1997: 180).
2. Confusion on these issues is rife and yet often unremarked; even skilled analysts have had trouble avoiding vague and ambiguous terms. Thus an outstanding environmental policy scholar, Daniel Esty (1999: 290–314), in a recent essay refers to "overseas environmental harms," "environmental security threats," "environmental effects on state stability," "direct environmental threats," and "direct environmental spillovers" as various ways to link environmental concerns with security. I believe Esty uses "environmental effects on state stability" to imply violent consequences of environmental change, and both "direct environmental threats" and "direct environmental spillovers" to describe non-violent threats. But none of his terms has a clear and unequivocal meaning. Moreover they make no explicit mention of population at all, although in his case examples Esty focuses heavily on population-related causes of conflicts.
3. A recent *Aviso* bulletin providing an excellent survey of water and security issues notes that over 3,600 treaties have been signed over different aspects of international waters, with remarkable elegance and creativity in dealing with water issues; moreover, in the last 3,000 years, "there has *never* been a war fought over water" (Wolf 1999: 2).
4. Homer-Dixon and his colleagues have in fact recognized this and, in their most recent work, point to population growth pressing on resources, and political barriers constraining access to vital resources, as the major pathways involving the environment and population in the origins of conflict (Homer-Dixon and Percival 1996; Percival and Homer-Dixon 1998).

References

Albala-Bertrand, J. M. 1993. *The Political Economy of Large Natural Disasters.* Oxford: Clarendon Press.

Baechler, Günther. 1998. "Why Environmental Transformation Causes Violence: A Synthesis." *Environmental Change and Security Project Report of the Woodrow Wilson Center* 4: 24–44.

Brennan, Ellen. 1999. *Population, Urbanization, Environment, and Security: A Summary of the Issues.* Comparative Urban Studies Occasional Paper Series No. 22. Washington, D.C.: Woodrow Wilson International Center for Scholars.

Brown, Neville. 1989. "Climate, Ecology, and International Security." *Survival* 31: 519–532.

Choucri, Nazli. 1997. "Environmental Flash Points in the Near East and North Africa." In *Consequences of Environmental Change—Political Economic, Social* (Proceedings of the Environmental Flash Points Workshop, Reston, Virginia, 12–14 November 1997). Edited by Robert S. Chen, W. Christopher Lenhardt and Kara F. Alkire. University Center, MI: Consortium for International Earth Science Information Network (CIESIN), pp. 177–196.

de Sherbinen, Alex. 1995. "World Population Growth and U.S. National Security." *Environmental Change and Security Project Report of the Woodrow Wilson Center* 1: 24–29.

Deudney, Daniel. 1990. "The Case Against Linking Environmental Degradation and National Security." *Millennium* 19: 461–476.

Diehl, Paul. 1998. "Environmental Conflict: An Introduction." *Journal of Peace Research* 35: 275–277.

Doyle, William. 1984. "The Price of Offices in Pre-Revolutionary France. *Historical Journal* 27: 831–860.

Drury, A. Cooper, and Richard Stuart Olson. 1998. "Disasters and Political Unrest: An Empirical Investigation." *Journal of Contingencies and Crisis Management* 6: 153–161.

Eberstadt, Nick. 1988. *The Poverty of Communism.* New Brunswick, NJ: Transaction Books.

———. 1993. *North Korea: Reform, Muddling Through, or Collapse?* Monograph 4(3). Seattle: National Bureau of Asian Research.

Esler, Anthony. 1971. *Bombs, Beards, and Barricades: 150 Years of Youth in Revolt.* New York: Stein and Day.

Esty, Daniel. 1999. "Pivotal States and the Environment." In *The Pivotal States: A New Framework for U.S. Policy in the Developing World.* Edited by Robert Chase, Emily Hill, and Paul Kennedy. New York: W. W. Norton.

Esty, Daniel, Jack A. Goldstone, Ted Robert Gurr, Barbara Harff, Pamela Surko, and Alan N. Unger. 1995. *Working Papers: State Failure Task Force Report.* McLean, VA: Science Applications International Corporation.

Esty, Daniel, Jack A. Goldstone, Ted Robert Gurr, Barbara Harff, Marc Levy, Geoffrey D. Dabelko, Pamela Surko, and Alan N. Unger. 1998. *State Failure Task Force Report: Phase II Findings.* McLean, VA: Science Applications International Corporation.

Feierabend, Ivo K., R. L. Feierabend, and B. A. Nesvold. 1969. "Social Change and Political Violence: Cross-National Patterns." In *Violence in America: Historical and Comparative Perspectives.* Edited by H. D. Graham and T. R. Gurr. New York: Praeger.

Foran, John, ed. 1997. *Theorizing Revolutions.* London: Routledge.

Gleditsch, Nils Petter. 1998. "Armed Conflict and the Environment: A Critique of the Literature." *Journal of Peace Research* 35: 381–400.

Gleick, Peter H. 1989. "The Implications of Global Climate Changes for International Security." *Climate Change* 15: 303–325.

———. 1998. *The World's Water: The Biennial Report on Fresh Water Resources.* Washington, D.C. and Covelo, CA: Island Press.

Goldstone, Jack A., ed. 1998a. *The Encyclopedia of Political Revolutions.* Washington, D.C.: Congressional Quarterly.

———. 1998b. "The Soviet Union: Revolution and Transformation." In *Elites, Crises, and the Origins of Regimes.* Edited by Mattei Dogan and John Higley. Lanham, MD: Rowman and Littlefield.

———. 1999. "Population and Pivotal States." In *The Pivotal States: A New Framework for U.S. Policy in the Developing World.* Edited by Robert Chase, Emily Hill, and Paul Kennedy. New York: W.W. Norton.

Gurr, Ted Robert. 1980. *Handbook of Political Conflict.* New York: Free Press.

Gurr, Ted Robert, and Barbara Harff. 1994. *Ethnic Conflict in World Politics.* Boulder, CO: Westview Press.

Hauge, Wenche, and Tanja Ellingson. 1998. "Beyond Environmental Scarcity: Causal Pathways to Conflict." *Journal of Peace Research* 35: 299–317.

Haynes, Viktor, and Marko Bojcun. 1990. *The Chernobyl Disaster.* London: Hogarth Press.

Hill, Richard, Swarupa Ganguli, and Dede Naylor. 1998. "Environmental Flashpoints in South Asia." In *Consequences of Environmental Change—Political Economic, Social.* Proceedings of the Environmental Flash Points Workshop, Reston, Virginia, 12–14 November 1997. Edited by Robert S. Chen, W. Christopher Lenhardt, and Kara F. Alkire. University Center, MI: Consortium for International Earth Science Information Network (CIESIN).

Homer-Dixon, Thomas. 1991. "On the Threshold: Environmental Changes as Causes of Acute Conflict." *International Security* 16: 76–116.

———. 1994. "Environmental Scarcities and Violent Conflict: Evidence from Cases." *International Security* 19: 5–40.

Homer-Dixon, Thomas, and Valerie Percival. 1996. *Environmental Scarcity and Violent Conflict: Briefing Book.* Toronto: Project on Environment, Population, and Security, University of Toronto and the American Association for the Advancement of Science.

Huntington, Samuel P. 1968. *Political Order In Changing Societies.* New Haven: Yale University Press.

Kahl, Colin. 1998. "Population Growth, Environmental Degradation, and State-Sponsored Violence: The Case of Kenya, 1991–1993." *International Security* 23: 80–119.

Lane, David. 1996. "The Gorbachev Revolution: The Role of the Political Elite in Regime Disintegration." *Political Studies* 44: 4–23.

Levy, Marc A. 1995. "Is the Environment a National Security Issue?" *International Security* 20: 35–62.

Lipschutz, Ronnie D. 1997. "Damming troubled waters: Conflict over the Danube, 1950–2000." Paper presented at Environment and Security Conference, Institute of War and Peace Studies, Columbia University, New York, October 24, 1997.

Lowi, Miriam R. 1993. *Water and Power: The Politics of a Scarce Resource in the Jordan River Basin*. Cambridge: Cambridge University Press.

Matthews, Jessica Tuchman. 1989. "Redefining Security." *Foreign Affairs* 68: 162–177.

Moller, Herbert. 1974. "Rebellious Youth as a Force for Change." In *The Youth Revolution: The Conflict of Generations in Modern History*. Ed. Anthony Esler. Lexington, Mass: D.C. Heath.

Myers, Norman. 1993. *Ultimate Security: The Environmental Basis of Political Stability*. New York: W.W. Norton.

O'Boyle, L. 1970. "The Problem of an Excess of Educated Men in Western Europe, 1800–1850." *Journal of Modern History* 42: 471–495.

Percival, Valerie, and Thomas Homer-Dixon. 1998. "Environmental Scarcity and Violent Conflict: The Case of South Africa." *Journal of Peace Research* 35: 279–298.

Remington, Thomas. 1990. "Regime Transitions in Communist Systems: The Soviet Case." *Soviet Economy* 6: 160–190.

Rothschild, Emma. 1995. "What is Security?" *Daedalus* 124: 53–91.

Shefner, Jon. 1999. "Pre- and Post-Disaster Political Instability and Contentious Supporters: A Case Study of Political Ferment." *International Journal of Mass Emergencies and Disasters*, 17: 137–160.

Skocpol, Theda. 1979. *States and Social Revolutions*. Cambridge: Cambridge University Press.

Soroos, Marvin S. 1997. *The Endangered Atmosphere: Preserving a Global Commons*. Columbia, S.C.: University of South Carolina Press.

Teitelbaum, Michael S., and Jay Winters. 1998. *A Question of Numbers: High Migration, Low Fertility, and the Politics of National Identity*. New York: Hill and Wang/Farrar, Straus, Giroux.

Terborgh, John. 1999. *Requiem for Nature*. Washington, D.C. and Covelo, CA: Island Press.

Tilly, Charles. 1973. "Does Modernization Breed Revolution?" *Comparative Politics* 5: 425–447.

U.S. Bureau of the Census. 1999. *World Population Profile 1998*. Report WP/98. Washington, D.C.: U.S. Government Printing Office.

Urban, Michael, Vyacheslav Igrunov, and Sergei Mitrokhin. 1997. *The Rebirth of Politics in Russia*. Cambridge: Cambridge University Press.

Weiner, Myron. 1971. "Political Demography: An Inquiry into the Political Consequences of Population Change." In *Rapid Population Growth: Consequences and Policy Implications*. Compiled by the National Academy of Sciences. Baltimore, MD: Johns Hopkins University Press.

Whitmeyer, Joseph, and Rosemary L. Hopcroft. 1996. "Community, Capitalism, and Rebellion in Chiapas." *Sociological Perspectives* 39: 517–539.

Wolf, Aaron T. 1999. "Water and Human Security." *Aviso: An Information Bulletin on Global Environmental Change and Human Security*. No. 3: 1–7.

Wolf, Eric R. 1973. *Peasant Wars of the Twentieth Century*. New York: Harper and Row.

Woodrow Wilson Center. 1998. "Bibliographic Guide to the Literature." *Environmental Change and Security Project Report*. 4: 141–179.

World Bank. 1998. *World Development Indicators 1997* (CD-ROM).

CHAPTER 3

Demographic Change and the Sources of International Conflict

Ronald R. Krebs and Jack S. Levy

With the close of the Cold War, concerns about the global balance of power and strategic stability have diminished, while other threats to international security and the future world order have acquired greater salience among scholars and policymakers. Although some have continued to worry about a rising China or a resurgent Russia, many have identified new types of threats and have constructed new frameworks to explain and grapple with them. While some have augured conflict along civilizational lines (Huntington 1996) and others have trumpeted democracy as the foundation of peace,[1] both pundits and the press have increasingly warned that rapid population growth in the developing world poses dangers to international stability and may spark wars. Some argue that demographic growth in the developing world contributes to social and political turmoil that is conducive to domestic and international violence, while others maintain that declining fertility among the advanced industrialized countries portends a shift in the global military and economic distribution of power, undermining the postwar international order.[2] That American policymakers have recently devoted greater thought to the international implications of demographic patterns is further reason to examine these claims more carefully.[3]

The ramifications of demographic change have received relatively little attention in the mainstream international relations literature, particularly before the end of the Cold War.[4] Although the postwar conventional wisdom has portrayed rapid population growth as injurious to a country's economic health and potentially politically destabilizing, an equally long tradition has depicted population growth as increasing the state's basis for international influence.[5] Nearly every textbook on international politics contains an obligatory discussion of the elements of national power (for example, Morgenthau 1993 [1948]; Organski 1968), and population size is typically treated unproblematically as contributing to a state's power resources. The relationship between population and national power is a good deal more complicated than that, however, and scholars have explored other connections between demographic change and international conflict. In this review we systematically and critically assess the relationship between these two phenomena by focusing on several intervening variables and their respective causal pathways: national power, resource scarcity, communal conflict, and international migration (see Fig. 3.1).[6]

We argue that many of the predictions forecasting widespread international conflict as a consequence of rapid population growth and the corresponding proposals for drastic reduction of the birth rate in the developing world rest on unsubstantiated premises that deserve greater scrutiny. While these powerfully worded warnings and recommendations satisfy our intuitive sense that population growth gives rise to international conflict, that link is not obvious and certainly not direct. Policymakers may have good reasons—rooted in humanitarian goals, fear of environmental degradation, concern for women's quality of life (Mazur 1994; Sen 1994; Oppong 1996), and domestic political interests— for endorsing policies aimed at curbing population growth in poor countries. However, we take issue with the attempt to justify such policies on the basis of threats to international peace and security. Population growth may, on occasion, contribute to international conflict, but it does so only in combination with other factors and under particular circumstances.[7] The literature commonly posits straightforward links that are neither theoretically nor empirically convincing; what is needed is a better understanding of the conditions under which these hypotheses hold. To deny

FIGURE 3.1   Demographic Change and International Conflict: Possible Linkages

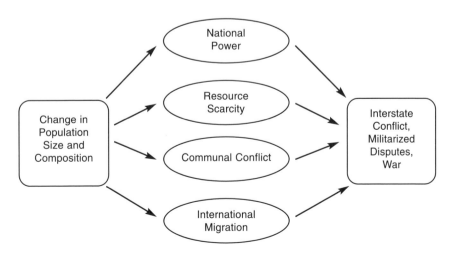

the relevance of demographic factors to international politics would be foolish, but polemics that portray runaway population growth as the next great threat to peace and that recommend population control as a panacea are equally misleading.

Population, National Power, and International Conflict

Realist writers on international relations trace their lineage to Thucydides and take as a fundamental truth of international politics the famous lesson of the Melian Dialogue—the strong do what they can, the weak suffer what they must. They argue that in an anarchic international environment force is the *ultima ratio*, and that the distribution of power, both at the dyadic and systemic levels, is the primary determinant of foreign policy choices and international outcomes. Realists have never been as insensitive to economics as their critics have charged, however, and a strong economic foundation has always been seen as essential to projecting military power and attaining great power status (Earle 1986; Doyle 1997). In the following three sections we explore the relationship between population growth and military power, population growth and economic development, and finally between national power and international conflict.[8]

Population and Military Power

Realists typically endorse two hypotheses relating population and military power. First, they argue that the static indicator of relative population size correlates with the relative *size* of the army and hence with relative military power; a country with a larger population can summon a larger military than can its opponent. While scholars of international relations often eschew the most crude correlations between population size and military power, Hans Morgenthau (1993 [1948]:140–141) is hardly alone in declaring that "no country can remain or become a first-rate power which does not belong to the more populous nations of the earth."[9] Similarly, Katherine and A. F. K. Organski (1961: 15) have written that "though few nations arm to the hilt, the size of the sword is significant.... It is the size of the total population that sets the limit." Second, realists have, in a more dynamic vein, contended that population *growth* bequeaths a larger population and ensures that more young men will enter military service, boosting a state's military resources. As Morgenthau (1993 [1948]:140–141) averred, "shifts in the distribution of power within Europe in recent history have been roughly duplicated by the changes in population trends."

For some realists, the advent of the nuclear era has not significantly weakened the relationship between population and national power. Conventional forces and weaponry remain necessary for small (non-global) wars. Even in a nuclear conflict, some have argued, population would remain a critical element of power, albeit in the form of technicians and scientists rather than infantry; troops would also be needed as occupying forces once the bomb had been dropped (Organski and Organski 1961; Tapinos 1978). It is worth recalling that the nuclear contest of the Cold War did not render the superpowers' conventional forces irrelevant. In the mid-1980s American military strategists intensely debated the state of the balance on the European front, and the possession of nuclear weapons did not prevent the Soviet Union and China from massing troops along their borders.

This reasoning has justified pro-natalist policies from Hitler to de Gaulle. British Prime Minister Winston Churchill clearly articulated this logic in a 1943 radio broadcast:

> One of the most somber anxieties which beset those who look thirty, or forty, or fifty years ahead … is the dwindling birth-rate…. If this country is to keep its high place in the leadership of the world, and to survive as a great power that can hold its own against external pressures, our people must be encouraged by every means to have larger families. (Quoted in Morgenthau 1993 [1948]: 143)

This thinking also underlies contemporary concerns about the ability of the advanced industrialized nations to raise and maintain effective military forces as their fertility falls below the replacement rate and as their populations age, leaving them with a smaller manpower pool of military age and a smaller supporting labor force (Saunders 1991; Sarkesian 1989). As Geoffrey McNicoll (1995: 321) notes, "This old conviction that population means power clearly persists: in the United States it is seen in support for international population control efforts in branches of government (National Security Council, Defense Department) not given to welfarist concerns."

Both key links in these hypotheses' causal logic are overly simple, however. Population growth is neither necessary nor sufficient for an increase in the size of the military, nor does a larger army necessarily bring battlefield success. First, whether a country's army is commensurate with its population depends on various factors, including the character of its social and political institutions as well as the expansiveness of the state's definition of its interests. As Nazli Choucri (1974: 29) has written, "only through the mediated influence of technology, social organization, capital and military equipment, and political structure, among other variables, does population become an important consideration." For example, population growth will obviously have very different effects, all else being equal, on the size of the military in a state with mandatory service and in one with an all-volunteer force; however, if state leaders believe that the current armed forces are capable of performing their tasks, population growth can induce a state to abandon conscription.[10] In recognition of this fact, Organski and his colleagues (1972) refined earlier discussions by introducing the concept of "effective population"—that portion of the population that contributes most directly to furthering national goals—to capture the population's skill level and the ability of the political and economic system to aggregate individual contributions into a common pool of national capabilities. Increments of national power thus result from changes in effective population, not total population.[11]

The mediating effect of state and social institutions between national resources, including population, and state power, particularly the size of the military, cannot be ignored. In the latter half of the nineteenth century, the United States compared favorably with the European great powers in population and industrial production, but ranked low on measures of state autonomy and capacity. With a limited ability to convert national resources into state power, the United States remained, until the early 1890s, relatively inactive in foreign affairs and possessed of a military befitting a far smaller and less wealthy state. As the power of the American federal state grew relative to the state governments, and as the executive branch extended its reach over policy, the military and the scope of the nation's ambitions overseas swelled accordingly.[12] Similarly, the size of the French population under the old regime was obviously not dramatically different from that of Revolutionary France, but the turn to the *levée en masse*, wrapped up with changing conceptions of the state and its purpose, produced a vastly larger military force and a starkly different form of warfare. Of course, the success of the Revolutionary armies did not lie in their size alone, but in the marriage "of the professionalism of the ancien régime with the enthusiasm of a Nation in Arms," and later in the brilliance of Napoleon (Howard 1976: 80).

Nor does the second step in the realist causal chain hold, for the size of a state's army does not translate smoothly into military effectiveness, whether in winning wars or helping states prevail in crises and disputes. Numbers may matter, but the historical record does not demonstrate that, to paraphrase Voltaire, God is always on the side of the bigger battalions.[13] From the Greek defeat of the Persian armies at Marathon in 490 B.C.E. to the English victory at Crécy in 1346 to Germany's triumph in the 1940 battle for France, superior doctrine and armaments have overcome overwhelming numbers. Raw manpower is not sufficient, as the failure of "human wave" tactics, employed by China against Vietnam in 1979 and by Iran against Iraq in the 1980s, has demonstrated (Freedman 1991). States with relatively small populations have compensated with advanced technology, better tactics and strategy, the advantage of surprise, or a more efficient military organization.[14] A severely outmanned Israel has repeatedly defeated its Arab neighbors in various wars, and Britain succeeded in conquering India despite far fewer troops and armaments that were at best equal.[15]

Just as the size of an army is not a powerful predictor of military success, there is evidence that the dyadic balance of power, reflecting overall military capabilities including industrial capacity, is not the primary determinant of the diplomatic outcomes of crises that do not escalate to war.[16] As Maoz (1983: 221) argues, "initiators of serious interstate disputes tend to disproportionately emerge as victors not because they are stronger than targets but because they are able to demonstrate that the stakes of the dispute are more important to them than to their opponents." This conclusion regarding the balance of resolve is consistent with George and Smoke's (1974) emphasis on the importance of the "asymmetry of motivation," with rational choice models that incorporate preferences as well as power-based constraints (Bueno de Mesquita and Lalman 1992), and with a number of studies that attempt to explain "why big nations lose small wars" (Mack 1975; Paul 1994).[17]

Pessimistic prognostications regarding fertility patterns and the West's ability to raise adequate military forces implicitly assume that war today is much as it was in the time of Frederick the Great.[18] However, technological developments are increasingly rendering the military's size even less relevant to the outcome of international conflict.[19] Nuclear weapons, which require a relatively limited number of technical and strategic staff to maintain and operate them, would render differentials in population less important were they to proliferate widely (Deudney 1990: 472–473). More important, the heralded information revolution in military affairs will likewise privilege an army's skill and training over its absolute size. As Eliot Cohen has noted,

> At long last, after a reign of almost two centuries, the age of the mass military manned by short-service conscripts and equipped with the products of high-volume military manufacturing is coming to an end.... Future technologies may create pockets of military capability that will allow very small states to hold off larger ones, much as companies of Swiss pikemen could stop armies sweeping through their mountain passes or a single, well-fortified castle could hold immensely larger forces at bay for months. (Cohen 1996: 47, 53)

In assessing the lessons of the Gulf War, scholars may dispute whether superior American skill, inferior Iraqi tactics, and better American arms were all essential to the complex story of a crushing U.S. victory, or whether skill and technology were each sufficient, but no one believes that numbers were critical to the outcome (Biddle 1996, 1997; Press 1997).[20] The most advanced and effective armaments require more highly educated and technically proficient manpower to operate and maintain them, skills that are in relative abundance in the industrialized world.[21] As the information revolution continues to transform the battlefield over the coming decades, sheer numbers, never the sole determinant of war's outcome, will in all likelihood continue to decrease in importance.[22]

In terms of national strategy, the impact of declining birthrates must be judged in the context of missions that need to be performed. If peace enforcement operations in the former Yugoslavia in the 1990s—low-intensity, regional conflicts rather than massed forces along a central front—represent the future of warfare and of NATO's likely missions, the

West's military power, though perhaps not its willpower, will suffice. None of this is to deny, of course, that demographic factors are important considerations for military planners. The composition of the population determines the overall numbers of service-age men, affects the gender balance of the armed forces, and influences government options regarding its policies for raising forces. The size of the army influences how strategists weigh their options. None of these "demographic" facts is independent of social and political institutions, however, and numbers may be far less important than factors such as technology and level of education. Population growth alone does not translate into a larger army, and a larger military is not the same as a more effective or successful one.

Although the link between population growth, the size of the armed forces, and military power is tenuous, state leaders have often found this logic persuasive. Throughout the Cold War, American and European strategists worried about the huge Warsaw Pact numbers advantage along the central front, and Israeli generals have expressed concern about similar disparities with their neighbors to the east. Such thinking was most pervasive before World War I, when European statesmen, influenced by the Prussian model of the short-service conscript army, were engaged in "the increasingly obsessive numbers game of comparative demography" (Best 1989: 14; Howard 1976: 99–100, 105–107). Dispassionate analysis may reveal that such connections are far weaker than many suppose, but perceptions are the stuff of politics. To the extent that this strategic belief, no matter how erroneous, influences military manpower policies and strategy, it affects the likelihood of war.

Let us now turn from change in the size of the population to change in its composition. Some have suggested that if rapid population growth contributes to segmental cleavages (differences among classes, ethnicities, age groups, gender, and so on), these divisions within the populace will undermine the nation's integration and cohesion and hence its capacity for collective action (Choucri 1974: 74; Sarkesian 1989).[23] One clear example of ethnic cleavages undercutting military strength is Austria-Hungary prior to World War I. Austrian leaders had to form a cohesive military organization out of eleven different nationalities while dealing with the continued refusal of the Magyars to support army reform or increases in military recruitment without guarantees of more autonomy and other concessions that would weaken centralized command (Williamson 1991).

We will assess a related set of arguments in greater detail in the section on ethnic composition, but for now two points will suffice. First, in modern, large-scale societies, an individual must construct a political identity out of a host of possible identities—ethnicity, religion, race, class, gender, nationality—and there is nothing given about which will seem most apposite. Segmental cleavages will affect national power only if they are highly salient and politically mobilized. Identity is, then, as much a product of political context and contest as it is their source (Dirks,

Eley, and Ortner 1994). Moreover, one need not be a radical constructivist to recognize that the meanings individuals attach to their identification with a larger group are subject to flux. Under urban political machines in the United States, ethnic identification was a critical marker of one's political loyalties, and the number of new Irish or Italian immigrants portended shifts in power; however, even as these hyphenated Americans have maintained a connection with their immigrant ancestors' homelands, these groups have largely melded into the single category of white ethnic. These identities have become less politically and economically relevant, mass ethnic political machines have declined, and the old ethnic foundation of politics has eroded (Waters 1990).[24]

Second, this hypothesis, although intuitively plausible, requires far greater specification regarding the expected outcomes and the causal mechanisms that lead to them. Rapid population growth would more likely be disruptive to national cohesion when it either upsets the balance between two or more ethnic or religious groups nearly equal in size or narrows the gap between two groups that are far apart, than when it further widens an already large disparity. When a far weaker group declines in influence, its capacity to fracture the nation and undermine the country's ability to project power on the international stage is correspondingly circumscribed. These hypotheses must be qualified, however, for a group's population size alone does not reveal a great deal about its political power, even in a democracy. In addition, changes in the population's age structure might have little impact on national cohesion. Although the large youth cohort might, for example, strenuously object to a military venture in which it would suffer disproportionately, it may have relatively few political resources at its disposal. As noted earlier, assuming a particular institutional and technological context, a larger youth cohort may simply increase the size of the army and add to military capability, while remaining largely incapable of altering national policy. Thus the hypothesis must further specify which trends in which segments have what political effects under what types of political institutions.

Population and Economic Development

The relationship between population growth and the economic components of national power involves a long-standing debate in demography and economics, one with important implications for national security. For some, population growth underpins a rise in national income and industrial wealth, and the expanded economy can then serve as the foundation for potential military power as well as for economic coercion (Organski and Organski 1961: 21–26; Davis 1958). Others, drawing on the work of Malthus and his followers, see rapid population growth as undermining the economy and contributing to resource scarcities.[25] The strength of both sets of theoretical arguments, under varying conditions, prevents any easy resolution of this still-raging debate, and the empirical evidence is inconclusive. Amartya Sen (1994: 62) has elegantly characterized these positions as "dismissive smugness" and "apocalyptic pessimism," warning that such a polarized debate prevents a more nuanced and genuine understanding of the relationship between population and development.

The Malthusian tradition presents the best known reasoning regarding the negative effects of population growth. Although population growth raises total productive capacity, that rise in productivity will fall short of the increase in labor supply. Given fixed natural resources, particularly land, agricultural productivity progressively diminishes, and population invariably outruns food supplies. The persuasiveness of the neo-Malthusian case turns on the highly contested concept of "carrying capacity," defined as the optimum population that a given resource base can support. The hypothesis that crisis ensues when the population exceeds the land's carrying capacity is meaningful, however, only if the point at which this occurs can be objectively identified independent of its predicted social and political consequences. This accomplishment has eluded scholars, for different societies define the minimally acceptable standard of living in different ways at different times. Moreover, the possibility of trade for food resources renders a particular country's "carrying capacity" meaningless (McNicoll 1995: 317; Bharadwaj 1996: 5; Davis 1991: 5–8). Although analysts of a Malthusian bent continue to invoke the concept when they decry "overpopulation," this critical point can be identified only after the fact.

Empirically, the Malthusian model, while perhaps adequate as an explanation of dynamics in the preindustrial period, cannot comprehend Europe's "demographic transition" over the eighteenth and nineteenth centuries, when decreasing mortality contributed to rapid population growth but combined with steady economic gains.[26] Nor can neo-Malthusian accounts make sense of the industrialized world's fertility decline in the context of continuing economic growth (Wrigley 1996). Some scholars have even challenged these accounts on their own turf, dating Europe's escape from its Malthusian chains not to the Industrial Revolution, but to the discovery of the New World, the invention of the printing press, the Reformation, and so on (Weir 1991).

The proposition that population growth is beneficial to development in the long run is based on three lines of argument. First, since Adam Smith, economists have argued that larger internal markets are more likely to be capable of exploiting economies of scale; the larger the population, the greater the possible productivity gains (Easterlin 1996; Weiner 1971). This claim is weakened by the fact that international trade permits states to specialize in particular sectors and still reap the higher productivity generated by economies of scale.

Second, Julian Simon (1981, 1986, 1989) has argued that the Malthusian model is excessively static and ignores the possibility of technological advance, which engenders productivity gains and increased output despite the exponential growth in population. In fact, Simon has averred that in the long run population growth encourages such innovation by producing intense demand for higher levels of output to maintain aggregate social satisfaction, and by boosting the supply of useful ideas by inducing changes in resource prices, thereby providing incentives to entrepreneurs. In addition, population growth increases the supply of creative intelligences: more heads means more good ideas. As Simon has argued, the short-term economic problems generated by rapid population growth

> eventually lead to increases in technology, by way of both the "demand-side" increase in payoff to invention, as well as from the "supply-side" increase in potential investors in the larger population.... Nor is there a physical limit upon capacity. Should the need arise, processes such as hydroponics can produce incredible amounts of food in tiny compass of space, even without soil. (Simon 1989: 178–179)

Richard Easterlin (1996) attributes population growth primarily to new techniques of disease control, which reduce mortality rates, but these advances also promote societal attitudes favorable to further innovation and hence material progress (Eberstadt 1991). This cycle of population growth, short-run pressure on resources, and long-term adjustment by way of technological change has been enacted repeatedly over the course of human history, and faith in human ingenuity sustains the optimists' confidence in the future.[27]

Finally, akin to Simon, others have maintained that the neo-Malthusian model is unrealistic in assuming that human beings are incapable of recognizing threats to their well-being and adjusting to their environment, and have argued that temporary Malthusian pressures are ultimately resolved by adaptive changes in individual behavior. As McNicoll argues,

> Human economic and demographic history has been a long story of unsustainable growth somehow sustained.... The assertion that things are now closing in, that long-standing adjustment processes can no longer be taken for granted, has much weight: but expressed without allowance for adaptive response, or with blanket condemnation of responses that do take place, it invites (and often receives) disregard. (McNicoll 1995: 315)

Similarly, Kingsley Davis (1963) has argued that human beings will tailor their demographic behavior, opting for later marriage, celibacy, abortion or contraception, or emigration. Ester Boserup (1965) has pointed to the possibility of adopting different methods of production; advanced techniques that yield higher output are also more labor-intensive, requiring the sacrifice of leisure time, and people do not turn to them until compelled.[28]

Another response, though posed more at the societal than at the individual level, is to narrow the meaning of "scarcity." Beyond some minimal level of caloric intake and nourishment, "scarcity" (or "necessity") is a cultural construct.

> Faced with overpopulation, we have occasionally invented or adopted new technologies to increase production, but we have also accepted a wider range of foods as "edible" and accepted altered and often increased labor inputs in production while settling for declining nutritional quality.... Resource scarcity may not be so much a function of population density vis-à-vis fixed and immutable resources as it is a function of socially defined demand against technologically augmented supply.[29] (M. Cohen 1984: 27, 31)

Although the "revisionist" challenge to the Malthusians has usefully broadened the population debate, its claims have hardly been widely accepted. The assumption that technological advancement will always eventually outrun population growth is neither sufficiently justified theoretically nor confirmed empirically (Tir and Diehl 1998: 325–326; Homer-Dixon 1991, 1994). Critics have noted that technological change is a product of investment in research and education, which are policy choices located at the firm and national levels, while population growth results from inputs at numerous levels, including that of the individual, and there is no necessary link between the two phenomena. Furthermore, these explanations generate as many anomalies as they answer. Within Boserup's model, for example, without rising numbers there is no incentive to innovate (Wrigley 1996: 10).

Homer-Dixon (1995) has suggested that future environmental problems, partly a product of population growth, may reduce the supply of ingenuity in society. The concomitant resource scarcity will intensify distributional conflict, and dominant elites will impede efforts to reform existing social institutions and practices or to establish new ones if these encroach on their interests. Moreover, many poor societies lack the financial and human capital needed for vigorous, timely research; under conditions of resource scarcity, the needed capital is even harder to come by, since saving is depressed and capital is diverted to short-term necessities. The result in such societies is a chronic "ingenuity gap," preventing smooth response to emerging scarcity.[30]

Small cultural or ethnic minorities often play the dominant roles in entrepreneurship and innovation, however, and there is no evidence that their decisions are linked to the size of the population, as Simon's claims would lead one to expect (McNicoll 1984: 199, 201). Finally, in developing countries innovations are largely imported from abroad, limiting the effect of population growth on the pace and direction of technological change (Horlacher and Heligman 1991: 363).

Unfortunately, the historical record does not allow for a definitive resolution of this debate regarding the relationship between population growth and development. As several recent studies have noted, the revisionist view appears to have become the new conventional wisdom. The

many cross-national studies, based on the experiences of the industrialized West as well as the more recent experiences of the less-developed
regions, have failed to document that population change either slows or
bolsters economic growth. At a recent United Nations-sponsored meeting
on the subject, the consensus was that "past population growth may not
have played a dominant role in either enhancing or retarding the economic progress of developing countries. Non-demographic factors such
as technical and institutional adjustments, the choice of technologies, and
specific public policies appeared far more important" (Horlacher and
Heligman 1991: 368; National Research Council 1986; Eberstadt 1991,
1998; McNicoll 1995; Easterlin 1996). In a recent study prepared for the
Overseas Development Council, Robert Cassen (1994: 2) concluded that
"the available evidence does not clearly show that population growth
exerts a negative influence on development.... The issue of whether per
capita economic growth is reduced by population growth remains unsettled. Attempts to demonstrate such an effect empirically have produced
no significant and reliable results." However, these conclusions are based
on research that has examined the experience of developing countries in
the aggregate rather than individually.

Over the course of the twentieth century, as demand for goods and
services has surged, income has also risen, and, perhaps most surprisingly, long-term real prices for primary commodities have fallen sharply
(Eberstadt 1998). Where population growth has coincided with a decline
in real per capita income, as in sub-Saharan Africa, the main reasons for
the region's economic collapse have been attributed to its political, not
demographic, troubles. As Amartya Sen has written,

> [W]hat we have to ask is not whether things are just fine in the third world
> (they obviously are not), but whether population growth is the root cause of
> the deprivations that people suffer. The question is whether the particular
> instances of deep poverty we observe derive mainly from population growth
> rather than from other factors that lead to unshared prosperity and persistent
> and possibly growing inequality.[31] (Sen 1994: 65–67)

While demographers and economists continue to sort through these
hypotheses and the evidence and seek to establish more restrictive scope
conditions for their theories, political scientists must at the very least
conclude that the relationship between population growth and economic
growth is largely indeterminate outside specific societal and institutional contexts.

National Power and International Conflict.

Although national power (or the dyadic or systemic distribution of
power) plays a role in a variety of theories of international conflict,[32] it is
most central in realist approaches to international relations.[33] Drawing on

the insights of the classical realists, some contemporary foreign policy theorists, commonly known as "offensive realists," relate increases in relative state power, defined as national power discounted by limitations on state extractive capacities, to more expansive conceptions of the national interest and a more assertive foreign policy. In this view, the international system's competitive imperative drives states to seek to maximize their relative power and influence (Mearsheimer 1990; Schweller 1994; Zakaria 1998).[34] This hypothesis does not necessarily imply violent conflict, for that depends on the responses of other states. However, *ceteris paribus*, as states grow more powerful, they will become more active on the international scene, more likely to endure tense international episodes and foreign relations, and more likely to get into violent scrapes.

This theory captures important elements of foreign policy: States that lack substantial military power and potential know their limits and refrain from challenging the status quo. However, the link between state power and the definition of the national interest is far more problematic than this hypothesis suggests. First, while many would agree that "much imperial expansion is unproblematic: the strong conquer the weak because it pays" (Snyder 1991: 10), states whose power is on the rise do not seek to extend their influence continuously or uniformly. In its most general formulation, this offensive realist hypothesis does not seem to allow for variation of this kind. In fact, its proponents have conceded that states are not blind, power-mad revisionists, but prudent actors who calculate the costs and benefits of particular moves, refraining from expansion when they anticipate a strong balancing reaction. Other scholars have offered a series of hypotheses laying out the conditions most amenable to and those most resistant to aggression by systematically combining an analysis of relative power with an additional critical variable, such as the offense-defense balance or the degree of threat (Jervis 1978; Walt 1987; Glaser 1994; Van Evera 1999).

Second, although rising challengers may seek to shape the international rules of the game in a way that promotes their interests, those interests, and the way in which they are pursued, do not follow deterministically from the possession of power. As John Ruggie (1983) has pointed out, Germany's plans for the postwar international economic and political order diverged greatly from those the United States actually put into effect: the social purpose informing states' ambitions matters to the outcome. Moreover, the strong have multiple instruments at their disposal—coercive diplomacy, military force, economic statecraft, covert operations—and the offensive realist hypothesis yields little insight into which they will seek to employ. Increasing relative power may provide states with the opportunity to expand, but the motive and the intensity with which it is held do not automatically follow.[35]

A second important line of thinking is power-transition theory (Organski and Kugler 1980; Kugler and Organski 1989; Kugler and Lemke 1996) or the closely related hegemonic transition theory (Gilpin

1981).[36] According to these theorists, international politics has been a story not of recurrent formations of the balance of power, but of cycles of international dominance, decline, and transition. In nearly every period, a single state sits atop the international system, having used its power to shape the rules of the game and international political, economic, and legal institutions in a manner highly beneficial to itself. Differential rates of economic growth, technological diffusion, and hegemonic overextension eventually lead to a shift in the distribution of power, however, and a challenger arises. The probability of war is greatest when the power of the rising challenger overtakes that of the declining leader, though there is some debate as to whether the challenger initiates the war in order to accelerate the power transition and secure the benefits of hegemony for itself (Organski and Kugler 1980; Kugler and Organski 1989), or whether the declining leader initiates a preventive war to block the rising adversary and secure its own position while that opportunity is still available (Levy 1989a; Van Evera 1999).[37]

Although both Organski and Gilpin developed power transition theory to apply to the system hegemon and its leading challenger, the theory can also be applied to regional systems (as developed by Lemke [1996] in his "multiple hierarchies" model) or at the dyadic level to any pair of states (or non-state actors, for that matter), and the preventive war hypothesis is essentially dyadic in nature. The basic power transition hypothesis is that a preponderance of power within a dyad is stabilizing in the sense of minimizing the probability of war, while parity is destabilizing. A power shift combined with parity is highly dangerous, in part because conditions do not facilitate a negotiated settlement between the declining and rising states. No settlement is enforceable because the rising state cannot credibly commit to not using its preponderant power in the future to overturn the settlement and exploit the formerly dominant power (Fearon 1995).[38]

Another link between national power and international conflict has been proposed by Edward Luttwak (1994, 1996), who argues that the declining birthrate in the industrialized world has resulted in a general reluctance to lose soldiers in battle and has contributed to the widespread societal aversion to war. Luttwak concludes that the world is no longer inhabited by classic great powers which pursue claims and use force in matters far beyond their immediate security, and that without great powers to impose international order there will be chronic chaos. A further implication of Luttwak's argument is that countries with a "youth bulge," with larger youth cohorts, which are located in the developing world, will be more comfortable with war and may be tempted to undertake aggressive military ventures that threaten the interests of a West devoid of the martial spirit; thus falling fertility renders the West vulnerable.

This argument is logically flawed and empirically unsupported.[39] First, according to Luttwak parents with many children care less deeply when one falls in battle than do their counterparts with fewer progeny.

Luttwak's argument is based on the assumption that parents' concern for their children's safety is finite and that the more children there are, the less love for each—hence his reliance on the metaphor of "the family's emotional economy"—which is highly implausible. Second, birthrates everywhere in the West began declining by the early twentieth century, but that hardly prevented Europe from suffering the consequences of two world wars, often with enthusiastic popular support, and the postwar baby boom does not appear to have sparked any unusually aggressive impulses in the West as those children came of military age. Third, even were Luttwak correct that public attitudes toward war are rooted in demographic trends, the public does not control the decision to engage in warfare, even in democracies. While popular opinion is critical in the long term, policymakers often make decisions that run against the popular vein in the short term. Whether they can succeed in shaping the public's view of the operation and its implications over the long haul is an open question, but the limited decision to go to war may be made relatively independently of public views.

Throughout this discussion of population, national power, and international conflict, we have consistently skirted around one central issue: the conceptualization of power. As Robert Dahl suggested long ago, the scope (influence over which issue), domain (target of influence attempt), and weight (quantity of resources) of power must be specified if the concept is to be meaningful (Dahl 1957; Baldwin 1989). Often in international relations, power is portrayed as a *property* of an individual state, rather than as a *relation* between units.[40] The large number of quantitative research efforts, and many qualitative ones, that aim to discover correlations between the distribution of national capabilities and international outcomes proceed in precisely this fashion, focusing only on the question of weight and assuming that power defined in terms of objective indicators is a fungible instrument of political influence. This makes for parsimonious theories of power and international conflict, but at the cost of ignoring the critical questions of power over whom and for what purposes. Great military resources or economic capacity or population may then be useful in some contexts but not others (Keohane 1986), and whether a growing or shrinking population contributes to a nation's influence may depend on the issue area and the target. However, discussions of population and power, whether by demographers or international relations specialists, have not yet extended much beyond the crudest of such claims.

Population Growth, Resource Scarcity, Economic Decline, and International Conflict

Another important path from rapid population growth to international conflict proceeds through the intervening variable of resource scarcity, and more broadly, poor economic prospects. A basic hypothesis is that once the population passes a certain threshold, it exceeds the nation's carrying capacity, and the result is a dearth of resources and a reduction in individual living standards. We have argued that the concept of carrying capacity is problematic, in that it is hard to specify a priori, that it cannot be separated from its political and social institutions and the distribution of resources, and that it is somewhat dependent on the society's (or individuals') definition of what constitutes the minimally acceptable standard of living (Gurr 1985: 54–55). Nevertheless, numerous studies have discovered that population growth and resource scarcity are closely intertwined, with important political effects. Less explored, and more often simply asserted, in this literature is the further link to international conflict.[41]

Although the revisionists, led by Julian Simon, have often seemed to argue that resource scarcity driven by population growth has been more myth than reality—and that is certainly an important aspect of their work—a crucial caveat has often been lost: the dynamics of technological advance usually kick in only in the long term, leaving an opening for resource scarcity and its political consequences in the short run (Tir and Diehl 1998; Goldstone 1997). Debilitating shortages may develop even more quickly today due to the size of populations and the resource-intensive nature of their economies (Homer-Dixon 1994: 155–156).[42]

Scholars have offered three explanations for how resource scarcity and economic decline contribute to political instability and civil strife. First, relative deprivation stemming from poverty and resource competition produces feelings of frustration and impulses toward aggression, which in turn cause social upheaval (Gurr 1970, 1985). However, although the deprivation hypothesis yields insight into the motives of dissatisfied individuals, the poor, who have suffered significant relative deprivation, lack the resources and opportunity to rebel and are faced with a classic collective action problem. Second, and in response to the inadequacies of the first, resource scarcity produces internal conflict only when it undermines state capacity, provides incentives for vigorous elite distributional conflict, and breeds discontent among the masses. Consequently, long before societies reach the nadir of privation, state institutions for resolving social conflicts and distributing goods may collapse in the face of persistent population pressure and limited resources, opening windows for individuals and groups to engage in violence (Goldstone 1991, 1997). Third, state elites may seek to capitalize on resource scarcities and related social grievances and to advance their parochial interests by instigating intergroup violence (Kahl 1998). Thus, regardless of their position on the broader, long-term relationship between population and economic development, many scholars recognize that rapid population growth can in the short run contribute to political instability.[43]

A number of empirical studies have examined the links between population pressure, resource scarcity, and international conflict, with mixed results. Many, conducted in a behavioral vein, are far stronger on findings than on an explanatory framework. Choucri (1974) analyzed the role of four dimensions of population—size, change, distribution, and composition—in producing conflict in 45 cases in the developing world between 1954 and 1972.[44] She concludes that population factors were important in 38 of these, with size and change less important than composition and distribution; population pressures on resources were important in 19 of these cases, and were the central or sole determinants in 10 out of 45. However, Choucri also notes that population density is, by itself, not particularly important, and that even when the concentration of numbers is judged in relation to available or mobilizable resources, there is no necessary link to external aggression. When states do expand, she further argues, they may conquer a territory prized for its symbolic value, not its resources or ability to reduce high population density.

Some have criticized Choucri's study for analyzing only cases in which conflict has occurred, leaving open the possibility that the same conditions she hypothesizes to be associated with conflict may also be present in cases in which that is not the outcome,[45] and for exaggerating the contribution of population to international conflict. Kleinman (1980: 50–51) remarks that Choucri's "listing of population factors is so inclusive that it is surprising that it was not possible to find a population factor for the remaining seven instances of violence."

A contemporaneous study, conducted by Bremer, Singer, and Luterbacher (1973), is more skeptical of population's importance, defining the critical aspects of population more narrowly, but is quite consistent with Choucri's findings. Examining the war-proneness of European nations between 1816 and 1965, Bremer and his colleagues found that there was little correlation between population density and the propensity of states to initiate or participate in war.

Comparing the Choucri and Bremer studies, it is worth noting that their samples are quite different and that the temporal periods overlap only slightly. Although Choucri found distribution variables, like population density, occasionally important, it was the location with regard to borders and population that was critical, not density per se. Finally, Bremer and his co-authors acknowledged that their findings might not be applicable in less technologically advanced areas outside the European context, and that they had not tested for a non-linear relationship between density and conflict, so that they could not rule out the possibility that conflict is more likely above a particular, if as yet unspecified, crowding threshold.

Most recently, a study by Tir and Diehl (1998) confirms a modest correlation between population growth, although not population density, and states' involvement in militarized interstate disputes between 1930 and 1989. However, population growth shows little relationship in this study to the likelihood of a state initiating the conflict, which raises questions about hypothesized causal mechanisms and the likelihood of the conflict escalating to war.[46] Two points are worth noting. First, the causal mechanism supposedly being tested is that states with growing populations will have difficulty adjusting to resource scarcities and attendant environmental problems. As Tir and Diehl (1998: 330) acknowledge, the empirical analysis does not include a variable specifically devoted to resource scarcity or perceptions of it, leaving the causal claims entirely unexamined. Second, the study raises, but does not resolve, an interesting conundrum in its findings—why does population growth contribute to militarized interstate disputes, but have no correlation to the initiation of the conflict or its escalation to war?

There are at least three possible ways of linking resource scarcity and economic ill health (and short-term political instability) with international conflict (see Fig. 3.2). First, decision-makers may use military force in an effort to eliminate scarcity—what Homer-Dixon (1991, 1994) calls "simple scarcity conflicts."[47] Conflicts over renewable resources (for example, fisheries, forests, cropland) are fairly rare, but conflicts over oil and other non-renewable resources have played a significant role in the history of the twentieth century, as illustrated by Japan in World War II and also by the Gulf War. Homer-Dixon has conjectured that war is more likely over non-renewable resources such as petroleum and mineral resources, since these can be more directly and immediately converted into state and military power than can arable land and fish. One exception is water, which is essential for personal and national survival and has been central to political conflicts in various regions (Gleick 1993; Lowi 1993). It is important to note that war for oil and minerals is then undertaken not as a consequence of domestic political instability, but as a strategic decision for national security.

A related, but still broader, argument is Choucri and North's (1975, 1989) "lateral pressure theory" of international conflict, in which a growing population and advancing technology generate increasing domestic demands for resources that cannot be satisfied by a state's domestic

FIGURE 3.2   Resource Scarcity and International Conflict

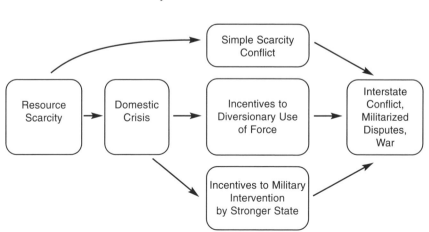

endowments or existing levels of trade. These demands produce "lateral pressure" for access to raw materials and markets and often for political control. As these empires expand and compete for territory and resources, action-reaction cycles of arms buildups and alliance-building ensue, culminating in violent conflict and possibly full-scale war. Aside from narrow methodological difficulties, several theoretical problems arise. Choucri and North fail to consider the conditions under which free trade might be a viable alternative to colonization as a means of acquiring the external resources that promote economic growth, although in a more recent study they construct a revised model that seeks to explain the behavior of both autarkic Japan before World War II and free-trading Japan after World War II (Choucri, North, and Yamakage 1992). Moreover, the link between colonial expansion and war requires further development, especially because others have argued that colonial expansion served as a "safety valve" that diverted great power competition from the core to the periphery of the system (Morgenthau 1993 [1948]). The fact that a number of serious colonial rivals became allies during World War I runs counter to the model's expectations.

However frequently resource wars have occurred in the past, some have argued that they are less likely to occur in the future. First, some suggest that because of the nature of the global trading system, states no longer experience resource dependency as a major threat to their security and political autonomy (Deudney 1990; Lipschutz 1989).[48] There is some truth to this claim: during the Gulf War, increased drilling by Saudi Arabia and Venezuela kept petroleum prices from rising too rapidly, and despite serious restrictions on Iraqi oil production since, global crude prices remained low. However, one clear motivation (among others) for American and UN intervention in the Gulf War was to maintain access to oil supplies at acceptable prices, given the centrality of oil to the economies of the United States, its allies, and indeed the industrialized world. Moreover, the United States has continued to stockpile strategic reserves of oil and other resources, which suggests that American leaders continue to believe that resource dependency is a potential threat to national security. It has also been argued that the possibility of substitution of resources makes scarcity an unlikely cause of war (Deudney 1990: 471). Although substitution is possible, alternatives to petroleum and various other strategic minerals are simply not yet cost effective, and thus war for resource access may be perceived as rational.

Second, with the spread of small arms and national consciousness, some argue, conquest is now more expensive than ever before; consequently, "schemes of resource imperialism are now more appealing to romantic militarists than practical policy-makers" (Deudney 1990: 470–471; Kaysen 1990). However, neither nationalism nor small arms were in short supply in the middle decades of this century, and that hardly prevented Germany, Japan, and the Soviet Union from undertaking imperialist ventures. Recent research has demonstrated that the conquest of industrial society can be quite profitable from a narrow economistic perspective, and that the very institutions and infrastructures of modern society that were thought to provide the backbone of resistance can also be used to enforce rule. A ruler willing to be sufficiently brutal can stamp out serious resistance (Liberman 1996).[49] Finally, even were this argument valid regarding the industrialized world, resource imperialism might still make sense in the developing world.

Second, resource scarcity may also create incentives for political leaders, faced with crisis at home, to provoke external conflict to quiet their domestic opposition. They may seek to distract their detractors by launching a "diversionary war" or, perhaps more likely, engage in the diversionary use of force short of war, which may escalate to war through a conflict spiral. Leaders understand this, and, by coupling hard-line foreign policies with patriotic and nationalistic rhetoric, they can forge domestic unity against a common enemy.[50] The resulting "rally 'round the flag" effect may be temporary, but it nearly always follows from the use of military power abroad, regardless of the wisdom or success of that action (Russett 1990a).

Although early quantitative studies did not find strong relationships between internal and external conflict, they were theoretically mis-specified and empirically problematic (Levy 1989b); more sophisticated recent studies have generally confirmed that the use of external force is a function of domestic economic and electoral cycles and of presidential approval ratings (Ostrom and Job 1985; Russett 1990b). These findings have been reinforced by historical studies of diversionary behavior in a variety of cases, including World War I (Austria-Hungary, Russia, and Germany), the Falklands/Malvinas War, and the Arab-Israeli Wars.

Finally, it is also conceivable that resource scarcity and concomitant political weakness in one state will invite a stronger state to intervene militarily (Blainey 1988). Political crisis has historically often served as an incentive to attack, in two ways. First, the stronger state may seek to exploit a temporary window of opportunity created by the disruptive effects of political turmoil, as illustrated by Iraq's attack on Iran in 1980 in the wake of the revolution (Walt 1996). Second, the stronger state may desire to influence the outcome of the struggle for political power. The Soviet invasions of Czechoslovakia in 1968 and of Afghanistan in 1980 took this form, as did U.S. interventions in Latin American countries. This has been one of the traditional motives for the strong to intervene in the domestic political affairs of their weaker neighbors.

Population Growth, Ethnic Composition, and Conflict

One common hypothesis in the literature is that differential population growth among communal groups, both within and across borders, revises the existing and likely future distribution of power among the relevant groups and disrupts political arrangements, engendering ethnic tension and conflict. Within the Soviet Union, fertility rates among Muslims far outpaced those of Slavic and other non-Muslim citizens; had the Soviet Union not collapsed, Russians would soon have been a minority. As the non-European republics became less Russian, and as the European republics became more so, the country's changing ethnic composition had far-reaching implications for the composition of the army as well as for demands for education, housing, and social services in general (Anderson and Silver 1995: 168).[51] More dramatically, the changing Christian-Muslim balance in Lebanon has been blamed for upsetting that country's finely tuned political system in the 1970s and throwing it into decades of turmoil. Other within-border examples include Belgium, Nigeria, and South Africa. Across-border cases include Western Europe and North Africa; Israel and the Arab states; Greece and Turkey; and Mexico and the United States (Weiner 1971; Choucri 1974; Tapinos 1978; Azar and Farah 1984; Eberstadt 1991; Freedman 1991; Homer-Dixon 1994; Goldscheider 1995; Brown 1997; Teitelbaum and Winter 1998).[52]

Although the proposition that differential growth in the populations of ethnic communities produces tension and conflict is widely held, it lacks a firm theoretical grounding. First, it overpredicts ethnic conflict. Since ethnic groups within a society generally have different fertility rates and different rates of immigration, one would expect to see nearly all societies riven with paralyzing ethnic conflict, but large-scale ethnic violence remains the exception rather than the rule (Fearon and Laitin 1996). Second, the hypothesis fails to recognize that identity is a variable. A particular identification, whether along gender, class, ethnic, or religious lines, is neither constant nor exclusive, and thus a full explanation of the dynamics of ethnic conflict must explain why a particular ethnic identity comes to dominate all other possible identities and why violent conflict follows. For example, despite significant economic disparities between Hindus and Muslims in Kashmir, and Hindu dominance of most political and economic institutions, prior to 1989 there was little widespread communal tension because the two communities shared a common Kashmiri identity (Ganguly 1996). Similarly, English workers embraced a class identity that joined home and work, while their American counterparts were mobilized along ethnic lines in residential communities (Katznelson 1985). To be convincing, these propositions regarding the relevance of demographic trends to ethnic conflict must be reformulated as either relying on the caveat that the ethnic cleavage is highly salient or persuasively linking the salience of ethnicity to population patterns.[53]

From the first perspective, recent, more explicitly theoretical work offers a foundation for hypotheses elaborating the link between demographic change and ethnic conflict. Direct conflicts of interest may explain ethnic tension, but they are not sufficient to account for actual violent conflict among ethnic groups. James Fearon has modeled ethnic conflict as a form of "commitment problem." Under conditions of deteriorating state power, ethnic majorities cannot convincingly guarantee that they will not take advantage of their superior resources to exploit ethnic minorities, and the latter may see fighting now, for an independent or autonomous region, as the superior alternative to forging an unstable pact with the former and having to fight later (Fearon 1998; Lake and Rothchild 1996).[54] Ethnic conflict, argues Fearon, is a species of preventive war.[55]

For these authors, "state weakness" is apparently a necessary precondition for violent ethnic conflict, but more careful reading reveals that they are, despite strong rhetorical claims to the contrary, highly ambiguous regarding this scope condition. State weakness, some acknowledge, cannot be limited to objective state collapse, but may be based on groups' time horizons or state strategies for coping with dissent. Lake and Rothchild (1996: 44) concede that "if plausible futures are sufficiently threatening, groups may begin acting today as if the state were in fact weak, setting off processes … that bring about the disintegration of the state. Thus, even though the state may appear strong today, concerns that it may not remain so tomorrow may be sufficient to ignite fears of physical insecurity and a cycle of ethnic violence." They conclude that "in the end, ethnic groups are left without reliable safety nets. There is no form of insurance sufficient to protect against the dilemmas that produce collective fears and violence" (Lake and Rothchild 1996: 57). Ethnic entrepreneurs can create the structural conditions and mindsets that are conducive to violent ethnic conflict—the state weakness that makes credible commitment problematic—rather than merely taking advantage of such conditions when they present themselves (Gagnon 1994/1995).[56] Thus it is not clear that these attempts to specify the scope of violent ethnic conflict have made much progress and have solved the overprediction tendency.

Demographic trends can also affect the salience of ethnicity. Recent work in sociology has suggested that an individual's social network affects the likelihood of identification along ethnic lines. "Young adults living alone," writes Goldscheider (1995: 6), "may be less likely to identify themselves ethnically, while families with young children may be linked to ethnic communities through family networks, jobs, schools, friends, and neighborhoods." Given the multiplicity of social identities in modern pluralistic societies, ethnic social networks—tied to places of residence and family connections, to economic activities and enclaves, expressed in political ties and cultural forms of expressions—are important to understanding why ethnic populations may fear future shifts in the balance of power. One limitation here is that networks are not a purely structural phenomenon, and insofar as individuals choose which networks to join, social networks are less a cause of ethnic identification than a reflection of it.

Rogers Brubaker's (1996: 21, 19) recommendations regarding the study of nationalism are apropos here: he recommends focusing on "the processual dynamics of nationalism," on "nationness as an event, as something that suddenly crystallizes rather than gradually develops, as a contingent, conjuncturally fluctuating, and precarious frame of vision and basis for individual and collective action." His suggestion is both troubling and suggestive, troubling because the focus on nationalism's dynamics as "governed by the properties of political fields, not by the properties of collectivities" (Brubaker 1996: 17) fails to provide strong grounding for explanations of the varying success of nationalist appeals, but suggestive in its attention to the ways in which the salience of ethnicity and nationalism is highly contingent. This is an under-explored area within the ethnicity and nationalism literature, and answering that question is key to understanding how and when demographic change contributes to national/ethnic tensions and conflict and when it has relatively little impact.

Finally, several causal mechanisms can link domestic ethnic violence to international conflict (see Fig. 3.3). First, political leaders may seek to smooth over ethnic divisions by attacking (and sometimes creating) a common external adversary. Although much theoretical work remains to be done fully to explicate the dynamics of this scapegoat hypothesis, the validity of this link is borne out by numerous historical incidents. Second,

FIGURE 3.3   Communal Conflict and International Conflict

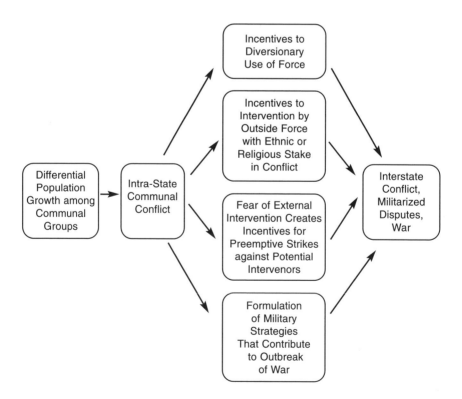

ethnic conflict undermines the capacity of the central state, possibly to the point of collapse, thereby providing an incentive for other states to exploit its current weakness. Such ventures may, however, backfire if the warring ethnic groups band together and overcome their differences to repel the invader. In anticipation of ethnic problems, concomitant state weakness, and external attack, leaders may have incentives to launch preventive strikes against likely adversaries. Variants on both these mechanisms were discussed at greater length earlier.

Third, ethnic conflict may compel states to adopt military strategies that hamper their effectiveness and, under some conditions, possibly contribute to the outbreak of war. A notable example of diminished military effectiveness is the Russian armed forces at the start of World War I. Before 1914, the Russian military, fearful of the political consequences of concentrating troops of any single ethnicity in one location, widely dispersed its armies, which significantly slowed the process of mobilization. The slow pace of Russian mobilization encouraged Germany to believe that it could successfully execute the Schlieffen Plan, which focused on defeating France quickly in the west before turning to face the delayed but potent threat from Russia in the east.

Fourth, if differential population growth among ethnic or religious groups results in the poor treatment of minorities, outside parties with an ethnic or religious stake in the outcome may come to their aid, threatening conflict across boundaries. Ill treatment of Greek minorities in Turkey and of Turks in eastern Thrace, whether real or perceived, has certainly contributed to tensions between these Aegean neighbors.[57] Shortly after the dissolution of the Soviet Union, concerns about the fate of ethnic Russians in other former Soviet republics fueled the popularity of nationalists and their calls for more assertive policies in the "near abroad." More clearly still, Islamic fighters from Afghanistan, out of work in the early 1990s with the installation of a stable central government, found a cause in the plight of their Muslim brethren in Bosnia-Herzegovina.

Migration and International Conflict

Rapid population growth can lead to migration within and across borders. Short-term resource scarcities generate incentives for people to move to locations where supplies are more plentiful, and ethnic conflict may force refugees to flee their homes for safer ground. By changing regional population balances among ethnic groups, overwhelming urban infrastructures, creating pressure on limited water and food supplies, and suppressing agricultural and industrial production, internal migration, driven by population growth, can create additional stresses on social and political institutions (Swain 1996). External migration can also produce tension within the host country if it poses new economic or social burdens. Migration may also provide elites with incentives to play the nativist card and incite intergroup conflict as a means of shoring up their political base (Swain 1996: 969–970; Saunders 1991: 2). The internal implications of these dynamics have been explored above. Finally, migration, as a source of population change, may indirectly contribute to international conflict by bolstering or undermining national power, altering a country's ethnic or communal composition, or giving rise to resource scarcities—the three other causal pathways examined in this paper. This section of the essay will instead assess the hypotheses offered regarding the direct international consequences of migration across borders.

There are several paths by which migration can contribute to international conflict:[58] First, migrants may seek to influence their host government to pursue aggressive policies vis-à-vis their country of origin. As Myron Weiner (1985: 451) notes, migrants "have been critics of their country of origin and pressured their host government to influence the domestic politics of their country of origin." In several cases, migrants have actually succeeded in pulling the host country into war: East Pakistan and India; Khmer refugees in Thailand; Afghan refugees in Pakistan (Freedman 1991; Weiner 1992/93: 198–201; Sheffer 1993; Shain 1993; Miller 1998: 23–24).[59] However, others have argued that this problem is quite limited, since migrants, politically marginal in their home country, normally possess a limited ability to organize politically and successfully make demands on the government of the receiving country (Homer-Dixon 1994: 159).[60] With either position capable of citing a large number of relevant examples, neither has succeeded in establishing a convincing generalization; whether migrants are politically powerful or powerless depends on the particular context.

Second, mistreatment—real, perceived, or manufactured—of migrants can lead their country of origin to seek to intervene on their behalf (Organski and Organski 1961: 138, 242). As noted above, this dynamic has often led to international tension in the past. Russian sensitivity in the post–Cold War period to the treatment of ethnic Russians in the former Soviet republics is a case in point, and just a few years ago American hawks were pointing to Russian nationalist rhetoric regarding the "near abroad" as representing a real threat to international security (Brubaker 1993). Other cases include tensions between India and South Africa over the latter's treatment of its Indian minority, Chinese concern over the status of Chinese communities throughout Southeast Asia, and Mexican denunciations of perceived discrimination against Mexican nationals in the United States (Poku and Graham 1998).

Further, classifying migrants as refugees with a well-founded fear of persecution implicitly accuses and condemns the country of origin, fostering an antagonistic relationship (Weiner 1992/93: 198–199). In the early 1990s, China regarded the American debate over whether Chinese students should be permitted to remain in the United States as interference in its internal affairs. The United States' relations with Russia and Cuba are other good examples. While such moves may contribute to worsening diplomatic relations, it is unlikely that they could, in the absence of further provocation and deeper conflicts of interests, lead to international violence.

Fourth, further conflict can emerge over a state's migration policies. Where one state permits, promotes, or forces emigration to a state that forbids or restricts entry, the situation has the potential for international tension, creating a "high" politics over population movements. The United States has been involved in a series of such incidents with Cuba and Haiti over the last two decades (Zimmermann 1995; Zolberg 1995). Where one country restricts emigration that another seeks to promote, migration policies may become a bargaining chip in a larger negotiation package. A key example here is wrangling between the United States and the Soviet Union over the fate of Soviet Jews (Weiner 1985; Swain 1996).

In addition, the presence of combatants in refugee camps can make the host country into a target for foreign attack. Foreign forces may feel justified in pursuing the enemy across the border, commonly threatening the safety of host country citizens. This story has been enacted repeatedly across Africa. Moreover, in many regions, ethnic groups straddle national boundaries, and ethnic conflicts are not easily confined to the country in which they originated (Jacobsen 1993).

Sixth, migrants can themselves become a threat to the security of the host country by launching terrorist attacks, illegally smuggling weapons, trafficking in drugs, and so on. Palestinians have posed a security problem for Arab states, such as Lebanon and Jordan; Pakistan's decision to arm the Afghan refugees has in turn limited its dealings with the governments of Afghanistan and the Soviet Union (Weiner 1992/93: 201–202; 1993). Fighting among rival factions in refugee camps can spill over into the local community (Jacobsen 1993).

At present the literature on the consequences of international migration consists of a set of generalizations, each with relevant examples, rather than a set of testable propositions laying out the conditions under which one expects to see international conflict as a consequence of migration. This is an essential first step, generating a series of puzzles and a wide range of expectations, but the literature has not yet made the move to theory, leaving unclear which of these causal paths is most likely and when. Whether migration heightens tensions between states often depends on whether it is viewed as undermining national security or domestic harmony, but the process by which threats are constructed and by which boon is transformed into bane remains poorly understood and under-theorized.[61] Nor has the literature generally distinguished between the possible international repercussions of migration: a rise in international tension, a militarized interstate dispute, or war. As scholars continue to pin down the relationship between migration and these phenomena, they must remain attentive to the different levels of international conflict and offer clear hypotheses regarding when one would expect to see one rather than the other as a consequence of migration.

Conclusion

Few would deny that population growth and decline and other demographic factors are dynamic processes with important ramifications for international politics. Specifying the precise paths through which they might impair national security and contribute to international conflict is another matter. In the preceding discussion of four important causal factors joining these phenomena—national power, resource scarcity, ethnic composition and communal conflict, migration—we have questioned the theoretical logic and empirical validity of many of the hypotheses that proliferate in the relevant fields of international relations and demography.

The intersection of demography and international relations is marked by a paucity of well-developed theory, partly because scholars in each discipline rarely devote attention to these questions and because they generally do not read the literature of the other discipline. Consequently students of international relations often blithely assert that a growing population underpins a country's increasing ability to project power and exert influence on the international scene, ignoring the raging debate in economics and demography over the relationship between population growth and development. Meanwhile, demographers often offer simplistic hypotheses regarding the international consequences of population growth without sufficiently considering how political processes might affect those dynamics.

Moreover, while the prevailing literature addresses some plausible mechanisms linking a variety of population factors to interstate conflict, it has not generally recognized that this process is analytically distinguishable from that leading to militarized disputes or war. One of the earliest modern students of international relations to write on the subject, Quincy Wright (1958: 260–263), recognized this: "[Population] movements may affect the balance of power and the prosperity of peoples, but there are always alternative methods for meeting these problems. Population differentials or population pressures never create a necessity to go to war though they may create a necessity for action." More recently, Tir and Diehl (1998) indicated their sensitivity to this difficulty by testing separate hypotheses on militarized interstate disputes and wars. This review has sought to demonstrate the advantages that a broader perspective, rooted in international relations theory but familiar with demographers' findings, can bring to this project at the nexus of these two disciplines.

Reviewing the literature of the last several decades, one is struck by how little progress has been made since Wright wrote on the subject over forty years ago. Although Wright clearly believed political demography was of great import, he concluded that a country's population is indeterminate with respect to foreign policy, that both overpopulation and underpopulation had been associated in the past with peaceful and escalatory national policies. Moreover, Wright found no correlation between war and either rising or declining world population. He noted and cautioned against "the temptation to state over-precisely and without adequate qualification, the international consequences, of, or the remedies for, population conditions" (Wright 1955: 365). Many contemporary scholars have been much less sensitive to Wright's concerns.

There are also important methodological issues to consider. The linkages between population growth and international conflict are admittedly convoluted and difficult to trace, but scholars should not entirely sacrifice rigor on the altar of richness, abandoning the quest for spare, generalizable causal models. For example, although Thomas Homer-Dixon's project on environment, population, and security has made a significant contribution by generating an intricate set of hypotheses as to the conditions under which demographic change fosters conflict, and by illustrating these hypotheses with a series of richly detailed case studies, the complexity of these models and their excessive particularity undermines their utility for theory construction.[62] History is messy, but social science usefully employs narrower lenses, focusing on a limited number of variables while recognizing that such an account is necessarily incomplete. As in so many other areas, we need to strike a better balance between richness and rigor in the study of demography and international conflict.

Although scholars of international relations have not yet devoted much attention to demographic factors, we anticipate that this will prove a productive area of future research along the lines of the four causal paths presented above. Past work on the relationship between population growth, national power, and international conflict has been marked by bold claims that upon further examination appear far weaker and more contingent. The still-raging debate between neo-Malthusians and revisionists leads to the conclusion that outside of specific societal, cultural, and institutional contexts the relationship between population growth and economic growth is indeterminate. As demographers and economists sort out the evidence and establish more restrictive scope conditions for their theories, political scientists can begin to incorporate them into more determinate hypotheses regarding the sources of international influence.

While many students of international relations have commented on the link between population growth and military strength, a rising population does not imply an increase in the size of the armed forces, and a larger military has never smoothly translated into military effectiveness. Nonetheless, state leaders have often pursued pro-natalist policies and decreed mass conscription in the belief that a large youth cohort is the key to military success, and such beliefs—not scholars' findings—shape political decisions. Thus numbers will, given a particular strategic culture, affect how policymakers assess the balance of power, weigh their policy choices (for example, to wage preventive war, to appease, or to stand firm), and design their military strategy. Whether and how population growth affects military power and the causes of war and peace are contingent upon the prevalence of a particular set of beliefs among policymakers.

Even if the population revisionists' expectations are borne out in the long run, resource scarcity may set in and economic performance may suffer in the short term. Through this intervening path, population growth may contribute to international conflict in one of three ways: the seizure of resource-rich territories to alleviate scarcity, the diversionary use of force to rally public support around the political leadership, and opportunistic military intervention in the suffering country by an outside power. All three mechanisms are plausible, but the theories that would help identify when each is most likely to operate remain insufficiently developed. Similarly, scholars have so far examined a number of ways in which migration might contribute, and has in the past contributed, to international tension and conflict, but these remain a set of unintegrated hypotheses, empirical generalizations not grounded in a strong theoretical edifice. Although work on the causes of migration and refugee flows is becoming increasingly theoretically sophisticated, more thought must be applied to their consequences, to the conditions under which they are most and least likely to exacerbate international tensions.

Finally, one of the more intriguing hypotheses in the literature is that differential population growth among ethnic groups sparks conflict, as growing groups employ their newfound power to restructure existing political, economic, and social institutions at the expense of declining groups. This proposition takes the mobilization of ethnic/national identity for granted, however, and the process by which identities are mobilized is not particularly well understood. Demographic change, including population growth and movement, may play an important role in highlighting the salience of particular cleavages, thus allowing for their exploitation by ethnic entrepreneurs. Moreover, as some sociologists have argued, particular age cohorts may be more likely to take part in ethnic networks, and thus fertility patterns may have a great impact on the degree of ethnic identification across society. These claims await further theoretical analysis and empirical examination.

Rapid population growth in the developing world is hardly welcome, but it does not by itself pose a serious threat to international peace and security. While we have identified several mechanisms through which demographic change may contribute to international conflict, the more common result is domestic disruption and perhaps violence. Inspired by humanitarian ideals or pressured by domestic interest groups, policymakers in the industrialized world may strive to devote resources to combating rapid population growth and to offer aid to developing nations as they cope with exploding populations. Their counterparts in poorer countries may, confronted with economic crisis and resource scarcity, be eager for help in containing the seemingly inexorable rise in numbers. International conflict is a possible outcome, but the links between it and population growth are complex and indirect, with social institutions, political considerations, and the international environment all mediating. By successfully manipulating these intervening factors—by no means an easy task—Western policymakers whose central concern is preserving international peace could achieve their goal even as rapid population growth rages unabated. At stake is the kind of world in which we wish to live, the international milieu, but not international order.

Acknowledgments

The authors are grateful for the helpful comments and criticisms of Myron Weiner, Sharon Stanton Russell, Edward Rhodes, and participants in the MIT Demography and Security Conference, December 1998.

Notes

1. While democratic states are involved in war as frequently as non-democratic states, liberal democracies rarely, if ever, go to war with each other. Although a consensus has formed around the law-like status of this finding—it has been described as coming "as close as anything we have to an empirical law in international relations" (Levy 1989a: 270)—the theoretical explanation for this phenomenon remains highly contested (Brown et al. 1996).

2. For a sampling of such views, see Wattenberg 1987; Foster 1989; Myers 1989; Ehrlich and Ehrlich 1990; Homer-Dixon 1991; Helman and Ratner 1992/93; Kaplan 1994, 1996; Luttwak 1994; Chase, Hill, and Kennedy 1996. For a variety of European concerns regarding declining fertility, see Michael Specter, "Population Implosion Worries a Graying Europe," *New York Times*, 10 July 1998, A1; Teitelbaum and Winter 1998.

3. Both President Clinton and Vice President Gore reportedly read carefully Robert Kaplan's jeremiad, "The Coming Anarchy" (1994). In 1994 Thomas Homer-Dixon briefed Gore and other top administration officials; see Saul Friedman, "'Failed States' Bring World Crisis Nearer," *Newsday*, 18 August 1994, A6. On the new ecological focus of U.S. foreign policy, see also Gore 1992; Steven Greenhouse, "The Greening of U.S. Diplomacy," *New York Times*, 9 October 1995, A6; Dabelko and Simmons 1997; Pirages 1997.

4. Important exceptions include Sprout and Sprout 1971; Choucri 1974; Choucri and North 1975; and, more recently, Homer-Dixon 1991, 1994. Also relevant here is Leroy 1978.

5. On the association of population with power, particularly among the encyclopedists of eighteenth-century France, see Keegan 1987.

6. In the earlier literature on rapid population growth, much was made of the effects of "overcrowding" derived from studies of animal behavior. We have not discussed these approaches because their claims regarding intrasocietal conflict have been severely criticized in the last two decades. Moreover, the distinctive prediction of these hypotheses was social anomie and violence, not international conflict. See various essays in Choucri 1984.

7. For the purposes of this essay, we adopt a traditional conception of "security." On the problems with casting the environment debate in national-security terms, see Deudney 1990; M. Levy 1995. Broader definitions of security

have been offered by Ullman 1983; Mathews 1989; Rothschild 1995. It is worth noting that Ullman has himself retracted his earlier, highly influential claims; see Ullman 1991.

8. We focus here on the consequences of population growth for economic development and military power and potential. Many of these hypotheses can be reversed to generate expectations regarding the consequences of population decline. On the political implications of population decline, see McNeill 1990.

9. To be fair to Morgenthau, he recognizes that "the largeness of population" has also at times served as an obstacle to the development of national power and that the age distribution within a given population is also important (1993 [1948]: 142). But the dominant thrust of the text is that a large population bequeaths great international influence, and at best Morgenthau provides no guidance to the analyst seeking to understand when population augments, and when it undermines, a nation's power.

10. Depending on the extractive capacity of the state, population growth can also affect military strategy, particularly with respect to the tradeoff between the internal mobilization of manpower and armaments and the formation of military alliances. On the tradeoffs (or lack of such) between arms and alliances, see Barnett and Levy 1991; Morrow 1993; Christensen 1997. On intra-alliance dynamics, see Krebs 1999.

11. Although Organski et al. (1972) recognize that the level of contribution varies across individuals and across issue areas, that contributions are intermittent, and that specific individuals drop in and out of the effective population, they nonetheless proceed to operationalize the category in terms of the number of employed agricultural workers, a measure that takes none of this into account. Moreover, this figure ignores the political activist class, the military, and the fact that agricultural workers in the industrialized world produce for both national and international markets. Finally, the authors note that beyond some optimum level, effective population becomes dysfunctionally large, as nongovernmental groups come to dominate the state. As we argue later, it is not clear how to ascertain that optimum point except in post hoc fashion.

12. On the American case, see Zakaria 1998. On the bulky, but nonetheless useful, concept of "state strength," see Skocpol 1985; Ikenberry et al. 1988.

13. This widely cited saying has been ascribed to many sources, often Napoleon, occasionally Frederick the Great. John Keegan (1987) asserts that it comes from Voltaire.

14. The size of the military certainly influences doctrine. A small army is unlikely to engage in a war of attrition against a larger enemy, while a larger force might find that option more attractive. However, strategy is not *determined* by circumstances and always involves an element of choice; accounts of the process by which militaries actually reach their doctrinal decisions stress the importance of individual decision-makers and chance. Two examples: Germany would not have adopted blitzkrieg in 1940 without a plane crash that led to fear that the war plans had been divulged to the Allies, the postponement of the attack, and a search for alternative strategies, and without Hitler's eventual endorsement of blitzkrieg. Moshe Dayan's return to the Israeli government in June 1967 ensured the rejection of a limited-aims strategy, which Yitzhak Rabin had favored. See Mearsheimer 1983.

15. On the latter case, see Rosen 1996; for further examples, see Howard 1976.

16. This section builds on Levy 1989c.
17. The influence of the balance of resolve relative to the balance of capabilities reflects how such crises originate in the first place. Since states tend to challenge the status quo only when they are very highly motivated, any analysis that fails to endogenize the role of resolve in crisis bargaining, including the diplomatic or domestic political costs of backing down ("audience costs"), may be seriously flawed (Fearon 1994a, b).
18. Note that such arguments seem to favor indigenous growth over population growth from other sources (e.g., migration). Were the actual population levels considered at risk, Western countries could easily rectify the situation by adopting more open borders and looser citizenship policies. The racist subtext of such concerns is much more explicit in the rhetoric of extreme Russian nationalists, such as Vladimir Zhirinovsky, who see the country's demographic decline as boding ill for its status as a great power.
19. For a contrary view, see Wright 1958. Wright has suggested that as developing countries become more technologically proficient, technology will equalize across the international system, and population can be expected to become more salient, a more critical determinant of national power. Wright's implicit claim that technology will achieve some ultimate stasis is problematic, for technology is a process marked by ever-present flux. Technological diffusion is also gradual and uneven.
20. For an argument that is skeptical of the power of technology alone to yield victory, and even of the military advantages of advanced arms, see Handel 1981.
21. Some scholars have expressed alarm over the current and expected skill-level of the U.S. armed forces. They note that if the military continues to employ more complicated weaponry, it may be caught between the need for highly educated technicians and specialists and a diminishing supply of recruits able to absorb the complex training (Handel 1981; Binkin 1986; Foster et al. 1987). This is a far more serious problem for developing countries.
22. However, technology does not diffuse evenly or always rapidly across the globe, and states outside the advanced industrialized world will be slower to absorb such technological developments into their armed forces and military doctrines. Consequently, in such states the relative impact of numbers will decline more slowly.
23. Choucri (1974: 184–185) acknowledges later that the evidence regarding segmental differences and national power is highly mixed.
24. Even as older ethnic categories have lost their political relevance, "new" ethnic groups, notably Latinos and Asian-Americans, have become major players in their own fashion on the American political scene.
25. The following discussion of the effects of population growth, both positive and negative, draws, in addition to sources cited below, on McNicoll 1984, 1994, 1995; Bharadwaj 1996; Easterlin 1996: chapter 7.
26. A large literature has persuasively criticized the so-called "demographic transition theory" as less a theory, or even a set of empirically testable propositions, than a description of and generalization from the European experience. Even as the latter, it is inadequate as anything more than a first cut, for the timing and pace of the eventual declines in fertility bore no relationship to the level or pace of economic development: Fertility rates declined in France and in China while their respective economies were still largely agrarian, but declined in England long after the onset of industrialization. Nor did

demographic transition theory predict either the spectacular postwar mortality decline in the developing countries, in the absence of significant economic development, or the baby boom in the advanced nations. Finally, it is not clear that the model is applicable outside the European context, for, as McNicoll has observed, "such 'surface' characteristics as family forms, tenurial arrangements, local authority structures, and political traditions have played a significant part in both economic and demographic outcomes" (1995: 319). See Organski et al. 1984; Davis 1991: 13–17; McNicoll 1994, 1995; Teitelbaum and Winter 1998: 197–198.

27. An amusing and relevant anecdote: in 1980, three environmentalists bet Julian Simon that the price of a basket of five metals would rise over a ten-year period; Simon, who thought it would decline, won the bet. See Myers and Simon 1994: 99, 206.

28. Along similar lines, see Ruttan and Hayami 1991; Wrigley 1996. Kleinman (1980) weaves together elements of all these arguments.

29. Similarly, an anthropologist reports that "I ask my students how they feel about being increasingly crowded by the growing population, and they reply, 'We're not crowded.' … Whatever environment you're born into is the one that seems normal." See Malcolm W. Browne, "Will Humans Overwhelm the Earth? The Debate Continues," *New York Times*, 8 December 1998, D5.

30. See also Gurr 1985. Homer-Dixon (1995) also notes that the supply of ingenuity will be limited by market failures and constraints on scientific advance, but these factors are independent of resource scarcity and population growth.

31. Sen (1994) is careful to note that a lower population growth rate could have reduced the magnitude of the fall in per capita GNP, but argues that rising population was much less important than exploitative and combative political rulers (and the Cold War) in undermining economic stability.

32. For reviews of theories of war, see Levy 1989a, 1998; Vasquez 1993; Van Evera 1999.

33. "International conflict" encompasses a wide range of phenomena, from war to militarized interstate disputes to nonmilitarized interstate tensions. With occasional exceptions, the literature on demography and conflict has failed to distinguish among the large number of possible conflictual international outcomes to which population growth may contribute. At each stage in the analysis we will attempt to clarify these relationships more precisely.

34. On the debate between offensive and defensive realism, see Lynn-Jones 1998; Rose 1998.

35. As Lynn-Jones (1998: 179–180) argues, offensive realism does not "offer predictions about the magnitude and character of a state's expansion." In fact, models of war that attempt to incorporate actors' utilities as well as power give significantly better predictions than do more narrow balance of power models (Bueno de Mesquita and Lalman 1992).

36. Although differing in important ways, the two approaches are sufficiently similar for our purposes.

37. The declining state has a number of strategies at its disposal, ranging from retrenchment to appeasement to preventive war (Gilpin 1981), but there has been very little research on the conditions under which each response is most likely.

38. Note that the power transition/preventive war hypothesis, possibly reinforced by hypotheses of loss aversion that predict risk-acceptant behavior to

avoid losses or recover recent losses (Levy 1997), implies that the main threat to the peace comes not from those increasing in power, but rather from those decreasing in relative power. International conflict, in this view, is driven more by fear than by ambition.

39. One might dismiss Luttwak out of hand if not for the fact that his suggestion has been approvingly cited over the years. Two recent mentions are Kupchan 1998: 52–53; and Charles Lane, "TRB: Casualty Attitude," 26 October 1998, *The New Republic*, 6.

40. The power literature is extremely large and "essentially contested," to borrow Steven Lukes's term. We need not burrow deeply into these debates here to note that many thinkers on power would decry the crude treatment of the concept by mainstream IR theorists.

41. Some make the strong claim that overpopulation, presumably operating through resource scarcity, is one of the driving forces of international conflict. McNeill (1982), for example, argues that the Revolutionary and Napoleonic Wars were a consequence of French population pressures, while Great Britain coped with its demographic problems by establishing an overseas empire and exporting both goods and people. Similarly, both World Wars erupted in an effort to cope with overcrowding in East-Central Europe: "the statesmanship of the Great Powers surely reflected the aggressive politics of expanding populations." (McNeill 1990: 20–21)

42. For a contrary view, which argues that advanced industrial societies rely less on minerals, energy, and raw materials to produce wealth ("dematerialization"), see Farinelli 1996. Drawing particularly on the cases of Japan and Germany, Prodi (1996: 126) argues that today the key to economic success is not investment in physical capital, but in human capital, in education: "The novel characteristic of the last generation of economic development is the weak correlation between the availability of resources and prospects for long-term growth in all countries of the world.... All empirical data demonstrate that land and raw materials have not been the foundations of the economic growth of the last generation."

43. For many, the question is not one of whether rapid population growth has negative short-term economic impact—Sen (1994), for example, despite his attention to political factors, concedes that it does—but whether it is the most important variable. Occupying middle positions on the continuum, Sen (1994) and Goldstone (1997) simply have different emphases, but not starkly different arguments.

44. Choucri (1974: 90–91) operationalizes international violence or conflict as "any armed conflict involving regular armed forces, a certain degree of organized fighting, and sustained violent encounters and armed clashes." Choucri's study is based on an MIT data set—the Computer Aided System for the Analysis of Local Conflict—from which she extracted only the Third World cases and incorporated a number of "additional cases which seemed particularly revealing from a political perspective." A number of relevant cases, notably conflicts between India and Pakistan, were excluded because they would have involved too much additional coding.

45. In more technical terms, Choucri has committed the methodological sin of selecting on the dependent variable (Tir and Diehl 1998: 326).

46. Tir and Diehl (1998) control for geographical proximity (contiguity), military capability, and level of development. Because capability is correlated with

population, however, controlling for military power misses some of the effect of population growth. In addition, population may wield its effects through development, either by retarding economic growth (neo-Malthusian position) or promoting it (Julian Simon and other revisionists).

47. See also Gurr 1985: 65. Note that militarized conflict may arise either through the direct use of force or as a result of a conflict action-reaction spiral beginning with responses to lower-level threats.

48. This may also be because economic growth is no longer dependent on investment in raw materials (see n. 46 above). This hypothesis reflects the broader view of "commercial liberalism" that an open trading system and extensive economic interdependence is a force for peace. Although the majority of recent empirical studies support the liberal hypothesis on interdependence and conflict (Oneal and Russett 1997; McMillan 1997), some research points in the other direction (Barbieri 1996), supporting the realist argument that economic interdependence either has no systematic impact on the outbreak of war or that asymmetric interdependence actually increases the probability of war.

49. Notwithstanding the title of his book, Liberman is not arguing that conquest pays in the broadest sense: Clearly it did not for Germany, Japan, and the Soviet Union, who provoked overwhelming balancing coalitions. Nonetheless his analysis is apposite, demonstrating that the conquest of industrialized nations is worthwhile in a more limited sense. Although Liberman does not examine whether his conclusions remain valid given the "postindustrial" turn in national economies, we are skeptical that it would render obsolete his insights regarding the cumulativity of industrial resources; physical and even human capital is relatively immobile and can still be exploited by a conqueror. Moreover, much of the developing world still awaits industrialization.

50. Among writers on demography and international relations, this possibility was noted by Organski and Organski (1961: 243–244): "if a nation cannot or will not solve the problem by economic change at home, it may seek to solve it by arming and threatening others, for an army affords employment; military production provides more jobs; and militant nationalism takes people's minds off other problems."

51. For some, population trends within the United States are cause for concern, as increasing numbers of Latino and Asian Americans augur a shift in political power from the north and east to the south and west, from Europe-centered issues to Hispanic/Pacific problems. These demographic patterns, according to this view, are forecast to spark an intense contest for entitlement priorities between predominantly Caucasian retirees and predominantly nonwhite children, mothers, and unemployed, and are likely to provoke ethnic and racial conflict as African-Americans fear their jobs will go to Hispanic-Americans and as poor whites dread a diverse gray/brown threat— that is, from the aging population and from other ethnic groups (Kennedy 1993: 50–51).

52. The discussion that follows will focus more extensively on the arguments linking demographic change to internal ethnic conflict; many of the same arguments are applicable at the international level.

53. Ethnic identity is not the only possible salient political cleavage. Consequently Fearon 1998, as well as Lake and Rothchild 1996, explicitly assume that ethnicity is the society's focal political division.

54. Numerous other theoretical frameworks have been offered to explain violent ethnic conflict (Brown et al. 1996, 1997) and some are quite convincing, both theoretically and empirically, but these are less useful for making sense of its links to demographic change.
55. For an attempt to model ethnic conflict as a security dilemma, see Posen 1993.
56. For other ambiguous statements, see Lake and Rothchild 1996: 48, 52, 55. A further problem of characterizing violent ethnic conflict as the consequence of a commitment problem (and hence as a form of preventive war) is that this implies that the conflict is initiated by the declining minority, but ethnic conflict is also at times (and perhaps more often) undertaken by the majority group seeking to exploit its greater power and attain its ends at the expense of minorities.
57. On the postwar Greco-Turkish conflicts, and particularly the role of NATO, see Krebs 1999.
58. Causality of course goes both ways. International and internal conflict have been important sources of migrants and refugees. The resulting endogeneity problems force the analyst to give careful attention to questions of causation.
59. Migrants also sometimes become pawns in, rather than causes of, inter-state conflict, as the host country, for its own reasons, actively supports them in their quest to change the regime of their homeland. The United States' support for Cuban exiles is well known. For other examples, see Weiner (1992/93: 199).
60. Suhrke 1993 partially endorses this claim, arguing that refugees, as opposed to migrants, are unlikely to successfully foment conflict, and hence the consequence of their efforts is more often oppression than destabilization.
61. For an interesting, suggestive discussion of changing Australian views on migration, from "populate or perish" to "diversify or decline," see Freeman 1993.
62. For the most recent statement, and a set of case studies on Mexico, Gaza, South Africa, Pakistan, and Rwanda, see Homer-Dixon and Blitt 1998.

References

Anderson, Barbara A. and Brian D. Silver. 1995. "Demographic Sources of the Changing Ethnic Composition of the Soviet Union." In *Population, Ethnicity, Nation-Building*, ed. Calvin Goldscheider. Boulder, CO: Westview.
Azar, Edward E., and Nadia E. Farah. 1984. "Political Dimensions of Conflict." In *Multidisciplinary Perspectives on Population and Conflict*, ed. Nazli Choucri. Syracuse, NY: Syracuse University Press.
Baldwin, David. 1989. *Paradoxes of Power*. New York, NY: Basil Blackwell.
Barbieri, K. 1996. "Economic Interdependence: A Path to Peace or Source of Interstate Conflict?" *Journal of Peace Research* 33 (February): 29–49.
Barnett, Michael N., and Jack S. Levy. 1991. "Domestic Sources of Alliances and Alignments: The Case of Egypt, 1962–1973." *International Organization* 45 (summer): 369–395.
Best, Geoffrey. 1989. "The Militarization of European Society, 1870–1914." In *The Militarization of the Western World*, ed. John R. Gillis. New Brunswick, NJ: Rutgers University Press.

Bharadwaj, Lakshmi. 1996. "Theories of Demographic Change." In *Demographic and Structural Change*, eds. Dennis L. Peck and J. Selwyn Hollingsworth. Westport, CT: Greenwood Press.

Biddle, Stephen. 1996. "Victory Misunderstood: What the Gulf War Tells Us about the Future of Conflict." *International Security* 21 (fall): 139–179.

———. 1997. "The Gulf War Debate Redux: Why Skill and Technology Are the Right Answer." *International Security* 22 (fall): 163–174.

Binkin, Martin. 1986. *Military Technology and Defense Manpower*. Washington, D.C.: Brookings.

Blainey, Geoffrey. 1988. *The Causes of War*, 3rd ed. New York, NY: Free Press.

Boserup, Ester. 1965. *The Conditions of Agricultural Growth: The Economics of Agrarian Change under Population Pressure*. Chicago, IL: Aldine.

Bremer, Stuart, J. David Singer, and Urs Luterbacher. 1973. "The Population Density and War Proneness of European Nations, 1816–1965." *Comparative Political Studies* 6 (3): 329–348.

Brown, Michael E. 1997. "The Causes of Internal Conflict: An Overview." In *Nationalism and Ethnic Conflict*, eds. Michael E. Brown et al. Cambridge, MA: MIT Press.

Brown, Michael E., et al., eds. 1996. *Debating the Democratic Peace*. Cambridge, MA: MIT Press.

———. 1997. *Nationalism and Ethnic Conflict*. Cambridge, MA: MIT Press.

Brubaker, Rogers. 1993. "Political Dimensions of Migration From and Among Soviet Successor States." In *International Migration and Security*, ed. Myron Weiner. Boulder, CO: Westview.

———. 1996. "Rethinking Nationhood: Nation as Institutionalized Form, Practical Category, Contingent Event." In his *Nationalism Reframed*. Cambridge: Cambridge University Press.

Bueno de Mesquita, Bruce, and David Lalman. 1992. *War and Reason*. New Haven, CT: Yale University Press.

Cassen, Robert, ed. 1994. *Population and Development: Old Debates, New Conclusions*. New Brunswick, NJ: Transaction Publishers.

Chase, Robert, Emily Hill, and Paul Kennedy. 1996. "Pivotal States and U.S. Strategy." *Foreign Affairs* 75 (1): 33–51.

Choucri, Nazli. 1974. *Population Dynamics and International Violence*. Lexington, MA: D.C. Heath.

———. 1983. *Population and Conflict: New Dimensions of Population Dynamics*. New York, NY: United Nations Fund for Population Activities.

———, ed. 1984. *Multidisciplinary Perspectives on Population and Conflict*. Syracuse, NY: Syracuse University Press.

Choucri, Nazli, and Robert C. North. 1975. *Nations in Conflict*. San Francisco, CA: W.H Freeman.

———. 1989. "Lateral Pressure in International Relations." In *Handbook of War Studies*, ed. Manus I. Midlarsky. London: Allen and Unwin.

Choucri, Nazli, Robert C. North, and Susumu Yamakage. 1992. *The Challenge of Japan before World War II and After: A Study of National Growth and Expansion*. London: Routledge.

Christensen, Thomas J. 1997. "Perceptions and Alliances in Europe, 1865–1940." *International Organization* 51 (winter): 65–97.

Cohen, Eliot A. 1996. "A Revolution in Warfare." *Foreign Affairs* 75 (2): 37–54.

Cohen, Mark N. 1984. "Population Growth, Interpersonal Conflict, and Organizational Response in Human History." In *Multidisciplinary Perspectives on Population and Conflict*, ed. Nazli Choucri. Syracuse, NY: Syracuse University Press.

Dabelko, Geoffrey, and P.J. Simmons. 1997. "Environment and Security: Core Ideas and U.S. Government Initiatives." *SAIS Review* 17 (1).

Dahl, Robert. 1957. "The Concept of Power." *Behavioral Science* 2 (June): 201–215.

Davis, Kingsley. 1958. "Population and Power in the Free World." In *Population and World Politics*, ed. Philip M. Hauser. Glencoe, IL: Free Press.

———. 1963. "The Theory of Challenge and Response in Modern Demographic History." *Population Index* 29 (4): 345–366.

———. 1991. "Population and Resources: Fact and Interpretation." In "Resources, Environment, and Population: Present Knowledge, Future Options" (supplement to *Population and Development Review*, volume 16), eds. Kingsley Davis and Mikhail S. Bernstam. Oxford: Oxford University Press.

Deudney, Daniel. 1990. "The Case Against Linking Environmental Degradation and National Security." *Millennium* 19 (3): 461–476.

Dirks, Nicholas, Geoff Eley, and Sherry Ortner, eds. 1994. *Culture/Power/History: A Reader in Contemporary Social Theory*. Princeton, NJ: Princeton University Press.

Doyle, Michael W. 1997. *Ways of War and Peace*. New York, NY: W. W. Norton.

Earle, Edward Mead. 1986. "Alexander Hamilton, Friedrich List: The Economic Foundations of Military Power." In *Makers of Modern Strategy: From Machiavelli to the Nuclear Age*, ed. Peter Paret. Princeton, NJ: Princeton University Press.

Easterlin, Richard A. 1996. *Growth Triumphant: The Twenty-First Century in Historical Perspective*. Ann Arbor, MI: University of Michigan Press.

Eberstadt, Nicholas. 1991. "Population Change and National Security." *Foreign Affairs* 70 (3): 115–131.

———. 1998. "Demography and International Relations." *Washington Quarterly* 21 (spring).

Ehrlich, Paul R. and Anne H. Ehrlich. 1990. *The Population Explosion*. New York, NY: Simon and Schuster.

Farinelli, Ugo. 1996. "Materials and Mineral Resources." In *Resources and Population: Natural, Institutional, and Demographic Dimensions of Development*, eds. Bernard Colombo, Paul Demeny, and Max Perutz. Oxford: Clarendon Press.

Fearon, James D. 1994a. "Signaling versus the Balance of Power and Interests: An Empirical Test of a Crisis Bargaining Model." *Journal of Conflict Resolution* 38 (June): 236–269.

———. 1994b. "Domestic Political Audiences and the Escalation of International Disputes." *American Political Science Review* 88 (September): 577–592.

———. 1995. "Rationalist Explanations for War." *International Organization* 49 (summer): 379–414.

———. 1998. "Commitment Problems and the Spread of Ethnic Conflict." In *The International Spread of Ethnic Conflict: Fear, Diffusion, and Escalation*, eds. David A. Lake and Donald Rothchild. Princeton, NJ: Princeton University Press.

Fearon, James D., and David D. Laitin. 1996. "Explaining Interethnic Cooperation." *American Political Science Review* 90 (4): 715–735.

Foster, Gregory. 1989. "Global Demographic Trends to the Year 2010: Implications for U.S. Security." *Washington Quarterly* 12 (2).

Foster, Gregory, Alan Ned Sabrosky, and William Taylor, Jr., eds. 1987. *The Strategic Dimension of Military Manpower*. Cambridge, MA: Ballinger.

Freedman, Lawrence. 1991. "Demographic Change and Strategic Studies." In *Population Change and European Security*, eds. Lawrence Freedman and John Saunders. London: Brassey's.

Freeman, Gary. 1993. "From 'Populate or Perish' to 'Diversify or Decline': Immigration and Australian National Security." In *International Migration and Security*, ed. Myron Weiner. Boulder, CO: Westview.

Gagnon, V. P. 1994/95. "Ethnic Nationalism and International Conflict: The Case of Serbia." *International Security* 19 (winter): 132–168.

Ganguly, Sumit. 1996. "Explaining the Kashmir Insurgency: Political Mobilization and Institutional Decay." *International Security* 22 (fall): 76–107.

George, Alexander, and Richard Smoke. 1974. *Deterrence in American Foreign Policy*. New York, NY: Columbia University Press.

Gilpin, Robert. 1981. *War and Change in World Politics*. New York, NY: Cambridge University Press.

Glaser, Charles. 1994. "Realists as Optimists: Cooperation as Self-Help." *International Security* 19 (winter): 50–90.

Gleick, Peter. 1993. "Water and Conflict: Fresh Water Resources and International Security." *International Security* 18 (summer): 79–112.

Goldscheider, Calvin, ed. 1995. *Population, Ethnicity, Nation-Building*. Boulder, CO: Westview.

Goldstone, Jack A. 1991. *Revolution and Rebellion in the Early Modern World*. Berkeley, CA: University of California Press.

———. 1997. "Population Growth and Revolutionary Crises." In *Theorizing Revolutions*, ed. John Foran. London: Routledge.

Gore, Albert. 1992. *Earth in the Balance*. Boston, MA: Houghton Mifflin.

Gurr, Ted Robert. 1970. *Why Men Rebel*. Princeton, NJ: Princeton University Press.

———. 1985. "On the Political Consequences of Scarcity and Economic Decline." *International Studies Quarterly* 29 (March): 51–75.

Handel, Michael. 1981. "Numbers Do Count: The Question of Quality Versus Quantity." *Journal of Strategic Studies* 4 (3): 225–260.

Helman, Gerald, and Steven Ratner. 1992/93. "Saving Failed States." *Foreign Policy* 89: 3–20.

Homer-Dixon, Thomas. 1991. "On the Threshold: Environmental Changes as Causes of Acute Conflict." *International Security* 16 (2): 76–116.

———. 1994. "Environmental Scarcities and Violent Conflict: Evidence from Cases." *International Security* 19 (1): 5–40

———. 1995. "The Ingenuity Gap: Can Poor Countries Adapt to Resource Scarcity?" *Population and Development Review* 21 (3): 587–612.

Homer-Dixon, Thomas, and Jessica Blitt. 1998. *Ecoviolence: Links Among Environment, Population, and Security*. Lanham, MD: Rowman and Littlefield.

Horlacher, D. E., and L. Heligman. 1991. "Recent Findings on the Consequences of Rapid Population Growth in Developing Countries." In Proceedings of the United Nations, *Consequences of Rapid Population Growth in Developing Countries*. New York, NY: Taylor and Francis.

Howard, Michael. 1976. *War in European History*. Oxford: Oxford University Press.

Huntington, Samuel. 1996. *The Clash of Civilizations and the Remaking of World Order*. New York, NY: Simon and Schuster.

Ikenberry, G. John, et al., eds. 1988. *The State and American Foreign Economic Policy*. Ithaca, NY: Cornell University Press.

Jacobsen, Karen, with Steven Wilkinson. 1993. "Refugee Movements as Security Threats in Sub-Saharan Africa." In *International Migration and Security*, ed. Myron Weiner. Boulder, CO: Westview.

Jervis, Robert. 1978. "Cooperation under the Security Dilemma." *World Politics* 30 (January): 186–213.

Kahl, Colin H. 1998. "Population Growth, Environmental Degradation, and State-Sponsored Violence: The Case of Kenya, 1991–93." *International Security* 23 (fall): 80–119.

Kaplan, Robert D. 1994. "The Coming Anarchy: How Scarcity, Crime, Overpopulation, Tribalism, and Disease Are Rapidly Destroying the Social Fabric of Our Planet." *Atlantic Monthly* 273 (2): 44–67.

———. 1996. *The Ends of the Earth*. New York, NY: Random House.

Katznelson, Ira. 1985. "Working-Class Formation and the State: Nineteenth-Century England in American Perspective." In *Bringing the State Back In*, eds. Peter Evans, Dietrich Rueschemeyer, and Theda Skocpol. Cambridge: Cambridge University Press.

Kaysen, Carl. 1990. "Is War Obsolete? A Review Essay." *International Security* 14 (spring): 42–64.

Keegan, John. 1987. "The Role of Manpower in Traditional Strategic Thought." In *The Strategic Dimension of Military Manpower*, eds. Gregory Foster, Alan Ned Sabrosky, and William Taylor, Jr. Cambridge, MA: Ballinger.

Kennedy, Paul. 1993. "The American Prospect." *New York Review of Books* 41 (5): 42–53.

Keohane, Robert O. 1986. "Theory of World Politics: Structural Realism and Beyond." In *Neorealism and Its Critics*, ed. Robert O. Keohane. New York, NY: Columbia University Press.

Kleinman, David S. 1980. *Human Adaptation and Population Growth: A Non-Malthusian Perspective*. New York, NY: Universe Books.

Krebs, Ronald R. 1999. "Perverse Institutionalism: NATO and the Greco-Turkish Conflict." *International Organization* 53 (2): 343–377.

Kugler, Jacek, and Douglas Lemke, eds. 1996. *Parity and War*. Ann Arbor, MI: University of Michigan Press.

Kugler, Jacek, and A. F. K. Organski. 1989. "The Power Transition: A Retrospective and Prospective Evaluation." In *Handbook of War Studies*, ed. Manus I. Midlarksy. London: Unwin and Hyman.

Kupchan, Charles A. 1998. "After Pax Americana: Benign Power, Regional Integration, and the Sources of a Stable Multipolarity." *International Security* 23 (fall): 40–79.

Lake, David A., and Donald Rothchild. 1996. "Containing Fear: The Origins and Management of Ethnic Conflict." *International Security* 21 (fall): 41–75.

Lemke, Douglas. 1996. "Small States and War: An Extension of Power Transition Theory." In *Parity and War*, eds. Jacek Kugler and Douglas Lemke. Ann Arbor, MI: University of Michigan Press.

Leroy, Marcel. 1978. *Population and World Politics*. Leiden: Nijhoff.

Levy, Jack S. 1989a. "The Causes of War: A Review of Theories and Evidence." In Philip E. Tetlock, Jo L. Husbands, Robert Jervis, Paul C. Stern, and Charles Tilly, eds. *Behavior, Society, and Nuclear War*, Vol. 1. New York, NY: Oxford University Press.

———. 1989b. The Diversionary Theory of War: A Critique. In *Handbook of War Studies*, ed. Manus I. Midlarsky. London: Allen and Unwin.

———. 1989c. "Quantitative Studies of Deterrence Success and Failure." In *Perspectives on Deterrence*, eds. Paul Stern et al. Oxford: Oxford University Press.

———. 1997. "Prospect Theory, Rational Choice, and International Relations." *International Studies Quarterly* 41 (March): 87–112.

———. 1998. "The Causes of War and the Conditions of Peace." *Annual Review of Political Science* 1: 139–166.

Levy, Marc A. 1995. "Is the Environment a National Security Issue?" *International Security* 20 (2): 35–62.

Liberman, Peter. 1996. *Does Conquest Pay? The Exploitation of Occupied Industrial Societies*. Princeton, NJ: Princeton University Press.

Lipschutz, Ronnie. 1989. *When Nations Clash: Raw Materials, Ideology and Foreign Policy*. New York, NY: Ballinger.

Lowi, Miriam. 1993. *Water and Power: The Politics of a Scarce Resource in the Jordan River Basin*. New York, NY: Cambridge University Press.

Luttwak, Edward N. 1994. "Where Are the Great Powers?" *Foreign Affairs* 73 (4): 23–28.

———. 1996. "A Post-Heroic Military Policy." *Foreign Affairs* 75 (4): 33–44.

Lynn-Jones, Sean M. 1998. "Realism and America's Rise: A Review Essay." *International Security* 23 (fall): 157–182.

Mack, Andrew. 1975. "Why Big Nations Lose Small Wars: The Politics of Asymmetric Conflict." *World Politics* 27 (January): 175–200.

Maoz, Zeev. 1983. "Resolve, Capabilities, and the Outcomes of Interstate Disputes." *Journal of Conflict Resolution* 27 (June): 195–229.

Mathews, Jessica. 1989. "Redefining Security." *Foreign Affairs* 68 (2): 162–177.

Mazur, Laurie, ed. 1994. *Beyond the Numbers*. Washington, D.C.: Island Press.

McMillan, Susan M. 1997. "Interdependence and Conflict." *Mershon International Studies Review*, 41, Supplement I (May): 33–58.

McNeill, William H. 1982. *The Pursuit of Power: Technology, Armed Force, and Society since A.D. 1000*. Chicago, IL: University of Chicago Press.

———. 1990. *Population and Politics since 1750*. Charlottesville, VA: University Press of Virginia.

McNicoll, Geoffrey. 1984. "Consequences of Rapid Population Growth: An Overview and Assessment." *Population and Development Review* 10 (2): 177–240.

———. 1994. "Population and Institutional Change." *International Social Science Journal* 46 (3): 307–316.

———. 1995. "On Population Growth and Revisionism: Further Questions." *Population and Development Review* 21 (2): 307–340.

Mearsheimer, John. 1983. *Conventional Deterrence*. Ithaca, NY: Cornell University Press.

———. 1990. "Back to the Future." *International Security* 15 (summer): 5–56.

Miller, Mark J. 1998. "International Migration and Global Security." In *Redefining Security: Population Movements and National Security*, eds. Nana Poku and David T. Graham. Westport, CT: Praeger.

Morgenthau, Hans. 1993 [1948]. *Politics Among Nations*. Brief ed. Revised by Kenneth W. Thompson. New York, NY: McGraw Hill.

Morrow, James D. 1993. "Arms versus Allies: Tradeoffs in the Search for Security." *International Organization* 47 (spring): 207–234.

Myers, Norman. 1989. "Environment and Security." *Foreign Policy* 74: 23–41.
Myers, Norman, and Julian Simon. 1994. *Scarcity and Abundance? A Debate on the Environment.* New York, NY: W. W. Norton.
National Research Council, Working Group on Population Growth and Economic Development. 1986. *Population Growth and Economic Development.* Washington, D.C.: National Academy Press.
Oneal, John R., and Bruce M. Russett. 1997. "The Classical Liberals Were Right: Democracy, Interdependence, and Conflict, 1950–1985." *International Studies Quarterly* 41 (March): 267–294.
Oppong, Christine. 1996. "Population Change: The Status and Roles of Women." In *Resources and Population: Natural, Institutional, and Demographic Dimensions of Development*, eds. Bernard Colombo, Paul Demeny, and Max Perutz. Oxford: Clarendon Press.
Organski, A. F. K. 1968. *World Politics*, 2nd ed. New York, NY: Knopf.
Organski, A. F. K., Bruce Bueno de Mesquita, and Alan Lamborn. 1972. "The Effective Population in International Politics." In *Political Science in Population Studies*, eds. Richard L. Clinton, William S. Flash, and R. Kenneth Godwin. Lexington, MA: D.C. Heath.
Organski, A. F. K., and Jacek Kugler. 1980. *The War Ledger.* Chicago, IL: University of Chicago Press.
Organski, A. F. K., et al. 1984. *Births, Deaths, and Taxes: The Demographic and Political Transitions.* Chicago, IL: University of Chicago Press.
Organski, Katherine, and A. F. K. Organski. 1961. *Population and World Power.* New York, NY: Alfred A. Knopf.
Ostrom, Charles, and Brian Job. 1985. "The President and the Political Use of Force." *American Political Science Review* 80 (June): 541–566.
Paul, T. V. 1994. *Asymmetric Conflicts: War Initiation by Weaker Powers.* New York, NY: Cambridge University Press.
Pirages, Dennis. 1997. "Demographic Change and Ecological Insecurity." Environmental Change and Security Project Report 3. Washington, D.C.: Woodrow Wilson International Center for Scholars.
Poku, Nana, and David T. Graham, eds. 1998. *Redefining Security: Population Movements and National Security.* Westport, CT: Praeger.
Posen, Barry R. 1993. "The Security Dilemma and Ethnic Conflict." In *Ethnic Conflict and International Security*, ed. Brown et al. Princeton: Princeton University Press.
Press, Daryl G. 1997. "Lessons from Ground Combat in the Gulf: The Impact of Training and Technology." *International Security* 22 (fall): 137–146.
Prodi, Romano. 1996. "The Evolution of Economic Organization in Contemporary Societies." In *Resources and Population: Natural, Institutional, and Demographic Dimensions of Development*, eds. Bernard Colombo, Paul Demeny, and Max Perutz. Oxford: Clarendon Press.
Rose, Gideon. 1998. "Neoclassical Realism and Theories of Foreign Policy." *World Politics* 51 (October): 144–172.
Rosen, Stephen Peter. 1996. *Societies and Military Power: India and Her Armies.* Ithaca, NY: Cornell University Press.
Rothschild, Emma. 1995. "What is Security?" *Dædalus* 124 (summer): 53–98.
Ruggie, John. 1983. "International Regimes, Transactions, and Change: Embedded Liberalism in the Postwar International Order." In *International Regimes*, ed. Stephen D. Krasner. Ithaca, NY: Cornell University Press. Pp. 195–231.

Russett, Bruce. 1990a. *Controlling the Sword*. Cambridge, MA: Harvard University Press.

———. 1990b. "Economic Decline, Electoral Pressure, and the Initiation of International Conflict." In *The Prisoners of War*, eds. Charles Gochman and Alan Sabrosky. Lexington, MA: D.C. Heath.

Ruttan, V.W., and Y. Hayami. 1991. "Rapid Population Growth and Technical and Institutional Change." In Proceedings of the United Nations, *Consequences of Rapid Population Growth in Developing Countries*. New York, NY: Taylor and Francis.

Sarkesian, Sam. 1989. "The Demographic Component of Strategy." *Survival* 31 (6): 549–564.

Saunders, John. 1991. "Introduction: Population and Security." In *Population Change and European Security*, eds. Lawrence Freedman and John Saunders. London: Brassey's.

Schweller, Randall. 1994. "Bandwagoning for Profit." *International Security* 19 (summer): 72–107.

Sen, Amartya. 1994. "Population: Delusion and Reality." *New York Review of Books* 40 (15): 62–71.

Shain, Yossi. 1993. "Democrats and Secessionists: US Diasporas as Regime Destabilizers." In *International Migration and Security*, ed. Myron Weiner. Boulder, CO: Westview.

Sheffer, Gabriel. 1993. "Ethnic Diasporas: A Threat to their Hosts?" In *International Migration and Security*, ed. Myron Weiner. Boulder, CO: Westview.

Simon, Julian L. 1981. *The Ultimate Resource*. Princeton, NJ: Princeton University Press.

———. 1986. *Theory of Population and Economic Growth*. New York, NY: Basil Blackwell.

———. 1989. "Lebensraum: Paradoxically, Population Growth May Eventually End Wars." *Journal of Conflict Resolution* 33 (1): 164–180.

Skocpol, Theda. 1985. "Bringing the State Back In." In *Bringing the State Back In*, eds. Peter Evans, Dietrich Rueschemeyer, and Theda Skocpol. Cambridge: Cambridge University Press.

Snyder, Jack. 1991. *Myths of Empire*. Ithaca, NY: Cornell University Press.

Sprout, Harold, and Margaret Sprout. 1971. *Toward a Politics of the Planet Earth*. New York, NY: Van Nostrand.

Suhrke, Astri. 1993. "Pressure Points: Environmental Degradation, Migration and Conflict." Washington, D.C.: American Association for the Advancement of Science and the University of Toronto.

Swain, Ashok. 1996. "Environmental Migration and Conflict Dynamics: Focus on Developing Regions." *Third World Quarterly* 17 (5): 959–973.

Tapinos, Georges. 1978. "The World in the 1980s: Demographic Perspectives." In *Six Billion People: Demographic Dilemmas and World Politics*, eds. Georges Tapinos and Phyllis T. Piotrow. New York, NY: McGraw-Hill.

Teitelbaum, Michael S., and Jay Winter. 1998. *A Question of Numbers: High Migration, Low Fertility, and the Politics of National Identity*. New York, NY: Hill and Wang.

Tir, Jaroslav, and Paul F. Diehl. 1998. "Demographic Pressure and Interstate Conflict: Linking Population Growth and Density to Militarized Disputes and Wars, 1930–89." *Journal of Peace Research* 35 (3): 319–339.

Ullman, Richard H. 1983. "Redefining Security." *International Security* 8 (1): 129–153.

———. 1991. *Securing Europe*. Princeton, NJ: Princeton University Press.

Van Evera, Stephen. 1999. *Causes of War: Power and the Roots of Conflict*. Ithaca: Cornell University Press.

Vasquez, John. 1993. *The War Puzzle*. New York, NY: Cambridge University Press.

Walt, Stephen M. 1987. *Origins of Alliances*. Ithaca, NY: Cornell University Press.

———. 1996. *Revolution and War*. Ithaca, NY: Cornell University Press.

Waters, Mary. 1990. *Ethnic Options: Choosing Identities in America*. Berkeley, CA: University of California Press.

Wattenberg, Ben. 1987. *The Birth Dearth: What Happens When People in Free Countries Don't Have Enough Babies?* New York, NY: Pharos Books.

Weiner, Myron. 1971. "Political Demography: An Inquiry into the Political Consequences of Population Change." In *Rapid Population Growth: Consequences and Policy Implications,* ed. National Academy of Sciences, Office of the Foreign Secretary. Baltimore: The Johns Hopkins University Press.

———. 1985. "International Migration and International Relations." *Population and Development Review* 11 (3): 441–455.

———. 1992/93. "Security, Stability, and International Migration." *International Security* 17 (3): 91–126. Reprinted in *Global Dangers: Changing Dimensions of International Security*, eds. Sean M. Lynn-Jones and Steven E. Miller. Cambridge, MA: MIT Press, 1995.

———. 1993. "Rejected Peoples and Unwanted Migrants in South Asia." In *International Migration and Security*, ed. Weiner. Boulder, CO: Westview.

Weir, D. R. 1991. "A Historical Perspective on the Economic Consequences of Rapid Population Growth." In Proceedings of the United Nations, *Consequences of Rapid Population Growth in Developing Countries*. New York, NY: Taylor and Francis.

Williamson, Samuel R., Jr. 1991. *Austria-Hungary and the Origins of the First World War*. London: Macmillan.

Wright, Quincy. 1955. *The Study of International Relations*. New York, NY: Appleton-Century-Crofts.

———. 1958. "Population and United States Foreign Policy." In *Population and World Politics*, ed. Philip M. Hauser. Glencoe, IL: Free Press.

Wrigley, E. A. 1996. "A Historical Perspective on Population and Resources." In *Resources and Population: Natural, Institutional, and Demographic Dimensions of Development*, eds. Bernard Colombo, Paul Demeny, and Max Perutz. Oxford: Clarendon Press.

Zakaria, Fareed. 1998. *From Wealth to Power*. Princeton, NJ: Princeton University Press.

Zimmermann, Warren. 1995. "Migrants and Refugees: A Threat to Security?" In *Threatened Peoples, Threatened Borders: World Migration and U.S. Policy*, eds. Michael S. Teitelbaum and Myron Weiner. New York, NY: W.W. Norton.

Zolberg, Aristide. 1995. "From Invitation to Interdiction: U.S. Foreign Policy and Immigration since 1945." In *Threatened Peoples, Threatened Borders: World Migration and U.S. Policy*, eds. Michael S. Teitelbaum and Myron Weiner. New York, NY: W.W. Norton.

PART TWO

State Responses to
Demographic Trends

CHAPTER 4

Keepers of the Gates: National Militaries in an Age of International Population Movement

William J. Durch

Defending the interests and borders of the territorial state against external threat is the second-oldest role of military institutions (after facilitating establishment of the state itself). In the waning years of the twentieth century, the principal external threats to many states' security on a day-to-day basis derive not from potential military aggression but from cross-border movements of people and goods not sanctioned by the destination state. The forces of nationalism, ethnic prejudice, and religious and racial intolerance produce record numbers of refugees, while misfiring economies, growing populations, and modern means of transportation have spawned historic numbers of economic migrants. Organized criminal groups facilitate the movement of refugees and migrants, for a steep price. Drug cartels exploit deprivation at one end of their supply chain, addiction at the other, and greed in the middle, to establish and expand complex networks for creating, moving, and marketing their product, for which the path of least resistance is through the weakest states.

In safeguarding the sovereignty of the state against these new cross-border challenges, regular militaries are assisted by a host of quasi-military institutions answerable to ministries of finance, internal affairs, transportation, and law enforcement. All collaborate, with varying degrees of effectiveness in different states, in strengthening national borders against "unwanted entry."

Although we will focus in this chapter on the human element in unwanted entry, consistent with the volume's larger emphasis on demography and security, the international movement of people and goods of all types is increasingly viewed by those responsible for safeguarding borders as an undifferentiated stream of potential threats. The greater the influx, moreover, the quicker any system for processing them can be overloaded and the more likely that even legitimate refugees become "unwanted."[1]

Regular militaries have been involved on both sides of the question of unwanted entry, that is, both protecting borders and producing mass population movements. The bulk of this paper is about the protective function, but national armed forces in many countries have a long and not especially glorious record of expelling unwanted groups, whether refugees who have overstayed their welcome or minority groups of longstanding residency. They have been used to disrupt the activities of "refugee warriors" among groups who were previously expelled or who may have fled the country after losing a revolution or civil war.[2] Militaries have on occasion made common cause with refugee warriors, arming them against the ruling regime in the refugees' own state. Combinations of these actions have occurred in the context of wars and revolutions over the last quarter century in Afghanistan, Cambodia, Cuba, El Salvador, Ethiopia, Guatemala, Nicaragua, Rwanda, Sudan, Tanzania, and Zaire. Expulsion of resident minorities has been national policy at various times in Burma, Iraq, Kuwait, Senegal, Mauritania, Nigeria, Uganda, and Vietnam.[3]

Nor has Europe been immune from such upheavals. Sizable westward population movements accompanied the fall of the Iron Curtain, although the psychology and politics of the Cold War meant that most of those immigrants were welcomed by destination states (Loescher 1992: 21–22, 75–76). On the other hand, the mass population expulsions—dubbed "ethnic cleansing"—that afflicted the sequential breakup of postwar Yugoslavia created unexpected floods of refugees and internally displaced persons. The secession struggle of Croatia (1991–1995) ultimately resulted in expulsion of much of the state's Serb minority by Croatia's armed forces. The three-way battle for Bosnia-Herzegovina (1992–1995), where Serbs and Croats each pushed Bosnian Muslim populations out of large swaths of territory, led to the imposition of a de facto international protectorate with heavily armed peacekeeping forces and equally heavy political oversight. Finally (as of this writing), actions by secessionist fighters in Yugoslavia's province of Kosovo triggered a government backlash that had escalated, by March 1999, into the wholesale uprooting and expulsion of the ethnic Albanian and Muslim population of the province by Serb-dominated government forces, despite punishing counteraction by the air forces of the North Atlantic Treaty Organization (NATO).

This chapter offers a tentative framework for categorizing state responses to unwanted entry and presents brief case histories of militarized immigration control that fit each category. The cases examined include the United States, the European Union, the Russian Federation, the Republic of India, and the Republic of South Africa. These cases do not exhaust the story of military involvement in controlling unwanted entry, but they illustrate a wide range of circumstances, actions, and institutional arrangements. The chapter closes with a preliminary judgment of the efficacy of militarized immigration control and its potential impact on the international refugee regime that has evolved over the past half-century.

Defining Unwanted Entry

States establish controls on entry, exit, and transit for a variety of political and economic reasons. From an economic perspective, entry limitations represent an effort by the state to control the supply of a major factor of production, keep domestic unemployment low, and maintain relatively high wages. Were labor allowed to be as mobile as capital, wages in unskilled and semi-skilled jobs, in particular, would drop (or at least that would be business's hope and organized labor's fear). Hence economic migrants are routinely turned aside by developed states except in recognized specialties where there are labor shortages. U.S. employers in high-technology industries, for example, face a shortage of skilled workers and would welcome more immigrant labor. Countries like South Africa face similar supply-demand mismatches: while most of the foreigners seeking employment there are unwanted, certain categories such as miners are in demand because, as the government acknowledges, South Africans are unwilling to endure the poor working environment (Mokoena 1999: 15).

Anyone without a valid official passport and/or visa who attempts to cross a state border, especially somewhere other than at an established point of entry (airport, seaport, traffic checkpoint) is an unwanted entrant, whatever his or her motivation. States want to validate entry to block not only unwanted economic migrants but obvious criminal elements and contraband (drugs, weapons, stolen goods, new ideas) that may pose threats to the security of the state and its citizens. Individuals coming from zones of conflict who seek asylum and formal status as refugees may find it difficult to substantiate either their identity or their fear of individual persecution or violence. Identity papers may have been lost or confiscated en route; they may have only an oral account of their experiences on which to base an asylum claim; or they may be making claims as members of a group whose members have experienced violence, although they themselves may have been spared. The OAU and Cartagena definitions of refugee status allow such claims; the UN Convention on the Status of Refugees does not.

Unwanted entry can and often does involve overstaying tourist or other short-term visas to work in a country illegally. Such behavior is facilitated by lax or deficient internal labor controls rather than problematic border controls, since the individuals involved conformed to legal requirements when entering the country.

Under international law, states have no duties or obligations to economic migrants, while refugees "have the right to apply for asylum and to demonstrate the political nature of their plight...." No state is obliged to grant asylum, but at least there are recognized criteria for securing refugee status, giving economic migrants every incentive to claim refugee status when challenged by authorities in transit or destination states (Loescher 1990: 9).

The situations of migrants and refugees are conflated when they become involved with professional smugglers who promise "irregular" entry into the country of desire. Clients are effectively at the mercy of their "coyotes" (as such smugglers are known on the U.S.-Mexican border) once the guided entry attempt begins, and the coyotes—sometimes lone operators, sometimes agents of criminal cartels—know it. Clients may be starved, suffocated, dumped on isolated islands, pushed into the sea, locked in freight containers, or merely stranded, whatever money or documentation they may have brought with them lost to the coyote toward the end of the journey. In the case of illegal economic migrants from China, the smugglers are "well-organized [and] extremely violent" (U.S. Coast Guard 1998). Because of the role of such gangs in irregular immigration, migrants tend to be lumped together with other smuggling activities in the eyes of law enforcement, and refugees may tend to be lumped together with migrants.

Once people seeking entry come to be viewed as threats, their potentially positive contributions to the economy of the destination state and whatever empathy asylum seekers may deserve for their plight can get lost in the perceived urgency of the need to secure national borders. Thus, while President Clinton may give a speech extolling the virtues of immigration, the U.S. Coast Guard advertises its success in dealing with the "migrant threat," cheek by jowl with discussion of the "drug threat," with interdiction counts as its measure of effectiveness (U.S. Coast Guard 1997). Stopping such threats can and does take on symbolic political value since, if the state cannot defend its borders against ragged civilian hordes, what can it defend against? In consequence, there is an increased burden of proof placed on those in the stream to prove eligibility for legitimate entry; increased tendencies to err in favor of the interests of the state that is facing unwanted entry; and increased incentives on the part of those attempting entry to seek ways around the state's border barriers and filters, including the use of criminal facilitators, reinforcing in turn the guardians' perceptions of incoming people as every bit as much a threat as incoming missiles.

The Dimensions of "Militarized" Immigration Control

States employ a wide array of military, paramilitary, and police forces to guard their borders and filter out unwanted entrants. Timothy Dunn, in his study of U.S. control policies and practices on the U.S.-Mexico border, provides a relevant definition of "militarization," linked to the U.S. military doctrine of Low Intensity Conflict (LIC):

The essence of LIC doctrine is the establishment and maintenance of social control over targeted civilian populations through the implementation of a broad range of sophisticated measures via the coordinated and integrated efforts of police, para-military, and military forces. One of the doctrine's distinguishing characteristics is that military forces take on police functions, while police forces take on military characteristics. (Dunn 1996: 4)

Militarized border control, then, involves cooperation and coordination among police, paramilitary, and regular military forces to prevent unwanted entry. Although national authorities in some of the cases discussed below might not consider themselves to be engaged in a low-intensity conflict with would-be immigrants, their forces are indeed attempting to control a specific class of people that is continually moving their way, probing, in effect, for weaknesses in the country's border defenses. The uppermost thought in the minds of enforcement authorities is likely to be how best to meet today's and tomorrow's "threat," not how to assure that asylum seekers are plucked from the threat stream, especially when seekers have chosen to cross borders at irregular points of entry.

Countries grapple with a wide variety of circumstances in attempting to control access to their borders. Some of those circumstances involve the state of relations with next-door neighbors (friendly, tense, hostile) and some have to do with a departure state's economic status relative to the destination state. Wealthy, stable countries are beacons for both political refugees and economic migrants from near and far; intervening lands are merely places to traverse en route to their ultimate goal. Such long-distance movement can pose problems for those seeking refugee status, however, as some destination countries, especially in Europe, employ the so-called "safe third country" concept, which denies to those who have already passed through a potential safe haven the right to apply for asylum at their preferred destination. Border forces may summarily reject entry attempts in such cases, regardless of whether the traveler's current statelessness is a product of poverty or political upheaval.

The political and economic circumstances behind entry attempts can be framed in a way that allows us to view such attempts and states' management measures in an orderly fashion. On the political side, one might differentiate circumstances of unwanted entry according to the level of persecution or violence associated with population movement, from very low (political issues were not a motive for emigrating) to very high (life-threatening dangers, either targeted at the individual or affecting broad groups, as in the case of civil war). One might expect that more militarized responses to unwanted entry would be associated with a combination of higher levels of hostility in the departure state and higher volumes of entrants. Thus, Turkey deployed forces to block the Iraqi-Turkish border and deny entry to large numbers of Kurds fleeing the Iraqi army in the spring of 1991 and has pursued forces of the Kurdish Workers Party (PKK) into Iraq.

On the economic side, one might define the circumstances of entry in terms of the differences in wealth, or "economic gradient," between the departure and destination countries. One might expect economic migrants to aim at the wealthiest destination that money and means of transport allow. The steeper the gradient, the more attractive the destination.

The cases discussed in this chapter are positioned along these two dimensions in Figure 4.1. While relations between the United States and Haiti, Mexico, and the Dominican Republic are peaceful, each year hundreds to thousands of Haitian and Dominican boat people risk everything to sail to the U.S. mainland or Puerto Rico, and hundreds of thousands of Mexicans try to cross the U.S. southwestern land border, to find work in the United States. Bangladeshi-Indian relations are also peaceful and the economic gradient between the two countries is not that steep, but it suffices to bring large numbers of Bangladeshis into India each year. War and ethnic cleansing in Kosovo produced massive outpourings of refugees into neighboring and equally poor Albania and Macedonia, and follow-on movement into the much wealthier European Union (EU).

More militarized approaches to unwanted entry would be expected for cases depicted in the upper half of Figure 4.1. Some states in the lower half, however, especially India and the United States, have heavily militarized border control practices, reflecting partly the multifaceted nature of their border issues and partly a political reflex in both countries to reach for military tools to solve a multitude of problems.

Trends in Military and Paramilitary Forces

Although regular military forces and their equipment are tracked from year to year by such publications as *The Military Balance* from the London-based International Institute for Strategic Studies (IISS), information on paramilitary and police forces is sketchier. Readily available numbers are provided in Table 4.1. Some organizational examples follow.

In the United States, the Customs Service, Border Patrol, and Coast Guard each has responsibility for elements of immigration control. The Customs Service, a branch of the U.S. Treasury Department, is a police force responsible for import inspections at the country's 301 official ports of entry, and for aerial surveillance of the U.S. coastline. The Coast Guard, a branch of the U.S. Department of Transportation, is responsible for maritime law enforcement. It operates in that capacity at a far remove from U.S. territorial waters and in wartime becomes a fully militarized service, reporting to the Department of Defense. The Border Patrol is a unit of the Immigration and Naturalization Service, a branch of the Department of Justice. It has responsibility for monitoring and halting people and goods that attempt to cross the U.S. border between official ports of entry. While the regular U.S. Army decreased in end strength by 38 percent between 1988 and 1998, the number of agents in the U.S. Border Patrol increased

FIGURE 4.1 Categorizing Circumstances of Unwanted Entry

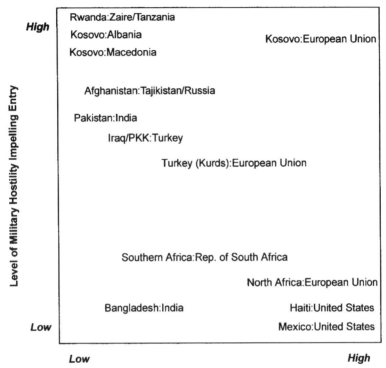

41 percent. The service is slated to grow by another 20–25 percent through 2001. Still, all U.S. border control forces combined are much smaller than the army (perhaps a tenth as large).

In the Russian Federation, the regular military is complemented by the quarter-million troops of the Interior Ministry and the roughly 200,000 troops of the Russian Federal Border Service (FPS) and its maritime wing (which accounts for 23,000 of that total). The FPS operates not only 1,700 armored personnel carriers and infantry combat vehicles, but also fleets of transport aircraft, helicopters, and patrol ships up to frigate-size. It reports directly to the President of the Russian Federation, rather than to the Ministry of Defense (IISS 1998b: 114).

Italy's paramilitary services, 255,700 strong, are nearly as large as its regular active duty armed forces (298,400). Some 113,000 carabinieri report to the Ministry of Defense, while 79,000 public security guards report to the Interior Ministry, and 63,500 members of the Finance Guards report to the Treasury (IISS 1998b: 59). The Finance Guards function as Italy's coast guard.

TABLE 4.1   Border Security Force Trends, Selected Countries

		1988			1998	
		Army	Para-military	Border Police	Army	Para-military	Border Police
North America	**United States**	776,400			479,400		
	Army National Guard		462,100			364,000	
	Coast Guard			36,300			36,000
	Border Patrol			5,530			7,800
	Customs Service			>2,000			>2,000
Europe	**France**	280,900			203,200		
	Gendarmerie (land, air)		83,750			90,300	
	Maritime Gendarmerie			1,150			not listed
	Germany (West, Unified)	332,100			230,600		
	Territorial Army		41,700			not listed	
	Federal Border Guard			20,000			33,800
	Coast Guard			1,000			not listed
	Italy	265,000			165,600		
	Carabinieri		90,000			113,200	
	Public Security Guard		80,372			79,000	
	Finance Guards			49,000			63,500
	Spain	323,000			127,000		
	Guardia Civil		72,700			75,000	
	Policia Nacional		47,000				
	Maritime Surveillance Force			not listed			760
	Turkey	522,900			525,000		
	Gendarmerie		75,000			180,000	
	National Guard		50,000			not listed	
	Coast Guard			1,100			2,200
	USSR/Russian Fed.	1,900,000			420,000		
	Internal Security Troops		340,000			237,000	
	Border Troops			190,000			200,000
	Forces for Protection of Russian Federation					25,000	
	Federal Security Service					9,000	
	Federal Communications & Information Agency					54,000	
Africa	**South Africa**	19,000			58,600		
	South African Police		55,000			129,300	
	Coast Guard			'to form'		part of police	
	SW Africa Territ. Force		22,000			disbanded	

TABLE 4.1 Border Security Force Trends, Selected Countries *(continued)*

		1988			1998		
		Army	Para-military	Border Police	Army	Para-military	Border Police
South Asia	**India**	1,200,000			980,000		
	National Security Guards		3,000			7,400	
	Central Reserve Police Force		90,000			165,300	
	Border Security Force			90,000			185,000
	Assam Rifles		40,000			52,500	
	Rashtriya Rifles		n/a			40,000	
	Ladakh Scouts		5,000			not listed	
	Indo-Tibetan Border Police			14,000			32,200
	Special Frontier Force			8,000		not listed	
	Central Industrial Security Force		55,000			88,600	
	Defence Security Force		30,000			31,000	
	Railway Protection Forces		70,000			70,000	
	Provincial Armed Constabulary or State Armed Police		250,000			400,000	
	Coast Guard			not listed			6,000
	Special Protection Group		not listed			3,000	
	Home Guard		not listed			416,000	
	Civil Defence		not listed			394,000	
	Pakistan	480,600			520,000		
	National Guard		75,000			185,000	
	Frontier Corps			65,000			35,000
	Pakistan Rangers			15,000			25,000
	Northern Light Infantry		7,000			not listed	
	Coast Guard or Maritime Security Agency			2,000			2,000
	Bangladesh	90,000			101,000		
	Bangladesh Rifles			30,000			30,000
	Armed Police		5,000			5,000	
	Ansars (security guards)		20,000			14,500	
	Coast Guard			not listed			200

Sources: Data from IISS, *Military Balance, 1988–89, 1998–99.* German government statistics, "The Federal Border Guard: A National Police Force," Internet: http://www.government.de/english/02/0204/index11.html. Accessed 10 May 1999.

Different countries take different organizational approaches to similar tasks. Germany has a single Federal Border Guard service (Bundesgrenzschutz, or BGS) that also provides protective services for railways, public buildings, and VIPs. India has separate services for each of these functions. While Germany gets by with 33,800 BGS officers, comparable Indian forces tally some 346,000.[4] However, in terms of officers per capita, Germany is actually the more densely policed in these categories, at 42 per 100,000 population versus India's 35. Russia has the highest density of border police per capita (162 per 100,000) but given the sprawl of Russian territory, this may still leave Russian borders relatively thinly manned (between 10 and 20 troops per kilometer of land border).

Where the Cold War was most intense, spending and emphasis generally have shifted from regular militaries to internal and border security forces. Regular armed forces in Europe declined substantially between 1988 and 1998 but paramilitary and border security forces in many cases gained strength. German, Italian, and Indian border control forces in particular grew substantially over the same period. (See Table 4.2 for percentage changes.)

Regular forces have shrunk very little, or even grown in size, in some of the other countries considered here. Turkey, for example, is embroiled in a serious civil conflict in which the regular army plays a direct role.

Techniques and Equipment of Militarized Border Control

Military or paramilitary units contribute heavier armaments to the task of border security than one would expect to find in the average police force. Depending on the fire power available to groups seeking to cross the border—from none at all for the average migrant, to a fair amount for organized criminals, to a considerable amount for guerrilla forces—such military-style armament and mobility may be necessary to meet those threats. Troops patrol landward borders to deter entry, and on occasion stage pre-emptive raids across borders to disrupt the logistics of guerrilla forces, or armed elements in refugee camps (whose arms violate their international refugee status). States anticipating immigrant influxes may establish joint patrols with departure states. They may engage in open-ocean interdiction of migrants and asylum seekers. Depending on the circumstances, and on bilateral agreements between departure and destination states, those picked up at sea may be carried onward to their hoped-for destination for processing, or repatriated directly home.

Militaries may contribute types and/or quantities of technology less readily available to other border protection agencies. Aside from the obvious, like enhanced radio communications, these contributions may include sophisticated command, control, and intelligence networks, radar surveillance, aerial or (in a few cases) satellite surveillance; infrared scopes and low-light night vision goggles and scopes for ground forces; infrared sensors

TABLE 4.2   Trends in Security Forces, Selected Countries, 1988–1998

		Army	Paramilitary	Border Police
North America	**United States**	-0.38		
	Army National Guard		-0.21	
	Coast Guard			-0.01
	Border Patrol			0.41
	Customs Service			n/a
Europe	**France**	-0.28		
	Gendarmerie (land, air)		0.08	
	Germany (West & Unified)	-0.31		
	Federal Border Guard			0.69
	Italy	-0.38		
	Carabinieri		0.26	
	Public Security Guard		-0.02	
	Finance Guards			0.30
	Spain	-0.61		
	Guardia Civil		0.03	
	Turkey	0.00		
	Gendarmerie		1.40	
	USSR/Russian Fed.	-0.78		
	Internal Security Troops		-0.30	
	Border Troops			0.05
Africa	**South Africa**	2.08		
	South African Police		1.35	
South Asia	**India**	-0.18		
	National Security Guards		1.47	
	Central Reserve Police Force		0.84	
	Border Security Force			1.06
	Assam Rifles		0.31	
	Indo-Tibetan Border Police			1.30
	Central Industrial Security Force		0.61	
	Defence Security Force		0.03	
	Railway Protection Forces		0.00	
	Provincial Armed Constabulary		0.60	
	Pakistan	0.08		
	National Guard		1.47	
	Frontier Corps			-0.46
	Pakistan Rangers			0.67
	Coast Guard, Maritime Security			0.00
	Bangladesh	0.12		
	Bangladesh Rifles			0.00
	Armed Police		0.00	
	Ansars (security guards)		-0.28	

Source: Table 4.1, for services with entries in both years.

for aircraft; electronic and acoustic motion sensors to monitor border crossings; and high-endurance, drone aircraft with surveillance cameras.

Techniques employed to make border areas more difficult to traverse include fortifications like border fences, with or without barbed wire or electrification and with or without embedded motion sensors; and buffer zones, either inside one's own country or inside a neighbor's territory. Examples of the latter include the Israeli security zone in south Lebanon and the free-fire zone established by Russian border troops on the Afghan-Tajik border. Pre-emptive or disruptive actions undertaken against threats based in neighboring states (engaging refugee warriors, for example) require military-style firepower, mobility, and logistical support if they are to be sustained. Even the best regular army can find itself bogged down in such engagements however, as Israel found over more than 20 years in southern Lebanon.

Managing Unwanted Entry: Selected Cases

This section looks in greater detail at the involvement of military and paramilitary forces in managing unwanted entry, drawing examples from all parts of Figure 4.1 (high and low levels of violence impelling population movement and high and low economic gradients between departure and destination states). The examples include the United States, Russian Federation, European Union, Turkey, India, South Africa, and Central Africa.

United States

The United States at one time prided itself on being a nation of immigrants, and immigration continued at high rates in the 1990s. In 1996, for example, the United States granted permanent resident status to more than 900,000 legal immigrants. That same year, however, the U.S. Immigration and Naturalization Service (INS) apprehended and expelled 1.6 million illegal immigrants, the vast majority of them from Mexico, while the U.S. Coast Guard interdicted over nine thousand "boat people" (U.S. Dept. of Justice 1997a: 12–13). Since 1996, the Illegal Immigration Reform and Immigrant Responsibility Act (IIRIRA), has allowed INS officials at entry points and the border to formally deport, not merely expel, irregular/undocumented immigrants within hours of apprehension, without judicial intervention, as a deterrent to "recidivism." Once deported, individuals are at risk of criminal prosecution and prison time should they be apprehended trying to enter the United States again within five years (Ojito 1998).

The U.S. military became actively involved in stemming illegal immigration largely as a byproduct of its growing role in the war on drugs. Until 1981, the military rendered only modest support to the INS. However, the fiscal year (FY) 1982 defense authorization law relaxed the 1879 *posse comitatus* statute so that the U.S. military could render active assistance to law enforcement agencies, including the INS and the Drug Enforcement Administration (DEA). The defense authorization for FY 1989 gave the U.S. military further powers to assist law enforcement, including interdiction of vessels on the high seas suspected of carrying contraband headed for U.S. shores, and informational intercepts of aircraft similarly suspect (Dunn 1996: 117–121). It also authorized military pursuit of vessels and aircraft into U.S. waters and airspace. The legislation stopped short of giving defense agencies arrest powers, so U.S. naval vessels on the contraband blockade line in the Caribbean carry Coast Guard Law Enforcement Detachments.

U.S.-Mexico border: The United States always maintained some control over the land border with Mexico, but only relatively recently did parts of it come to be fortified with triple steel fences separated by drag roads of soft dirt that show the footprints of attempted entrants. The first electronic movement detection sensors were installed along parts of the border in the early 1970s, and by the mid-1980s the INS and its Border Patrol had acquired substantial quantities of military-style night vision equipment and observation helicopters.

In 1994, the Border Patrol inaugurated Operation Gatekeeper in its San Diego Sector, traditionally the locale in which 40 percent of illegal entry attempts had been made. Gatekeeper and a counterpart operation called Hold-the-Line in the El Paso sector marked a change in emphasis for the Border Patrol from reactive to deterrent operations, that is, from chasing down individuals and groups who had already crossed into U.S. territory, to preventing their initial entry. Gatekeeper established a three-layer border defense, with the first tier deployed in high-visibility, fixed positions along the border itself. Agents staffing those posts "were instructed to remain in their assigned positions rather than chase alien traffic passing through adjacent sectors." The second tier was deployed further north "in corridors heavily traveled by aliens," and the third tier was assigned to chase down aliens who made it past the first two tiers. Gatekeeper also increased the density of night vision equipment, seismic sensors, electronic fingerprinting systems (Project IDENT), and all-terrain vehicles used by the Border Patrol in the San Diego sector (U.S. Dept. of Justice 1998).

Like the Green Revolution in agriculture, Gatekeeper is a resource-intensive approach. The INS more than doubled the number of agents in the San Diego sector, to about 2,300 in 1997, and doubled the number of seismic sensors deployed there (to 1,200) while extending the fence line 70 kilometers inland (U.S. Dept. of Justice 1997b: Booth 1998: A2). By early 1999, the Border Patrol had installed 185 infrared detectors along the southwest border, a five-fold increase over 1994, and 8,600 seismic sensors, double the number in 1994. Encrypted radio sets, radio frequency scanners, remote video surveillance cameras, and Skywatch mobile night vision watch towers round out the newer technology in use along the border (Dunn 1996: 69, 182–183; Branigin 1999: A21).

If successful, the new approach would decrease overall apprehension rates by deterring would-be immigrants from attempting entry. Based on comparative apprehension statistics from the San Diego, El Paso, and Tucson sectors, the new approach appears to be having some impact: apprehension rates for the first two sectors using the intensive new approach were the same or lower in 1994–1996, while the rates for the Tucson sector roughly tripled over the same period, presumably as entrants sought to circumvent the tougher crossing barriers of the San Diego and El Paso sectors (Legomsky 1997: 1, 3). The Border Patrol has shifted some resources eastward from San Diego in response, but the terrain east of San Diego County is rural, desert-like and/or mountainous, more difficult and risky for migrants to attempt to cross, regardless of man-made obstacles. Overall, apprehension rates along the border may exceed 90 percent since the new policies were inaugurated.[5] On the other hand, civil rights groups charge that 360 migrants have died along the California border between 1994, when Gatekeeper was inaugurated, and early 1999 (Booth 1998: A2; Dillon 1999: A12).

The border technology initiatives have contributed to substantial seizures of illegal drugs. In the easternmost McAllen sector that runs 450 kilometers up the Rio Grande River from Brownsville, Texas, where the technology initiative is called Operation Rio Grande, drug seizures in 1998 and 1999 averaged about 12 tons of marijuana and one to two hundred kilos of cocaine per month (U.S. Dept. of Justice 1999).

U.S. government efforts to stem illegal immigration and its efforts to stem illegal drugs have been merging since the late 1980s, when the Border Patrol was designated the primary agency for drug interdiction between ports of entry, with emphasis on the southwest border, where more than three-quarters of its agents work. INS and Customs Service Inspectors coordinate coverage of the 24 official southwestern ports of entry (U.S. Dept. of the Treasury 1999a). The Border Patrol also cooperates closely with the DEA and the military, via Joint Task Force Six (JTF-6) headquartered at Fort Bliss, near El Paso, Texas. JTF-6's task is to coordinate military support for law enforcement within 80 kilometers of the U.S.-Mexico border (Dunn 1996: 133–138).

In fiscal year 1997, Marine Corps teams "conducted 96 logistical and operational missions with domestic law enforcement agencies along the southwest border" (U.S. Dept of the Navy 1997). After an incident in mid-1997 in which a Marine patrol on the Texas border shot and killed a young Mexican-American herdsman, the Defense Department suspended all armed patrols and would prefer to remain entirely out of the border ground patrol business (NNIRR 1998). An amendment by Representative James Traficant (D-Ohio) to give the military a more direct role in patrolling the Mexican border with up to 10,000 troops made it into the House version of the FY 1998 defense authorization bill, although it was opposed by the Departments of Defense and Justice and the Office of National Drug Control Policy. It subsequently died in conference committee with the Senate.[6]

Boat people and smuggling rings: Although the land border with Mexico is the primary source of illegal entry into the United States, the country's coastlines and the island of Puerto Rico are also informal entry points. The largest numbers of would-be entrants have come from Cuba, Haiti, and the Dominican Republic. Cuban and Haitian sailors tend to head toward Florida; Dominicans for Puerto Rico.

The largest single influx of boat people occurred between April and September 1980. The Cuban economy had just suffered major crop failures in sugar and tobacco, its primary exports, and unrest was rising. Ten thousand Cubans took refuge in the Peruvian embassy in early April 1980, seeking to emigrate. A three-week standoff ended when the Castro regime agreed to let them, and any Cubans with relatives in the United States, leave by private boat, and opened the port of Mariel, west of Havana, to that end (IISS 1981: 25, 135). Rumors of this impending action had attracted small craft of all sorts, piloted largely by Cuban exiles, to Mariel to pick up their countrymen, yet Castro's move caught Washington by surprise. U.S. policy during the Cold War was to welcome as refugees those who escaped communist rule, but the volume of the Mariel exodus was unexpected. Initially, U.S. officials fined boat owners $1,000 for every immigrant brought across the Strait, then reversed course and welcomed them as political refugees (1980 was a presidential election year and the Cuban vote in Florida was influential). Three weeks into the exodus, U.S. policy changed again and the Coast Guard set up a ten-ship picket line to keep additional boats from crossing over to Cuba. A thousand boats were already in Mariel, however, and the Castro regime refused to let them leave empty. By the time the port was closed again, nearly 125,000 people had left the island, with the Cuban government adding many of the occupants of Cuba's jails and asylums to the flux. Had the United States let boat owners make additional trips, another quarter million people might have opted to leave. The Coast Guard assisted nearly 1,400 vessels over the course of the boat lift and intercepted as many as 3,700 immigrants per day (Blechman and Durch 1981: 95; U.S. Coast Guard 1999a).

One year after the Mariel boat lift ended, the Coast Guard was formally directed by the President to assist in the enforcement of U.S. immigration laws (Presidential Proclamation 4865, 29 September 1981). Over the next ten years, the service's Alien Migrant Interdiction Operation (AMIO) intercepted 30,000 migrants at sea, three-fourths of them from Haiti. Under a 1981 agreement with the Haitian government, the United States was permitted to stop vessels originating in Haiti on the high seas and to repatriate any Haitians found on them (U.S. Dept. of State 1997).

Between 1991 and 1995, the number of migrants intercepted at sea leaped to 120,000, mostly reflecting the exodus from Haiti following the 1991 coup against President Jean Bertrand Aristide. Between October 1991 and May 1992, U.S. forces intercepted 34,000 Haitians and held them at U.S. facilities in Guantánamo Bay, at the easternmost tip of Cuba. (In one of the Cold War's stranger arrangements, the United States retained base rights at Guantánamo that dated back to the Spanish American War, analogous to the Russians keeping a toehold in Juneau.) By presidential Executive Order 12807 (24 May 1992), the Coast Guard was directed to transport interdicted Haitians directly back to Haiti, without asylum hearings. This process continued for two years until deteriorating conditions in Haiti prompted the White House to resume off-shore processing of asylum requests, whereupon Haitians again began to take to the boats at a rate of 5,000 a week. In January 1993, the Coast Guard commenced Operation Able Manner, using up to 17 cutters and U.S. Navy assistance to interdict Haitian boats in the Windward Passage between Haiti and Cuba. Guantánamo was pressed into service once again. Of the 21,000 Haitians "granted safe haven" there between July and September 1994, when U.S. forces landed in Haiti to restore the Aristide government, 20,700 were returned to Haiti. About 5,000 Haitian asylum requests were granted through May 1995, but most such requests were processed in Haiti itself (U.S. Coast Guard 1999b; U.S. Dept. of State 1997).

As the Haitian exodus continued, a spate of hijackings of Cuban vessels by would-be emigrants caused the Cuban government to threaten the United States with another mass exodus. In August 1994, Cubans who wished to leave were allowed to do so once again, without government assistance. The U.S. Coast Guard implemented Operation Able Vigil, which replayed some of 1980's script by blocking boats headed toward Cuba to pick up emigrants. Those Cubans who did manage to find a boat or build a raft were picked up by the Coast Guard and shipped to Guantánamo or holding facilities in Panama. In the first week of the new exodus, over 10,000 Cubans were interdicted by U.S. forces, more than in the previous ten years. A total of 30,244 left the island in the five weeks the ports remained open. On 10 September, the United States and Cuba reached a bilateral accord to increase legal immigration from Cuba to the United States and to return illegal emigrants interdicted at sea. Between late 1994 and early 1999, roughly 1,200 illegal emigrants were returned to Cuba, either directly by the Coast Guard or via Guantánamo. Under the U.S.-Cuba agreement, however, those who make it to U.S. shores get to stay, so there is great incentive to develop techniques to evade Customs and Coast Guard patrols (U.S. Coast Guard 1999c).

A final Coast Guard operation intercepted Dominicans headed for Puerto Rico. Between April 1995 and October 1997, 9,500 migrants were "interdicted or forced to turn back." In contrast to the politically motivated Cuban boat lifts, which exile groups viewed as rescues, and in contrast to Haitian émigrés, who paid individual boat builders, owners, and operators for passage to the United States, Dominican emigration involved smuggling gangs (U.S. Coast Guard 1999d; Soros Foundation 1997). Asian illegal migrants to the United States are also brought in by gangs, many Chinese; as of November 1998 there were thought to be as many as 500,000 undocumented Chinese immigrants in the United States, many of whom end up in New York sweatshops to work off the $30,000–$48,000 smuggling fees (*Migration News* 1998). Some are brought directly to the United States, while others make landfall in Central America or Mexico and join the flow of those attempting to cross the U.S. border on land. In the largest people-smuggling operation broken up by the government to date, 31 indictments were returned in November 1998 against a ring that had smuggled 12,000 South Asian and Middle Eastern migrants to the United States over a three-year period, via Russia, Cuba, and elsewhere in Latin America, for a fee that averaged $20,000 per migrant. The International Organization for Migration estimates that, worldwide, some four million persons are smuggled across borders each year, earning seven billion dollars for the smuggling networks (*IOM News* 1998; Rosenbaum 1998).

With illegal immigration associated with old ideological feuds, failing states, criminal gangs, and the same entry routes used by narcotics traffickers, little wonder that migrants tend to be viewed as one element of a larger skein of transnational threats to U.S. interests rather than as individuals or groups of people in need of assistance or entitled to due process, even asylum. Indeed, the U.S. Customs Service views every single individual who crosses U.S. borders as a potential threat. Its World Wide Web site lists land, sea, and air border crossing statistics for all individuals, private vehicles, and common carriers for 1998, that is, for tourists, business people, government officials—everyone—but the data table is entitled "Fiscal Year 1998 Windows of Opportunity for Drug Smuggling" (U.S. Dept. of Treasury 1999b). The Defense Intelligence Agency has a data base designed to support the military missions of Combating Terrorism and Force Protection (provision of security against terrorist threats). Significantly, it calls this the Migration Defense Intelligence Threat Data System (U.S. Dept. of Defense 1998).

Russia/CIS

Under the Soviet system, external borders were indeed supposed to be an iron curtain through which nothing passed unnoticed or unchallenged. When the Soviet Union broke up, the construct of the Commonwealth of Independent States (CIS) was originally designed to maintain common central control of the armed forces of the new states born of the break-up. Plans for joint control by Russia and the new states of former Soviet military forces on these states' territories had fallen apart everywhere but in Turkmenistan by 1995, and one year later, even Turkmenistan had assumed sole control over ex-Soviet ground forces on its territory. All but Azerbaijan agreed, however, to maintain a joint air defense system (IISS 1992: 89–90, 245–246; IISS 1993: 93–94; IISS 1995: 107; IISS 1996: 105; IISS 1997: 101; IISS 1998b: 103).

Control of the external borders of the CIS also remained, in part, a joint effort. In May 1995, Armenia, Belarus, Georgia, Kyrgyzstan, Russia, and Tajikistan signed an accord in Minsk on external border protection. Azerbaijan, Kazakhstan, and Moldova opted not to sign, and Russian border guards in Ukraine reportedly only "monitor" rather than "guard" its borders (O'Prey 1996: 412, 450 n.11). In August 1996, Russia, Armenia, Kyrgyzstan, and Tajikistan signed a further agreement permitting Russia to recruit local citizens to serve in Russian Border Service (BPS) units stationed in their countries, a point to be discussed further below (IISS 1995: 105; 1996: 106).

By mid-1998, Georgia was making efforts to renegotiate its border protection arrangements with Russia and was working with U.S. Coast Guard advisers to develop its own coast guard infrastructure. Under agreements initialed in June, Georgia would first take over its seaward borders and then the border with Turkey. BPS troops withdrawn from Georgia were expected to redeploy to the Special Caucasus Border Guards District north of the mountains, bordering Chechnya, where a three-kilometer buffer zone was to be set up (Kiyampur 1998: 8; UN DHA, 1998). By February 1999, Georgia had decided to pull out of the CIS altogether, as had Uzbekistan. Kyrgyzstan planned to form a border service in 1999 to replace Russian guards who serve along the Kyrgyz-Chinese and Kyrgyz-Tajik border. Whether Russia was equally agreeable to the replacement was less clear (RFE/RL Newsline 1998; Stanley 1999b; DePalma 1999).

The current BPS command structure was created in June 1992, using forces that had previously been part of the Soviet Committee for State Security (KGB). Its forces remained deployed on what had been the external borders of the USSR partly because the new states had no border forces of their own, partly because Russia wanted to keep an active hand in their affairs, and partly because forward defense of Russian Federation territory along familiar terrain was easier and cheaper than pulling back and attempting to seal thousands of kilometers of the new Russian borders in the Central Asian steppes. However, Russia has been taking steps—first announced at a CIS summit in Almaty in October 1996—to build a secondary line of defense against smugglers and illegal immigration within its own borders. Increasingly short of funds (BPS received just about half of its budgeted funds in 1996 and 1997), Moscow will be using largely local part-time volunteers to staff its new checkpoints.[7] These volunteers include, somewhat controversially, "non-army Cossack units" who are paid for each border violator they nab. Cossack-manned checkpoints were established just a few kilometers north of the Russia-Kazakh border, to the dismay of Kazakh leaders.[8]

In the first half of 1998, claimed BPS Director Nikolay Bordyuzha, border guards seized 800 kg of illegal drugs and 700 tonnes of contraband alcohol (the ratio being eloquent commentary on the Russian market) and stopped 1,000 would-be entrants with forged/invalid documents (Plotniknov 1998). Ninety percent of the immigrant traffic that Russia faces involves "forced migrants," Moscow's term for Russians who were living within the USSR but outside the Russian Federation at the breakup, and who are now returning to Russia proper because, for example, local educational authorities are closing Russian-language schools. UNHCR estimates that 3–4 million of 25 million expatriate Russians moved to the Russian Federation between 1990 and 1996. Convention refugees make up a very small portion of the influx: only about 12,000 foreigners apply for refugee status annually to Russia's Federal Migration Service. Status is granted to fewer than 800, and no asylum cases have been processed since 1993. The migration service also estimates that 700,000 illegal immigrants live in Russia. Juxtapose that number against the roughly 2,000 arrests of illegal entrants reportedly made each year and divide by the number of years since the iron curtain collapsed to get an idea of the effectiveness of current Russian border management—about two percent (Blagov 1998; Ivanov and Perea 1998).

The most acute border threat managed by the BPS, with Army backing, is in Tajikistan. That country continues to suffer from the aftereffects of civil war despite a supposed peace accord reached in 1997. What really worries the Russians, however, is Tajikistan's long, mountainous, southern border with Afghanistan and the continuing extension of Taliban control toward that border (Saradzhyan 1998). Russia has kept the 201st Motor Rifle Division in Tajikistan, but largely as a backup to BPS forces with Russian officers but locally recruited (*Military Balance* says "conscripted") troops. Kazakhstan, Kyrgyzstan, and Uzbekistan also contribute company- to battalion-sized units to the border control task. The BPS reportedly has fortified the Tajik-Afghan border with guard points on high ground every 2–3 kilometers, with tactical and operational reserve troops positioned behind the front lines, and with support from up to 300 artillery tubes. Across the border, the Russians have declared a 15–20 kilometer-deep "demilitarized" zone, monitored with the assistance of aerial and orbital reconnaissance and special operations units. BPS chief Andrei Nikolayev has argued, not unself-servingly, of course, that the regular army would not be as adept at such border defense: "[T]his is not a frontal clash of two military forces, it is a far more subtle business. The army would, by the mere fact of its full-scale inclusion in a conflict, be taking it to an entirely different level. This, incidentally, is what happened in Chechnya" (Smirnov 1998).

In sum, Russia has attempted to craft a system of militarized forward border defense where the threat is most acute, backed by an informal, decentralized, non-military system on its borders with the rest of the CIS. The risk is that the latter, intended to combat common smuggling, will become all too self-sustaining by collaborating with the smugglers, the only certain source of income in the region for those who do not own an oil or gas field. Meanwhile, the forward border strategy, designed to keep out mujahideen and drugs, is becoming financially unsustainable. Andrei Kokoshin, Secretary of the Russian Security Council, has stated that the BPS will be transitioning to "mainly non-military forms of service" with a reduced military component (IISS 1998b: 103).

European Union

An agreement signed in 1985 in Schengen, Luxembourg, and a follow-up accord in 1990 established the principle of open internal borders and common external borders for participating states, which also happened to be members of the European Union (EU). The so-called Schengen system came into force for its five original signatories (France, Belgium, Netherlands, Luxembourg, and Germany) in 1995. Spain and Portugal joined the agreements in 1991, Greece in 1992, Austria in 1995 (joining and fully implementing the agreement are separate steps). Britain and Ireland are, to date, the only EU members that have not signed on, arguing that island nations have special border requirements.

The 1997 Treaty of Amsterdam brought Schengen under the wing of the EU. The updated Schengen system provides for a common visa policy, police and judicial cooperation, and computerized data sharing on cross-border crime (for example, involving drugs and illegal immigrants), but it also requires effective controls on the system's external borders (BBC News Online 1997).[9] Italy and Austria had been held back from full participation until 1998 by other members' concerns about the relative porosity of their respective borders.

Austria has only had to face the challenges of modern border control since the end of the Cold War, the demise of the Warsaw Pact, and the breakup of Yugoslavia: its formerly Communist neighbors were efficient minders of the East-West divide. In March 1990, however, Austria faced its first mass population movement in the form of 30,000 Romanian migrants who transited Hungary looking for work. In September, the Interior Ministry, which has responsibility for border and customs police, asked for "temporary" assistance from the army, which has deployed two battalions (roughly 1,500 to 1,900 troops) on the 350-kilometer eastern border with Hungary ever since. The troops serve two-month rotations on the border, with a third battalion kept in reserve. Since Austria's full-time army has only 15,000 troops, these border duties occupy a significant portion of its end strength. Moreover, most of these troops are "national servicemen" (draftees) on seven-month tours of duty, so border patrolling absorbs more than one quarter of their training and duty cycle, with potentially serious impact on the army's combat readiness. Austria has formed a new "border gendarmerie" to take the army's place, but the cost of supporting a full-time border force that is equal in strength to three army battalions will be much greater than the cost of the conscript-based military units. In their first eight years, army border patrols seized 35,000 illegal immigrants, nearly three-quarters of the total number stopped (Fowler 1992; *Vienna Oesterreich Eins* 1998; Austria 1999).

Once a country like Austria becomes an active participant in the Schengen system, its borders become part of the external membrane of the EU, a membrane that has been punctured regularly in the 1990s, especially by migrants and asylum seekers from North Africa, the Balkans,

Afghanistan and other conflict zones of Asia, plus the various Kurdish areas of Turkey and the Middle East. Yugoslavia's wars—first Croatia, then Bosnia, then Kosovo—and Albania's all but complete political and economic collapse, have generated successive waves of refugees and jobless migrants. Nearly 40,000 Moroccans reportedly tried to cross the Strait of Gibraltar in 1998; perhaps 1,000 drowned in the first eight months of the year; about 17,000 were caught and returned by the Spanish Civil Guard, while the rest seem to have made it to Europe. Most paid steep fees to smugglers to take them across. Spain, meanwhile, has built double electric fences around its North African enclaves of Ceuta and Melilla and is reinforcing them with metal barricades, video surveillance, and closely spaced watchtowers (Drago 1998).

The Tunisian town of Sfax, midway down that country's eastern coast, is home to a smuggling operation known as the "Sfax mafia" that ferries emigrants to southern Italy, sometimes dumping its clients on the tiny Italian islands of Pantelleria or Lampedusa in the Strait of Sicily. The 63,500 members of Italy's Finance Guard are responsible for patrolling the country's 7,500 km of coastline, including the islands. Calls for the regular navy to join in the effort to intercept the smugglers have thus far been resisted, although the navy apparently contributes surveillance support in the Adriatic. Coordination with landward enforcement authorities is, however, frequently lacking, so that the probability of escaping apprehension once landfall has been made in Italy is perhaps 70 percent (*Rome RAI* 1998a; *La Repubblica* 1998).

Italy has signed accords with Morocco and Tunisia offering financial and technical assistance—boats, coastal radars—to improve those states' own border/seacoast management in return for their agreement to accept immediate return of their own nationals who are caught trying to enter Italy illegally (Pina 1998). Italy has inked a similar instant deportation accord with Albania, offering $120 million over three years to help rebuild that country's economic infrastructure and keep its people at home (Gilbert 1998; *Rome ANSA* 1998). The amount seems a relatively small down payment on a new Albanian economy. The old one was wrecked in 1997 by the collapse of a government-supported pyramid scheme into which most Albanians, for whatever reason, contributed their life savings. When it went bust, riots broke out and security services dissolved, leaving national armories open to mobs that stole at least one-half million assault rifles and other armaments. As a result, Albania is awash in guns but has little that resembles a functioning economy. As UNHCR's chief in Albania observed, "illegal immigration and exile are, together with money laundering and drug trafficking, the nation's only expanding industry. Exile is a business" (Cianfanelli 1998; Galluzzo 1998).

The smuggling is, moreover, a highly organized business, as a series of first-hand reports in the *San Francisco Chronicle* documented in early 1999, before the Kosovo crisis had fully erupted. Emigrants from all over the world arrive in the Albanian port of Vlore on the Otranto Strait, 70 kilometers from the heel of Italy's boot, seeking entry into the European Union on the final stage of often long journeys that are paid for in advance and coordinated by criminal smuggling organizations across several continents and many borders. Between 800 and 1,000 reach Italian shores nightly; others are lost in Adriatic storms or tossed over the side of the fast boats called "gommones" that smugglers use, to force pursuing Finance Guard vessels to stop and attempt a rescue. The combination of such ruthlessness and rules of engagement that appear to prevent the pursuers from firing the first shot keeps Italian vessels from interdicting the gommones on their way to Italy or apprehending them on the way back. Albania's heavily armed anarchy has impeded efforts to confiscate Vlore's 200 gommones in the face of resistance by the families who collectively own them (Viviano 1999a; 1999b).

The scope of the Kosovo refugee emergency had become so great by spring 1999 that refugee assistance and management became a task taken on by NATO governments, international aid agencies, and relief-oriented international NGOs. Smugglers were nonetheless reported to be active in the refugee camps, offering European destinations of choice for $5,000, roughly five times the previous going rate simply to take Kosovars across the Strait to Italy (*Migration News* 1999e; Viviano 1999b).

The conflict in Kosovo threatened to destabilize ethnically mixed Macedonia, which by late April was seeing 5,000 refugees per day cross its northern border. Most refugees were housed among Macedonia's own ethnic Albanian minority and the rest in UNHCR-supervised camps. By early May 1999, some 200,000 refugees had entered the country (and about twice that number had entered Albania itself). Worried about the potential political impact of the influx on its Albanian minority, the Macedonian government insisted that the late-April/early-May total not be exceeded, and that it would accept new refugees only as others were transferred to third countries. Macedonian troops and riot police were first used to load refugees on buses bound for locations in southern Albania and then to block further border crossings. The latter move, in early May, rapidly produced international pledges of emergency assistance totaling $252 million. By mid-May, the UNHCR's "humanitarian evacuation program" had moved 44,000 Kosovars out of Macedonia and had pledges from 39 countries to accept a total of 135,000 (UNHCR 1999).

It was an early 1998 wave of Kurdish asylum claimants, however, rather than Albanian migrants or refugees from Kosovo, that brought the issue of Italy's porous borders to a head and led the country to tighten its immigration laws. Undocumented immigration per se is not a crime under Italian law, and unwanted entrants previously had been handed deportation orders and given 15 days to leave the country. Most headed north. The law was changed in late March 1998 so that irregular immigrants would be held in special camps "where they are identified and, if found to be without proper papers, sent home." By a continuing quirk of Italian law, however, such people can only be held for 30 days and, in a further Catch 22, if their nationality cannot be demonstrated, they cannot be deported (the same is true for Germany). So asylum seekers and others tend to "lose their documents on arrival" (Sharma 1998; Kumin 1998).[10] The Kurds presented a particular political problem, since Italy tends to treat them as asylum seekers, which nettles the Turks, who are thus painted as persecutors of minorities, and angers the Germans, whose population includes perhaps 500,000 people of Kurdish descent but whose laws treat new Kurdish émigrés as "criminal migrants" (*Economist* 1998a: 42). When Italy permitted entry to Abdullah Ocalan, the founder and leader of Turkey's militant PKK, in November 1998, and then denied a Turkish request for extradition, an international uproar ensued. Ocalan was allowed to leave Italy in January and was tracked by U.S. intelligence to the Greek embassy in Nairobi, Kenya. Induced to leave Greek protection, he was seized by Turkish commandos and brought back to Turkey for trial (Hughes 1998; Stanley 1999a; T. Weiner 1999).

In response, violent demonstrations by expatriate Kurds erupted across Europe, focused on Greek embassies in twenty cities. Some thought the demonstrations far too focused to be spontaneous, indicative of a well-organized PKK network within Western Europe.

Italy's immigration problems are not something that a beefed-up Italian military/naval patrol presence would be able to resolve, although less restrictive rules of engagement in the Adriatic might be a step in the right direction. The problems run deeper, however, than better coordinated or more aggressive interdiction efforts. As Turin's *La Stampa* editorialized,

> How come the illegal landings seem to target Italian shores more frequently than others in the Mediterranean? Spain is much closer to Morocco … Greece has infinitely more islands.… The truth is, no matter what the laws are, it is easier to violate them in Italy than in any other European country. Anyone who has seen tens of thousands of scooters racing against traffic in the streets of Rome;… anyone who has seen entire metropolitan areas transformed into encampments of foreigners, drug dealers, and criminal henchmen … along with the infinite number of other violations tolerated out of unconcern, laziness, or pity from a society that does not defend itself, knows what I am trying to say. The captain of the Turkish ship or the Tunisian boatman knows it, too. (Bianchieri 1998)

In the relatively near future, as other states join the European Union, they will become the Union's new eastern borders. If those borders are not as effectively sealed as Schengen demands, the EU will be slowly transformed by immigration and risk right-wing backlash in the process. If they are indeed well-sealed but the southern borders of the CIS are not, then, as the deputy head of Belarus' Border Troops Committee observed, the result will be to "reduce the role of the CIS member-states to a peculiar migrants' sedimentation tank" (Kahkan 1998).

Turkey

In the 1990s, the Turkish military has been used for a very specific border
control purpose related to the country's fight against the insurrection of
the PKK. Much of Turkey's substantial Kurdish minority lives in the
southeastern portion of the country, where a bi-directionally brutal insurgency has been underway since 1984. That part of the country borders
Iraq, Iran, and Syria. After the end of the Gulf War and the abortive Iraqi
Kurd uprisings against Saddam Hussein in April 1991, much of northern
Iraq's Kurdish population fled toward the Turkish border to escape
onrushing Iraqi military forces. Turkey ordered its military to seal the
border rather than accept upwards of two million Iraqi Kurds as refugees
(who certainly were subject to persecution upon return to Iraq). U.S. military and humanitarian intervention saved Turkey from having to explain
the deaths of so many asylum seekers within reach of assistance, but
much of northern Iraq has been without a government ever since. In this
power vacuum, two Iraqi Kurdish factions have fought for dominance
and the PKK has set up base camps.

Several times since 1992, the Turkish Army has moved in force into
northern Iraq to destroy those camps and has attempted to create a border
buffer zone along the lines of the one maintained by Israel in southern
Lebanon for nearly 20 years. The 1992 incursion ended when Turkey had
obtained the agreement of the two main Iraqi Kurdish factions to prevent
the PKK from establishing new bases in Iraq, in exchange for economic
aid. When the factions fell into internecine fighting in early 1995, Turkey
intervened again. On 20 March 1995, 35,000 Turkish troops and tanks
rolled 40 km into northern Iraq on a search and destroy mission. They
withdrew completely within two months. In September 1996, Iraqi
armored forces rolled into the U.S.-patrolled northern zone to support one
Iraqi Kurdish faction. Turkey declared a Temporary Danger Zone near the
two countries' common border and Turkish forces moved as much as 15
km into Iraq to "deny ... use of the zone for infiltration of PKK terrorists
into Turkey" (Kohen 1995; Rohde 1995; Gellman 1996; Turkey 1996).

After May 1997, the Turkish military established a more or less permanent presence on the Iraqi side of the frontier. In February 1998, that
presence was augmented by deployment of 7,000 additional troops as a
precautionary measure. The United States was threatening to bomb Iraq
unless it permitted UN weapons inspections to continue unimpeded, and
Ankara wanted to stop any Kurdish exodus indirectly produced by the
bombing well before it reached the mountain passes between the two
countries. In late 1998, 25,000 Turkish troops pushed 30 km into northern
Iraq, looking for guerrillas who had fled Syria following Turkish pressure
on Damascus to expel the PKK and Abdullah Ocalan (Kinzer 1998; AP
1998; *Economist* 1998b: 46–47).

Although pursuit of the PKK and prevention of mass Kurdish immigration into Turkey are key goals of Turkish border policy, other issues

are at work as well. Turkey hosts U.S./NATO air forces that patrol northern Iraq and supports the United Nations economic embargo on Iraq, but
that support has cost Turkey a great deal in lost trade, and further
depressed the economy in the Kurdish-dominated southeastern part of
the country. By the mid-1990s, therefore, the government was looking the
other way regarding certain kinds of cross-border smuggling. Turkish
truckers were reported to be swapping flour for diesel fuel in Mosul, Iraq,
at a rate of 1.5 tons to 2,250 gallons, bringing up to 40 million gallons of
diesel a day back across the border, where the diesel could be sold for a
factor-of-ten profit. The proceeds reportedly sustained the extended families of the 60,000 largely Kurdish truckers. Iraq gained food supplies and
hard currency in the exchange, the Iraqi Kurdish faction that controlled
the border areas (the Kurdish Democratic Party) earned a substantial
income from "transit duties" imposed on the contraband, and the extra
cash perhaps brought a measure of stability to the southeast—win-win all
around, except perhaps for international law (Pomfret 1995).

India

The modern Republic of India dates from the end of the British Raj in
South Asia and the Partition of 1947, which created the independent
states of Burma, India, and Pakistan, the latter's eastern and western
halves separated by 1,500 kilometers of Indian territory. In 1971, after a
year of civil disturbances and Pakistani army repression that generated
10 million refugees and Indian military intervention, the eastern part of
Pakistan split off to become the present-day state of Bangladesh.

India's border issues are entangled with the legacy of the original
Partition, the 1971 repartition of Pakistan, and a half-century of stalemate
over the status of Jammu and Kashmir, the northernmost juncture of
India and Pakistan. Pakistan was founded as a homeland for Muslims
and, in 1947–1948, millions of Hindus and Muslims who found themselves in the wrong "homeland" either crossed voluntarily from one state
to the other or were pushed out by communal rioting. As many as one
million people died in the process of population resettlement.

Britain's Indian Independence Act of 1947 also liberated nearly 600
mostly minor princely states within the subcontinent. Most of these prin-
cipalities opted to join either India or Pakistan, but three did not. Indian
forces invaded and annexed two, Hyderabad and Junagadh, which were
Muslim-ruled but had Hindu majorities. The third state, Kashmir, had a
Muslim majority but a Hindu maharaja who, shortly after independence,
faced a mutiny by his mostly Muslim troops and an invasion from Pakistan of several thousand well-armed Pathan tribesmen roundly considered to be proxies for Pakistan. The maharaja sought military help from
India, which agreed to help provided Kashmir joined India first. The
maharaja signed an Instrument of Accession in late 1947. Fighting
between Indian and Pakistan-supported forces lasted until a UN-brokered

cease-fire took effect in January 1949 along what was then called the "line of control" and is now known as the "line of actual control" or LAC. India regards the areas north and west of the LAC as "Pakistan-Occupied Kashmir" (POK), while Pakistan views areas east and south of the line as "India-Held Kashmir" (IHK). Brief wars in 1965 and 1971 jostled the line but the basic political-military stalemate continues.

Today, India's Muslim population alone is greater than the total population of Pakistan and this, together with the existence of mostly Muslim Bangladesh, vitiates part of Pakistan's founding rationale, the so-called "two nation" theory that Hindus and Muslims required separate states (Burns 1997). The corollary of that theory was that a multinational state such as India, with a dozen major ethno/linguistic groups and a "national" language that is the primary tongue of just 30 percent of its people, could not be held together. Indian analysts contend that Pakistan has over the years tried to help that theory along by supporting subnational separatist causes within India, not only in Kashmir but in the adjacent Indian state of Punjab. Indian analysts argue that Pakistani provision of arms and sanctuary encouraged the terrorist campaigns begun in the 1980s by Sikh militants in Punjab on behalf of independence for "Khalistan," as well as the 1989 upwelling of secessionist terrorism in Kashmir (Marwah 1995: chaps. 2–3).

Pakistan and India both tested nuclear weapons in May 1998, ending international speculation about their respective capabilities that dates to the mid-1970s in the case of India and to the late 1980s in the case of Pakistan. The risk of nuclear escalation is thought to make national leaders cautious about the use of conventional military force against a nuclear-armed neighbor. With Indian conventional superiority presumed to be neutralized, argues Indian author Shekhar Gupta, Pakistan could support terrorist action in Kashmir with relative impunity (Gupta 1995: 21).

India also faces unrest among the many ethnic groups in its northeastern states, which are all but separated from the bulk of India's territory by a 150-kilometer-wide spur of Bangladesh. Some of that unrest, especially in Assam, the largest of these states, focuses on illegal immigrants and especially the influx of Bangladeshis, who cross 2,000 kilometers of joint border, only 200 km of which is fenced. Another 150 km of low-voltage electrified fencing was under consideration in mid-1998. (Marwah 1995: 301; Namboodiri, Chakravarti, and Sen 1998; *Asiaweek* 1998).[11]

While the number of Bangladeshis illegally resident in India is uncertain, some sources estimate that up to one quarter of the 10 million who fled into India to escape Pakistani army action in 1971 remained in India when the emergency ended, and that as many as 300,000 new infiltrators (a term applied to all illegal entrants, including terrorists) enter the country each year. Estimates of the total number now resident in India range from 10 to 20 million. Although Bangladesh refuses to accept deportees, some states like Maharashtra in southwestern India, ruled by the Hindu nationalist Bharatiya Janata Party (BJP), and city administrations in

Bombay and New Delhi, have at different points in the 1990s adopted policies of "pushing out" suspected Bangladeshis, shipping them eastward and handing them over to Indian border security, who simply dump the pushees across the border. Unwanted in Bangladesh, many return (Namboodiri, Chakravarti, and Sen 1998; Padmanabhan 1998; K. Chaudhuri 1998; Kakodkar 1998; Nair 1997).[12]

India, in short, faces several different border security problems. In the east, they take the form of economic migrants and smuggling, while in the northeast they are a combination of illegal immigration, the violent responses to it, and a long, unsettled mountain border with China. The two countries agreed in principle in late 1996 on troop withdrawals, and pledged not to resolve their dispute by force, but details remained to be worked out (Burns 1996). In the northwest, the tense, decades-old standoff with Pakistan has created a highly militarized frontier (what Indian analysts call a "live border") where the chief concern is infiltration of terrorists and the contraband that supports them. In the frozen northern reaches of Kashmir, Indian and Pakistani troops face one another high on the Siachen Glacier, near unsettled borders with China (Noorani 1994: 5–13). Along the LAC in Kashmir, Indian and Pakistani border security forces have shelled one another for years and have even targeted civilians near the line, leaving dozens dead and farmland along the LAC fallow. A cease-fire agreement between India's Border Security Force (BSF) and its counterpart Pakistan Rangers in February 1999 allowed farms to be reopened along 210 kilometers of the line. Kashmir as a whole remained unsettled and violent, however (Ramachandran 1998; *Lokma Times* 1999).

Over the years, the Indian government has established a number of security forces to police its borders and/or deal with its internal security problems. In almost all cases, forces raised and trained for one purpose have been used for another, as circumstances demanded. Forces raised for service in one region have been deployed to others. Duplication of effort and charges of "empire building" have led a number of former high-level military and police officials to call for substantial consolidation.

Some of India's forces and their functions date back to the pre-independence era, when the Indian Army used about 40 percent of its strength for internal security purposes. The Assam Rifles, established in 1945 to maintain order in the largely inaccessible northeastern part of the country, was at first locally recruited and assigned to the state government. By the 1990s, it was recruited nationally, reported to the Ministry for Home Affairs, and was led by an army lieutenant general (Marwah 1993: 16; Apte 1994: 53–54). The locally recruited Indo-Tibetan Border Police (ITBP) was set up in October 1962, during or shortly after India's disastrous border war with China. During the crisis in Punjab in the mid-1980s, several ITBP battalions were raised and assigned to bank security duty there, 300 km from the Tibetan border (Marwah 1993: 16).

The BSF, founded after the Indo-Pakistan war of 1965, is a paramilitary organization that was raised to guard the border with Pakistan and (after 1971) Bangladesh. When the Punjab crisis erupted in the 1980s, however, the BSF was assigned internal security duties there. When terrorist violence broke out in Jammu and Kashmir in 1989, one third of the BSF were deployed there to conduct counter-insurgency operations, for which they had not been trained. In its first three years fighting the insurgency, the BSF was accused of numerous human rights violations, and as late as 1997 accused of torture and extra-judicial killings. BSF leaders say that more than 200 officers and men have been indicted, dismissed, or imprisoned for such violations, and emphasize that a constant, high level of stress takes its toll on men who serve largely uninterrupted two-year assignments in Kashmir at relatively low pay (Intelligence Resource Program 1998; Bedi 1995).

The regular army's mishandling of the crisis in Punjab in 1984, and especially the siege of the Golden Temple in Amritsar (which is to Sikhs roughly what the Vatican is to Roman Catholics) helped stimulate the establishment of the National Security Guards, a force of seconded military and police personnel specially trained to handle terrorist standoffs (Apte 1994: 59; Marwah 1993: 17). India also has a small coast guard whose duties include anti-smuggling patrols and protection of the country's 200-mile maritime economic zone (Chaudhury 1993).

Other Indian paramilitary forces managed by elements of the central government include the Rashtriya Rifles (the Army's internal security force) and the Central Reserve Police Force (CRPF), designed to assist state police forces in maintaining law and order. Several large guard forces protect government infrastructure: the Defence Security Force (for military installations), the Central Industrial Security Force (for other public buildings), and the Railway Protection Force (see Table 4.1 for statistics).

As noted earlier, a number of analysts argue that duplication in duties and haphazard use of many of these border and internal security forces suggest the need for wholesale consolidation. Some suggest that all forces primarily oriented toward border security be merged under the auspices of the regular army, and that all internal security forces be merged into the CRPF. Others offer a more selective approach: keep the BSF, because dealing with smugglers and immigration is a specialized law enforcement function quite different from combat and deterrence of military aggression; merge the ITBP into the BSF as a regional/specialized unit; and relieve the whole institution from internal security duties. Make the National Security Guards a specialized anti-terrorist unit of the CRPF and reduce regular army involvement in internal security matters to a minimum, implying disbandment of forces such as the Rashtriya Rifles (Apte 1994: 54–56; Marwah 1998: 76–77).

South Africa

Like the Soviet Union, the Republic of South Africa is a country that died and was reborn; unlike the USSR, it was reborn with intact territorial boundaries. Previously built up to protect apartheid from its enemies, South Africa's borders now serve to help keep out the thousands of economic migrants from worse-off countries in the region who think that South Africa, like the EU or the United States, offers them a new start or at least a source of remittances to send back home. Border controls do not do the job all that well, however, as estimates of the number of illegal immigrants in the country range from four to five million. The end of apartheid has increased the influx of illegals. With unemployment running at 33–45 percent and an economy that is not growing, South African officials and public alike feel that they cannot afford to be the rest of southern Africa's employer of last resort. Articles on the new South Africa stress a circle-the-wagons mentality, a new xenophobia that an old-style Afrikaaner might have understood well (Christie 1997; Blanchfield 1997). The mix of people within the kraal is just more diverse.

South Africa is not a signatory to the 1951 UN Convention on the status of refugees, nor to the OAU Convention of 1969 on the subject. In 1993, it did sign an agreement with UNHCR that set up a process for recognizing asylum requests.

The long civil war in Mozambique, which the old South Africa sustained after its Rhodesian instigators had fallen from power, produced a relatively large number of Mozambican refugees in South Africa (some 300,000). Once the war in Mozambique ended (elections were held in 1994, six months after South Africa's own national elections), Pretoria proceeded with forced repatriation of about 5,000–6,000 people per month. Most of the border with Mozambique is taken up by the Kruger National Park game preserve, about 50 km deep on average, where "an unknown number of the thousands of Mozambicans trying to cross are eaten by lions," which must then be destroyed. South of the park runs a 2-meter high, 62-km-long electrified fence built in 1986. The fence, which is now set to stun, can be run up to a lethal 3,300 volts and is reported to have killed at least 78 people in its first four years of operation under the old regime. Some would like to see it restored to full power and a similar fence built along the 108 km border with Zimbabwe, which suffers a reported 40 percent unemployment rate. Responsibility for monitoring incursions along the current fence line falls to Army Group 33, which in 1997 stopped 22,000 illegal entrants. The recidivism rate is quite high, however. The army holds migrants only overnight, then sends them back over the border where they try again (*Migration World* 1996; Daley 1998).

In its annual report on the "Landward Defence Programme" for 1997, the South African Department of Defence lists border protection as a main task of the new South African National Defence Force (SANDF), in cooperation with the South African Police Service (SAPS). The army has primary responsibility for managing the influx of illegal immigrants, deploying 26 light infantry companies for this task and the related one of combating cross-border crime. Considering the magnitude of South Africa's crime problem (and, apparently, its illegal immigration problem), the statistics listed in the report seem meager: 15 assault rifles seized, plus 56 other weapons, and 224 suspects. (In addition, 1,013 head of stolen cattle were recovered, along with 2,884 head of "small stock.") Much greater effort seems to have been expended on maintenance of internal law and order in cooperation with SAPS, with a reported four thousand road-blocks; 43 thousand foot patrols; 16 thousand observation posts; and 3,414 "ambushes" (South African Department of Defence 1998). Internal security clearly seems a higher priority for the military than does border security, and rightly so since, for a substantial plurality of its citizens, South Africa has not yet been able to fulfill the promise of freedom and opportunity held out by the end of apartheid, and that has led to escalating crime and violence.

In May 1997, a long-awaited report on South Africa's migration policies, the "Green Paper," was submitted to the Ministry of Home Affairs. The Green Paper called for, among other things, greater military intelligence support to customs and immigration officials, "to identify strategic entry points and to concentrate in successfully counteracting these" (James et al. 1997: para. 3.4.3). Military surveillance of cross-border routes, it argued, could identify typical patterns of activity and promote better responses. The report noted that, while SANDF estimated one (illegal) border crossing every 10 minutes, or 50,000 a year, this figure included many repeat attempts, implying that the total number of individuals involved could be many fewer than 50,000 (James, et al. 1997: para. 3.4.4). Other estimates of illegal immigration are higher (see below).

Except for its training for peacekeeping operations, and assuming that it stays out of the fighting in the Democratic Republic of Congo, the primary functions of the South African army are currently law and order-related, focused on the border and on internal matters. In effect, the army provides the military muscle that the police services used to have under the apartheid regime, when they were paramilitary units.

These functions would change if the government were to accept the recommendations of its Task Team on International Migration, which submitted its White Paper on International Migration in late March 1999. The team acknowledged the recommendations of the 1997 Green Paper and its classification of the causes of illegal immigration into "push" factors (such as economic hardship in the rest of Africa), "pull" factors (especially South Africa's image as a new land of opportunity), and the effectiveness of border controls. The White Paper argued that South Africa could have little impact on push factors in other countries, and that a visit to the southwestern border of the United States convinced the team that, if the United States could not stop illegal immigration with the billions of dollars in people and equipment that it devoted to control of the U.S.-Mexico border, South Africa had even less chance of doing so "in the short to medium term." Nor could enforced deportations solve the problem of illegal aliens already in the country: although the government managed to deport 160,000 persons a year, it would take 25–30 years at that rate to repatriate all illegal aliens, assuming perfectly sealed borders and no natural population increase. Instead of relying on deportation or border controls, the White Paper concluded, South African policy would have to emphasize the pull factors, addressing, in particular, "the perception, or the reality, that vast job opportunities are made available to foreigners at worse workplace conditions than those at which such jobs are available for South African nationals." South African immigration policy, it argued, should rely primarily on rigorous enforcement of internal labor laws designed to remove the incentives for illegal immigration and to promote the voluntary repatriation of migrants already in the country (Mokoena 1999: sect. 4).

The White Paper recommended that a new Immigration Service (IS) be established under the Director General of Home Affairs, to "enforce the immigration laws within each community" in cooperation with the police, and to check (as the INS does in the United States) employer compliance with employment laws. The IS should include a "professional security service" that is neither police nor regular military to assume border control duties from the SANDF. Personnel and equipment for that service might be transferred from the military, "provided both are reconditioned to fit the substantially differing requirements." The IS would also have responsibility for customs functions at the border. The White Paper's recommendations would involve, in short, a substantial transfer of responsibility and budget from the Department of Defence to the Department of Home Affairs, as part of a strategy that emphasized the rule of law and market incentives over barriers and foot chases. The White Paper emphasizes economic issues and economic migrants, however, and makes only cursory reference to arms and narcotics trafficking, both serious problems for South Africa (Mokoena et al. 1999: sect. 5; Batchelor 1997:108–109; *Mail and Guardian* 1998).

Central Africa: Great Lakes Region

A principal example of pre-emptive border defense comes from the Great Lakes region of central Africa. As is well known, in late 1993, Burundi erupted into one of the periodic spasms of intergroup violence that have marred its and neighboring Rwanda's entire history of independence. Six months later, Rwanda suffered an even greater spasm, orchestrated by the then-ruling party, its army (the Force Armée de Rwanda, FAR) and its militia henchmen, known collectively as the Interhamwe ("those who fight together"). The perpetrators of the 1994 genocide in Rwanda were members of the majority Hutu group (although historical patterns of intermarriage were such that group belonging was as much socially constructed as genetic or cultural in nature). Civil war between Hutu government and Tutsi rebel forces based in Uganda (1990–1993) had been brought to a halt, it was thought, by the August 1993 Arusha Peace Accords. When the killings broke out, rebel forces (the Rwanda Patriotic

Front, RPF), swept south and routed government troops, triggering a mass exodus of Hutu people along with governing party personnel, virtually the entire FAR, and the Interhamwe. Most headed west into Zaire, where their subsequent travails (short on food, short on water, long on cholera) attracted the attention of Western media, relief providers, and the U.S. military, all of which descended upon the camps and initiated public health and feeding programs—for the *genocidaires*, their friends, their relatives, and their sympathizers (Vaccaro 1996: 369–373, 391–392). Other camps on a somewhat smaller scale were established in Tanzania.

Howard Adelman of York University has tracked subsequent events through late 1996, documenting how the FAR went about re-establishing itself as a fighting force based in the camps, how it financed and rearmed itself, and how it set about planning to finish the job it had started in Rwanda in spring 1994. The FAR had at its disposal between 18,000 and 48,000 troops, plus an equivalent number of Interhamwe. The failing government of Mobutu Sese Seko did not live up to its obligations to prevent hostile cross-border actions against Rwanda on the part of these refugee-warriors. Indeed, the Interhamwe paid government soldiers to attack Zairean Tutsi, the so-called Banyamulenge (not a tribal referent but a place referent: "people from Mulenge"), from late 1995 onward. In May 1996, Mobutu made the harassment policy official, and thereafter sought to force the Banyamulenge out of North and South Kivu provinces, which border Uganda, Rwanda, and Burundi. Although long resident in Zaire, the Banyamulenge were regarded as outsiders by other Zairean tribal groups and as fair game for ethnic cleansing. They turned to the RPF, now the recognized government of Rwanda, and to its Rwandan Peoples Army (RPA) for support. As Adelman notes, when the Zairean provincial government in South Kivu finally issued an expulsion order in October 1996, the Banyamulenge were trained and ready to counterattack. In December 1996, the Banyamulenge and the RPA overran the camps used as bases of operations by the ex-FAR and the Interhamwe, and pursued them further into Zaire. The bulk of the refugees (some 640,000) went back to Rwanda.[13]

The government of Tanzania, at the time host to 750,000 refugees, two-thirds of them Rwandan, chose this moment to demand that the Rwandans return home, giving them less than 30 days notice and a deadline of December 31. Under pressure from ex-FAR/Interhamwe elements in some of the camps, some 300,000 refugees instead headed deeper into Tanzania, reportedly bound for Kenya or Malawi (a 600–900 km trek). Turned around by Tanzanian troops and police, who also blocked re-entry to the camps, the refugees walked to Rwanda. Tanzanian troops used tear gas and rifles fired into the air to control the crowds and herd them toward their destinations. On the Rwandan side of the border, UNHCR lined up fleets of trucks to take returnees to their home prefectures. Criticized by human rights groups, Tanzania's Foreign Minister, Jakaya Kikwete, replied, "We won't listen, we won't apologize to anyone. Let them talk until they get tired and keep quiet" (UN DHA/IRIN 1996f). By Christmas day 1996, UNHCR estimated that 415,000 of an estimated 535,000 Rwandan refugees in Tanzania had returned (UN DHA/IRIN 1996a–g).

Shortly after the mass exodus was finished, the same Tanzanian forces involved in pressing the repatriation began rounding up Rwandan residents of Western Tanzania, many who had been resident since much earlier times of trouble in Rwanda. By December 30, 1997, some 28,000 people of Rwandan origin had been rounded up by troops and police for deportation (USAID 1997).

The ease with which the intervenors pushed aside Zairean government forces and the welcome they received from local peoples tired of Mobutu's long, corrupt, inattentive rule, led the Rwandans to believe that they might be able to take care of their troubles at the source, and actually bring about a change of government in Zaire. The RPA made common cause with Laurent Kabila, a Katangese with a desultory career of opposition to Mobutu who became the figurehead leader of the forces that swept down the Congo River and into Kinshasa in May 1997. Kabila was soon installed as president of a newly renamed Democratic Republic of Congo (DRC) (IISS 1998a: 209–210).

The RPA's campaign to rid itself of the ex-FAR/Interhamwe border threat by pursuing them into Zaire and even forcing a change in Zaire's ruling regime was only partially successful. Its enemies regrouped. An estimated 15,000 ex-FAR/Interhamwe resumed attacks into northwestern Rwanda from North Kivu, recruiting new members "from refugee camps in Tanzania, Uganda, Congo-Brazzaville, and Central African Republic." Moreover, since late 1996, a group calling itself the Allied Democratic Forces (ADF) has been waging a terrorist campaign in southwestern Uganda from bases in North Kivu.[14]

With armed forces that were Rwandan-led and roughly half Banyamulenge in composition, Kabila grew increasingly restive with charges that his government was really a proxy for foreigners. In July 1998, Kabila ordered all Rwandan and Ugandan troops out of the country. Within a week, the second "rebellion" in as many years was underway again, starting as had the first one in the eastern provinces. The RPA and Banyamulenge banded together again, with assistance from the Ugandan Army and substantial numbers of Congolese Army forces (especially the 20th Brigade, based in Goma), and former members of Mobutu's military elite. In September, official Congolese radio stations began to broadcast exhortations to kill Tutsi that were reminiscent of broadcasts in Rwanda at the time of the genocide (Duke 1998).

Without the Rwandans and the Banyamulenge, Kabila's military capabilities rapidly collapsed. Kabila first turned to contract troops (mercenaries) like the South African-based Executive Outcomes, but he also invited neighboring states to send troops. Within weeks of the outbreak of the new rebellion, Zimbabwe, Angola, and Namibia had dispatched troop contingents into the DRC. By early 1999, Zimbabwe had 6,000–8,000

142142 | William J. Durch

troops in the DRC, Angola 2,500 (reduced from 6,000 by the resumption of large-scale fighting in Angola itself), Namibia 2,000, Chad 1,000, and Sudan perhaps 1,000. Kabila also made common cause with remaining ex-FAR/Interhamwe. Roughly one-third of the DRC was reported to be under rebel control by late December 1998 and perhaps half by March 1999, but rebel forces had begun to splinter and neither "side" was operating under unified military or political command (IISS 1999: 235–237, 282–283; Brittain 1999). The Kabila government refused to negotiate face to face with the rebels, and the rebels refused all peace deals in which they were not direct participants.

What began—twice—as an effort by Rwanda and Uganda to secure their own borders against armed insurgents had bloomed into regional conflict by mid-1998. By early 1999, the war had not only subtended the DRC into several equally ungoverned and ungovernable parts, but threatened to make Central Africa "a wasteland of wandering, starving people excluded from tiny pockets of economic activity conducted by foreign mining companies and guarded by heavily armed private security outfits" (Barrell 1999; Fisher and Norimitsu 1999). South African proposals for a multinational peacekeeping force seemed to pale before the enormous size of the DRC, the complexity of the interests involved, the recrudescence of neighboring Angola's own decades-long civil war, and the multiplication of heavily armed irregular armies, some of whom, like the Interhamwe, were supporting themselves by running drugs (UN Security Council 1998: 6, 16).

Efforts to Prevent Unwanted Entry: Estimates of Effectiveness

As South Africa's White Paper observed, states can take basically three approaches to reducing unwanted entry: reduce the push factors in countries of departure; reduce the pull factors that make one's own country an attractive destination for undocumented aliens; or raise and maintain barriers that are impervious to penetration. The push and pull factors may be either political or economic in nature, that is, people may seek safety from conflict and persecution or they may seek a solution to poverty and unemployment. Strategies to reduce political push factors include diplomacy, conflict resolution, peacekeeping, and military intervention, for example NATO's 1999 campaign against Yugoslavia. Strategies to reduce economic push factors include bilateral or multilateral development assistance, private investment, and population planning. None of these is cheap, easy, or short term in nature.

Strategies to reduce economic pull factors may make the destination country less attractive to illegal immigrants by enforcing internal labor laws that reduce the likelihood of employment, but also by setting those laws so that immigrant labor can be legitimately recruited and used when the domestic supply is inadequate. Tracing the economic impacts and nuances of such policies goes well beyond the scope of this paper, but the linkages between economy and security issues, domestic and international, are unavoidable and probably will grow in the decades to come.

Political pull factors are both more difficult to alter and at times irrelevant. A destination state is what it is in terms of political development, and such a state can alter its political attractiveness to asylum seekers only by offering them less safety or comfort than do other similarly attractive destinations, implying a race to the bottom in political protection, rights and relief, an approach that rests on shaky moral grounds. On the other hand, those in mass flight from conflict cannot afford to be too selective about potential shelter and may crash imperfectly sealed borders despite disincentives, or for marginal improvements in security, resulting in ad hoc responses at the destination that focus on containment or segregation, for example, the circumscribed world of the refugee camp and its international supply lines. The new border to be guarded becomes that of the camp perimeter, the new task is repatriation when conditions are ripe, including forced repatriation when patience runs thin or domestic politics dictate, international law notwithstanding.

Border controls are the default short-term option but are difficult to apply in cases of mass exodus unless the destination state is willing to pay the moral and political price of people and bodies stacked up at the fence. In 1991, Turkey had the capability to seal its mountainous border with Iraq but U.S. action kept the worst from happening by providing both security and sustenance. In 1994, Zaire had no capability to stop the hundreds of thousands of people who poured out of Rwanda in the wake of the RPF's sweep into power, and had neither the capability nor interest to stop subsequent raids on Rwanda staged from the camps. The ultimate breakup of those camps by the forces of what turned into Zaire's first rebellion scattered the immediate threat to Rwandan security but did not end it, leading to the further outbreak of multi-national fighting that continued into 1999.

The efficacy of border controls varies widely, even under more normal circumstances. Summary assessments of the effectiveness of controls in the cases analyzed earlier are presented in Table 4.3, using the level of violence/economic gradient categorization scheme presented in Figure 4.1. ("High violence" cases are listed in order of population volume/flow.) Nowhere, except perhaps in U.S. dealings with Mexican migrants, does the day-to-day percentage effectiveness of border controls seem very high. In the Mexican case, a high percentage of migrants may opt to storm the battlements of the southwestern border, whereas other nationalities use official ports of entry and opt for an overstayed visa. Europe's southern tier, the EU's first line of defense against illegal immigration, seems rather porous, if sketchy reporting on Spanish and Italian border police effectiveness is even reasonably accurate. Other countries and regions, like Russia, may do rather worse in controlling their borders. If such controls are infeasible or, as South Africa concluded after inspecting the U.S. southwestern

TABLE 4.3   Varying Efficacy of Border Controls

	Low Economic Gradient	High Economic Gradient
High Violence		
Rwanda: Zaire/Tanzania	no Zairean controls; two years of refugee warrior action, Rwandan counter-attack with trained Zairean allies. Simultaneous Tanzanian action to empty refugee camps on its territory.	
Kosovo: Albania/Macedonia	sporadic Macedonian closures as leverage for international aid; accepted 200,000 refugees	
Kosovo: European Union		limited humanitarian transfers accepted (135,000); deterrent strategy through NATO failed
Iraqi Kurds: Turkey	1991: seal border against Kurdish exodus. 1994: selective customs and sanctions enforcement to relieve economic strain in southeast	
PKK: Turkey	1992–present pre-emptive sanctuary raids; cross-border presence in Iraq	
Afghan: Tajikistan/Russia	fortified borders and demilitarized zone may keep out raiders but do not seem to work for drugs	
Pakistan: India	most crossings politically motivated; no physical barriers in Kashmir	
Low Violence		
Bangladesh: India	weak controls; few physical barriers; dumping of unwanteds; high recidivism	
Southern Africa: Rep. of So. Africa	semi-effective controls (electric fencing, lions) on part of border; high levels of recidivism; can't afford US-style barrier strategy	
NIS: Russia	porous borders; freelance border management (Cossacks); perhaps 2% effective	
Mexico: United States		estimated 91% against Mexican migrants; 30-40% against others; alien/drug smuggling conflated
No.Africa: European Union		30% effectiveness in Southern Italy; 45% effectiveness in Spain (both maritime borders)

border strategy, simply too costly, then altering pull factors, at least for economic migrants, may be the most effective strategy in the medium term. It requires well-organized and comprehensive enforcement efforts but remains something that states can effect internally.

Over the longer term, however, push factors cannot be ignored. On the economic side, expanding populations, lagging investment and education, marginal infrastructure, and corrupt governance may well bring ever more economic migrants to the gates and fences of the developed world. On the political side, arbitrary, autocratic governance, ethnic and religious violence, and gross abuses of human rights will continue to generate asylum seekers—maybe not in a wave from right next door, but from close enough given modern means of communications and transport to assure eventual impact, one gommone at a time.

Militarized Borders and the International Refugee Regime

These trends and dilemmas bode ill for the refugee regime. The West designed the current UN refugee convention for individuals, not masses, and for transit across the Iron Curtain, not the Caribbean or the Adriatic. While the OAU recognizes a broader class of refugee than does the UN convention, the OAU's member states do not have the resources, singly or together, to support the waves of refugees who flee the continent's civil and border wars, and so they rely upon international largesse, periodically push refugees back home, or subsidize their efforts to fight their way home. In the old home of the Iron Curtain, refugees from conflicts in the Balkans strain the even-tempered tolerance for which European integration has been striving for decades.

The borders of the countries considered in this chapter are all at least partly militarized. The greater the actual or latent level of violence, the greater the militarization, as on the Indo-Pakistani frontier, or the border between Turkey and Iraq, or between Kosovo and the outside world. Where borders do not demarcate the territories of enemies, there may be violent drug traffickers, ruthless smugglers of human cargo, and heavily armed gun runners who keep the danger level high enough to foster official perceptions of ongoing, low intensity conflict, and to blur the common enemy image enough to include desperate but ordinary people looking for a job or a home. The risk of harm, mistreatment, or sudden death for asylum seekers may grow disproportionately with that blurring, as much from the migrants' association with organized crime transport networks—the better to breach official barriers—as from any encounter with border police or military forces. This merger of the desperate and the diabolic is occurring on borders all over the world.

Acknowledgments

The author is grateful for the research assistance provided by Caroline R. Earle and Jolie M. F. Wood, for research advice offered by Stephen P. Cohen and Erwin A. Schmidl, and for the comments on an earlier draft offered by participants in the Demography and Security Workshop, in particular Sharon Stanton Russell, Susan Forbes Martin, and Barry R. Posen.

Notes

1. The 1951 UN Convention Relating to the Status of Refugees and its 1967 Protocol define refugees as persons forced to flee their own states to avoid a well-founded fear of persecution "for reasons of race, religion, nationality, [or] membership of a particular social group or political opinion" (so-called "convention refugees"). The 1969 Convention on Refugee Problems in Africa of the Organization for African Unity and the 1984 Cartagena Declaration (with respect to Central America) broaden the definition to include those who have fled their homelands to avoid generalized conflict, external aggression, serious disturbances of public order, or human rights abuses (Loescher 1992: 6–7).
2. Howard Adelman attributes the phrase "refugee warriors" to Astri Suhrke (Adelman 1998: n.13; Zolberg, Surhke, and Aguayo 1989: 44, 275). Adelman defines them as people who have fled a homeland (or whose forebears fled); who use violent means aimed at overthrowing the regime in power in their homeland, from bases normally located within refugee communities in neighboring states; and who are not "fighting on behalf of their host state as surrogates of that state." Both sources note that the label is a contradiction in terms under international law, as a refugee may not resort to violence and still qualify for refugee status (Adelman 1998: 6). The 1951 UN Convention on the Status of Refugees requires only that refugees "conform to the laws and regulations of the host country," but the 1969 OAU refugee convention "prohibits 'subversive activities' by verbal means or arms." Thus to exist, refugee warriors "require sanctuary in a neighboring country permitting military operations from its territory.... Because the warriors are engaged in military operations across the border that associate the host country in an act of war, communities of this type cannot persist for long unless they secure substantial external partisan support" (Zolberg, Suhrke, and Aguayo 1989: 276–277).
3. For a good historical reviews, see M. Weiner 1992/93 and Loescher 1992: chaps. 1 and 2.
4. Personnel totals for Germany's Bundesgrenzschutz may be found on the German government's web site. Internet: Accessed 10 May 1999.
5. The U.S. Immigration and Naturalization Service estimates that the population of illegal Mexican immigrants in the United States grew by an average of 154,000 per year between 1992 and 1996. In 1996, the INS apprehended roughly 1.6 million illegal immigrants from Mexico, implying an entry success

rate of 8.8 percent. Other nationalities' success rates are closer to 60 percent; many of these overstay their visas rather than attempting to "enter without inspection" (U.S. Dept. of Justice 1999).

6. Reintroduced as a separate bill in November 1997, it was referred to a military personnel subcommittee, where it remained when the Congress adjourned for the 1998 elections.

7. The new "protective cordon" would run initially along the "Orenburg-Chelyabinsk-Omsk axis," or the bulk of the Russian-Kazakh border. In addition to the risk that the "volunteers" would seek to be self-financing, budget deficits have meant that Moscow has had to rely increasingly on regional budgets to fund this initiative, offering local satraps greater opportunity for independent revenue generation, as well (Yemelyanenko 1996).

8. As Kazakhstan's president, Nursultan Nazarbayev, observed in an interview, "The Kazakhs have a clear recollection of who the Cossacks are ... [a]nd now these greedy creatures are standing on our borders and shaking out old ladies' bags" (Kuzovkikov 1997).

9. For an unofficial translated text of the Schengen agreements, see Internet: <http://users.patra.hol.gr/~cgian/schengin.htm.[sic]>.

10. Italian authorities manage to identify about ten percent of the immigrants held at detention centers in Sicily; those who cannot be identified are released from the centers with old-style, 15-day expulsion orders in hand (*Rome RAI* 1998b).

11. The Indo-Pakistani border in Punjab and Rajasthan, on the other hand, is completely fenced and posted with guard towers. In Kashmir, Indian efforts to erect fencing along the LAC in 1994 attracted Pakistani military intervention, as fencing would contravene Pakistani policy that all of Kashmir is "disputed territory." More recently, Indian authorities have been testing ground sensors built in Israel that emit an electromagnetic field easily altered by passing objects. Indian border guards would be alerted to infiltrators, in effect, by disturbances in the Force. (Marwah 1995: 219; Khosa 1998)

12. Neither India, nor Bangladesh, nor Pakistan is a signatory to the 1951 UN Convention on the Status of Refugees.

13. Adelman has extensive discussion on the disputed numbers of refugees, and refugee-warriors, who fled into the Zairean bush, noting that unjustifiably high baseline estimates of the number of refugees in Zaire (as high as 1.2 million versus UNHCR estimates of 910,000) led to unjustifiably high estimates of people unaccounted for after the camps were broken up. The same over-counting, Adelman concludes, applied to subsequent reports of wide-scale killings of the remnants, with up to 200,000 said to have perished in reprisals by the RPA and Banyamulenge, among others. Tallying eyewitness accounts and adding a substantial margin of error, Adelman concludes that a more likely number is 20,000; still large, and still reflecting some large-scale killings, but 90 percent less than the commonly used statistic (Adelman 1998: 6–7, 14–18).

14. The Allied Democratic Forces are a largely Muslim force that is a blend of "Tabliq Moslem extremists, rebels from the moribund National Army for the Liberation of Uganda and soldiers from the overthrown governments of Rwanda and the ... DRC ... financed by the Salaf Muslim sect, based Iran and Sudan" (ICG 1998: 3, 5–6).

References

Adelman, Howard W. 1998. "Early Warning and Humanitarian Intervention: Zaire—March to December 1996," paper written for the Forum on Early Warning and Early Response, revised Sept. 1998. Mimeo.

Apte, Brigadier A. S. (ret'd). 1994. "One Military, One Police." *U.S.I. Journal* 124 (515): 51–64.

Asiaweek. 1998. "Newsmap: Bangladesh, week of July 17." Internet: <http://pathfinder.com/asiaweek/98/0724/newsmap/bangade.html>. Accessed 2 Nov. 1998.

Associated Press. 1998. "Report: Turkish Troops Sent to Iraq." 8 Nov., 1703EST. Internet: <http://wire.ap.org/AP.../center_story.html?FRONTID= MIDEAST&STORYID=APSI6P31AB0>. Accessed 9 Nov. 1998.

Austria. *Bundesheer.* 1999. "Austrian Armed Forces Facts and Figures," Internet: < http://www.bmlv.gv.at/facts.html>. Accessed 10 May 1999.

Barrell, Howard. 1999. "Failed Congo peace endangers neighbors." *Mail and Guardian* (Johannesburg), 26 Feb. Internet: <http://www.mg.co.za/mg/news/99feb2/26feb-congo.html>. Accessed 8 May 1999.

Batchelor, Peter. 1997. "Intra-state Conflict, Political Violence, and Small Arms Proliferation in Africa." In *Society Under Siege: Crime, Violence and Illegal Weapons*, ed. Virginia Gamba. Halfway House, South Africa: Institute for Security Studies.

BBC News Online. 1997. "Background to Schengen Agreement" and "Britain and Ireland Opt Out." Special Reports, 28 Nov. Internet: <http://www.news.bbc.co.uk/>.

Bedi, Rahul. 1995. "Jane's Defence Weekly Interview: Daya Kishore Arya." *Jane's Defence Weekly*, 24 June. Internet: <http://www.thomson.com/janes2/defence/interviews/kishore.html>.

Bianchieri, Boris. 1998. "Commentary Assessing Immigrant Phenomenon." *La Stampa* (Turin), 22 July. Translated by FBIS, Doc. No. FTS19980723000917.

Blagov, Sergei. 1998. "Refugees: Russia Faces Continuing Influx of Displaced People." *Inter Press Service*, 4 Jan. Internet: http://www.oneworld.org/ips2/jan98/russia.html>. Accessed 15 Nov. 1998.

Blanchfield, Mike. 1997. "From Apartheid to Xenophobia." *The Ottawa Citizen.* Internet: <http://www.queensu.ca/samp/migdocs/artic26.htm>. Posted 6 Jan. 1998; accessed 13 Nov. 1998.

Blechman, Barry M., and William J. Durch. 1981. "Bay of Pigs +20." *The Washington Quarterly* 4(4): 86–100.

Booth, William. 1998. "7 Illegal Immigrants Die as Heat Raises Peril of Border Crossings." *Washington Post*, 14 Aug.

Branigin, William. 1999. "Border Patrol Adds High-Tech Tools to Its Arsenals." *Washington Post*, 19 Feb., A21.

Brittain, Victoria. 1999. "The Congo war redraws African alliances." *Mail and Guardian* (Johannesburg), 26 Mar. Internet: <http://www.mg.co.za./mg/news/99mar2/26mar-congo.html>. Accessed 20 May.

Burns, John F. 1996. "China and India Pledge to Withdraw Troops on Disputed Border." *New York Times*, 30 Nov.

———. 1997. "India's Five Decades of Progress and Pain." *New York Times*, 14 Aug., A11.

Chaudhuri, Kalyan. 1998. "Protest in West Bengal." *Frontline* (India). 15–28 Aug. Internet: <http://www.the-hindu.com/fline/fl1517/15170430.htm>. Accessed 2 Nov. 1998.

Chaudhury, Rahul Roy. 1993. "The Indian Coast Guard in the 1990s." *Indian Defence Review* (October): 64–68.

Christie, Kenneth. 1997. "Security and Forced Migration Concerns in South Africa." *African Security Review* 6(1). Online at <http://iss.co.za>.

Cianfanelli, Renzo. 1998. "Albania: Refugee Nightmare." *Corriere della Sera* (Milan). Internet version, 21 Sept. Translated by FBIS, Doc. no. FTS19980921000367, 21 Sept.

Daley, Suzanne. 1998. "New South Africa Shuts the Door on Its Neighbors." *New York Times,* 19 Oct. A1.

De Palma, Anthony. 1999. "Georgia: Quitting the Defense Pact." *New York Times,* 23 Feb., A6.

Dillon, Sam. 1999. "More Deaths on Border, Groups Say." *New York Times,* 11 Feb., A12.

Drago, Tito. 1998. "Immigration-Spain: Not even 1,000 Deaths Have Stemmed the Flow." *Inter Press Service,* 11 Aug. Internet: <http://www.oneworld. org/ips2/aug98/18_26_094.html>.

Duke, Lynne. 1998. "Revolt in Congo Had Multiethnic Genesis." *Washington Post,* 27 Oct., A20.

Dunn, Timothy J. 1996. *Militarization of the US-Mexico Border: Low Intensity Conflict Doctrine Comes Home.* Austin: CMAS Books, University of Texas.

Economist. 1998a. "Frontier Wars." 10 Jan., 42.

———. 1998b. "International: Watch out for the Kurds." 14 Feb., 46–47.

Fisher, Ian, and Onishi Norimitsu. 1999. "Congo's Struggle May Unleash Broad Strife to Redraw Africa." *New York Times,* 12 Jan., A1.

Fowler, Brenda. 1992. "Vienna Journal: Guards Now Patrol the Other Side of the Frontier." *New York Times,* 6 June, A2.

Galluzzo, Marco. 1998. "Intelligence Services: Most Dangerous Threat from the East." *Corriere della Sera* (Milan). Internet version, 7 Aug. Translated by FBIS, Doc. no. FTS19980807001534, 7 Aug. 1998.

Gellman, Barton. 1996. "In Iraqi Thrust, New Power Shift?" *International Herald Tribune,* 2 Sept. Internet: <http://www.turkey.org/news/selected/ 10029631.htm>. Accessed 6 Nov. 1998.

Gilbert, Sari. 1998. "Government Pleased with Accord with Tirana to Facilitate Identification of Illegal Immigrants." *Il Sole-24 Ore* (Milan). Internet version, 14 Aug. Internet: <http://www.sole24ore.iol.it>. Accessed 8 Dec. 1998.

Gupta, Shekhar. 1995. "Nuclear Weapons in the Subcontinent." In *Defense and Insecurity in Southern Asia,* Chris Smith et al. Occasional Paper No. 21. Washington, D.C.: The Henry L. Stimson Center.

Hughes, Candice. 1998. "Italy Releases Kurd as Turkey Protests." *New York Times,* 22 Nov., A37.

Intelligence Resource Program. 1998. "Border Security Forces." Federation of American Scientists. Washington, D.C. Internet: <http://www/fas/org/ irp/world/india/bsf.html>. Accessed 12 May 1999.

International Crisis Group (ICG). 1998. "North Kivu: Into the Quagmire? An Overview of the Current Crisis in North Kivu." Report, 13 Aug. Internet: <http://www.crisisweb.org/projects/cafrica/reports/ca02main.htm.> Accessed 15 May 1999.

International Institute for Strategic Studies. 1981. *Strategic Survey, 1980–81.* London: IISS.

———. 1988. The Military Balance, 1988–89. London: IISS.

———. 1992. *The Military Balance, 1992–93.* London: Brassey's.

———. 1993. *The Military Balance, 1993–94.* London: Brassey's.

———. 1995. *The Military Balance, 1995–96.* London: Oxford University Press.

———. 1996. *The Military Balance, 1996–97.* London: Oxford University Press.

———. 1997. *The Military Balance, 1997–98.* London: Oxford University Press.

———. 1998a. *Strategic Survey, 1997–98.* London: Oxford University Press for the IISS.

———. 1998b. *The Military Balance, 1998–99.* London: Oxford University Press.

———. 1999. *Strategic Survey, 1998–99.* London: Oxford University Press for the IISS.

IOM News. 1998. "Smuggling Asian Migrants into the United States: A Booming Business." North American Supplement no. 6 (June/July): 1.

Ivanov, Andrei, and Judith Perera. 1998. "Migration: Millions Still on Move as Russian Refugee Crisis Eases," *Inter Press Service,* 4 Jan. Internet: <http:// oneworld.org/ips2/fed98/russia.html>. Downloaded 15 Nov. 1998.

James, Wilmot G., et al. 1997. *Draft Green Paper on International Migration,* Task Team on International Migration, presented to the Minister for Home Affairs, Pretoria, South Africa, 13 May. Internet: <http://www.polity. org.za/>. Downloaded 13 Nov. 1998.

Kakhan, Col. Mikalay. 1998. "On the Edge of the Fight Against Illegal Immigration." *Vo Slavu Rodiny* (Minsk), 23 Sept., 2. Translated by FBIS-SOV-98-273, 30 Sept. 1998.

Kakodkar, Priyanka. 1998. "Deportees were released into a forest or jute field on the border." *The Times of India,* 29 July. Internet: <http://www.indian-express.com/ie/daily/19981209/34350274.html>. Accessed 3 Nov. 1998.

Khosa, Aasha. 1998. "India to bury Israeli devices on J&K border to check infiltration." *Indian Express,* 9 Dec. Internet: <http://www/indian-express.com/ie/daily/19981209/34350274.html.> Accessed 12 May 1999.

Kinzer, Stephen. 1998. "Turkish Troops Reported in Iraq to Block Kurd Refugees." *New York Times,* 22 Feb. Internet: http://www.nytimes.com/ library/world>. Accessed 3 Nov. 1998.

Kiyampur, Saidksasym. 1998. "Georgia Starts Protecting Its Borders: Celebrations in Poti May Turn Out to Be Premature." *Russkiey Telegraf (Moscow).* Trans. in FBIS Daily Report. FBIS-SOV-98-201, 20 July 1998.

Kohen, Sami. 1995. "A Little Mideast War Tests Turkey." *Christian Science Monitor,* March 24. Internet: http://www.csmonitor.com/cgi-bin/ getasciiarchive?tape/95/mar/day24/24071. Accessed November 6, 1998.

Kumin, Judith. 1998. "Asylum in Europe: Sharing or Shifting the Burden?" *World Refugee Survey, 1995,* reprinted by the US Committee for Refugees, Internet: http://www.refugees.org/ world/articles/europe_wrs95.htm. Accessed December 10, 1998.

Kuzovkikov, Sergei. 1997. "Cossacks Guarding Russian Borders." *Moscow News,* August 7. Downloaded from Lexis-Nexis Universe, 3 October 1998.

La Repubblica (Rome). 1998. "Coastal Patrols Against Illegal Landings to be Stepped Up." Internet edition, 22 July. Translated by FBIS, Doc. No. FTS19980722000599, 22 July 1998.

Legomsky, Stephen H. 1997. "Non-Citizens and the Rule of Law: the 1996 Immigration Reforms." *Research Perspectives on Migration* 1(4). May/June.

Loescher, Gil. 1990. "Introduction: Refugee Issues in International Relations." In *Refugees and International Relations,* ed. G. Loescher and L. Monahan. Oxford: Clarendon Press.

———. 1992. *Refugee Movements and International Security.* Adelphi Paper 258. London: International Institute for Strategic Studies.

Lokma Times. 1999. "Indian farmers back on field in border areas with Pakistan." February 24. Internet: http://www.lokmatimes.com/24/nation.html. Accessed 12 May 1999.

Mail and Guardian. 1998. "South Africa: SA Crime is Getting Organised." Johannesburg, 13 February. Downloaded from Lexis-Nexis Universe, 3 October 1998.

Marwah, Ved. 1993. "The Problems and the Challenges Faced by the Police and the Paramilitary Forces." *Indian Defence Review* (January 1993): 13–18.

———. 1995. *Uncivil Wars: Pathology of Terrorism in India.* New Delhi: Harper-Collins Publishers India.

———. 1998. "Police and Paramilitary Structure in 2010." *Indian Defence Review* (April–June 1998): 73–77.

Migration News. 1998. "North America, INS: Sanctions, Detention, Fees." 5(11).

Migration News. 1999. "Europe: Kosovar Refugees" 6(5). Internet: http://www.migration.ucdavis.edu/ archive/May_1999-09.html. Accessed 8 May 1999.

Migration World Magazine. 1996. "Immigrants, refugees, and displaced people in southern Africa." 24(4): 34 ff.

Mokoena, A. S., et al. 1999. *White Paper on International Migration.* Task Team on International Migration, presented to the Minister of Home Affairs, Pretoria, South Africa, 31 March. Internet: <http://www.polity.org.za/govdocs/white_papers/migration.html>. Accessed 12 May 1999.

Nair, Ravi. 1997. "Refugee Protection in South Asia." *Journal of International Affairs* 51(1): 201–220.

Namboodiri, Udayan, Sayantan Chakravarti, and Avirook Sen. 1998. "Political Pawns." *India Today,* 10 Aug. Internet: <http://www.india-today.com/itoday/10081998/bangl.html>. Accessed 2 Nov. 1998.

National Network for Immigration and Refugee Rights (NNIRR). 1998. "Pentagon Wants to End Armed Military Patrols of Border." Internet: <http://www.policy.com/issuewk/98/0413/041398i.html>. 15 Jan.

Noorani, A. G. 1994. "Easing the Indo-Pakistani Dialogue on Kashmir." Occasional Paper No. 16. Washington, D.C.: The Henry L. Stimson Center.

O'Prey, Kevin P. 1996. "Keeping the Peace in the Borderlands of Russia." In *UN Peacekeeping, American Politics, and the Uncivil Wars of the 1990s,* ed. William J. Durch. New York: St. Martin's Press.

Ojito, Mirta. 1998. "Change in Laws Sets Off Big Wave of Deportations." *New York Times,* 15 Dec.

Padmanabhan, R. 1998. "The Deportation Drive." *Frontline* (India). 15–28 Aug. Internet: <http://www.the-hindu.com/fline/fl1517/15170410.htm>. Accessed 2 Nov. 1998.

Pina, Jorge. 1998. "Italy-Tunisia: Accord Brings Start of Deportation Proceedings." *Inter Press Service,* 7 Aug. Internet: <http://www.oneworld.org/ips2/aug98/16_51_077.html>.

Plotniknov, Nikolay. 1998. "Interview with Federal Border Service Director Nikolay Nikolyevich Bordyuzha," *Nezavisimoye Voyennoye Obozeniye* (Moscow), 17 July. Translated in FBIS-UMA-98-210, 29 July 1998.

Pomfret, John. 1995. "Iraq-Turkey Fuel Smugglers Back in Business." *New York Times,* 7 Apr., A1.

Ramachandran, Hari. 1998. "More Than 80 Dead in Attacks across India-Pakistan border." Reuters, 4 Aug., 0719 PDT. Internet: <http://www.seattletimes.com/news/nation-world/html98/altkash_080498.html>. Accessed 12 May 1999.

RFE/RL Newsline. 1998. "Kyrgyzstan Will Guard Its Own Borders." Transcaucasia and Central Asia segment, relaying a report from ITAR-TASS. 25 Aug.

Rohde, David. 1995. "Might Makes Flight in Two Rebel Wars." *Christian Science Monitor,* 3 April. Internet: http://www.csmonitor.com/cgi-bin/getasciiarchive?tape/95/apr/day03/03011. Accessed 6 November 1998.

Rome ANSA. 1998. "Bilateral Accord Signed, Aid Accepted." 6 Aug., in English. FBIS Doc. No. FTS19980806002744, 6 Aug. 1998.

Rome RAI. 1998a. "Illegal Immigrant Influx Said Testing Authorities." *Radio Uno Network,* 15 July. Translated by FBIS, ID FTS19980715000743, 15 July 1998.

————. 1998b. "Immigrants Arrested, Deadline Nears for Release of Others." *Uno Television Network,* 10 Aug, 1130 GMT. Translated by FBIS, Doc. no. FTS19980810000867.

Rosenbaum, David E. 1998. "U.S. Breaks a Ring Smuggling Aliens." *New York Times,* 21 Nov., A1.

Saradzhyan, Simon. 1998. "Taliban March Strikes Fear in Russia." *The Moscow Times,* 15 Aug. Downloaded from Lexis-Nexis Universe, 3 Oct.

Sharma, Yojana. 1998. "Rights-Germany: Bonn May Cut Aid to Nations that Refuse Deportees." *Inter Press Service,* 20 May. Downloaded from Lexis-Nexis, 3 Oct.

Smirnov, Petr. 1998. "The Result of Our Operations in Tajikistan is of Considerably Larger Scale than Military Success Proper." Interview with Andrey Nikolayev, head of the Russian Federal Border Service. *Nezavisimaya Gazeta* (Moscow), 20 May, 1. Translated in FBIS-SOV-98-154, 3 June.

Soros Foundation. 1997. Forced Migration Projects (FMP). *Haitian Boat People.* Special report, April. Internet: <http://www.soros.org/fmp2/html/haitian_full.html>. Accessed 15 Nov. 1998.

South African Department of Defence. 1998. *Annual Report 1997: Defence in a Democracy.* Internet: <http://www.mil//za/Secretariat/annualR/AnnualR97.htm>. Downloaded 29 Nov. 1998.

Stanley, Alessandra. 1999a. "Kurdish Rebel Leader, Who Is Wanted by Turkey, Leaves Italy." *New York Times,* 17 Jan., A13.

————. 1999b. "Uzbekistan, Russia: Dropping Out." *New York Times,* 5 Feb: A8.

Turkey, Government of. 1996. "Turkey Declares Temporary Danger Zone Along Turkish-Iraqi Border." Press Release, 6 Sept. Internet: <http://www.turkey.org/releases/090996.htm>. Accessed 6 Nov. 1998.

UN Department of Humanitarian Affairs (DHA). 1998. "Chechnya, Russian Federation Situation Report, 1 Nov–15 Dec 1997." Internet at <http://www.soros.org/migrate.html>. Accessed 5 Oct. 1998.

UN DHA Integrated Regional Information Network (IRIN). 1996a. *Emergency Update on Eastern Zaire,* No. 50, 6 Dec. Internet: <http://www.reliefweb.int>. Accessed 9 May 1999.

————. 1996b–g. *Emergency Update on the Great Lakes.* Nos. 56–58, 60, 62, 66, Dec. 13–27. Internet: <http://www.reliefweb.int>. Accessed 9 May 1999.

UN High Commissioner for Refugees (UNHCR). 1999. "Kosovo Crisis Update: 14 May 1999." On UN Relief Web. Internet: <http://wwwnotes.reliefweb.int>. Accessed 14 May 1999.

UN Security Council. 1998. *Final Report of the International Commission of Inquiry (Rwanda).* UN document S/1998/1096/Annex. 18 Nov.

U.S. Agency for International Development (USAID). 1997. *Great Lakes Complex Emergency Situation Report.* No. 3 for fiscal year 1998, December 30. Available from UN Relief Web.

U.S. Coast Guard, Office of Law Enforcement. 1997. "Alien Migration Year in Review: FY 1997." *Current Reports and Other Information.* Internet: <http://www.uscg.mi./hq/g-o/g-opl/lawweb2/ link13.htm>. Accessed 8 Dec. 1998.

————. 1998. "Alien Migrant Interdiction." Internet: <http://www.uscg.mi./hq/g-o/g-opl/lawweb2/link10.htm>. Accessed 2 Nov. 1998.

————. 1999a. "Alien Migrant Interdiction: Mariel Boat Lift." Internet: <http:///.uscg.mil/hq/g-o/g-opl/ lawweb1/mariel.htm>. Accessed 12 May 1999.

————. 1999b. "Alien Migrant Interdiction: Operation Able Manner." Internet: <http://www.uscg.mil/hq/g-o/g-opl/lawweb2/AbM.htm>. Accessed 12 May 1999.

———. 1999c. "Alien Migrant Interdiction: Operation Able Vigil." Internet: <http://www.uscg.mil/hq/g-o/g-opl/lawwb2/AbV.htm>. Accessed 12 May 1999.

———. 1999d. "Alien Migrant Interdiction." Internet: <http://www.uscg.mi./hq/g-o/g-opl/lawweb2/link10.htm>. Accessed 12 May 1999.

U.S. Department of Defense Intelligence Agency. 1998. *Migration Defense Intelligence Data System.* Internet: <http://www.acq.osc.mil/at/mdi.htm>. Accessed 18 Dec. 1998.

U.S. Department of Justice, Office of the Inspector General. 1998. "Operation Gatekeeper; An Investigation into Allegations of Fraud and Misconduct." U.S.DOJ/OIG Special Report, July 1998. Internet: <http://www.usdoj.gov/oig/gatekpr/gkexsum.htm>. Downloaded 29 Aug. 1998.

U.S. Department of Justice, Immigration and Naturalization Service (INS). 1997a. *1996 Statistical Yearbook of the INS.* Washington, D.C.: U.S. Government Printing Office (October).

———. 1997b. "INS Launches Next Phase of Operation Gatekeeper: New Focus on Alien Smuggling in El Centro as San Diego Border Patrol Arrests Plunge to 17-Year Low," INS Press Release, 7 Oct.

———. 1999. "Statistics: Country of Origin." Internet: http://www.ins.usdoj.gov/stats/ 199.html>. Accessed 17 May 1999.

U.S. Department of Justice, INS, Border Patrol, Del Rio Sector, Texas. 1999. "Headquarters." Internet: <http://www.ins.usdoj.gov/delrio/drsechq.htm>. Accessed 12 May 1999.

U.S. Department of State. Bureau of Population, Refugees, and Migration. 1997. "Haiti: Haitian Migrants." Fact sheet, 23 Jan. Internet: <http://www.state.gov/www/global/prm/Haiti.html>. Downloaded 15 Nov. 1998.

U.S. Department of the Navy. 1997. *1997 Posture Statement, Pt. III: Operational Primacy, Counter-drug Operations.* Internet: <http://www.chinfo.navy.mil/navpalib/policy/enforem/bord.htm>.

U.S. Department of the Treasury, Customs Service. 1999a. "Border Coordination Initiative." Internet: <http://www.customs.ustreas.gov/enforcem/bord.thm>. Accessed 12 May 1999.

———. 1999b. "Fiscal Year 1998 Windows of Opportunity for Drug Smuggling (National Statistics)." Internet: <http://www.customs.ustreas.gov/enforcem/hardline/int98w.htm>. Accessed 12 May 1999.

Vaccaro, J. Matthew. 1996. "The Politics of Genocide: Peacekeeping and Disaster Relief in Rwanda." In *UN Peacekeeping, American Politics, and the Uncivil Wars of the 1990s,* ed. William J. Durch. New York: St. Martin's Press.

Vienna Oesterreich Eins. 1998. "Fasslabend Says Army at Border Mission to Continue." Broadcast 1000 GMT, 3 Sept. Translated in FBIS/West Europe, ID: FTS19980903000701, 3 Sept. 1998.

Viviano, Frank. 1999a. "Crest of a Human Wave: Illegal Immigrants Flood Albania to Be Smuggled across Adriatic." *San Francisco Chronicle,* 12 Feb., A1.

———. 1999b. "Global Mob Cashing in on Human Cargo: Criminal Network Smuggles Thousands across Adriatic." *San Francisco Chronicle,* 16 Feb., A1.

Weiner, Myron. 1992/93. "Stability, Security and International Migration." *International Security* 17(3): 91–126.

Weiner, Tim. 1999. "U.S. Helped Turkey Find and Capture Kurd Rebel." *New York Times,* 20 Feb., Al.

Yemelyanenko, Vladimir. 1996. "Russia Reinforces Its Southern Border." Moscow News, 19 Oct. Downloaded from Lexis-Nexis Universe, 3 Oct. 1998.

Zolberg, Aristide, Astri Suhrke, and Sergio Aguayo. 1989. *Escape from Violence: Conflict and the Refugee Crisis in the Developing World.* New York: Oxford University Press.

CHAPTER 5

Plural Nationality: Facing the Future in a Migratory World

T. Alexander Aleinikoff and Douglas Klusmeyer

In a perfectly symmetrical world, each individual citizen or national would be a member of one and only one state.[1] Many political theorists and legal scholars in the past imagined such a world. They denounced the very idea of dual nationality as unnatural, and likened it to a bigamous marriage. Today defenders of post-national and transnational understandings of polity membership see in the phenomenon of dual nationality the harbinger of a new world no longer dominated by the nation-state. Whether one sees the rising trend of plural nationality as positive or negative, there is no denying that its incidence is widespread and growing. One recent study, for example, has estimated that over a half million children born each year in the United States have at least one additional nationality (Aleinikoff 1998: 28). Another study reports that 60 percent of Swiss nationals who live abroad do so as dual nationals (Schuck 1998: 223).

How should we understand the rising incidence of plural nationals? This chapter will address this question by first examining the concept of nationality under domestic and international law. Then it will focus on the issue of plural nationality and state responses to it. With this background, the chapter will conclude by assessing traditional objections to the phenomenon of plural nationality, arguing that the threats seemingly posed by plural nationals have historically proved to be more hypothetical than real.

The Concept of Nationality under Domestic and International Law

Nationality is a legal-political category that constitutes the most basic legal nexus between an individual and a state. It involves reciprocal relationship, obligating a state to protect the individual and investing that individual with allegiance to the state.

The right of a state to determine its own nationality policy has long been considered an essential attribute of sovereignty, although emerging international legal norms have somewhat qualified this authority. Nationality has traditionally been defined as a term of municipal law, subject to the domestic jurisdiction of the state. While under the direct province of municipal law, nationality also has certain functions under international law. The first concerns a state's right to protect its nationals in relation to other states: It allows one state to protect persons or property in another. A second function is to give an individual the right to be admitted to and reside in the territory of the state of nationality. This right rests on the premise that the international order requires a territorial allocation of persons according to membership in states. These twin functions establish a link between the individual and international law, whose primary subjects are states.

Nationality can be acquired by a variety of means. Among the most common means are by: (i) birth on the sovereign's territory (*jus soli*); (ii) descent from one or both parents who are nationals (*jus sanguinis*); (iii) marriage; (iv) adoption or legitimation; (v) naturalization; (vi) territorial transfer from one state to another. Because there is no international uniformity among states in their application of these criteria, the acquisition of multiple nationalities can occur in any number of ways. Children can acquire them from parents having different nationalities; children may obtain multiple nationalities when they are born in states that recognize the principle of *jus soli*, but whose parent(s) are nationals of states that base acquisition on the principle of *jus sanguinis*; spouses of different nationalities may acquire their partners' nationalities without having to renounce their own. States that have experienced large-scale emigration may offer their emigrants the right to retain their nationality alongside any new nationality obtained, and may facilitate their descendents' acquisition of their parents' nationality.

Determining criteria of acquisition can be especially complex when one state succeeds another as sovereign over a territory. Under international law, successor states cannot impose nationality on their new territorial inhabitants, and any conferment must be construed as an offer which must be accepted to be valid. An offer is never automatic, and is governed by the municipal law of the successor state (if not by treaty). Nevertheless, the presumption in international law is that the municipal law of the succeeding state will result in the conferral of nationality on the residents of the transferred territory. For nationals residing outside the transferred territory, the municipal law of the transferring state (presuming the state has not lost its sovereignty through conquest or other means) determines whether or not they retain their nationality. If the predecessor state does withdraw nationality from such persons, the successor state cannot confer nationality without the permission of the state of residence. In cases of territorial cession, the ceding state must remove its nationality from those persons who receive the nationality of the acquiring state and respect the municipal law of the acquiring state.[2] Should the ceding state not fulfill this obligation, third-party states have a duty to recognize only the nationality of the acquiring state. Article 10 of the United Nations Convention on the Reduction of Statelessness (1961) imposes a duty on Contracting Parties to include provisions in every treaty involving territorial transfer that are "designed to secure that no person shall become stateless as a result of the transfer. A Contracting State shall use its best endeavors to secure that any such treaty made by it with a State which is not a party to this Convention includes such provisions."

Nationality can be lost in several ways: (i) some states permit children who have acquired multiple nationalities to renounce their nationality upon reaching majority; (ii) some states treat service in another state's military or government as an act of expatriation; (iii) some states (but increasingly fewer) consider the acquisition of a new nationality as an act of expatriation; or it can be lost through (iv) territorial transfer between states; by (v) mass deprivations, such as the Third Reich's policy toward German Jews; or by (vi) adoption.[3] The distinction between "voluntary" and "involuntary" has traditionally been a common criterion by which states determine whether an individual will be required to renounce his or her nationality before acquiring a new one and whether the acquisition of a new nationality will be treated as an act of expatriation.[4] Germany, for example, permits foreign nationals to acquire German nationality without renouncing their foreign allegiance if the states to which they owe allegiance do not recognize expatriation. Many states do not consider the involuntary acquisition of nationality, such as when children receive different nationalities through their parents or through birth on a territory where the principle of *jus soli* applies, to be grounds for expatriation. Likewise, when spouses (invariably wives) automatically acquire the foreign nationality of their husbands, many states do not treat such acquisition as an act of expatriation.[5]

The problem with using this distinction is that it assumes that voluntary acquisition of another nationality is a valid test for a lack of allegiance, but the validity of this test is by no means clear. The circumstances of foreign residence might induce an individual to obtain the nationality of the state of his or her residence for many different reasons other than a lack of allegiance. Individuals may seek another nationality in order to obtain stronger legal protections, including broader rights of employment, residence, travel, and family re-unification. In addition, often the acts of acquisition categorized as "involuntary" may, in fact, be voluntary, such as using marriage as a means to obtain another nationality.

Many of these problems can be effectively resolved through international agreements and bilateral treaties.[6] As one commentator has observed:

The absence of far-reaching limitation of municipal nationality law by international law and the scarcity of positive rules of international law in the matter of nationality ... is bound to lead to ... conflicts.... But they also result in giving States considerable freedom to prescribe rules for the solution of [... such] conflicts, in the absence of treaty obligations. (Weis 1979: 169)

Consider, for example, the conflict that can arise when nationals of one state visit another state wherein they also hold nationality. Under international law, a state can extend no diplomatic protection to its nationals when in the jurisdiction of a state of nationality.[7] Through the Convention Establishing the Status of Naturalized Citizens (1906), a number of states in the Western hemisphere adopted rules to regulate nationality effects of those naturalized citizens who returned to their country of origin. Under this Convention, naturalized persons who resume permanent residence in the state of their original nationality and who do not intend to return to the country in which they were naturalized are deemed to have renounced their naturalized nationality.[8] Article 1 of the 1930 Protocol Relating to Military Obligations in Certain Cases of Double Nationality[9] provides that: "A person possessing two or more nationalities who habitually resides in one of the countries whose nationality he possesses, and who is in fact most closely connected with that country, shall be exempt from all military obligations in the other country or countries."[10]

The limitations that international legal norms impose on a state's authority over nationality policy are unclear but remain decidedly modest. The 1948 Universal Declaration of Human Rights sets forth two general principles with direct bearing on nationality. Article 13(2) recognizes that: "Everyone has the right to leave any country, including his own, and to return to his or her country." Article 15 proclaims the right of everyone to a nationality. It further stipulates that "no one shall be arbitrarily deprived of his nationality nor denied the right to change his nationality." This latter provision can (arguably) be interpreted to mean that no one should be compelled to surrender a nationality involuntarily irrespective of having another nationality.[11] As the preamble makes clear, the Universal Declaration is not legally binding on State Parties, but it may be invoked as evidence of a customary international human rights law.[12]

Since the UN General Assembly adopted the Universal Declaration, a series of human rights covenants that implicate different aspects of nationality have been adopted that are legally binding on Contracting State Parties. Article 1 of the 1957 Convention on the Nationality of Married Women, for example, stipulates that "neither the celebration nor the dissolution of a marriage between one of its nationals and an alien, nor change of nationality by the husband, shall automatically affect the nationality of the wife." Article 2 provides further: "Each Contracting State agrees that neither the voluntary acquisition of the nationality of another State nor the renunciation of its nationality by one of its nationals shall prevent the retention of its nationality by the wife of such

national." Article 1 of the 1961 Convention on the Reduction of Statelessness obligates a Contracting State to "grant its nationality to a person
born in its territory who would other be stateless," while Article 7 stipulates limitations on a Contracting State's discretion to revoke nationality.

Article 5 of the 1966 International Convention on the Elimination of
All Forms of Racial Discrimination "guarantee[s] the right of everyone,
without distinction as to race, color, or national or ethnic origin, to equality before the law, notably in the enjoyment of the following rights...."
These rights expressly include: (d)(ii) "The right to leave any country,
including one's own, and to return to one's country"; and (d)(iii) "The
right to nationality." This Convention then links an individual's right to
nationality to the principles of equality and freedom from discrimination.[13] The adoption of the 1979 Convention on the Elimination of All
Forms of Discrimination against Women was intended promote these
principles with respect to the rights of men and women. Article 9(1) of the
Convention stipulates: "State Parties shall grant women equal rights with
men to acquire, change or retain their nationality. They shall ensure in particular that neither marriage to an alien nor change of nationality by the
husband during marriage shall automatically change the nationality of the
wife, render her stateless or force upon her the nationality of her husband." Article 9(2) provides further that: "State Parties shall grant women
equal rights with men with respect to the nationality of their children."[14]

Despite the steady growth of these human rights instruments, commentators who have studied nationality law most closely in both its
domestic and international contexts have emphasized the decisive role
and relative autonomy of states in regulating their nationality policy
(Weis 1979: 248–249). Instruments like the UN Convention on the Nationality of Married Women have probably had their greatest effect by influencing the development of domestic legislation in particular states rather
than as binding international legal norms. Nonetheless, these instruments do provide a body of international standards and are laying the
foundation for the emergence of an international customary law of
nationality (Donner 1994: 389).

The Issue of Plural Nationality

Traditional theories of the modern state posited that subjects of a state
owed an exclusive duty of loyalty and obedience to their sovereign. By
this view, multiple ties of loyalty were unthinkable, and an individual
could not transfer obligations of allegiance from one sovereign to another.
For example, the old common-law doctrine of "perpetual allegiance"
denied an individual the right to renounce obligations to his sovereign.
The bonds of subjecthood were conceived in principle to be both singu-
lar and immutable. In the early nineteenth century, England invoked this
doctrine to justify impressing naturalized Americans, who had been born

in the United Kingdom, into the British navy, a policy that helped precipitate the War of 1812. The refusal of many states to recognize expatriation posed a chronic problem for a country with a large immigrant population, like the United States. Naturalized American citizens visiting their native homelands remained liable for duties of citizenship imposed there. To address this problem, the United States in the nineteenth century negotiated a series of bilateral agreements with foreign governments to secure at least a limited right to expatriation for its naturalized citizens. In 1868, George Bancroft, U.S. Ambassador to the North German Confederation, concluded a treaty that recognized the naturalized status of German-born Americans. Similar treaties soon followed with Austria-Hungary, Belgium, Denmark, Norway, Sweden, and the United Kingdom.

The most important international agreement regulating plural nationalities is the Convention on Certain Questions Relating to the Conflict of Nationality Laws, which was opened for signature at The Hague on 12 April 1930.[15] The Hague Convention offered international tribunals a modest number of rules to decide when jurisdiction existed in cases concerning plural nationality.[16] It did not deal with fundamental questions regarding the loss or acquisition of nationality, nor with the function of nationality in international law. The preamble to this Convention reaffirmed the traditional view that every person "should have one nationality only," but also acknowledged that "under the economic and social conditions which at present exist in various countries, it is not possible to reach immediately … [this goal]." Articles 1 and 2 recognized that each state has the right "to determine under its own law who are its nationals" and the right to decide "[a]ny question as to whether a person possesses the nationality" of that state. Article 3 provides that "a person having two or more nationalities may be regarded as its national by each of the States whose nationality such person also possesses." Article 5 enjoins third-party states to treat plural nationals as if they had only one nationality based either on where they resided habitually or where they had the closest connections, but failure to perform military service can still be grounds for a state to withdraw its nationality. Given the multiple ways in which the principles of *jus soli* and *jus sanguinis* intersect to produce dual nationals, the Convention's potential effectiveness to reduce their incidence was significantly impaired from the outset by its failure to set forth a uniform principle for the acquisition of nationality at birth. The failure of the Convention to address this issue may also reflect the drafters' recognition of the deeply divided interests at stake in defining criteria for the conferral of nationality.

Given the difference in interests among states, the rising incidence of plural nationality should hardly come as a surprise. The most important factor behind this rising incidence has been the lack of agreement among states over the rules governing the acquisition and loss of nationality.[17] If all states practiced a pure form of *jus soli* or *jus sanguinis*, then the issue of plural nationality would be minor except in cases of mixed marriages.

Conversely, the conflicting combinations of these forms among states almost ensure that the incidence of plural nationality will continue to grow, although there are additional causes behind this growth, such as changes in gender policies behind the rules governing the acquisition and loss of nationality. Where before women of a different nationality were expected to assume the nationality of their husbands at marriage, this norm has been amended. Now women increasingly have the option (the right) to retain their own nationality irrespective of marital status, which increases the likelihood that parents within such a marriage will pass on different nationalities to their children. Finally, advances in travel technology and the globalization of commerce have made the movement of people across states much faster, easier, and more common. The incidence of plural nationality is growing because people increasingly have the means to live with concrete connections to multiple states.

The traditional posture of states against plural nationality is now changing. The 1997 European Convention on Nationality demonstrates a trend in the recognition of states that plural nationality is not a short-term abnormality to be eliminated but rather a growing reality that must be accommodated.[18] Article 14(a)(b), for example, provides: "A State Party shall allow: children having different nationalities acquired automatically at birth to retain these nationalities; its nationals to possess another nationality where this other nationality is automatically acquired by marriage," while Article 16 provides: "A State Party shall not make the renunciation or loss of another nationality a condition for the acquisition or retention of its nationality where such renunciation or loss is not possible or cannot reasonably be required."

To deal with the problem of reconciling conflicting rights and duties of plural nationals as well as defining the diplomatic authority of states to protect them, international tribunals have adopted a connection test through the "doctrine of dominant (or effective) nationality." In the Nottebohm Case, the International Court of Justice explained the basis for this doctrine. The case involved Liechtenstein's attempt on behalf of one of its naturalized citizens to assert a claim against Guatemala, which argued that the person concerned was not a genuine Liechtenstein national because he had had little substantive contact with Liechtenstein. The Court found:

> International arbitrators have decided in the same way numerous cases of dual nationality, where the question arose with regard to the exercise of protection. They have given their preference to the real and effective nationality, that which accorded with the facts, that based on stronger factual ties between the person concerned and one of the States whose nationality is involved. Different factors are taken into consideration, and their importance will vary from one case to the next: the habitual residence of the individual concerned is an important factor, but there are other factors such as the center of his interests, his family ties, his participation in public life, attachment shown by him for a given country and inculcated in his children, etc.

Similarly, the courts of third States, when they have before them an individual whom two other States hold to be their national, seek to resolve the conflict by having recourse to international criteria and their prevailing tendency is to prefer the real and effective nationality.... National laws reflect this tendency when, inter alia, they make naturalization dependent on conditions indicating the existence of a link, which may vary in their purpose or in their nature but which are essentially concerned with this idea.

The same tendency prevails in the writings of publicists and in practice. (*Liechtenstein v. Guatemala* p. 22)

The Italian-United States Conciliation Commission relied on this Nottebohm precedent in applying the doctrine in the Mergé Case—Decision No. 55.[19] Citing both these cases for precedent, the Iran-United States Claim Tribunal (1984) declared the doctrine to be settled international legal principle.

This principle of international law creates the foundation for recognizing plural nationality as an active/passive status whereby domestic rights and duties are tied to place of residence. Active rights and duties would vest where a person resides without requiring a renunciation of passive affiliations with other states. Only individual states have the authority to determine the mix of these rights, but a long history suggests ample precedents for states to reach settlements with one another over such issues through bilateral and multilateral agreements.

State Responses to Plural Nationality

Through international cooperation, states could drastically reduce the incidence of plural nationality by agreeing on an enforceable set of uniform standards by which nationality is acquired and lost. The prospect of any such agreement is highly doubtful, because the perceived domestic interests of states differ widely in defining their respective nationality policies. The most basic division of interests is between those states that receive large inflows of immigrants and those that send out high numbers of emigrants. The former, such as the United States, have the strongest interest in encouraging the effective transfer of allegiances from former homelands to new countries of permanent residence. The latter have traditionally shown the strongest interest in preserving ties of affiliation with their emigrant nationals in order to facilitate their potential return, afford diplomatic protection, maintain inheritance and other rights, or to encourage them to invest financially in their countries of origin. Origin states also have self-interest at stake. Remittances from emigrant nationals have often been important sources of income for these states.[20] However, the nationality policies of different states are governed by other considerations as well, and so do not easily fit into a pattern that this simple dichotomy may suggest.

One of the ironies of U.S. citizenship rules is that prospective American citizens are required to renounce citizenship elsewhere as a condition of naturalization, but on the other hand American citizens by birth cannot be deprived of their citizenship even when they naturalize elsewhere, unless they demand to do so. The first rule is designed to uphold the exclusivity of allegiance to the United States by its citizens, while the second almost ensures a rising incidence of plural nationality. The first rule is exemplified in the oath of loyalty that naturalizing Americans are required to swear "abjur[ing] all allegiance and fidelity to any foreign prince, potentate, state, or sovereignty, of whom or which ... [the individual has] heretofore been a subject or citizen." The second rule has been codified through a series of Supreme Court decisions over the last three decades that have significantly restricted the authority of Congress to revoke U.S. citizenship or expatriate anyone. In reaching these decisions, the Court has emphasized the need to deter statelessness and the high value of American citizenship to its bearers.[21]

Although the loyalty oath that naturalized U.S. citizens are required to swear presumes the exclusivity of state allegiance, the United States government recognizes the de facto status of plural nationality as a practical matter. Thus, for example, the U.S. State Department has included this statement in U.S. passports: "Dual Citizens. A person who has the citizenship of more than one country at the same time is considered a dual citizen. Citizenship may be based on facts of birth, marriage, parentage, or naturalization. A dual citizen may be subject to all of the laws of the other country that considers that person its citizen while in its jurisdiction. This includes conscription for military service. Dual citizens who encounter problems abroad should contact the nearest American Embassy or Consulate."

The formal insistence by the United States on exclusive allegiance in the naturalization process may seem like the hallmark characteristic of a classic land of immigration in which consensual loyalty to a common political creed rather than shared ties of blood and ancestry bind its people together. However, other classic lands of immigration have proven far more tolerant in their formal law of plural nationality than the United States. Canada, for example, requires no loyalty oath from prospective naturalizing citizens and no repudiation by them of prior national allegiances. But it also treats the mere act of naturalizing elsewhere as a sufficient ground for the revocation of Canadian citizenship. As a signatory of the Hague Convention, Australia will revoke citizenship from an Australian over 18 who naturalizes elsewhere, but does not require prospective citizens to swear an exclusive oath of loyalty or renounce prior allegiances. Naturalizing Australians are required to take an oath pledging loyalty to their new country and its democratic principles, but the oath does not stipulate any relinquishment of prior national loyalties. Israel, another major center of immigration, does not require the renunciation of earlier national affiliations to become a citizen or demand as a matter of formal law that Israeli citizens treat their allegiance to Israel as primary. Rather, Israel assumes that no one would accept the considerable

duties of Israeli citizenship, such as military service, if one's highest allegiance were not vested in Israel.

Like Israel, the Russian Federation does not attach legal significance
to the holding of plural citizenship by its citizens. Article 62 of the Russian Federation's Constitution permits a Russian Federation citizen simultaneously to hold the citizenship of a foreign state. The government has
further been considering legislation that permits citizens of foreign states
to acquire Russian Federation citizenship without being required to
renounce their foreign citizenships. One of the clear purposes behind the
legislation is to discourage large-scale repatriation by Russians living
outside the Federation by offering them a guarantee that they will always
be able to settle in the Federation if they choose.

Enforcement of a policy against plural nationality can be an effective
deterrent to naturalization—which, in turn, can pose a major challenge to
societies that have been receiving large numbers of migrants by perpetuating a permanent subclass of aliens. Consider the example of the Federal
Republic of Germany. Almost nine percent of its population are aliens,
but it has long had a policy that naturalization should be the exception
rather the rule. Consistent with this policy, the Federal Republic of Germany has always insisted on expatriation as a condition for naturalization.[22] In justifying this policy, the Federal Republic's Constitutional
Court has also made one of most sweeping contemporary statements
against plural nationality:

> It is accurate to say that dual or multiple nationality is regarded, both domes-
> tically and internationally, as an evil that should be avoided or eliminated in
> the interests of states as well as in the interests of the affected citizen.… States
> seek to achieve exclusivity of their respective nationalities in order to set clear
> boundaries for their sovereignty over persons; they want to be secure in the
> duty of loyalty of their citizens—which extends if necessary as far as risking
> one's life—and do not want to see it endangered by possible conflicts with a
> loyalty to a foreign state (Opinion of German Federal Constitutional Court
> 1974: 254–255).

The Court did not consider whether or not permitting plural nationality
will in the long run facilitate the integration of minorities into German
society and thereby promote a deeper attachment to the Federal Republic. Despite liberalization of its naturalization rules in early 1990s, naturalization rates in the Federal Republic remain low when compared with
many other European states (Clarke, van Dam, and Gooster 1998). Critics
of German naturalization policy point out that liberalization will not be
effective until the prohibition of plural nationality is eliminated.
(Brubaker 1992: 173.)

Whereas receiving states such as Germany traditionally have been
more concerned with issues of allegiance, states of origin have typically
shown a strong interest in extending protection to their nationals abroad,
and these nationals often retain a direct interest in preserving their rights

in their former homelands. In the last decade, for example, sending states, such as the Dominican Republic, Ecuador, Italy, and Colombia have moved to facilitate the retention of their nationality after emigrants acquire a new one. However, as the 1998 amendment to the nationality provisions of the Mexican Constitution illustrates, sending countries can strike a careful balance between protecting the rights of their nationals living abroad and respecting the domestic interests of foreign sovereigns under whom their nationals reside. The change allows naturalized U.S. citizens of Mexican origin to apply for the re-acquisition of Mexican nationality, which permits them to travel on Mexican passports, to guarantee inheritance rights within Mexico, and to own properties in areas where property ownership is restricted from aliens. The change will not confer political rights on Mexican nationals residing in the United States, most especially not the right to vote in Mexican elections. Whether this constitutional amendment will lead to the creation of more Mexican-American dual nationals remains an open question, but the change does foreclose the possibility that third generation Mexican-Americans born in the United States may retain Mexican nationality.

Problems (Real and Imagined) Associated with Dual Nationality

Theoretical arguments can be made that dual nationality is a potential time bomb in a world of nation-states—or to use a different metaphor, dual citizens are walking contradictions. The argument would run as follows. For reasons of administrability and international peace, a regime of nation-states needs to know where individuals belong. Belonging means membership or citizenship. The fundamental rule of the international regime is that states should look after their own, and only their own; to do more is to interfere in the affairs of other states. Persons with no state affiliations (those who are stateless or refugees) are a troubling anomaly: Who is charged, states may ask, with their protection and assistance? To answer that no one is, is to admit the existence of persons outside the state system (hence, we have international conventions on the protection of refugees and promoting the reduction of statelessness in order to bring such persons back within the regime of states).

So, too, persons with two or more state memberships might be seen as causing headaches for states. Which state has the right to demand the citizen's allegiance? Which has the duty to protect? Suppose different states give conflicting orders; which is the dual citizen bound to obey? Assume X is a citizen of States A and B. May (should) State A intervene on X's behalf if it believes that X is being mistreated by State B—or would such intervention violate the "sovereignty" of State B to deal with its citizens as it sees fit (subject, of course, to international human rights obligations)? The "solution" to these problems adopted in the early twentieth century was an international regime dedicated to the proposition of at least one but no more than one citizenship for all (Spiro 1997).

Now, in the next century, we are witnessing a significant increase in dual nationality. There are literally millions—indeed, tens of millions—of persons who live in one state, and are citizens of that state, but who are also subject to the call of another state of which they are also citizens. Either we have a radically altered conception of the singularity of the state-citizen relationship, or we have a large number of accidents waiting to happen. So the argument might run.

Yet, to a remarkable degree dual nationality has not occasioned a noticeable increase in world tensions. The fact that many Israelis are dual nationals is not a cause of the tension in the Middle East; that 25 percent of Australians have more than one nationality has not produced a hot or cold war in Asia. The Mexican constitutional amendment sparked a few media reports and editorials, but not (at least, not yet) a congressional hearing, a plank in a political party platform, or a démarche from the U.S. Department of State. Military service of dual nationals—an issue that produced a mutilateral European convention in 1930—is not even on today's radar screen.

It is unlikely that the significant increases in dual nationality will pass by wholly unnoticed in days ahead. Thus, we can identify several possible points of tension that may arise in the future: (1) voting by dual nationals; (2) office-holding by dual nationals; (3) the "unfair advantage" of dual nationality; and (4) the (in)divisibility of loyalty and community building. We should stress at the outset that while we find these kinds of controversies of intellectual interest, we do not believe that, in the scheme of things, they will represent the major flash points between and among states. Economics, environmental issues, nuclear proliferation, religious fundamentalism, and (closer to home) migration, seem to present far more significant challenges for states.

Voting

Voting by dual nationals raises two separate concerns. First, if the country in which the dual citizen is not residing permits absentee voting, then he or she is entitled to vote in two sets of national elections. Second, it is sometimes supposed that a dual national (particularly one who has been naturalized in the current country of residence) may vote the interests of his or her other country. There is much less to these problems than meets the eye.

As to dual voting, it is hard to see exactly what the nature of the objection is here. Suppose Juan Smith is a citizen of the United States and the Dominican Republic, living in New York. Suppose also that he flies to Santo Domingo on election day to cast a ballot in the Dominican elections, returning to New York the next day. It is arguable that Smith's interest in Dominican elections may take away from the time he can spend thinking about U.S. political issues. Perhaps a more important argument against double voting is, as David Martin has argued, that "[f]ocusing political activity in the place where you live encourages a deeper engagement in the political process—perhaps even civic virtue—and also helps develop affective citizenship and a sense of solidarity" (Martin 1998: 19). Finally, double voting allows someone a vote in a polity in which he is not living and therefore avoids the consequences of the electoral outcome (it is, to adopt Hirschman's terms, voice and exit at the same time [Hirschman 1972]). These objections appear more symbolic than real—as Martin acknowledges (Martin 1998: 21). It is equally likely that those persons who double-vote are more politically engaged in both polities than the usual citizen. Indeed, there is evidence that U.S./Dominican citizens who take an active interest in Dominican politics also are politically active in the United States (Graham 1996). Accordingly, there does not appear to be a zero-sum game here. If, under ideas as old as Aristotle, we believe that participation in politics is a primary goal of citizenship, then it not clear on what basis we should condemn such conduct.

It is true that double nationality allows one to avoid the consequences of one's vote; but this is really an objection to the very idea of dual citizenship—which always endows the dual national with the ability to "flee" to another state if circumstances begin to turn sour in his or her current country of residence. (The phrase "sunshine patriot" springs to mind.) It is plausible that this option may produce less of a community spirit than would be possessed by a mono-national who must deal with the bad times as well as the good, but it seems that dual voting is a minor part of this broader problem (which we address below).

Another objection to dual voting might be that the dual citizen has an extra benefit not afforded a person with only one citizenship: He or she can seek to attain his or her interests by casting ballots in two separate polities. This inequality seems far down on the list of world unfairnesses—certainly below the claim that those with money and resources may exert far more influence in elections than those without.

The second major concern about dual nationality and voting is that a dual citizen might be (too) likely to reflect the interests of one state when voting in the elections of the other. We suppose that this might, under some circumstances, be so—although we are not aware of any empirical evidence either way. However, it seems far more likely that voting is an intensely local affair, reflecting perceived costs and benefits as they pertain to a voter (and perhaps groups with which he or she affiliates) in situ. There is also little reason to suppose that dual nationals vote "the national interest" (of either country) any more than mono-nationals do. Furthermore, if there is a "marching orders" problem, the requirement that dual nationals shed their "foreign" citizenship does not solve it. A citizen of Ecuador who at naturalization in the United States forswears all prior allegiances does not at that moment give up all psychological or cultural attachment to Ecuador. If he or she were inclined to vote "Ecuadorian" interests before naturalization, it is far from clear why he or she would be not so inclined after naturalization. So too, a mono-national may have a significant interest in the affairs of a foreign state whether or not he or she is a citizen (some U.S. citizens of Irish descent and American Jews may be examples). In short, the problem of divided loyalty and the franchise is not peculiar to dual nationals. Rather it appears to be the price of immigration.

Office Holding

Over the past few years, several naturalized U.S. citizens have returned to their native lands in Eastern European states to assume high govern-ment posts.[23] Under these circumstances it may begin to make sense to talk about a possible conflict of loyalties (Schuck 1998: 245–246; Aleinikoff 1986). Interestingly, however, the domestic politics of the home state usu-ally produces a dénouement, leading each of these government officials to announce his intention to renounce U.S. citizenship.

Unfair Advantage over Non-citizens (the "Exit" Option)

Robert Frost, in his poem "The Death of the Hired Man," defined home as "the place where, when you have to go there, / They have to take you in." In this sense, dual nationals have two homes because, under interna-tional law, states must permit their nationals free ingress to state terri-tory—and dual nationals are likely to possess two passports to facilitate inter-state travel. A dual national, then, has an exit option that mono-nationals do not: When times get tough in one state the dual citizen can move to the other state. Not only might this be said to give dual citizens an "unfair advantage" over mono-nationals, it might also cause the dual national to take less interest in contributing to the solution of problems in his or her current state of residence.

Again, it would be difficult to acquire evidence one way or the other on this point. However, whether or not there is some factual support for dual citizens voting with their feet, such movement is not likely to cause or increase inter-state tensions. They will not come close to the tensions induced by the large-scale movements of persons we regularly witness in migrant and refugee flows around the world.

The (In)divisibility of Loyalty

We might be correct about everything we have said so far and still be accused of not getting to the heart of the matter. The issue, some might argue, is not material or electoral, but rather symbolic. In a world divided among competitive and mutually exclusive nation-states, we need ulti-mately to know which side everyone is on. The domestic laws of western-style democracies prohibit bigamy—not for economic reasons, but because of our belief that certain relationships, to be true and successful, cannot be plural. Many would argue that citizenship is one such relationship, based on the following kind of considerations: Nation-states are increasingly fragile entities, under attack from both supra- and subnational forces. To maintain their efficacy they need members willing to contribute to, perhaps even sacrifice for, a common good. That kind of commitment can be watered down and rendered too weak if it is not made exclusive. Just as persons do not belong to two religions or two political parties, so too it is sensible to affirm loyalty to a single state. The power of this line of argument need not appeal only to strong nationalists, who see in the state the embodiment of a national identity or ideology.

Communitarians who seek to promote national policies addressing, say, deep inequalities in a state may find such programs achievable only if persons and groups are fully committed to the welfare of all within state territory; again, such commitment may require the kind of identification with a polity that is not indivisible.

From this perspective, dual nationality is not so much a problem between states as within one state. It might be seen as sapping the national commitment that states need and have a right to demand of their citizens. The problem with this argument, however, is that it is probably false—at least at current levels of dual nationality. Whatever decline we are witnessing in civic commitment and pride, no one has made the case that dual nationality is the cause. Rather, it appears to be a problem with the institution of citizenship itself, caused perhaps by a number of late twentieth-century phenomena. Indeed, persons who attain dual nationality through naturalization in the United States have shown a fair degree of commitment—a degree not required of the (sometimes alienated, take-citizenship-for-granted) native-born. Those who are dual citizens at birth might feel the tug of two nationalities. But they are considerably more likely to feel committed (at whatever level) to the place of their birth and continued residence. Does the existence of a second citizenship undermine the first to the point of endangering the state? If that be so, there is a disease in the polity that is probably afflicting all citizens, not just dual nationals.

At the most extreme, some worry that dual nationals will form a potentially dangerous "Fifth Column" committed to subverting the domestic politics of their country of residence. Alternatively, might country X use the presence of its nationals in country Y as a pretext to intervene? Searching the historical record it is difficult to find examples to support such fears. It is comparatively easy, however, to point to examples where national minorities with no legal affiliation to an outside power worked for the cause of that power. One such classic example is the German minority in Czechoslovakia during the 1930s. That minority had no formal affiliation with Germany—they had been part of the Austrian-Hungarian Empire and not the German Empire. Hitler never claimed that they had any legal status as dual nationals of his Reich or proposed such a status as a pretext for intervention. The German minority in Czechoslovakia may have understood themselves to be German as a matter of ancestry and culture, but not because of any shared legal affiliation with citizens of the Reich.

Likewise, in deciding to intern Japanese-Americans, suspicion about their presumed divided loyalties was directed at their ethnic ancestry and not their legal status. Plural nationality as a legal matter, as a conflict between formal obligations to different states, never emerged in the debate. The federal government did not distinguish between "citizens," "dual citizens," or "permanent residents" in launching its internment policy. In choosing to target Japanese-Americans for internment as opposed to German-Americans or Italian-Americans, the criterion was not the perceived relative threat to national security. Arguably, German-Americans and the German naval war posed more of an immediate threat to the United States than Japan and Japanese-Americans even in the wake of the attack on Pearl Harbor. Rather, perceptions of race and the greater political muscle of German-Americans and Italian-Americans made the crucial difference in internment policy (Report of the Commission 1997: 286–287).

If we consider in our own time the tragedy of ethnic cleansing that has broken out in such places as the former Yugoslavia and Rwanda, the legal status of the victims, whether they be citizens, dual citizens, or permanent residents, is never the stated pretext for acting against them. The cause that triggers these conflicts is always rooted in more concrete differences of ethnicity, caste, and religion. Legal status is often sadly irrelevant.

The Acquisition of Nationality for Commerce and/or Convenience

The Caribbean islands of Dominica, Grenada, and St. Kitts/Nevis all offer second passports for investments ranging from $50,000 to $250,000 without requiring any enduring residential or familial ties. The selling of nationality unquestionably cheapens its value as a form of allegiance, but no one knows how frequently this practice occurs and its long-term consequences remain unclear. If evidence emerges that these consequences are becoming a serious problem, then concerned states will always have the option to discourage this practice through diplomatic means.

This example may be extreme, but it may also point to an emerging trend in which individuals are able to purchase or otherwise acquire second and third nationalities without any substantial connection with the state conferring it. This acquisition without a substantial connection may occur in less extreme ways—for example under some versions of *jus sanguinis* rules, children are able to inherit the nationality of their parents even when neither generation has preserved or established any concrete relationship with the state in question. The emerging consensus in international law suggests that some sort of substantial connection should tie the individual to the state of which he or she is a national. Nationality should not become a commodity that individuals can purchase to further their business or personal interests for purely instrumental reasons. However, there is no clear means available at present to prevent or discourage states like the Commonwealth of Dominica from selling nationality as a commodity.

* * * *

Dual nationality is a product of the movement and settlement of people across state boundaries. In a world of nation-states, state members located beyond state borders present complications for inter-state relations. One might suppose that membership in two states makes things only more complicated. But we have suggested above that the problems of dual nationality, while real, are hardly likely fundamentally to subvert the international order. Indeed, if the movement of peoples across state borders presents problems, the fact that some of those persons might have two nationalities appears to add suprisingly little to inter-state relations. Why might this be so?

First, like politics, the practice of citizenship tends to be local. That is, most citizens are most concerned about events immediately before them: schools, local crime, traffic, drugs, the cost of housing, the availability of day-care. On these issues, it matters little whether a Mexican-American has one or two nationalities—or indeed whether he or she votes in elections in both the United States and Mexico.

Second, it is difficult to identify situations around the world where tensions approaching hostilities exist among nations with significant numbers of shared dual nationals. Australia and China are not on the verge of war; nor are the United States and Mexico, or Israel and the United States. Indeed, it may well run just the other way: The increasing ties among the populations of such paired states may create greater opportunities for peaceful interactions.

Third, the number of dual nationals is dwarfed by the number of cross-border migrants and refugees. Conceding, for the sake of argument, that such "out-of-state" persons create tensions and complications on the world scene, the relatively small number of dual nationals is hardly likely to be noticed. Put another way, states will be concerned about the treatment of their nationals residing in other states, whether or not those nationals have the citizenship of the other state.

Fourth, dual nationality appears more as an individual than as a group phenomenon. Most persons acquire dual nationality as an accident of birth—being born in one state to a parent or parents who are citizens of another state. The nationality passed on by the parents may have little real meaning to the dual national, other than giving him or her a sense of ethnicity or a romantic tie to a distant homeland. To be sure, those emotions can be mobilized at times (although so can the ethnic ties of persons with just one citizenship). Generally, however, lives are lived locally, and one's second nationality is more an aspect of identity than of practice. Perhaps the recent Mexican constitutional amendment could be viewed as the exception that proves the rule. The amendment might be seen, in part, as an attempt to assert a group-based dual nationality: One of its aims was to remove a disincentive to naturalization in the United States so that more Mexicans would naturalize and thereby obtain political rights in the United States that could be used to protect their interests. As noted earlier, there is, at this point, no evidence that the amendment has had an impact on Mexican naturalization rates; and indeed suprisingly few Mexicans who had naturalized in the United States have returned to U.S. Mexican consulates to reclaim Mexican nationality. Thus, even here, the concerns about dual nationality—at least for now—appear to be more symbolic and theoretical than real.

Conclusion: Prospects and Proposals

It is perhaps curious that we do not have an international regime that defines and regulates citizenship.[24] One might suppose that a system of nation-states would require firm, agreed-upon rules as to who belongs where; these decisions have been left, under international law, largely to the states themselves. The Universal Declaration of Human Rights may declare that "[e]veryone has a right to a nationality" (Article 15[1]); but international law does not pervasively regulate how citizenship may be acquired or lost, or how the issue of multiple citizenships should be resolved.

This is not to suggest that, were the international community to derive a set of rules or standards on dual nationality, such norms would seek to limit or prevent multiple citizenships. It does mean that the current sets of arrangements are largely the result of the (non-coordinated) decisions of individual states. These local citizenship rules are usually grounded in particular historical narratives about the state—for example, slavery in the United States, the idea of German nationality, Canada as a country of immigration and the Quebec issue—and perceived current needs—such as recent decisions by states to permit citizens to retain nationality despite naturalization elsewhere. Little reason exists to expect that such policies would yield a coherent whole at the world level. Indeed, there is good reason to believe that the goals of various states will not be compatible: "sending" states may adopt policies that create tensions for "receiving" states (witness reaction in the United States to the recent Mexican constitutional amendment); states with descent-based concepts of citizenship may embrace norms that conflict with norms of *jus soli* states.

In such a world, dual nationality results more from the overlap of differing rules than from any overall plan. It thus creates an area of potential conflict between and among states as each pursues its individual goals with little concern for system-wide effects. Economists might say that the world system does little to internalize the externalities of state citizenship norms.

What does this mean for the future? We are not prepared to make a firm prediction, but there appears to be little cause for serious concern. In all likelihood, dual nationality will continue to increase due to high levels of immigration, changes in state policies, and the continuation of both *jus sanguinis* and *jus soli* citizenship norms. In some states at some point, there will be backlashes against dual nationality: Nationalistic groups will condemn plural citizenship as undermining state strength and identity. However, the rise and apparent decline of Le Pen in France and Hanson in Australia may indicate that the majority of the populations in these states see no necessary conflict between dual nationality and loyalty. One can add to these the fairly remarkable proposals from the new Schroeder government in Germany which, although ultimately adopted in more modest form, constituted a dramatic shift in traditional German thinking on the issues. All told, we can see a world decidedly more tolerant of dual nationality than in the past.

If it is believed that increasing levels of dual nationality may contribute to inter-state or intra-state tensions, then various proposals might be entertained. David Martin has made several suggestions that are worthy of consideration, including the adoption of norms that permit dual nationals to vote only in the state in which they are residing, that require dual nationals who assume policy-level government positions to relinquish other nationalities, and that limit the indefinite continuation of nationality for future generations outside a state if a family has lost a genuine link with the state (Martin 1998).[25] Whether or not one agrees with these proposals, it is apparent that they tinker at the margins. Martin is not proposing a world of mono-nationals or international conventions that point us in that direction.

Notes

An abstract of this chapter appeared in *Research Perspectives on Migration* II: 2 (1999).

1. Nationality and citizenship are often treated as different sides of the same coin. Although any generalization here requires considerable simplification, nationality refers to a membership status and citizenship concerns the rights and duties connected with that status. For example, citizens of the European Union do not have a common nationality status. They are EU citizens (with rights to vote in European elections etc.), but nationals of their member states. As a general rule, when a person naturalizes, he or she acquires both nationality and citizenship simultaneously.

2. This obligation is grounded on the premise that a ceding state's refusal to withdraw nationality is tantamount to a state's imposing nationality on a foreign national residing outside of its territory. By this refusal, the ceding state has an "extraterritorial effect" on persons outside its territorial jurisdiction, and this effect can only be binding if the state of residence has given its consent because it has supreme authority within its own jurisdiction.

3. Article 17 of the Hague Convention (discussed below) provides that adopted children can only lose their original nationality on the condition that they receive their parent[s]' nationality. This Convention and its Protocols have been collected in Plender (1997).
4. Article 6 of the Hague Convention (discussed below) provides that "a person possessing two nationalities acquired without any voluntary act on his part may renounce one of them with the authorization of the State whose nationality he desires to surrender. This authorization may not be refused in the case of a person who has his habitual and principal residence abroad, if the conditions laid down in the law of the State whose nationality he desires to surrender are satisfied."
5. Articles 8–10 of the Hague Convention (discussed below) provide that wives should be deprived of their original nationality only on the condition that they acquire their husbands' and that wives cannot be forced to change their nationality should their husbands be naturalized.
6. With respect to conflicts over taxation, comparatively few have reached international tribunals. The practical constraints facing a state trying to tax a national who lives outside the state's jurisdiction and has no property within the jurisdiction discourage such conflicts from arising.
7. Article 4 of the Hague Convention (discussed below) stipulates: "A State may not afford diplomatic protection to one of its nationals against a State whose nationality such person also possesses."
8. This treaty is still in force (Donner 1994: 43).
9. Appended to the 1930 Hague Convention.
10. Similarly, the 1963 European Convention (as amended by additional protocol in the same year) resolved conflicts over military service for plural nationals.
11. The Hague Convention's protocol also recognizes that "every person should have a nationality."
12. The Preamble describes the Declaration as setting forth "a common standard of achievement for all peoples and nations …" which will "promote a common understanding of these rights and freedoms."
13. The Convention reiterates and expands on the principle enunciated in the 1961 Convention on the Reduction of Statelessness that provides: "A Contracting State may not deprive any person or group of persons of their nationality on racial, ethnic, religious or political grounds" (Article 9).
14. The 1989 Convention on the Rights of the Child recognizes a child's independent right to nationality. Article 7(1) provides that "The child shall be registered immediately after birth and shall have the right from birth to a name, the right to acquire a nationality…." Article 8(1) provides further that "State Parties undertake further to respect the right of the child to preserve his or her identity, including nationality … without lawful interference."
15. One of the primary objectives of the Hague Convention was to limit statelessness. Many of its provisions condition any loss of nationality on the acquisition of another nationality. The broader aim of the Hague Conference, which was sponsored by the League of Nations, was to promote the codification of international legal rules.
16. The Convention has been ratified by: Australia, Belgium (with reservations), Brazil (with reservations), Canada, China (with reservations), Great Britain, India, Monaco, the Netherlands (with reservations), Norway, Pakistan, Poland, and Sweden. It has been signed by 27 states.

17. Eugene Goldstein and Victoria Piazza have published the results of a survey on dual citizenship. One hundred twenty-eight countries responded to the survey question, If a citizen of (the country in question) acquires U.S. citizenship, does he or she retain or lose (the country in question's) citizenship? Of that number, sixty-two countries answered that their citizens would retain their citizenship, though some sort of procedure might need to be satisfied to do so (Goldstein and Piazza 1998).

18. As of this writing, 17 states have signed this treaty, but only Austria and Slovakia have ratified it.

19. "The principle, based on the sovereign equality of States, which excludes diplomatic protection in the case of dual nationality, must yield before the principle of effective nationality whenever such nationality is that of the claiming State" (p. 247). The case involved a claimant who sought compensation for property in Italy that had been lost during the Second World War. The claimant had been born in the United States, and so had U.S. citizenship. However, she also had acquired Italian nationality through marriage to an Italian citizen. The conciliation commission denied her claim on the grounds that she did not have substantial enough ties with the United States to be considered to hold dominant U.S. nationality since for many years she had not held habitual residence there or had professional ties with U.S. interests. The commission supported the Italian government's position that as an Italian national she could not assert a claim against it under the cover of another state's diplomatic protection.

20. Migrant-receiving states also have self-interest at stake. Immigrants often provide important means to fill labor market niches and to moderate demographic imbalances in aging developed societies.

21. See, for example, *Afroyim v. Rusk* (1967) and *Vance v. Terrazas* (1980).

22. Although it too has found it necessary to make exceptions for those foreign nationals whose countries do not recognize expatriation.

23. For example, Valdas Adamkus, a naturalized U.S. citizen who had served as a Regional Administrator for the Environmental Protection Agency, assumed the presidency of Lithuania in 1998. A day before his swearing-in, he formally renounced his U.S. citizenship.

24. In the United States, citizenship policy was largely left to the individual states for the first 75 years of the nation's existence because of the difficulties arising from the slavery question. The Supreme Court's 1857 decision in *Dred Scott* was a disastrous intervention in the citizenship debate that was soon overcome by the Civil War. The basis of modern U.S. citizenship law is the Fourteenth Amendment, which overturned *Dred Scott* and finally provided a constitutional definition of citizenship (Kettner 1978).

25. Other scholars are equally tolerant of dual nationality (Schuck 1998; Spiro 1997).

References

Afroyim v. Rusk. 1967. 387 U.S. 253.

Aleinikoff, T. Alexander. 1986. "Theories of Loss of Citizenship." *Michigan Law Review* 84: 1471–1503.

———. 1998. *Between Principles and Politics: The Direction of U.S. Citizenship Policy.* Washington, D.C.: Brookings Institution Press.

Brownlie, Ian, ed. 1992. *Basic Documents on Human Rights* (3rd edition, rev.). New York: Clarendon Press.

Brubaker, Rogers. 1992. *Citizenship and Nationhood in France and Germany.* Cambridge MA: Harvard University Press.

Clarke, James, Elsbeth van Dam, and Liz Gooster. 1998. "New Europeans: Naturalisation and Citizenship in Europe." *Citizenship Studies* 2(1): 43–67.

Convention Establishing the Status of Naturalized Citizens. 1906 (1913). *American Journal of International Law* 7:4 (Supp.): 226–229.

Convention on Certain Questions Relating to the Conflict of Nationality Laws [Hague Convention]. 1930. 179 L.N.T.S. 89. Reprinted in Plender 1997: 85–92.

Convention on the Elimination of All Forms of Discrimination against Women. 1979. 1249 U.N.T.S. 13, entered into force, 3 Sept. 1981. Reprinted in Brownlie 1992: 169–181.

Convention on the Nationality of Married Women. 1957. 309 U.N.T.S. 65, entered into force, 11 Aug. 1958. Reprinted in Plender 1997: 119–123.

Convention on the Reduction of Statelessness. 1961. 989 U.N.T.S. 175, entered into force, 13 Dec. 1975. Reprinted in Plender 1997: 123–130.

Convention on the Rights of the Child. 1989. Dec. A/Res/44/25, entered into force, 2 Sept. 1990. Reprinted in Brownlie, 1992: 182–202.

Donner, Ruth. 1994. *The Regulation of Nationality in International Law.* Irvington-on-the-Hudson, NY: Transnational Publishers, Inc.

European Convention on Nationality. 1998. *International Legal Materials* 37: 44.

Goldstein, Eugene, and Victoria Piazza. 1998. "Naturalization, Dual Citizenship and Retention of Foreign Citizenship: A Survey." *Interpreter Releases* 75(45): 1629–1632.

Graham, Pamela M. 1996. "Re-Imagining the Nation and Defining the District: The Simultaneous Political Incorporation of Dominican Transnational Migrants." Unpublished doctoral dissertation, University of North Carolina, Chapel Hill.

Hirschman, Albert O. 1972. *Exit, Voice and Loyalty: Responses to Decline in Firms, Organizations and States.* Cambridge, MA: Harvard University Press.

International Convention on the Elimination of All Forms of Racial Discrimination. 1966. 660 U.N.T.S. 195. Reprinted in Brownlie 1992: 148–161.

Iran-United States Claim Tribunal. 1984. No. A/18 Concerning the Question of Jurisdiction Over Claims of Persons with Dual Nationality, 23 International Legal Materials 489.

Kettner, James H. 1978. *The Development of American Citizenship, 1608–1870.* Chapel Hill, N.C.: University of North Carolina Press.

Liechtenstein v. Guatemala. 1955. [Nottebohm Case], 4 I.C.J 4-65.

Martin, David. 1998. *New Rules on Dual Nationality for a Democratizing Globe: Between Rejection and Embrace.* Document No. 19, CEPIC/FSNP/France.

Paris: CEPIC/FSNP International Conference on Nationality Law, Immigration and Integration in Europe and the USA.

Mergé Case. 1955. 14 R.I.A.A. 236, 247.

Opinion of German Federal Constitutional Court. 1974. Pp. 254–255.

Plender, Richard. 1997. *Basic Documents on International Migration Law.* 2nd ed., rev. Boston: Martinus Nijhoff Publishers.

Protocol Relating to Military Obligations in Certain Cases of Double Nationality. 1930. 179 L.N.T.S. 15, entered into force, 1 July 1937. Reprinted in Plender 1997: 93–96.

Report of the Commission on Wartime Relocation and Internment of Civilians. 1997. "Personal Justice Denied." Seattle: The Civil Liberties Public Education Fund and University of Washington Press.

Schuck, Peter H. 1998. *Citizens, Strangers, and In-Betweens.* Boulder, CO: Westview Press.

Spiro, Peter J. 1997. "Dual Nationality and the Meaning of Citizenship." *Emory Law Journal* 46: 1412–1485.

Universal Declaration of Human Rights. 1948. Reprinted in Brownlie 1992: 21–27.

Vance v. Terrazas. 1980. 444 U.S. 252.

Weis, P. 1979. *Nationality and Statelessness in International Law.* Germantown, MD: Sitjthoff and Noordhoff.

CHAPTER 6

Migration and Foreign Policy: Emerging Bilateral and Regional Approaches in the Americas

Susan Martin

Perhaps never before in history has international migration played as important a role in the foreign policy arena as it now does. Historically treated almost exclusively as a domestic policy matter, immigration's impact on international relations received little attention within or outside of government.[1] During the 1990s, however, immigration continually has crept onto foreign policy agendas, particularly in the context of discussions about regional economic and political integration.

The European Union has had the longest experience in this respect. Free movement of labor within the European Community first came into force in 1968. During recent years, however, discussions turned to broader themes raised by a common immigration policy. Debate about visa policy is a case in point. The intergovernmental Schengen Agreement, originally signed by five EU members in 1985, called for the abolition of internal borders between member states, largely to facilitate trade by reducing long waits at border crossings. The agreement contained the first provisions for the establishment of a single "Schengen visa" for travel throughout most of Western Europe. The 1991 Maastricht Treaty on European Union defined a common European visa policy as essential for the realization of the Union's long-term goal of establishing a single market in goods, capital, and labor. The later Amsterdam Treaty (1997) included the Schengen Agreement in the EU's formal political architecture. Five years after the treaty's entry into force,[2] it is envisioned that decisions on visa issuance will be decided by majority vote.

Less developed multilateral approaches to migration are to be found in other regions, some arising from the migration ramifications of economic integration and others focusing on alien trafficking, illegal migration, mass migration emergencies, and other security concerns related to large-scale movements of people. As an example of the former, the Asia-Pacific Economic Cooperation (APEC) Committee on Trade and Investment, spurred by the Business Advisory Council, has overseen the exchange of information on business visa requirements and is identifying mechanisms for regional cooperation to facilitate mobility. Under review are proposals for multiple entry visas, visa waiver arrangements, travel passes, harmonization of entry conditions, and information sharing and systems training for border management agencies (Luther 1998).

A regional process with a security focus stems from the regional conference on forced displacement in the Commonwealth of Independent States (CIS). In 1994, countries in the region requested the UN High Commissioner for Refugees, in combination with the International Organization for Migration and the Organization for Security and Cooperation in Europe, to provide a neutral and non-political forum for discussing refugee and migration issues, establishing a better understanding of the scale of population displacements, and devising a comprehensive strategy at the national, regional, and international levels to cope with problems arising from population movements. Recognizing that excessive migration within the CIS could disrupt the region's fragile economies and political stability, the conference prompted a range of initiatives, including projects to promote tolerance and prevent the type of violence that causes mass migration, although progress has been slow in funding and implementing them (UNHCR 1997).

The regional implications of migration for both economic and security interests has prompted a range of bilateral, regional, and hemispheric initiatives in the Americas, the focus of this chapter. The migration ramifications of Hurricane Mitch (1998) and the deportation of criminal aliens placed immigration matters squarely on the agenda of summit meetings in Central America. Immigration remains one of the most discussed issues on the U.S.-Mexico bilateral agenda, with only trade and drug trafficking matching it in importance. Because migration is not only controversial in itself but is connected with such diverse issues as international trade, drug smuggling, and ecological emergencies, discussion of these matters can be delicate, to say the least.

The agenda for discussion is complex, with issues ranging from control of unauthorized migration and deportation of migrants to regulation of legal crossings and issues of dual citizenship and absentee voting. The bilateral and regional mechanisms recognize that international migration proceeds from a set of complicated factors involving more than one country: push/supply forces in countries of origin that propel people to leave; pull/demand forces in countries of destination that attract would-be migrants; and the formal and informal networks that link the supply of workers with the demand of employers and often lead migrants to transit one country to reach another. Immigration cannot be managed properly unless all parts of this equation are taken into account. Hence, unilateral actions on the part of either receiving or source countries are unlikely fully to succeed in curbing emigration or immigration pressures. At the same time, such actions can have seriously damaging effects on bilateral relations and stymie efforts to build regional agreements on trade and other issues.

This chapter discusses four arenas in the Americas in which migration issues are addressed in a manner that recognizes their foreign policy implications. It begins with the North American Free Trade Agreement (NAFTA), which gave treaty status to specific immigration-related provisions, but, more importantly, set the tone for a new spirit of cooperation between the United States and Mexico. Next it discusses the U.S.-Mexico Binational Commission and the various other bilateral consultative mechanisms focusing on migration between the two countries. The chapter then moves to regional mechanisms, highlighting the so-called Puebla Process that involves the countries of North America, Central America, and the Dominican Republic. Finally, the treatment of migration issues within the Summit of the Americas is discussed.

NAFTA

The North American Free Trade Agreement has several important linkages to international migration. First, and most direct, NAFTA includes specific migration provisions affecting movements among the signatory countries. Second, proponents of NAFTA in both countries heralded it as a mechanism to reduce long-term emigration pressures in Mexico. Third, and most significant for the purposes of this chapter, NAFTA has provided an environment for constructive engagement, rather than endless recriminations, by Mexico and the United States in addressing migration issues of mutual concern. These three aspects of NAFTA will be discussed in turn.

During the NAFTA negotiations, immigration was largely off the table. The trade negotiators in all three countries understood that including provisions for the freer mobility of labor could well have spelled the demise of the treaty itself. Putting immigration issues squarely on the agenda also would have been inconsistent with broader U.S. trade policy. As an official of the office of the U.S. Trade Representative explained, "the exclusion of this issue from NAFTA negotiations is not unique; the free mobility of labor has never been negotiated as part of any trade agreement to which the United States is a party, including the current and previous rounds of the General Agreement on Tariffs and Trade (GATT) negotiations and the U.S.-Canada Free Trade Agreement" (U.S. GAO 1993: 125).

Although far from guaranteeing the free mobility of labor, the U.S.-Canada Free Trade Agreement (CFTA) had included several immigration-related provisions pertaining to the temporary entry of business persons that were included in NAFTA with some modifications. A "business person" is defined as "a citizen of a Party [to NAFTA] who is engaged in trade in goods, the provision of services or the conduct of investment activities."

Four categories of business persons are included: business visitors, traders and investors, intra-company transfers, and professionals.

Business visitors: Each Party to NAFTA is obliged to grant temporary admission to business persons seeking to engage in business activities related to research and design, growth, manufacture and production, marketing, sales, distribution, after-sales services, and other general services. Visas may be required (although in the case of Canada and the United States, no visa is needed); no numerical requirements may be imposed. The provisions are similar to those already in U.S. law under the B-1 visa category in the Immigration and Nationality Act (INA). Business visitors must present proof of citizenship of a NAFTA Party, documentation of the business activity in which the applicant for entry will be engaged, and evidence that the applicant is not seeking entry into the local labor market (generally by showing that his or her remuneration comes from outside the territory of the NAFTA Party granting entry).

Traders and investors: NAFTA permits temporary entry of traders who wish to carry on substantial trade in goods and services between their own country and another NAFTA Party. Also permitted is the temporary entry of investors seeking to commit a substantial amount of capital, provided that the persons seeking entry are in a supervisory or executive position or one that involves essential skills. In effect, NAFTA extended the E-1 (treaty trader) and E-2 (treaty investor) provisions of the Immigration and Nationality Act (INA) to Mexico, which was not previously covered because there was no bilateral treaty as required by the INA. Both Mexican and Canadian citizens must obtain visas, which are issued for five years and are renewable without any time limit. Having received the visa, the traders and investors are admitted for an initial one-year period and may be granted extensions of stay in two-year increments.[3] As in the next two categories, admission may be barred if the Secretary of Labor certifies that a strike or other work stoppage is occurring.

Intra-company transferees: NAFTA permits transfer of personnel already employed by a company in a managerial or executive capacity or one that involves specialized knowledge. The transferee must have worked for the employer at least one year abroad in the previous three years. The business may be a subsidiary or affiliate of the employer in the foreign country. This provision mirrors the L-1 intra-company transferee provision already in U.S. law. The Canadian or Mexican citizen transferring to the United States to take part in a new operation may be admitted for one year. Those transferring to offices in existence for one year or more may be admitted for three years. An extension of stay may be authorized in increments of up to two years to a maximum of five years for transferees with specialized knowledge and seven years for those in managerial or executive positions.

Professional workers: Certain professionals who meet minimum educational standards or who possess alternative credentials may enter under NAFTA provisions. To qualify, the applicant must possess credentials included in a list of about 60 professions. The applicant must generally possess a bachelor's degree and, if required, fulfill all licensing criteria. An employer must certify that the foreign worker is so qualified and is coming to a position which requires such a professional. The CFTA continues to guide admission requirements for Canadians: no visas are required; nor are labor market tests made. There are no numerical limits. Admission is for a one-year period but may be renewed indefinitely. NAFTA departs from the CFTA in that admission of spouses and children is permitted.

The provisions for Mexicans differ in several respects. Mexicans require a visa, and no more than 5,500 visas may be issued each year. The limit can be increased by agreement between Mexico and the United States and will automatically expire at the end of 2003. Companies seeking to employ Mexican professionals must file a labor condition attestation (LCA) specifying that prevailing wages will be paid, working conditions for the foreign worker will not adversely affect working conditions for similarly situated U.S. workers, there is no strike or lockout in the course of a labor dispute, and notice has been posted that the LCA has been filed. These requirements are modeled on the existing H-1B visa category for admission of specialty workers.

These provisions received relatively little attention in the debate about NAFTA. Although some labor unions protested that the provisions of entry of business visitors and professionals were too encompassing, the General Accounting Office summarized the prevailing view that "the agreement will allow the United States (1) to fully maintain its rights to protect the permanent employment base of its domestic labor force; (2) to implement its own immigration policies; and (3) to protect the security of its borders" (U.S. GAO 1993: 125).

This summation did not fully capture the situation, however. Significantly, these provisions now exist in treaty, not just in domestic law. A similar development occurred in the General Agreement on Trade and Services (GATS), which includes elements of the H-1B and L visas, setting minimum standards for admission of foreign professionals and executives. Having been ratified in these agreements, the flexibility to change the provisions is substantially reduced; the other parties to the agreements must acquiesce to the changes. Moreover, trade negotiators are not necessarily well enough informed about immigration policy to make decisions on what to include in the treaty. One critic of the practice summarized the potential problem: "Offering such 'concessions' in the context of a trade accord … is a bad precedent which dates only to the U.S./CTFA. In the hands of U.S. trade negotiators, availability of this provision becomes one more item to 'trade' for anything which they see as more important from a narrow trade perspective" (Papademetriou 1993: 21).

The GAO reflected the thinking of the time, however, that the immigration provisions in NAFTA merited little discussion. Far more prevalent was discussion about the effects of NAFTA on illegal migration from Mexico to the United States. The Bush administration argued that one important benefit of NAFTA was to decrease emigration pressures in Mexico. Concluding that NAFTA would raise Mexican wages and standards of living, the administration held that there would be decreased pressure for illegal immigration to the United States. The Clinton administration echoed the same theme, with Attorney General Janet Reno noting in an opinion piece in the Los Angeles Times: "Our best chance to reduce illegal immigration is sustained, robust Mexican economic growth. That is why passage of the NAFTA will help me protect our borders" (Papademetriou 1993: 10). Mexico made the same argument. President Salinas held that "more jobs will mean higher wages in Mexico, and this in turn will mean fewer migrants to the United States and Canada. We want to export goods, not people" (Martin 1993: 1). In more colorful language, Salinas cited his preference for Mexico to export tomatoes instead of tomato pickers.

Academicians exploring the relationship between NAFTA and emigration from Mexico tended to agree that economic development was the best long-term solution to illegal migration. Almost uniformly, however, they cautioned that emigration pressures were likely to remain and, possibly, increase before the long-term benefits accrued. In its final report to Congress in 1990, the U.S. Commission for the Study of International Migration and Cooperative Economic Development, a proponent of free trade, had described this seeming paradox: "The transformations intrinsic to the development process are at first destabilizing. They initially promote rather than impede migration. Better communications and transportation and other improvements in the quality of life of people working hard to make a living raise expectations and enhance their ability to migrate" (U.S. Commission 1990).

Several researchers posited what economist Philip Martin referred to as an "immigration hump," in reference to the proposition that, as levels of income rise, emigration would at first increase, then peak and decline, a relationship that is depicted graphically as an inverted U (Acevedo and Espenshade 1992; Cornelius and Martin 1993). Martin argued that short-term dislocations in the agricultural sector, in combination with continued pull of U.S. jobs and networks to link Mexican workers with those jobs, would increase illegal immigration. He concluded, however, that the issue was one of timing, since illegal migration would otherwise continue indefinitely: Despite the migration hump, "there will be less Mexico-to-U.S. migration over the next two decades with NAFTA than without NAFTA" (Martin 1993: 7).

Others believed that the evidence of a "hump" was highly speculative but agreed that NAFTA would reduce long-term emigration pressures. Demetrios Papademetriou, testifying at a congressional hearing, argued that

> there is no simple response to the concern about how the NAFTA might affect illegal immigration. We can safely assume, however, that even under the most

favorable NAFTA scenario (from Mexico's perspective) it will take Mexico considerable time to bring its un- and under-employment problems under control. During that time, it is indeed likely that some of the Mexicans who will by then have entered the Mexican internal migration stream will seek to enter the U.S. illegally and obtain unauthorized employment. What is even more clear, however, is that absent a successful conclusion of the NAFTA, the transitional period ... will be drawn out tremendously—with more consequential illegal immigration repercussions for the United States. (Papademetriou 1993: 12)

What is important for the purposes of this chapter is not the arguments themselves but the extent to which NAFTA placed immigration on a new footing in U.S.-Mexican relations. In both the policy and research communities, NAFTA fostered discussion of bilateral approaches to ease migration pressures and manage migration between the two countries. Previously, the debate within the United States about Mexican migration focused almost exclusively on unilateral actions that it could take to improve its border controls or reduce the lure of employment. In arguing that unauthorized migration stemmed primarily from the demands of U.S. employers, Mexicans also held that the United States had the principal responsibility for curtailing movements. Although border and worksite enforcement issues remained the principal focus of migration policy, NAFTA permitted consideration of other, more cooperative strategies.

NAFTA also shifted the tone of the U.S.-Mexico debate over immigration. A binational study team examining U.S. and Mexican responses to migration concluded:

The bilateral interaction on migration issues has altered in recent years from a lack of consultation to considerable discussion between the two governments. Negotiating NAFTA required a shift in bilateral political relations. Mexico's earlier reflexive opposition to U.S. international initiatives has given way to a more cooperative relationship. The United States gave political relations with Mexico a higher profile, and showed increased receptivity to Mexican overtures. (Mexico-U.S. Binational Study 1997: 61)

In effect, NAFTA introduced a far friendlier environment for discussion of controversial issues. Further, as the economies of Mexico and the United States grow more intertwined, the impetus to resolve such issues in a mutually beneficial way grows as well.

U.S.-Mexico Bilateral Mechanisms

A byproduct of NAFTA has been the strengthening of a range of bilateral mechanisms through which the United States and Mexico address immigration matters. The primary forum for increased communication and coordination is the Working Group on Migration and Consular Affairs of the U.S.-Mexico Binational Commission. The Binational Commission was created in the late 1970s by Presidents Carter and Lopez Portillo, and meets annually. It currently has more than a dozen working groups that meet throughout the year.

The Working Group on Migration and Consular Affairs was created in 1987. It is co-chaired by the Commissioner of the Immigration and Naturalization Service and Assistant Secretary of State for Consular Affairs, on the U.S. side, and the Under Secretary for Bilateral Affairs in the Secretariat of Foreign Affairs and the Under Secretary for Migration in the Secretariat for Government Affairs (Gobernación), on the Mexican side. The agenda includes such issues as consular protection, facilitation of legal movements, increased border cooperation, cooperative research initiatives, efforts against migrant trafficking, and migration legislation and policies in both countries.[4]

In 1992, the two countries established joint Border Liaison Mechanisms (the BLM) to discuss border relations. The BLM includes a number of subgroups to facilitate discussion of specific issues. Reducing violence at the border has been one of the principal areas of mutual concern. The Council for Public Safety was created in mid-1997, in part as a response to shooting incidents that had occurred along the border. The BLM provided a means of linking U.S. and Mexican law enforcement agencies (federal, state, and local) in the San Diego-Tijuana area. Another group, the Border Port Council, focuses on ways of improving ports of entry; a third focuses on the return to Mexico of unauthorized aliens who are apprehended.

The Binational Commission Working Group has been the forum through which the two governments have discussed placement of elite Mexican police units, referred to as Grupo Beta, in Tijuana and other locations. A highly selective, special force, Grupo Beta patrols the Mexican border to prevent and respond to violence by and against migrants, such as assaults, rapes, and robberies. A new level of trans-border law enforcement cooperation has followed deployment of Grupo Beta in Tijuana. Grupo Beta shares radio frequencies with the local American police and federal officials; it has cooperated in preventing the dangerous practice of "port running," wherein large groups of migrants run through customs and into oncoming highway traffic to elude capture, and has provided other assistance. Mexico has put over a half dozen other Grupo Beta-type units at other locations along the U.S. border and also along Mexico's southern border, where illegal immigrants and alien smugglers from Central America cross on their way north (Freedberg 1994, Rotella 1992).

One of the most prominent areas of discussion has been the protection of the rights of migrants. In May 1996, the U.S. and Mexican governments signed a Memorandum of Understanding on Consular Protection of Mexicans and United States Nationals. This memorandum ensures inclusion of issues related to consular protection and human rights in working group discussions; guarantees notification of rights to detained migrants, including contact with a consular representative; facilitates the presence of consular officials at any judicial procedures of their nationals; raises reports from the Border Liaison Mechanisms (BLM) and Consultation Mechanisms to the working group; promotes bicultural sensitivity related to human rights protection; and encourages cooperation at the highest levels regarding investigation of violent and serious incidents involving consular protection. Pursuant to the memorandum, the United States and Mexico have been working together to improve protection of migrant rights via such mechanisms as training for both Mexican and U.S. border officials on human rights issues; civilian review bodies to receive and hear complaints against officials; and locally based consultative groups that include U.S. officials and Mexican consular officers to review operations and their impact on the rights of migrants.

Another area of mutual interest has been enforcement against alien smuggling, particularly of third-country nationals transiting Mexico to reach the United States. A side effect of enhanced border controls has been an increase in the use of professional smugglers. The INS has worked closely with Mexico and other governments to break up the smuggling operations believed responsible for moving aliens of various nationalities through Central America and Mexico into the United States. More recently, cooperation has been evident in joint education campaigns to inform Mexican would-be migrants of the dangers posed by smuggling operations. Because of the tighter border enforcement in urban areas, more migrants are attempting to cross into the United States through rugged terrain that is highly inhospitable to life. A growing death toll, particularly of migrants whose smugglers deserted them in the desert and mountains, prompted the two governments to use the media to spread information about the dangers of illegal crossings in these areas.

A potentially explosive issue on the agenda, one with significant security ramifications, was the repatriation of criminal aliens. While Mexico recognized that the United States had a valid reason to deport those who commit crimes, the manner of the removals was a frequent matter for discussion. Mexican authorities asked for advanced notification that criminal aliens would be brought to border crossing points, in part to have time to determine if an outstanding arrest warrant would justify taking the migrant into Mexican custody. The U.S. authorities acknowledged the value in this approach, but violations of the agreed-upon procedures occurred frequently enough to place the issue on the agenda of the Working Group. Progress has been made, though, through the Border Liaison Mechanism. In 1997, Mexican consuls and INS officials formalized local arrangements for the safe and orderly repatriation of Mexican nationals at border-crossing ports.

Changes in U.S. law precipitated by the heightened domestic controversy about immigration tended to dominate the agenda of binational discussions once the legislation was introduced. In 1996, immigration, welfare, and anti-terrorism legislation was enacted, each containing provisions of particular import for future immigration. Although the laws pertain to migrants from all countries, the very size of the Mexican legal and unauthorized populations in the United States made the legislation of special interest to Mexico. In contrast to earlier periods when the Mexican government was largely silent on U.S. legislation and the U.S. government made little effort to keep Mexican authorities informed of new developments, the two governments exchanged frequent communications about the 1996 laws. Of particular concern to Mexico were the new restrictions on immigrant eligibility for certain public benefits, new income requirements placed on family sponsors, enhanced removal policies and procedures that reduced access to potential relief from deportation, and changes in policy that could result in a greater role for state and local police forces in the exercise of federal immigration law. This last issue took on new import after a well-publicized incident in Riverside, California in which police officers were videotaped beating Mexicans who had been apprehended.

A more positive focus of cooperation has been the development of commuter lanes to facilitate legal crossings at the border. Both countries saw the value of initiating pilot programs aimed at speeding up the crossing process. The INS proposed pilot programs in which frequent commuters would be pre-screened to determine their admissibility. Once approved, their automobiles would be fitted with transponders that would provide electronic information about their eligibility to enter. The system would not have worked, however, without the cooperation of Mexican authorities in clearing a highway lane to lead to the commuter entry point. Otherwise, the commuters would have had to stay in the same traffic as other border-crossers until they reached the inspection point. The BLM provided the opportunity for discussion of the changes needed to make the pilot programs successful.

In addition to discussing current policy issues and spurring cooperation on administrative initiatives, the Working Group has stimulated initiatives aimed at improving understanding of migration between the two countries. In a March 1995 meeting in Nuevo Laredo of the Migration and Consular Affairs working group, the governments of Mexico and the United States agreed to undertake a joint study, in which the Mexican Secretariat of Foreign Relations and the U.S. Commission for Immigration Reform would serve as national coordinators for their respective governments.[5] The study involved 20 researchers, ten from each country, working in five teams to examine the size, characteristics, causes, and impacts of migration, and responses to it. While most of the funding would be provided by the governments, the decision was also made to seek private foundation support to ensure maximum objectivity and flexibility in carrying out the research.[6]

Most notably, the Binational Study achieved a consensus among the independent researchers on issues that had eluded agreement in previous efforts to conduct binational research. The group reconciled data from U.S. and Mexican sources, a process that took some effort. For example,

Mexican research and data generally focused on circular migrants who had already returned to Mexico, while U.S. research and data generally focused on Mexicans who had settled in the United States, sometimes permanently. It was not surprising that the data showed different pictures of the factors precipitating migration or the effects of migrants. Nevertheless, careful review of the data allowed the binational research team to offer a more comprehensive picture of the characteristics, causes, and consequences for both countries of the different types of Mexican migration.

The Binational Commission meetings and other Presidential summits have been the occasion for a number of joint statements on migration. The frequency of these statements is testament to the important place migration has on the foreign policy agendas of both countries. The Declaration of Zacatecas (Joint Communiqué), adopted in Zacatecas, Mexico in 1995 during the first meeting of officials from the Zedillo and Clinton Administrations in charge of migration affairs, constitutes the framework for bilateral dialogue, cooperation, and management of migration issues. The 1996 Memorandum of Understanding on Consular Protection of Mexican and U.S. Nationals, discussed above, was followed by a 1997 presidential Joint Declaration on Migration "to ensure a proper and respectful management of this complex phenomenon, taking into consideration its diverse causes and its economic and social consequences for both countries" (Zedillo and Clinton 1997).

Several memoranda of understanding were signed during 1998. The Memorandum of Understanding of Consultation Mechanisms on INS Functions and Consular Protection formalized procedures to ensure information exchange between Mexico's 42 consulates throughout the United States and U.S. immigration officials. The Memorandum of Understanding between the INS and the Mexican National Council on Population (CONAPO) aimed "to pursue dialogue and sustained scientific cooperation to further understand the complexities of the migration phenomenon and develop a comprehensive vision of managing migration," in keeping with the recommendations of the Binational Study (U.S.-Mexico Binational Commission 1998b). In 1999 the two governments signed a Memorandum of Understanding on Cooperation against Border Violence. Signed during a presidential trip to Mexico, the MOU´s purpose was described as to help "prevent life-threatening border incidents whether they result from the use of deadly force by law enforcement personnel or by transboundary acts of aggression" (U.S.-Mexico Binational Commission 1999).

The activities of the two national governments represent only a fraction of the mechanisms now in place for facilitating cross-border exchanges that deal with migration matters. State and local government arrangements facilitate sustained discussion of border issues. The border governors, attorneys general and other officials meet regularly, and migration has been increasingly on their agendas. Private groups also convene forums for bilateral communication. The U.S.-Mexico Consultative Group of the Carnegie Endowment for International Peace engaged senior government officials and leaders in the research and advocacy communities from the United States and Mexico in off-the-record dialogue; the Inter-American Dialogue and the Brookings Institution's U.S.-Mexican Relations Forum engaged in similar bilateral discussions on controversial issues on the bilateral agenda, producing a report on Immigration in U.S.-Mexico Relations (U.S.-Mexican Relations Forum 1998).

These national, state and local government, and private initiatives tend to meet more frequently and with greater urgency when immigration between the two countries is at its most controversial. Between 1993 and 1996, the Binational Commission Working Group met every few months to discuss new developments. As immigration moved off of the political agenda after the 1996 elections, the meetings of the Working Group became less frequent, even though the two governments continued to sign agreements.

Some officials see the infrequency of meetings as a good sign, indicating that immigration is no longer as much of an irritant in U.S.-Mexico relations as it was heretofore. The ebb and flow of bilateral discussions is troubling to others, however, including this author. Responses to immigration tend to be episodic, most negative when the economy is in decline, and less intense as economic conditions improve. Both the United States and Mexico were in a period of economic growth in the late 1990s. As members of the Binational Study wrote, "This suggests that changes in immigration practices may be more feasible when the two economies are prospering and tensions are minimal" (Mexico-U.S. Binational Study 1998: 501). If the governments suspend their discussions just when responses to immigration drop, progress in finding mutually acceptable policies will prove all the more elusive.

The Regional Migration Conference

In 1996 the Mexican government took the initiative to convene a regional conference on migration. Convening in Puebla, Mexico, representatives from the countries of North and Central America agreed to meet regularly to promote multilateral coordination. The U.S. State Department described the intent as follows: "The group seeks to develop a long-term approach to multilateral cooperation in migration management, encompassing both an analysis of root causes of migration and activities to channel migration into safe, orderly, and authorized channels. The conference seeks balance in addressing concerns of countries of origin and of destination" (U.S. Department of State 1999). Initially, the Regional Migration Conference, better known as the Puebla Group, focused on cooperative law enforcement strategies, particularly to deter extraregional migrants from transiting one American state to reach another. The Puebla Group was also a forum for exchanging information about immigration-related developments in each of the participating countries.

Since its beginnings, the Puebla Group has enlarged its participation, venues, and agenda, reflecting the growing prominence of migration issues in regional relations. The annual vice-ministerial meeting has been held in Panama City, Ottawa, and San Salvador, with a fourth scheduled for Washington. More specialized workshops occur throughout the year. In 1999 the Dominican Republic was admitted as a full member, and membership was then closed. Colombia, Ecuador, Jamaica, Peru, Argentina, and several international organizations (the Economic Commission for Latin America and the Caribbean, the International Organization for Migration, and the UN High Commissioner for Refugees) have observer status; during the vice-ministerial meetings, time is also dedicated to formal discussion with representatives of non-governmental organizations.

The Puebla Group adopted a plan of action at the 1998 Ottawa meeting that focuses on migration policies, linkages between development and migration, activities to combat migrant trafficking, international cooperation for the return of extra-regional migrants, human rights, and technical cooperation (Regional Conference on Migration 1998). The objectives and proposed activities are as follows:

Migration policies: Three principal objectives were included: (1) formulation, review, and implementation of a national migration policy based on national interests, the dynamics of the phenomenon of migration, and the commitments agreed upon at the regional migration conference; (2) exchange of information on migration policies and legislation; and (3) identification of minimum standards related to the issuance of, information contained in, and security control of travel documents at the regional level. Activities would include carrying out a comparative analysis of the migration policies of the countries of the region; encouraging consultation with countries affected by new immigration measures prior to their adoption, with full respect for the sovereignty of each state; and analyzing existing standards related to travel documents and holding workshops on ways to enhance security.

Links between development and migration: The objective is to promote better understanding of regional migration phenomena through a long-term comprehensive approach to identify the origins, manifestation, and effects of migration in the region. Activities include a study and seminar at the regional level on the links between development and migration.

Migrant trafficking: The objectives are three-fold: to strengthen the fight against migrant trafficking with the aim of eradicating it; to promote information exchange; and to promote a better comprehension and societal awareness about the negative effects of migrant trafficking. The Puebla Group would encourage governments to characterize migrant trafficking in their legislation as a criminal offense, establish a regional network of liaison officers to exchange information, design a form to standardize the elements of information to be shared, and disseminate information about successful efforts to prevent migrant trafficking, legal proceedings against traffickers, and the negative consequences of migrant trafficking.

Return of extra-regional migrants: The objectives are international cooperation for the return of migrants from outside of North and Central America and development of a regional strategy and approach for facilitating the return of migrants in irregular situations. The Puebla Group would strengthen channels of communication among governments and international organizations to facilitate and expedite return, foster the exchange of information about procedures that prove effective for the return of migrants, explore ways to finance return, establish a joint and cooperative approach to air carriers to reduce fees and facilitate return, and work through diplomatic channels to secure travel documents with countries outside the region to ensure compliance with international obligations to accept the return of their nationals.

Human rights: The objective is full respect for existing provisions on human rights of migrants, irrespective of their immigration status, as defined in the Universal Declaration of Human Rights and other relevant international instruments. A further objective is to ensure the protection of refugees. Activities include: adopting regional cooperative mechanisms to prevent and fight against violations of human rights of migrants; disseminating and distributing information regarding human rights of migrants and refugees in order to enhance public awareness and counteract anti-immigrant attitudes; training officials as to appropriate treatment of migrants; giving particular attention to the special needs of women and children, the elderly, and the disabled; promoting regional consultative forums regarding consular protection of migrants between consular and immigration authorities; promoting regional meetings of those interested in the defense of human rights of migrants; and emphasizing the fundamental protection accorded refugees under international law.

Technical cooperation: The objectives are to equip and modernize information control and security systems, to have professionally trained personnel in government agencies working on migration issues, and to reintegrate repatriated migrants. The activities include acquisition of specialized equipment, training of officials in migration policy and procedures, and development of projects for the social and workforce reintegration of migrants.

The Plan of Action is most detailed and concrete on the joint enforcement issues raised at the first meeting in Puebla, particularly those related to the return of extra-regional migrants and combating migrant trafficking. Over time, however, the agenda has broadened significantly. The Joint Communiqué of the 1999 vice-ministerial meeting reflects the evolving agenda of the Puebla Group. Setting out the overall tone of the discussions, the delegates "reiterated that migration is a process with highly positive dimensions which should be addressed by taking a comprehensive, objective and long-term approach to its origins, manifestations and effects in the region" (Regional Conference on Migration 1999).

The migration ramifications of Hurricane Mitch received substantial attention, with the delegates recommending that international efforts concentrate in "strategic sectors that generate employment, guaranteeing that reconstruction and development projects presented for funding explicitly incorporate the variable of migration" (Regional Conference on Migration 1999). They also pledged to convene a Workshop of Experts to identify projects to generate employment and promote social welfare in communities of origin and to request that IOM design a project to evaluate the effects of Hurricane Mitch on migration movements.

What was not discussed about Hurricane Mitch's migration ramifications was just as illuminating as what was discussed, and reflects some of the strengths and weaknesses of the process. On 15 November 1998, Guatemala tightened border controls and suspended visa-free travel, despite an agreement among four Central American nations to allow free movement, saying that too many Central Americans were passing through en route to the United States. Salvadoran President Armando Calderon Sol called Guatemala's action "a step back in Central American integration" (*Migration News* 1999: 3). Guatemalan authorities reportedly refused to participate in the San Salvador meeting if discussion of its policy change were part of the official agenda. While the inability to discuss formally a policy change with major consequences reflected the weakness of a still very new mechanism, the Puebla meeting did permit informal discussions to take place.

The San Salvador meeting also addressed another controversial issue—return of migrants from within the region. Although there is general consensus on the need to return extra-regional migrants arriving in irregular circumstances, there is no such agreement when return involves nationals of the Puebla Group of countries.

Two major issues arise for countries of origin. First, the countries recovering from civil conflicts and natural disasters in Central America fear that premature return of their nationals will halt needed remittances and place a further burden on their fragile economies and political structures. Hurricane Mitch only exacerbated concerns that these governments had been expressing for many years. Second, all countries are troubled by the return of criminal aliens. Reintegrating individuals who grew up in the United States before committing crimes is a point of particular contention. Although the countries of the region recognize that they have an obligation to take back their nationals, they make the case that these migrants learned their criminal behavior in the United States. Moreover, many of them have few family or social ties to their countries of birth. At the San Salvador meeting, the delegates agreed to devote a May 1999 meeting to be held in Honduras to considering mechanisms for the orderly return of migrants.

The theme of orderly management of migration permeates the Puebla Group discussions. In San Salvador, the delegates concluded that "orderly and regulated migration permit[s] the exploration of new possibilities for positive links between migration and development through cooperation and coordination among the countries of the Conference.... Additionally, facilitating orderly migration maintains the circular flow of labor movement in specific geographic areas" (Regional Conference on Migration 1999). Guatemala and Mexico were to prepare a joint document on this issue for presentation at a consultation to be convened later in 1999. The practical implications of this conclusion, particularly if one or more governments propose to formalize seasonal guestworker programs, are likely to generate differences. To the extent that the Puebla Group can serve as a forum for developing greater consensus on a potentially divisive issue, however, it will make an important contribution to regional cooperation on migration matters.

The Summit of the Americas

Hemispheric discussions on migration are in their infancy in comparison with the still somewhat new bilateral and regional mechanisms. During the first Summit of the Americas in 1994 in Miami, newly elected Mexican President Zedillo urged placing immigration on the agenda. The Summit occurred just weeks after passage of the controversial California Proposition 187, the initiative that severely limited access of illegal aliens to state-funded public services, including public education. Attending the Summit, Guatemalan President Ramiro De Leon called Proposition 187 "a flagrant and massive violation of human rights, especially for children" (*Migration News* 1995: 7). In comments to the press, Vice President Gore acknowledged these concerns, stating that the Clinton Administration opposed 187. He held that the real answer to illegal immigration is "to create more opportunities for jobs and lives with dignity in the areas from which the immigration is taking place" (*Migration News* 1995: 7).

The Plan of Action at the Miami Summit included only brief mention of migration despite these discussions. It urged governments, within the section on human rights, "to guarantee the protection of the human rights of all migrant workers and their families" (Miami Summit 1994: I.2.). The Declaration of the Santiago Summit of the Americas in 1998 kept to the same theme, pledging: "We will make a special effort to guarantee the human rights of all migrants, including migrant workers and their families" (Santiago Summit 1998a).

The Santiago Plan of Action was more detailed, however, on what efforts should be made. In keeping with the Declaration, the actions pertained primarily to the rights of migrants working in other countries. The Plan of Action specified that governments will "reaffirm that the promotion and protection of human rights and the fundamental freedoms for all, without distinction by reasons of race, gender, language, nationality, or religion, is a priority for the international community and is the responsibility of every state" (Santiago Summit 1998b: II). At the same time, the Plan of Action reaffirmed the "sovereign right of each State to formulate and apply its own legal framework and policies for migration, including the granting of permission to migrants to enter, stay, or exercise economic activity" (Santiago Summit 1998b: II).

The Plan of Action urged governments, in exercising their sovereign rights, to conform with applicable international instruments relating to human rights and to act in a spirit of cooperation. In that context, governments would aim to comply with the applicable international human rights instruments and, consistent with the legal framework of each country, guarantee the human rights of all migrants, including migrant workers and their families. The governments would adopt effective measures, including the strengthening of public awareness, "to prevent and eradicate violations of human rights and eliminate all forms of discrimination against them, particularly racial discrimination, xenophobia, and related intolerance" (Santiago Summit 1998b: II).

More specifically, the Plan of Action asked governments to take the following steps to increase protection of the rights of migrant workers and their families: (1) provide, with respect to working conditions, the same legal protection as for national workers; (2) facilitate, as appropriate, the payment of full wages owed when the worker has returned to his/her country, and allow workers to arrange the transfer of their personal effects; (3) recognize the rights of citizenship and nationality of the children of all migrant workers who may be entitled to such rights, and any other rights they may have in each country; (4) encourage the negotiation of bilateral or multilateral agreements, regarding the remission of social security benefits accrued by migrant workers; (5) protect all migrant workers and their families, through law enforcement and information campaigns, from becoming victims of exploitation and abuse from alien smuggling; (6) prevent abuse and mistreatment of all migrant workers by employers or any authorities entrusted with the enforcement of migration policies and border control; and (7) encourage and promote respect for the cultural identity of all migrants.

Finally, the Plan of Action recognized the importance of international instruments and institutions. Governments should "seek full respect for, and compliance with, the 1963 Vienna Convention on Consular Relations, especially as it relates to the right of nationals, regardless of their immigration status, to communicate with a consular officer of their own State in case of detention" (Santiago Summit 1998b, II). Governments should also support the activities of the Inter-American Commission on Human Rights with regard to the protection of the rights of migrant workers and their families, particularly through the Special Rapporteur for Migrant Workers.

Interestingly, but perhaps not surprisingly, the Plan of Action makes no reference to compliance with the International Convention on the Protection of the Rights of All Migrant Workers and Members of Their Families, which is an attempt to reaffirm and establish basic norms of human rights and to embody them in an instrument applicable to migrant work- ers and their families. However, the number of ratifications is still very small, only nine States as of the end of 1998. At that time, only one State in the Western Hemisphere—Colombia—had ratified the Convention, although Mexico and Chile have signed it preparatory to ratification.

Conclusion

The growth of bilateral, regional, and hemispheric mechanisms to address migration issues of common concern represents a fundamental shift in perspective. From thinking about immigration as an issue of pure national sovereignty meriting unilateral policies, governments increas- ingly recognize the value of cooperation and coordination. President Clinton recognized the extent to which immigration matters have become part of the foreign policy agenda during his 1999 visit to Central Amer- ica. During the closing session of the Summit meeting in Guatemala, he reflected that "we talked a lot about immigration, as you might imagine."

That migration is on the foreign policy agenda is not to say that the route to bilateral and multilateral cooperation is smooth. Many issues are off the table in these discussions because they are too controversial or with- out obvious solution. When migration interests coincide with national security or economic integration interests, progress in finding multilateral solutions may be marked. However, when these interests diverge—as wit- nessed by the reactions within Central America to Hurricane Mitch- induced migration—migration matters are likely to take a back seat in foreign policy to the more traditional security and economic issues.

Nevertheless, the mechanisms described in this chapter, although they are at an early stage of development, hold the promise of a more com- prehensive approach to the management of migration. Beginning with basic exchanges of information and discussion of issues where agreement is possible—for example, curbing trafficking, reducing violence against migrants, repatriating extra-regional migrants—countries can develop the habit of cooperation. Then, when more difficult issues arise, as they no doubt will, this habit may lead to new breakthroughs in cooperative action for more effective management of international migration.

Notes

1. A clear exception is Myron Weiner's work. See, for example, Weiner and Teitelbaum (1995).
2. The Amsterdam Treaty entered into force on 1 May 1999. Consequently, sweeping changes in European migration policy are expected to take place by 2004, the close of the initial five-year test period envisioned in the treaty. This includes majority vote in the Council of Ministers on all areas of migration and asylum policy, as well as the acquisition by the European Commission of the sole right of initiative to introduce migration-related legislation.
3. This process reflects the separate phases of admission. A visa grants its recipient the right to seek entry (which can be done during a five-year period), but actual admission is controlled by immigration authorities at ports of entry who determine how long someone may remain within the country (in this case, an initial one-year period, with two-year extensions).
4. Based on the author's participation in meetings of the Working Group, 1995–1997.
5. This author served as U.S. National Coordinator in her capacity as Executive Director of the U.S. Commission on Immigration Reform.
6. The Ford Foundation, Hewlett Foundation, and Fundación Miguel Aleman contributed to the study.

References

Acevedo, Dolores, and Thomas J. Espenshade. 1992. "Implications of a North American Free Trade Agreement for Mexican Migration into the United States," *Population and Development Review* 18/4: 729–744.

Cornelius, Wayne A., and Philip L. Martin. 1993. *The Uncertain Connection: Free Trade and Mexico-U.S. Migration*. San Diego, CA: Center for U.S.-Mexican Studies.

Freedberg, Louis. 1994. "Mexico Slowly Getting Tougher On Illegals," *The San Francisco Chronicle*, 12 Aug., A1.

Luther, Dennis. 1998. "Progress in Recognizing and Regulating Global Professional Service Providers." *Industry, Trade, and Technology Review*. Washington, D.C.: Office of Industries. Publication 3134.

Martin, Philip L. 1993. *Trade and Migration: NAFTA and Agriculture*. Washington, D.C.: Institute for International Economics.

Mexico-U.S. Binational Study. 1997. *Migration Between Mexico and the United States*. Mexico City and Washington, D.C.: Mexican Ministry of Foreign Affairs and U.S. Commission on Immigration Reform.

———. 1998. *Migration Between Mexico and the United States*. Mexico City and Washington, D.C.: Mexican Ministry of Foreign Affairs and U.S. Commission on Immigration Reform.

Miami Summit of the Americas. 1994. Plan of Action.

Migration News. 1995. Vol. 2, No. 1.

———. 1999. Vol. 6, No. 2.

Papademetriou, Demetrios G. 1993. Testimony before the Subcommittee on International Law, Immigration, and Refugees of the Judiciary Committee, U.S. House of Representatives, 3 November.

Regional Conference on Migration. 1998. *Plan of Action*. Ottawa: Citizenship and Immigration Canada.

————. 1999. Joint Communiqué. San Salvador: Regional Conference on Migration.

Rotella, Sebastian. 1992. "Reducing the Misery at the Border: Immigration: Grupo Beta Is an Elite Mexican Multi-Agency Force with the Task of Protecting Migrants. It Has Cut Violence and Improved Relations Between U.S. and Mexico," *Los Angeles Times*, 10 Mar., A3.

Santiago Summit of the Americas. 1998a. *Declaration*.

————. 1998b. *Plan of Action*.

UN High Commissioner for Refugees. 1997. *The State of the World's Refugees: 1997–1998*. Oxford: Oxford University Press.

U.S. Commission for the Study of International Migration and Cooperative Economic Development. 1990. *Unauthorized Migration: An Economic Response*. Washington, D.C.: Government Printing Office.

U.S. Department of State. 1999. Press Statement of 26 January.

U.S. GAO (General Accounting Office). 1993. *North American Free Trade Agreement: Assessment of Major Issues*, Vol. 2. Washington, D.C.: U.S. General Accounting Office.

U.S.-Mexican Relations Forum. 1998. *Immigration in U.S.-Mexican Relations*. Washington, D.C.: The Inter American Dialogue.

U.S.-Mexico Binational Commission. 1995. Declaration of Zacatecas (Joint Communiqué). Mexico City and Washington, D.C.: Mexican Ministry of Foreign Affairs and U.S. Department of State.

————. 1996. Memorandum of Understanding on Consular Protection of Mexican and U.S. Nationals. Mexico City and Washington, D.C.: Mexican Ministry of Foreign Affairs and U.S. Department of State.

————. 1998a. Memorandum of Understanding of Consultation Mechanisms on INS Functions and Consular Protection. Mexico City and Washington, D.C.: Mexican Ministry of Foreign Affairs and U.S. Department of State.

————. 1998b. Memorandum of Understanding between the Immigration and Naturalization Service (INS) and Mexican National Council on Population (CONAPO). Mexico City and Washington, D.C.: Mexican Ministry of Foreign Affairs and U.S. Department of State.

————. 1999. Memorandum of Understanding between the Government of the United Mexican States and the Government of the United States of America on Cooperation against Border Violence. Mexico City and Washington, D.C.: Mexican Ministry of Foreign Affairs and U.S. Department of State.

Weiner, Myron, and Michael Teitelbaum. 1995. *Threatened People, Threatened Borders: World Migration and U.S. Policy*. New York: WW Norton and Co.

Zedillo, Ernesto, and William Clinton. 1997. Joint Presidential Declaration on Migration. Mexico City and Washington, D.C.: Mexican Ministry of Foreign Affairs and U.S. Department of State.

PART THREE

Demographic Engineering and
National Security Objectives

CHAPTER 7

Demography and Security: Transmigration Policy in Indonesia

Riwanto Tirtosudarmo

Geography had a strong influence upon the course of Indonesia's history and has always conditioned severely the course of political development.

George McT. Kahin, 1965: 535

Transmigration, a government policy that involves the clearing and opening of land previously uncultivated or only sporadically or illegally cultivated, and the deliberate movement and resettlement of people, is an acknowledged instrument of population distribution policy in Indonesia. The idea of population transfer from Java, one of the most densely populated areas in the world, to other sparsely populated islands is far from new, having been in force since the beginning of the twentieth century.[1] Java's population problem, particularly its rapid growth and its large size, has become more pressing as it has coincided with the problem of poverty among a large part of the population. From the beginning, transmigration has been perceived as a way simultaneously to solve Java's demographic and welfare problems.

From a demographic perspective, it is clear that transmigration policy has had little effect on population reduction in Java. Assuming, for example, that the government target to resettle 150,000 families a year during the Fourth Five-Year Development Plan (1984–1989)—the highest target to date—had been realized, and assuming that every family consisted of five persons (two parents and three children), only 750,000 persons a year would have been moved. This number, taking the 1980 annual growth rate of two percent, and the size of the population of Java and Bali as approximately 100 million, suggests that a successful transmigration policy could have removed only just over one-third of Java's annual population growth and would not have prevented Java's total population from continuing to increase. It also is evident that the unbalanced population distribution between Java and the other islands would have been only marginally altered by transmigration.

While in the long term the transmigration program has had only a marginal effect on population growth in Java and little influence on population distribution in the archipelago, it has had a tremendous demographic impact on the receiving areas. Lampung and South Sumatra are classic examples of the remarkable contribution of transmigration to accelerating regional population growth. In other provinces, although the overall demographic impact of transmigration has been less salient, it has been very significant for some districts. In 1985, for example, 25 percent of the population in the district of Kampar in the province of Riau were transmigrants, as were more than 40 percent of the population in the district of Kotabaru in the province of South Kalimantan. (World Bank 1988: 21).

After Independence in 1945, the relationship between the central and regional governments became a crucial aspect of national integration and development.[2] Suharto's New Order regime began in 1966, and would end when he was forced to step down on 21 May 1998, during a severe political and economic crisis. Beginning with the New Order, the Indonesian state could be described as strongly centralized in character, for example, nearly 80 percent of national expenditures are planned and disbursed by the central government (Tirtosudarmo 1990). The transmigration program is perhaps the government policy that most reflects the strength of the central government in determining affairs in the regions, as it has been almost totally planned by the central government in Jakarta, while the regional governments, whose lands were designated as receiving areas for settlers from Java and Bali, were basically passive participants in the planning and implementation processes.

After the mid 1980s, the transmigration policy lost its economic rationale, since economic opportunities grew more rapidly in Java than on the outer islands. The macro-economic shift instigated by the collapse of oil prices forced the state to adopt a more export-oriented policy, replacing the previous import substitution strategy. The transmigration program, within the macro-economic context, therefore became counterproductive, as the overall development trend clearly promoted the creation of employment opportunities in Java rather than on the outer islands. Surprisingly, however, the transmigration policy is still highly regarded among the ruling elite, particularly the military, who believe it is pivotal to national security.

This chapter analyzes transmigration policy as the state's demographic engineering instrument for strategic and security purposes. In order to demonstrate both the continuity of and changes in the policy, the chapter adopts a chronological approach, tracing the policy's history since its formation at the turn of this century through the end of Suharto's New Order in May 1998.

Dutch Emigration Policy: Its Formation and Competing Interests

The end of the nineteenth and the beginning of the twentieth centuries were marked by several important social changes, whose impact significantly altered the course of history in Indonesia. Although each can be considered a single event, they can more usefully be regarded as complexes of interconnected events.

Ten years after the Dutch recovered from the Java War (1825–1830), they started paying attention to territories outside Java—the outer islands. From about 1840 onward, Dutch involvement expanded throughout the outer islands. There are basically two general reasons for this expansion: first, to protect the security of areas they already held, the Dutch felt compelled to subdue other regions that they thought might support or inspire resistance movements; second, as the European scramble for colonies reached its height, the Dutch felt obliged to establish their claims to the outer islands of the archipelago in order to prevent other Western powers from intervening there. By about 1910, the boundaries of the present state of Indonesia had been roughly drawn by colonial armed forces, at a great cost in lives and money and devastation of social cohesion, human dignity, and freedom. (Ricklefs 1981: 138).

At the dawn of the twentieth century Dutch colonial policy took on a new mission. The direct exploitation of Indonesia, which had culminated during the Culture System (1830–1870), began to weaken and was replaced by concern for the welfare of Javanese. One important element of the new policy was the introduction of a native welfare program, the nature of which is well illustrated by the slogan of the prominent colonial reformer van Deventer: irrigation, emigration, and education.[3] This policy has become well-known as the Ethical Policy.

The Ethical Policy was an outcome of social, political, and economic transformations in the Netherlands, with its roots in both humanitarian concern and economic advantage (Ricklefs 1981). The denunciation of Dutch rule presented in the well-known novel *Max Havelaar* (Multatuli [1860] 1982) and in other exposés, began to bear fruit. Voices were raised in favor of relief for the oppressed people of Java, and by the late nineteenth century new colonial administrators were on their way to Indonesia "… with Max Havelaar in their baggage and its message in their minds." During the "liberal" period (ca. 1870–1900) private capitalism came to exert a preponderant influence upon colonial policy. Dutch industry began to see Indonesia as a potential market that required a rising living standard to increase its purchasing power; Dutch and international capital sought new opportunities for investment and extraction of raw materials, especially on the outer islands. Thus there was a need for Indonesian labor, and business interests supported more intensive colonial involvement in the causes of peace, justice, modernity, and welfare.

Humanitarian elements justified what the businessmen expected to be profitable, and the Ethical Policy was born.

After the middle of the nineteenth century, Java, especially in its central and eastern parts, was becoming seriously overpopulated, while there were still vast areas of unpopulated or under-populated land in the outer islands. While the Dutch colonial government considered Java's growing population to be the underlying cause of the decline of its people's welfare, as the findings of the Declining Welfare Commission showed, it had no idea of developing policies that could directly solve the problem, offering only emigration from Java to the outer islands as a solution (van der Kroef 1956). As a result, the nation's wealth was used for the interests of foreign enterprises, hindering the development of indigenous industries. The main economic development took place on the outer islands, while the main welfare problems grew in Java.

The Ethical Policy was almost entirely concerned with raising agricultural productivity, and the colonial government apparently had no serious intention to introduce drastic changes in the colonial economic structure by such means as large-scale industrialization. As Legge (1965) argues, the measures taken by "ethical" colonial governments to improve the living standards of the indigenous population were only palliatives, providing some alleviation of particular areas of hardship, but not achieving—nor did they attempt to achieve—any thoroughgoing technological changes. The importance of large-scale industrialization was actually stressed by a number of Ethical reformers, but until the worldwide economic depression of the 1930s, none of the various plans suggested was implemented. As early as 1901, according to Penders (1969), the Calvinist Prime Minister Kuyper even stressed that the only way to develop the Indies was to lift the people from the agricultural to the industrial state. Penders also notes that the Minister of Colonies, Idenburg, strongly supported Kuyper and envisaged the establishment of indigenous industries owned by indigenous capital; the socialist van Kol dismissed the view that emigration was the proper means to balance production and consumption, saying it was delusive and would never come true.[4]

Three reasons have been proposed for why the Dutch colonial government was not interested in proposing industrialization: internal freight rates were too high; there was no widespread distribution apparatus; and import duties on industrial goods were too low to afford sufficient protection (Penders 1969). Penders argues, however, that none of these fully explains the fundamental reason why the attempts at industrialization failed, which is the strong opposition of the politically powerful plantation companies. Large-scale industrialization would have increased the demand for labor and therefore its price. This would have been damaging to the plantations, which were largely dependent on low wages for their profits. Furthermore, Dutch industrialists, as well as Dutch labor, were unwilling to be priced out of the Indonesian market. In the final analysis, then, the industrialization of Indonesia militated against the interests of the imperial economy as a whole (Penders 1969: 29–30).

In serving the interests of plantation companies, the Netherlands Indies' government issued the first Coolie Ordinance in 1880 to regulate labor relations, particularly in East Sumatra. This ordinance was later expanded to other regions on the outer islands. It protected the interests of plantation companies by retaining workers for the duration of the contract period, and sanctions were imposed on workers who violated their labor contracts. The first Coolie Ordinance was followed in 1884 and 1893 by other ordinances providing employers with effective legal control over their indentured workers. In addition to the penal sanctions, employers resorted to other means to keep their workers. A favorite way was to provide gambling opportunities for the workers on payday; often, workers became so deeply indebted that they had no choice but to sign a new contract with their employers (Thee 1969: 7–9). Until 1909, the recruitment of Javanese estate labor remained in the hands of professional agents, but in that year planters were encouraged by law to appoint their own agents, who were often aided by worker-recruiters. The Deli Planter's Association, for example, led the way by setting up its own agency in Semarang, Central Java, and direct recruitment of labor gradually became widespread. In 1930, it was found that 84 percent of the labor employed on plantations on the outer islands was Javanese, 13 percent was Chinese and three percent local (Thompson 1947: 134). From a different perspective, Kartodirdjo (1973), a noted historian, perceived that the rural history of Java in the nineteenth and early twentieth centuries was marked by sporadic movements of peasant unrest, many erupting in more or less violent clashes with the colonial authorities. Protest movements and social unrest occurred between 1900 and 1920 in various places in rural Java, such as in Tanggerang, Pamanukan, Sukabumi, Ciasem, Kuningan (West Java), Pekalongan, Gombong, Semarang (Central Java), Mojokerto, Sidoardjo, Kediri, and Jember (East Java).[5] Although a direct link between social unrest in rural Java and the initiation of the emigration policy cannot be established, it is not implausible to posit a cause-effect relationship.

A major complicating feature of agrarian unrest in Java has been its correlation with social change in general and with the colonial impact in particular. Kartodirdjo (1973) strongly argued that the social movements had their background in the rapid penetration of a colonial economy whose impact on rural Java reached a climax during the course of the nineteenth century. The colonial rulers introduced a new legal and social relationship covering agrarian and labor matters. Excessive demands for compulsory services and the levying of new taxes exacerbated popular discontent. Turning over some land to sugar cultivation and the exaction of a compulsory contribution of paddy rice had a direct bearing on some of the instances of social unrest (Kartodirdjo 1973: 1).

Emigration from Java to the other islands is considered to be the least successful measure of the government's Ethical Policy, since the number of families to move was small. The first organized attempt in this direction was made in 1905, when Gedong Tataan, an experimental agricultural colony of 155 families, was set up in Lampung, South Sumatra. By 1930, it had 30,000 colonists. Efforts to settle Javanese farmers in the southeast of Kalimantan and Sulawesi met with failure. The situation improved somewhat during the 1930s, when, as a result of more skillful propaganda, better selection methods, and more extensive preparatory work in the settlement areas, more farmers could be induced to leave. From 1933 to 1941, 222,586 migrants were resettled in Lampung and South Sumatra (Heeren 1979: 14), and almost 2,500 migrants in Kalimantan (Pelzer 1945: 223–225). During the Japanese occupation (1942–1945), the government's migration policy was at a standstill, and the economic situation in Indonesia deteriorated. Population numbers continued to increase, but the growth in economic productivity fell seriously behind that of the population, owing to the destruction of the economic apparatus during the Japanese occupation and the revolution that followed.

As one of the three Ethical Policy objectives, Dutch colonial migration policy (*emigratie*) was essentially formulated and maintained by a combination of three factors. First were the political changes in the Netherlands which allowed the Calvinist-Catholic Coalition to come to power in 1901. The outstanding feature of the policy outcomes from this new coalition was the official abandonment of the goal of economic exploitation and the introduction of direct intervention in the economic sphere to improve the conditions of the indigenous population. The second factor was economic opportunity, particularly as seen by the Dutch capitalists after the whole archipelago was successfully brought under effective colonial control. The vast land areas on the outer islands attracted private companies seeking to open plantations. Due to the scarcity of workers, Javanese were recruited as cheap labor for new economic activities. The third factor was social and political unrest in many parts of rural Java, resulting from simultaneous economic exploitation and population pressures. These, in turn, encouraged the colonial government to deal with social unrest by moving people to the outer islands. Emigration policy, as developed by the Dutch, can therefore be summarized as a useful instrument to serve the many goals and interests of the state and its ruling elite. The relocation of people to ease social and political tensions was a form of demographic engineering that served the state's security purposes.

Transmigration: Migration Policies after Independence (1945–1965)

One of the new national leaders after Independence in 1945, Mohammad Hatta, the first vice-president and an economist, argued forcefully that emigration should be continued, however, transmigration as he proposed it was somewhat different from the policy implemented by the Dutch colonial government. Transmigration, according to Hatta, was to be implemented in conjunction with the industrialization of the outer islands. Hatta's ideas were not surprising, as the superiority of industrialization to emigration was an old idea among socialists in the Netherlands, where he had been a student at a time when socialism was strong in Europe. Socialist politicians in the Low Countries demanded a genuine process of industrialization to improve the economic conditions of the indigenous peoples, rather than the simple emigration of Javanese to the outer islands. Hatta (1954) argued that transmigration without simultaneous industrialization would only postpone future problems.

Hatta also strongly criticized the colonial policy, which basically had only shifted landless farmers from Java to become farmers on the outer islands. He argued that transmigration under the Dutch resulted only "in shifting peasants to be peasants, there is no fresh spirit, their lives have only postponed the coming problems." Furthermore, Hatta also suggested that emigration or transmigration would only achieve its goal of producing prosperity if the people were given guidance and assistance in their new environment. After Independence, the Committee for Economic Strategies (Panitia Siasat Ekonomi), of which Hatta was the chairman, formulated a plan in which industrialization and transmigration were the two major components.[6] However, at this writing the idea of industrialization that formed the backbone of Hatta's transmigration policy has proved to be unattainable.

It is striking that the office in charge of implementing resettlement policy after Independence has itself migrated constantly from one ministry to another. The unsettled political climate that followed the Proclamation of Independence in 1945, as the Dutch attempted to regain their former colony, as well as the lack of preparation among Indonesians to lead the country, contributed to the failure to establish a single, solid implementing agency for transmigration. The first Transmigration Office was placed under the Ministry for Labor and Social Affairs; in 1948, it was shifted to the Ministry for Development and Youth Affairs, which was abolished later in that year, at which time the transmigration office was transferred to the Ministry of Interior; in January 1950, the government established a separate Office for Transmigration (Kantor Transmigrasi), which was placed under the Ministry of Social Affairs the following October. It was under the auspices of this ministry that the first group, consisting of twenty-three families, was resettled in Lampung shortly thereafter (Hardjosudarmo 1965: 127).

In 1951, the head of the Transmigration Office, A. H. O. Tambunan, formulated a plan to resettle 10,000 families per year to South Sumatra and Sulawesi. Because of financial constraints, only 653 families from the regencies of Purworejo, Kebumen, Banyumas and Probolinggo in Central Java were moved to South Sumatra, and most of these were resettled in areas adjacent to former Dutch colonization sites (Sjamsu 1960: 80). Approximately twenty-six more families were resettled in Sulawesi, also

close to a former colonization area. The Transmigration Office also resettled 114 families of refugees from East Priangan to Banten, West Java
because their villages had often been terrorized and ransacked by an
Islamic rebel group operating in the region.

Under the Ministry of Social Affairs, the stated goal of transmigration
was to improve the prosperity and welfare of the population by developing various sectors of the economy (Hardjosudarmo 1965: 128). In 1952,
Tambunan proposed another ambitious fifteen-year plan for transmigration, under which the government would open up 30,000 hectares of land
a year in South Sumatra and send 1,000 families annually to be employed
there. Moreover, the government also established a land-clearing agency,
JAPETA (Jajasan Pembukaan Tanah). In the end, however, this plan
achieved little. Only 3,855 hectares of land were cleared and only 3,851
families were moved, mostly to South Sumatra. After a while, the Tambunan plan faded.

In addition to the so-called general transmigration program (*transmigrasi umum*), there were basically two other types of government-sponsored transmigration programs during the 1950s. The first was the
resettlement of the Surinam repatriates. In 1954, the Transmigration Office
resettled almost 300 families, mainly the descendents of Javanese sugar
plantation workers who had just returned from Surinam, another Dutch
colony in South America, whom the government resettled in West Sumatra. The second was the resettlement program for ex-guerrilla fighters and
ex-army members, *Staat van Oorlog en Beleg*, or S.O.B., prisoners. The introduction of the second type of resettlement program around the mid 1950s
clearly marked the beginning of the new state's explicit demographic engineering activities, which were strongly motivated by political and security
considerations. The S.O.B. prisoners were people suspected by the government of having been involved in the Islamic rebel group in West Java
during the early 1950s. Under Presidential Instruction No. 54, 1954, they
and their families were sent to transmigration settlements in Sumatra and
Kalimantan. In 1954, approximately 500 families were resettled in North
Sumatra and another 242 families in East Kalimantan; in 1955, another 326
families were sent to those two regions (Sjamsu 1960: 64).

From the early 1950s, agricultural resettlement activities on the outer
islands were considered to be the most appropriate way to resocialize ex-
guerrilla fighters and former army personnel, and to prevent them from
being attracted to Islamic rebel groups in West Java. This fear was realistic, because more than seventy percent of the ex-guerrilla fighters who
were resettled in South Sumatra originated in West Java, mostly from
places around Jakarta, such as Bogor, Bekasi, and Krawang (Heeren 1979:
71–72). Under the auspices of the Ministry of Defense, the Bureau for the
Resettlement of Ex-military Members (BPBAT) was established to open
up land for plantations and agriculture and to provide better economic
opportunities for ex-army transmigrants. From 1950 to 1955, the government resettled more than 6,000 ex-soldiers, mostly in Lampung, South

Sumatra. According to Sjamsu (1960: 88), statistics on transmigration in South Sumatra are hard to evaluate, because the transmigrants mixed with previous settlers, and many of them moved voluntarily. Nevertheless, as many observers noticed, Lampung was becoming another Java: by 1957 there were almost 22,000 migrants in the new settlement areas, mostly in South Sumatra and mostly of Javanese origin.

The pre-war Dutch resettlement policy was directed toward the creation of typical Javanese enclaves in a purely Sumatran environment, with conditions made as close to those in the homeland as possible; after Independence, the Indonesian government adopted a different view, that the strict separation of Javanese and local peoples was a relic of colonial policy, and that Javanese and Sumatrans were equally Indonesian and had to live together on an equal footing. Neither policy, however, had to do with industrialization (Wertheim 1959: 149).

In the period 1956–1960, the government formulated its first Five-Year Development Plan, describing transmigration as an instrument to reduce population pressure in Java, to provide labor in sparsely populated provinces, to support military strategy, and to accelerate the process of assimilation (Hardjosudarmo 1965: 128–129). Apparently due to increased political unrest in some regions resulting from disappointment with central government leadership, the Plan emphasized that the goal of transmigration was no longer industrial or economic strategy. The important strategic role of transmigration was further emphasized in 1962 when President Sukarno proclaimed the so-called Guided Democracy system of government to replace the Parliamentary Democracy system that he considered to be a failure. The establishment of the autocratic Guided Democracy system took place with the support of the central military leadership (Kuntjorojakti 1978: 138–139).

The political role of the military increased considerably after it successfully put down the regional rebellions in West Sumatra and in North and South Sulawesi between 1956 and 1958. As Feith and Lev have argued (1963: 37), the end of the rebellion removed regionalists from the political and military scenes, clearing the way for the emergence of a new set of power relationships. Of the three main political forces of 1957 (the President, the central army leadership, and the regionalists) only the first two remained by mid-1958, and they were markedly distinct from, and in many ways competitive with, one another. Furthermore, the course of the regional rebellions had caused the government to adopt more center-oriented policy attitudes. As noted by Kuntjorojakti (1978: 139), several Presidential edicts on regional matters were issued at the national level treating the regions as simple administrative units within the framework of a highly centralized national bureaucracy.

The central government paid little attention to local concerns, and the local populations' resentment of its implementation of the transmigration policy in the 1950s and 1960s grew, mostly fuelled by land disputes which arose partly because the concept of land ownership on the outer islands was generally based on customary (*adat*) law, in which all land belonged to the *marga* or clan. During the Dutch period in Lampung, where the greatest population resettlement was implemented, the reluctance of local people to allow colonization of their lands had resulted in the formation of Javanese enclaves separate from the indigenous settlements (Heeren 1979: 47). When the local people refused to give up their homelands for colonization, the Dutch used *perintah halus* (gentle command) to gain permission to use land outside *marga* jurisdiction. The colonized areas, therefore, were usually located outside the local settlements.

Nitisastro, from a somewhat nationalist stance, criticized the Dutch assumptions that had led to enclave politics, holding that the typical Dutchman's conservative politics had hampered the assimilation process among ethnic communities in the resettlement areas. Furthermore, he argued that enclave politics were obviously in contradiction to the primary goal of Indonesian independence—to build one Indonesian nation —which would be reached partly through assimilating the Javanese with the local population. However, this goal proved to be more elusive than the government or nationalists like Nitisastro had anticipated. Wertheim, for example, noted from his observations in Lampung in 1956 that assimilation of Javanese migrants resulted in neither a Sumatran nor a general Indonesian society, but rather in a Javanese society modified by a Sumatran environment (Wertheim 1959: 198). This situation, according to Wertheim, led to an increasing resistance by Sumatrans to resettlement policies, which could seriously hamper further transmigration efforts, since the absorptive capacity of the outer islands is restricted not only by spatial and technical factors but also by social concerns.[7]

The change in national political structures after the declaration of the Guided Democracy system significantly affected the subsequent course of transmigration policy, whose goals were now stated to be increased national security and improved social welfare through the attainment of three intermediate steps: opening up new areas of natural resources and land; moving the population from densely populated areas to empty ones; and developing strategic regions in order to achieve greater national resilience (Hardjosudarmo 1965: 129–130). In conjunction with the declaration of Guided Democracy, in 1959 the central government introduced a change in local administration. Under the new system, the *marga* and *negeri* were abolished, regional authority was transferred to the *Bupati* (District Head), who was assisted by the *Camat* (Sub-district Head), both appointed by the higher authorities. Such structural arrangements contributed to circumstances in which neither the local people nor the migrants had the opportunity to influence the course of regional development.

The local populations strongly criticized government budgets that allocated more funds to transmigration settlements than to other areas. Road construction, schools, agricultural offices, health, and many other facilities were usually concentrated in transmigration areas, with smaller allocations to other places. However, regional disappointment with the central government had a much broader base. As Pauuw argued, resistance among the peoples of the outlying islands to the President's new development program reflected their fear of the centralization of authority, as well as their more moderate attitudes toward capitalism and foreign enterprise. Behind these attitudes we find both ethnic considerations and significant differences in historical experience (Pauuw 1963: 156). In such circumstances, a transmigration policy that was basically aimed at resettling a population from Java to the other islands further exacerbated local discontent toward the central government, which was clearly articulated at an *Adat* Congress, first in Palembang, South Sumatra, in January 1957, and later in Bukittinggi, West Sumatra, in March of the same year. Abandonment of the transmigration policy was one of the main demands of the PRRI rebel group between 1956 and 1958. Transmigration was suspended during these rebellious years but resumed in April 1958, immediately after the PRRI rebellion was crushed.

In 1961, another ambitious transmigration plan was presented as part of the so-called Eight-Year Comprehensive Development Plan (1961–1968) formulated by Muhammad Yamin.[8] In the plan, the goal was to move at least 250,000 transmigrants to agricultural sectors on the outer islands.[9] This transmigration policy was mentioned in the plan under the rubric of Government and Police. This was not surprising, since the military comprised an important part of the ruling elite of the time, as well as of the bureaucracy that formulated the plan. As might be expected, the actual number moved during the Yamin Plan—92,473 from 1961 to 1965—was much lower than the target. One of the main receiving areas during this period was the district of Siabu in Riau province; a study showed that strategic reasons had been partly responsible for this resettlement, in order to support military operations during the confrontation with Malaysia (Hamidy and Ahmad 1984: 10).

In 1964, an evaluation of the Yamin Plan and a review of transmigration problems led to a new policy promulgated in January 1965, the New Transmigration Model (*Transmigrasi Gaya Baru*). In one of his speeches, President Sukarno stated that "Indonesia does not need birth control, Indonesia can feed at least 250 million people … if they are properly distributed, if their energies are utilized adequately.…"[10] Under the new plan, the government aimed to resettle 100,000 families every year. The records show that in the first half of 1965 the government successfully moved almost 25,000 transmigrants. However, the political turmoil after the abortive coup of October 1965 significantly impeded the plan's implementation.

While the Dutch colonial government used transmigration policy only implicitly as an instrument of demographic engineering for security purposes, the government of the Republic of Indonesia used relocation explicitly to fulfill political and strategic goals. Demographic engineering became an important part of the state's strategic policy to reduce the increasing possibility of social and political tensions, particularly in areas surrounding the national capital, Jakarta. Transmigration policy, among other military strategies, was also explicitly used to support the state's foreign policy during the confrontation with Malaysia, by populating the border areas such as Riau and West and East Kalimantan provinces. After Independence, several ideological leaders, such as Yamin and Sukarno, also perceived transmigration as a tool for assimilating different ethnic groups to construct a homogenized cultural identity and national integration.

Transmigration Policy in the New Order Period

When the New Order government came to power in 1966, Indonesia began an attempt to integrate its economy into the regional and global capitalist economy. The emergence of a group of economists dedicated to the promotion of economic growth has been reflected in the establishment of a series of national and regional Five-Year Development Plans (*Rencana Pembangunan Lima Tahun*, or *Repelita*; see Tables 7.1 and 7.2). Preceding the launch of the First Plan in April 1969, the government reduced the inflation rate from a high of more than 600 percent in 1966 to around 10 percent in 1969.

Between the political upheaval of 1965 and the commencement of the First Plan, the government apparently paid very little attention to transmigration.[11] At the dawn of the New Order, an observer had even predicted that the program would no longer occupy a significant role in government policy (McNicoll 1966: 69). Another population observer argued that the future trend of migration in Indonesia would be toward voluntary internal migration (Heeren 1979: 171). These predictions were based partly on an assessment that the economic and political environment, unstable and fragile despite government control, did not favor such a policy. Although the economist-technocrats seemed to dominate the field of advice and expertise, various centers of economic power were essentially controlled by military personnel, who used the new development strategy not merely to improve the laggard economy, but also to secure the military elite's goal of social modernization, stability, and national resilience (Rudner 1976: 250).

The conventional view among Indonesia's economist-technocrats was that the rate of population growth is a significant indicator of the success of a country's economic development efforts, but they did not generally regard the uneven population distribution between Java and outer islands as an issue of urgency. Nitisastro, widely known as the architect of the New Order's economic development policies, strongly argued that what was needed to overcome the population problem in Indonesia was a massive development effort to create expanding employment opportunities, accompanied by a rapid spread of fertility control (Nitisastro 1970). Yet, curiously enough, the problem of uneven population distribution and the role of transmigration as a means to overcome it remained a focus

TABLE 7.1 Five-Year Plans I–VI: Transmigrant Families Moved, by Province of Origin

Province	First Plan 1969/70–1973/74		Second Plan 1974/75–1978/79		Third Plan 1979/80–1983/84		Fourth Plan 1984/85–1988/89		Fifth Plan 1989/90–1993/94		Sixth Plan 1993/94–1996/97	
	Number	%	Number	%	Number	%	Number	%	Number	%	Number	%
Jakarta	750	2	2,405	4	4,412	1	2,937	1	6,343	3	5,171	2
West Java	4,941	13	7,230	13	60,003	16	37,196	16	36,997	15	23,846	10
Central Java	10,966	29	20,148	37	96,099	26	45,851	20	40,754	16	24,707	11
Yogyakarta	5,260	13	5,150	9	19,998	5	8,950	4	10,352	4	5,761	3
East Java	12,044	31	15,390	28	93,314	25	44,512	19	37,783	15	24,451	11
Java (subtotals)	33,961	88	50,323	91	273,826	73	139,446	60	132,229	53	83,936	37
Bali	5,100	13	3,060	6	14,735	4	4,369	2	6,673	3	4,362	2
NTB (W. Nusatenggara)	300	1	1,700	3	12,718	3	4,236	2	8,292	3	7,045	3
NTT (E. Nusatenggara)	—						3,300	1	3,864	2	3,561	1
Lampung	—						787					
APPDT	75				22,284	6	43,531	19	95,942	39	53,567	23
Resettlement	—				42,414	12	26,896	12			76,513	34
Relocation	—						5,857	3				
General Transmigrants	39,436	100	55,083	100	365,977	100	228,422	100	247,000	100	228,984	100
Unassisted/Partly Ass't. Transmigrants	—	—	7,281		169,497		521,728		—		—	
Totals	39,436	—	62,364		535,474		750,150		247,000	—	228,984	—

Note: Due to rounding the totals may not add up exactly.

Sources: Presidential Address, 16 August 1985 (Departemen Penerangan RI, 1985: XII/48–50); Presidential Address, 16 August 1989 (Departemen Penerangan RI, 1989: XII/692–5); Presidential Address, 16 August 1993 (Departemen Penerangan RI, 1993: XII/18–18); Presidential Address, 16 August 1997 (Departemen Penerangan RI, 1997: XIII/34–37).

TABLE 7.2 Five-Year Plans I–VI: General Transmigrant Families Moved, by Province of Destination

Province	First Plan 1969/70–1973/74 Number	%	Second Plan 1974/75–1978/79 Number	%	Third Plan 1979/80–1983/84 Number	%	Fourth Plan 1984/85–1988/89 Number	%	Fifth Plan 1989/90–1993/94 Number	%	Sixth Plan 1993/94–1996/97 Number	%
Aceh	—	—	800	1	10,771	3	7,084	3	9,312	4	9,507	4
N. Sumatra	200	—	500	1	8,006	2	3,651	2	4,828	2	6,063	3
W. Sumatra	450	1	3,950	7	7,603	2	9,185	4	6,952	3	5,737	3
Riau	500	1	662	1	37,522	10	27,300	12	39,074	16	26,994	12
Jambi	2,450	6	10,362	19	16,682	5	19,737	9	16,529	7	14,748	6
S. Sumatra	6,254	16	6,598	12	91,340	25	24,446	11	24,832	10	14,965	7
Bengkulu	1,300	3	3,600	7	12,187	3	9,076	4	12,591	5	9,535	4
Lampung	11,397	29	4,500	8	42,876	12	17,893	9	12,515	5	8,412	4
Sumatra (subtotals)	22,551	56	30,972	56	227,047	62	118,372	54	112,633	52	95,961	43
W. Kalimantan	952	2	2,100	4	15,141	4	19,684	9	24,143	10	24,945	11
C. Kalimantan	1,253	3	700	1	28,221	8	17,907	8	12,880	5	17,117	7
S. Kalimantan	1,490	4	4,300	8	15,374	4	13,922	7	7,744	3	8,985	4
E. Kalimantan	1,775	5	3,311	6	11,878	3	15,179	7	16,525	7	14,054	6
Kalimantan (subtotals)	5,470	14	10,411	19	70,614	19	66,692	30	61,292	25	65,101	28
N. Sulawesi	1,060	3	950	2	4,154	1	2,811	1	1,312	1	1,016	—
C. Sulawesi	3,452	9	5,700	10	15,740	4	10,441	5	13,293	5	11,404	5
S. Sulawesi	4,441	11	3,300	6	3,607	1	5,325	2	10,262	4	6,713	3
S.E. Sulawesi	2,012	5	3,250	6	19,225	5	7,002	3	5,412	2	2,786	1
Sulawesi (subtotals)	10,965	28	13,200	24	42,726	11	25,579	11	30,279	12	21,919	9
Maluku	350	1	200	—	7,635	2	3,270	1	5,789	2	13,450	6
Irian Jaya	100	—	300	—	16,616	5	12,598	6	18,373	7	23,991	10
NTB (W. Nusatenggara)	—	—	—	—	1,289	—	977	—	2,254	1	2,047	1
NTT (E. Nusatenggara)	—	—	—	—	—	—	—	—	830	—	1,915	1
East Timor	—	—	—	—	50	—	934	—	1,550	1	4,600	2
Eastern Indonesia Provinces (subtotals)									28,796	11	46,003	20
Totals	39,436	100	55,083	100	365,977	100	228,422	100	233,000	100	228,984	100

Note: Due to rounding the totals may not add up exactly.
Sources: Presidential Address, 16 August 1985 (Departemen Penerangan RI, 1985: XII/49); Presidential Address, 16 August 1989 (Departemen Penerangan RI, 1989: XII/693); Presidential Address, 16 August 1993 (Departemen Penerangan RI, 1993: XII/17–18); Presidential Address, 16 August 1997 (Departemen Penerangan RI, 1997: XIII/34–37).

of government thinking, and became a very important policy within the national development plans during the New Order.

President Suharto's real motive for continuing transmigration at the beginning of the New Order is not difficult to identify: It lies in the idea of harmony among the Javanese, which in the Indonesian political context can be translated to mean national unity and national integration. Transmigration was perceived by the President and the military as an instrument to accelerate the process of national integration. Government policies to relocate people from overcrowded Java to other islands were also considered an alternative to land reform.[12] Despite this, the colonial legacy and the population policies of the Old Order (which were basically pro-natalist and viewed uneven distribution as the main population problem), could not be easily eliminated from the thinking of the ruling elite.[13]

The Indonesian elite's divergent perceptions of the nature of population problems are not unusual. Weiner (1975: 66) has suggested that many governments assume that some of the problems associated with rapid population growth can be alleviated by policies aimed at population dispersal, and notes that migration policies are frequently embraced for a variety of purposes, but almost never for exclusively demographic reasons. Transmigration, as a form of land settlement scheme, can also be a supreme rhetorical device for a government and its ruling elite. According to Hulme, if the popular expectation is that those in power should "do something," then resettlement schemes are a most effective means of being seen to do so (Hulme 1987: 413).

The 1969 First Plan, strongly influenced by economist-technocrat views, mentioned the problem of population redistribution briefly, and transmigration policy only in passing; the need to meet labor requirements for development outside Java, although stated as a secondary goal, was given more attention. The transmigration program was considered an important source of labor to serve these broader goals and was also expected to increase food production in the outer islands. No numerical transmigration targets were set.

The actual course of the transmigration program, however, was neither as predicted by many observers nor as stated in the plan documents. In 1970, under the patronage of Brigadier General Soebiantoro, a national seminar on transmigration was held to discuss its role in national development. The landmark seminar, attended by scholars and policy makers, restored transmigration to a position of national importance by formulating a positive basis for the program in national development policy. The consensus of the seminar was that uneven population distribution was detrimental to many aspects of national development and, more crucially, to the achievement of national integration and security, reflecting a strong perception within the government elite that once the demographic goals of transmigration were achieved and population distribution balanced, other goals, such as economic, social, and national integration, would automatically be reached.

An international workshop on transmigration followed in 1971, and in 1972 the President established a national transmigration law, in which seven policy goals were stated: (1) improvements in living standards; (2) regional development; (3) balanced population distribution; (4) equitably distributed development throughout Indonesia; (5) utilization of natural and human resources; (6) national union and unity; and (7) strengthening of national defense and security. These goals reflected the complexity of the role of transmigration policy, suggesting that transmigration was seen by policy makers as a cure for a wide range of social and economic weaknesses. In 1973, two further seminars were held involving several foreign aid agencies, including the UN Food and Agriculture Organization (FAO), the U.S. Agency for International Development (USAID), and the World Food Programme (WFP), centered on providing financial assistance for the transmigration program. The role of foreign donor agencies, particularly the World Bank, was later to become very significant in reshaping Indonesia's transmigration policy.

During the Second Plan (1974–1979), the transmigration program became more salient, as the increase in government revenues from the oil boom provided funds to support the program on a much larger scale. For the first time, the plan explicitly recognized transmigration as an important means for strengthening national integration, while only implying that it was a tool for population redistribution. The Second Plan also identified the First Plan's problems with transmigration program implementation, including those relating to resettlement preparation in the receiving regions, choices of location, the provision of equipment, and coordination with the regional governments and with other agencies.

Although the demographic rationale for transmigration was only implied in the plan, a numerical target was explicitly mentioned: to move 250,000 families within five years. According to the plan, in selecting the sending areas, priority was to be given to regions such as areas prone to flooding and to rural locations with population densities of more than 1,000 persons per square kilometer. South Sumatra, South and East Kalimantan, and South, Central, and Southeast Sulawesi were designated as the main receiving areas for transmigration settlement.

In 1976, a significant development in the transmigration program was begun with the approval of the first World Bank-assisted transmigration projects, consisting of two pilot schemes in southern Sumatra. The first was rehabilitation of an existing settlement in Way Abung and the development of a new settlement in Baturadja; the second was to conduct research and long-term monitoring and evaluation on cropping systems. In the first, new settlers in Baturadja were provided with 5-hectare farms, which included 1.25 hectares of cleared land for food crops and 1 hectare of rubber trees established for the small-holders by a public sector estate. These benefits were provided to the settlers as a grant. To promote food crop development, farmers were given cattle for plowing, and free agricultural inputs (seed, fertilizer, and pesticides) were provided for three years. The first pilot scheme was considered by the World Bank to have been successful. The second was intended to resettle 30,000 families along the new Trans-Sumatra Highway, particularly in Jambi province (World Bank 1988: 161).

By the end of the Second Plan, in 1979, it had become clear that its achievement was far below its aim; of the targeted 250,000 families only 55,083 had been resettled. One study (Guinness 1977: 11) indicated that the failure was largely due to a lack of coordination between the various government agencies assigned to carry out the program. Another problem was the limited capacity of transmigration-implementing agencies to use the financial resources allocated in the budget. A special report showed that in the first year 24 percent of the transmigration budget remained unspent; in the second year, 34 percent, and by the second half of the third year, 96 percent of the budget was unallocated (Beddoes 1976, cited in Guinness 1977: 11–12). These represented very large sums, since the transmigration budget had increased from Rp 800 million in 1969–1970 to Rp 6,652 million in 1974–1975 and Rp 14,936 million in 1975–1976.

In the Third Plan (1979–1983), the Directorate General of Transmigration became part of the Department of Manpower and Transmigration. Harun Zain, an economist and former governor of West Sumatra, was appointed Minister, while Martono, a senior politician, filled the new post of Junior Minister for Transmigration. Harun Zain's appointment, due to his experience as governor in one of the receiving provinces, indicated the economist-technocrats' interest in incorporating transmigration into regional economic development. However, the appointment of Martono to the position of Junior Minister for Transmigration indicated that the President did not want to hand over policy control completely to the technocrats. In fact, the division of responsibility between the Director General of Transmigration, who reported directly to the President, and the Junior Minister for Transmigration, created coordination problems among the transmigration agencies.

Although the numerical achievements of the Second Plan had been far from its objective, the Third Plan doubled the target, to 500,000 families, not only because of the general euphoria occasioned by the second oil boom, but also because the economist-technocrats expected an increase in support from many foreign donor agencies. The 1979 project was the second to be assisted by the World Bank. Concentrating on the resettlement of transmigrants in dry-land areas along the new Trans-Sumatra Highway, it was a significant departure from the Bank's successful first project based on tree-crop transmigration schemes. This was an important development in the evolution of World Bank involvement in transmigration for at least two reasons: It had failed to influence the policy makers in directing transmigration policy into more market-oriented types of population settlements; and although the economist-technocrat group had played a larger role in reshaping transmigration policy into the so-called "integrated regional development" mode, the ambitious targets of the Third Plan mirrored the influence of strong forces that continued to view transmigration as a population policy aimed at relieving population pressures in Java through the development of agricultural settlement on the outer islands.[14]

The beginning of the Third Plan, therefore, indicated an important change in transmigration policies, which could be seen as a revitalization of the non-economic forces, particularly those represented by the military elite and the government bureaucratic apparatus, or as an expression of the difficulties and declining role of the economic views represented, in particular, by the economist-technocrats and the World Bank. The fact that the World Bank also tolerated the more demographic orientation of transmigration policy suggests that the Bank and, in particular, its bureaucratic elements, had adopted a more pragmatic approach.

By the end of the Third Plan, 535,474 families were reported to have been moved under the transmigration program. According to Hardjono (1986: 29), to say that the target was achieved gives a slightly exaggerated picture of the extent to which people were moved from Java and Bali at government expense, because only 365,977 families were moved by the government transmigration agency as fully supported transmigrants, a designation including both local people who moved into transmigration projects and families that had to be resettled within the same province for other reasons. The remaining 169,497 families, representing 32 percent of the total, were actually spontaneous transmigrants who moved with little or no government assistance. Another observer (Babcock 1986: 182) described the government's claim that the Third Plan had achieved its goal as a manipulation to justify the overly ambitious target.

Transmigration as a Full Department: 1983 and After

At the beginning of the Fourth Plan (1983–1988) Presidential Decree No. 45/M/1983 established transmigration as a separate department. Previous rivalries with the Directorate General of Transmigration ended with the appointment of former Junior Minister Martono as Minister. The government expected that an independent ministry could solve the earlier coordination problems that had plagued the department during the Third Plan. The President appointed Emil Salim, one of the New Order's leading economists, to the new post of State Minister for Population and Environment, responsible for the formulation, management, and coordination of national population policies. Given the number of economists in the central government, including economist-demographer Professor Nitisastro, it is surprising that an integrated national population policy was such a long time coming.[15]

The paradox of population and development in Indonesia, however, is understandable given the very different perceptions of the "population factors" held by the President and his military elite and the economist-technocrats, whose political position was almost entirely dependent on their ability to convince the latter group that their expertise was essential (Glassburner 1978: 32–33). Similarly, Rudner has argued that having no political base other than military patronage, technocrat ministers and planners were ultimately dependent upon the confidence of the military elite in general, and the President in particular; whatever their formal functions in economic policy-making, the decisions of economist-technocrats became operative only when, and to the extent that, they acquired executive support from military leaders and local commanders (Rudner 1976: 255). In the Fourth Plan, therefore, it was likely that transmigration policy would remain largely beyond the influence of the Minister of Population and Environment, as transmigration had by then become an independent department with a minister close to the President.

The Fourth Plan showed how important the transmigration program had become in national development policy. The target number was increased to 750,000 families, due to the supposedly successful outcomes of the Third Plan. Foreign financial support, particularly from the World Bank, also increased dramatically. However, the appointment of Martono as the minister suggested that the technocrats were losing control of the program. In the Fourth Plan, instead of demographic and regional arguments for transmigration, national defense and security were cited; the decision making process, particularly in setting the five-year target number, was not based on demographic considerations. This is not unique, however. McIntosh and Finkle (1985: 321) noted that the main reason for the weak relationship between demographic data and policy is that population policy formulation is determined primarily by political rather than demographic rationality.[16]

In the Fourth Plan documents, transmigration was discussed in a separate chapter of fifty-eight pages; the First Plan had covered it in only one and a half. Its role in national defense and security was emphasized by the Chief of the Armed Forces, General Moerdani, who stated that transmigration policy was the only policy within the economic development framework that had a direct linkage with national security and defense. He argued that it was necessary for the military to be involved in site selection, primarily because transmigration location had a strong relation to the concept of territorial management.[17] One obvious attempt by the military to influence transmigration policy was the 1983 appointment of Major General Santoso, a former regional army commander in Irian Jaya, as Secretary General of the Department of Transmigration. According to Anderson, this appointment should be read as General Moerdani's move to take full control of the "explosive transmigration program in Irian Jaya" (Anderson 1985: 140).

The issues of national integration and national unity had been discussed from the early years of independence, becoming especially important during the 1956–1958 regional rebellions. The decisive role of the military in ending the rebellions has been a major factor in reshaping the military leadership's role ever since (Feith and Lev 1963: 37). National integration had become the key issue and prime concern for the military leaders, whose power was further entrenched by the political chaos of 1965. The conceptual links between transmigration policy and national integration, however, were rarely stated. One explicit explanation, however, was given by Brigadier General Edi Sugardo of the National Defense Institute (Lemhanas), the think tank of the Department of Defense:

> From the geo-politic and geo-strategic point of view, transmigration policy is an effort, method, and means to achieve geographic integration, which is a basic condition for the unity of the nation, to improve the people's welfare and awareness, and provide an opportunity to utilize natural resources. Achievement of geographic integration, on the one hand, will protect the nation from centrifugal tendencies, and on the other hand, strengthen centripetal forces. Geographic integration is also a medium to build understanding, friendship, and cooperation with other countries. From the point of view of national defense, transmigration is supportive of the Popular Defense and Security System [*Sistim Pertahanan dan Kemananan Rakyat Semesta* or SISHANKAMRATA], in order to resist the threat of subversion, infiltration and invasion from abroad, particularly through the provision of human resources. (Sugardo 1987: 4–5, translated by the author)

Thus in the view of the military, geographic integration, in which transmigration policy plays an important role by providing human resources, is a necessary condition for the attainment of national integration. Closely related to this view is the Indonesian Armed Forces Strategic Concept of Basic Defense, which is based on the military doctrine of Territorial Warfare, and requires that the defense forces, especially the army, be organized principally along territorial rather than functional lines, with territorial commands more or less parallel to the civilian administration. One of their major functions was to maintain contact with the local people, who could be quickly mobilized to support guerrilla operations whenever necessary; this territorial structure has also been very convenient for the purpose of political control.[18] During the early 1980s the transmigration program was designed to serve the military's strategic goals, particularly in the troubled provinces, such as Aceh, Irian Jaya, and East Timor.

Implementation of the program after the mid-1980s generally failed, as hopes that had emerged at the beginning of the Fourth Plan confronted hard realities and both internal and external problems. The internal problems were related to departmental management, particularly the problem of the unspent budget, which reflected the inefficiency of plan implementation. The external problems were related mostly to criticism from abroad, particularly on issues concerning the destruction of tropical forests and unfair treatment of the indigenous populations whose lands were allocated for transmigration. Approaching the end of 1984, in an attempt to find a solution to these problems, the Minister of Transmigration asked Professor Sumitro, the guru of the New Order's economist-technocrat group, to act as an adviser to the Minister on matters related to program planning and internal management, including the problem of unused funds. The report, completed in April 1985, was considered a reconnaissance phase and mainly focused on internal management. Its technocratic nature and its avoidance of more controversial issues, such as the influence of strategic military interests on the policy, were major limitations to its value as a basis for program improvement.

The external problems of transmigration implementation multiplied rapidly, especially after the government decided to focus the transmigration receiving areas in the eastern part of Indonesia, particularly the border between Irian Jaya and Papua New Guinea, a decision that resulted in many technical as well as social and political problems (Manning and Rumbiak 1987: 71–82). Due to issues such as environmental degradation, in particular tropical forest destruction, and the displacement of the indigenous population, international criticism of the transmigration policy began to mount. The World Bank, which for almost fifteen years had supported transmigration policy, also became the target of international criticism.[19]

In January 1985, a research team headed by Professor Mubyarto of Gajah Mada University was asked by Minister for Transmigration Martono to study and report on transmigration in Irian Jaya. Their observations were presented at a seminar held at Gajah Mada University, where they stressed the urgent need to revise and reschedule the transmigration target in Irian Jaya, an issue subsequently highlighted by the press. In addition to exacerbating social and political conflicts, the original transmigration program in Irian Jaya was criticized as economically unrealistic. In an apparently hasty reaction, after a quick consultation with the President, Minister Martono strongly emphasized that the transmigration target for Irian Jaya would not be reduced but would even be increased (*Kompas* 1985a: 1).

This intention was subverted by the collapse of oil prices in early 1986, which led the government to reduce the budget for transmigration by 44 percent in fiscal 1986/87, and by a further 65 percent in fiscal 1987/88.[20] Costs per transmigrant family had risen from U.S.$577 at the beginning of the First Plan, to nearly U.S.$6,500 in 1983/84 (Arndt 1984: 66), and, as extensively reported in the press, many transmigration projects had to be abandoned because of the budget cuts. On 24 November 1987, the Minister of Transmigration announced that 16,000 houses built for transmigration had been declared unusable, because the government had no money to send transmigrants to the receiving areas.[21]

This setback attracted much comment and criticism. Some critics suggested that the transmigration program should be overhauled or the department downgraded to its original status as a directorate general. However, in spite of the program's financial problems, at the commencement of the Fifth Plan (1988–1993) the President replaced Martono with Major General Soegiarto, a former Head of Social and Political Affairs in the Defense Department, as the Minister of Transmigration, evidence that transmigration would retain an important role in the national scene and that the economist-technocrat group had become less influential. Under the Fifth Plan, there was a new orientation toward more spontaneous transmigration schemes and promotion of cash-crop transmigration settlements. The Fifth Plan set a five-year target of 550,000 families, of which only 180,000 would be fully supported by the government. The remaining 370,000 families would be assisted through various schemes under the spontaneous transmigration program. The Fifth Plan also aimed at rehabilitating the poor conditions of existing transmigration settlements.

The implementation of the Fifth Plan proved difficult. Besides the limited budget allocated for transmigration, the program's public image had been severely affected by the previous mismanagement. Data on inter-provincial migration from the 1990 population census showed that many migrants were moved to urban rather rural areas (Mantra 1992), and that a remarkable shift from sponsored to voluntary migration had occurred in the mid-1980s as new economic growth centers developed in several urban areas on the outer islands (Tirtosudarmo 1994).[22] In this period, migrants were also attracted by labor opportunities in neighboring countries, particularly Malaysia (Tirtosudarmo 1996). The press reported that the new minister frankly acknowledged the difficulties faced by his government in recruiting potential transmigrants, since people had become less willing to move to transmigration settlements, preferring to move to other places, particularly to urban areas. At the end of the Fifth Plan, it was obvious that even though the target had been set very low, its achievement was generally even lower.

With the commencement of the Sixth Plan (1993–1998), in a clear move to boost the involvement of the private sector in the transmigration program, the President appointed a new Minister for Transmigration, Siswono Yudohusodo, a successful businessman. Although observers generally regarded transmigration as having lost its rational justification, President Suharto expanded its scope to include resettlement of the so-called forest squatters, including many isolated tribal groups in the outer islands who had been officially recognized as living below the poverty line. It now became the Department of Transmigration and Resettlement of Forest Squatters. The beginning of the Sixth Plan was marked by a Presidential statement about various groups living below the poverty line; the state's rhetoric on raising the living standards of such groups conveniently supported the new task of transmigration (Tirtosudarmo 1993).[23]

An economic and business information center was created in 1994, which, in a policy similar to that of the World Bank in 1976, attempted to attract private and business sectors to invest capital in transmigration areas, a move to integrate transmigration into the cash-crop market economy. The major problem with this venture, however, was the lack of legal and business expertise within the Department of Transmigration. The new minister had indeed pushed the transmigration policy toward a more business and market orientation, yet, as the existing system in the Ministry of Transmigration became overly bureaucratized, the private sector became less willing to participate in the transmigration program. A few viewed the attempt as a revival of the colonial state's economic strategy.

Conclusion

One of the enduring results of the colonial state's Ethical Policy was Indonesia's migration policy, which relied on sponsored population mobility from the inner island, Java, to the outer islands, a policy that has remained on the state agenda for almost a century. In a much broader sense, the colonial state's dichotomy between "inner" and "outer" islands has also persisted, apparently resulting from the perception that the outer islands are empty land and the main sources of economic revenue while Java, the center of political power, is plagued by a population surplus. The persistence of a population resettlement solution, rather than industrialization, reflects the continuation of the dominant interest within the state, which serves the elite of the day. Migration policies are merely palliative in nature, consciously avoiding any fundamental solutions that demand redistribution of productive land or capital. Although in the early years of independence it was assumed that transmigration would be integrated with industrialization, such hopes were soon dashed.

While the Dutch colonial government used resettlement as an instrument of demographic engineering and only implicitly for security purposes, after Independence the government of the Republic of Indonesia explicitly relocated people for political and strategic goals. Demographic engineering has become an important part of the state's strategic policy to reduce the increasing possibility of social and political tensions, particularly in areas surrounding the national capital city of Jakarta, and to support the state's foreign policy. After Independence, several ideological leaders, such as Yamin and Sukarno, also perceived transmigration as a strategy aimed at assimilating different ethnic groups in order to build a homogenized cultural identity and national integration.

In the New Order period that began after the military defeated the communists in the mid-1960s, while transmigration policy began to be redesigned as part of an economic development strategy, to perceive it as solely a demographic or an economic development endeavor would be naive and misleading. The elusive and multifaceted goals of the policy, and the constant changes in implementing agencies, were strong indications that the program had never been carefully monitored and evaluated. Furthermore, the unavoidable rivalry and conflicts between the economist-technocrats, who viewed the program mainly as an element of regional development, and the political bureaucrats, who were close to the military with its strategic interests, have undoubtedly distorted the process of plan formulation and implementation. In this situation, the

World Bank, which in the beginning saw transmigration as a means to promote commercial tree-crop cultivation, could not escape the pressure to use transmigration policy as a primary tool for population distribution. After the mid 1980s, the state's attempt to reorient transmigration policy toward a more market oriented economy apparently failed due to the lack of legal and management capacities within the Ministry of Transmigration.

As we have learned from history, transmigration is a policy that elegantly provides the ruling elite with a disguised tool for defending their political as well as economic interests. In the late 1990s, it was strongly indicated that business and the private sector, particularly the logging and mining companies, were among the beneficiaries of the new aim of the transmigration program—the relocation of people currently relying on the forest for their survival. The relocation of these people, who are still dominant in the upland regions in Sumatra, Kalimantan, Sulawesi, and Irian Jaya, has had a catastrophic impact on their social and cultural lives. The relocation of tribal groups, which are perceived as potentially undermining the state's political hegemony, for example the Dayaks in Kalimantan and several tribal groups in Irian Jaya, serves the strategic goal of the state to subjugate these latent rebellious indigenous groups. Looking to the future, given its significant instrumental value to the ruling elite, the transmigration program will very likely be retained in the state's policy agenda.

Notes

This is a revision of a paper originally prepared for a workshop on Demography and Security, organized by Professor Myron Weiner, at the Massachusetts Institute of Technology, Cambridge Massachusetts, 11–12 December 1998. An earlier version of this paper was published as a PSTC Working Paper #97-05, at Brown University. Comments are gratefully acknowledged from Judith Banister, Regina Bures, Lorraine Corner, Calvin Goldscheider, Sidney Goldstein, Terrence Hull, Gavin Jones, Geoff McNicoll, Paul Meyer, Sharon Stanton Russell, Myron Weiner, and Thee Kian Wie.

1. Transmigration, far from being an exception, is the archetype of resettlement policies. For an interesting comparison with other population resettlement policies in the world, see Levang (1995).
2. See studies on the center-regional relations, among others by Maryanov, 1958; Legge, 1965; Nawawi, 1968; Bachtiar, 1974; Mackie, 1980; Achmad, 1984; MacAndrews, 1986.
3. While "emigration" technically refers to migration out of one's country, the Dutch used it to mean what is now termed transmigration under a population relocation policy.

4. "I believe that his plan for salvation which is indicated by the trilogy: education, irrigation and emigration … is inadequate because the distress has taken on too vast proportions. He believes that in particular indigenous education will have an enormous impact on the well-being of the Javanese. I am of the opinion that this is an illusion which is completely out of touch with reality. The only solution is a more intensified production and this is only possible with industry, preferably large-scale indigenous industry …" (Penders 1969: 29).

5. These movements were comprehensively documented by the National Archives of the Republic of Indonesia (Arsip Nasional Republik Indonesia) in 1981.

6. The fact that migration became an important part of the government plan immediately after Independence was, according to some observers, rather strange. Newly independent Indonesia had been born of a rhetoric that called for the rapid destruction of colonial economic institutions (Pauuw, 1963: 155).

7. Wertheim's prediction about the probability of social conflict in Lampung as a consequence of rapid population growth and social tensions between migrants and local people was realized in the so-called Lampung Affairs, which broke out in February 1989.

8. Muhammad Yamin was a historian, poet, and politician, who was described by Benedict Anderson, a noted Indonesianist at Cornell University, as "Indonesia's best known political eccentric as long as he lived. It was said of him, not altogether unkindly, that he was like a horse: if you were in front of him, you were likely to get nipped; if you were behind him, to get kicked; and if under him, to get trampled on. But if you were on top of him, with reins in your hands, he would carry you fast and far" (Anderson 1972: 288).

9. As observed by Heeren (1979: 24), however, there is confusion among some sources as to whether the target number referred to individuals or families, and it is obvious that Yamin, in fact, gave little attention to transmigration.

10. Quoted from Sukarno's speech at the general meeting on National Movements for Transmigration, 28 December 1964, entitled "Transmigration Is a Matter of Life or Death for Indonesia" (Department of Information c. 1964: 13).

11. The First Plan (1969–1974), according to Mangkusuwondo (1970), one of the New Order's leading economists, was not an exhaustive plan of expenditure and was not grounded in any particular macroeconomic model.

12. Land reform, which was aggressively promoted by the Indonesian Communist Party (PKI) prior to the abortive 1965 coup, was identified by the New Order as a communist policy.

13. An illustration of how the elite, particularly the military, have persistently regarded transmigration as an important undertaking is shown by a request from General Suharto to the U.S. Ambassador to Indonesia, Marshall Green, at their first meeting on 29 May 1966. In the meeting Suharto asked for U.S.$500 million in grants or soft loans to assist the transmigration program.

14. The central government's obsession with promoting population resettlement based on food crop agricultural systems as practiced in Java, besides being a legacy of the colonial era, was also a manifestation of the agroecological mythology of the Javanese that has developed on Java and strongly influenced the thinking of many policy makers in the central government (Dove 1985: 32).

15. The lack of integration between population policy and national development policy seemed "paradoxical," at least to outside observers (Hugo et al. 1987: 315).

16. According to McIntosh and Finkle, among the most important determinants of the behavior of government leaders as they contemplate demographic data and advice are the ideology and values of the regime, which are often closely related to the historical experience of the nation.
17. Quoted from Moerdani's keynote address at the National Defense Institute seminar (*Kompas* 1985b: 12).
18. For a further explanation of this issue, see Crouch (1986: 3). In a similar vein, Tanter (1991, quoted in Sebastian 1996: 88–89) describes three elements that influence the territorial strategic concept of the military in Indonesia: *geography* as the framework, *demography* as the content, and *social conditions* as the factor of social life that results from the synthesis of the other two elements.
19. For example, *The Ecologist*, No. 2/3, 1986, in collaboration with Survival International and Tapol, published a special issue that strongly criticized the transmigration program in Indonesia.
20. This drastic reduction was referred to by Mubyarto, in a seminar attended by the author in February 1987, "… as the will of God." Such a comment given by a notable economist of Mubyarto's standing reflects how powerless the academics actually are in dealing with the issue of transmigration.
21. An unofficial source informed the author that the actual number was over 40,000 houses.
22. The increasing numbers of voluntary migrants to the outer islands in the 1990s have apparently resulted in increased conflicts between migrants and local people. In 1995 mass open conflicts broke out between migrants and local people in East Timor, Irian Jaya, and Flores, all in Eastern Indonesia provinces (Tirtosudarmo 1995). The latest incident occurred in Sanggau-Ledo, West Kalimantan, in the first week of January 1997, between the Madurese migrants and the indigenous Dayak people (*Kompas* 1997: 1). Many observers have argued that the economic inequality between migrants and local people are factors underlying of these ethnic group conflicts (see Tirtosudarmo 1997).
23. In 1995 and 1996 several riots occurred in which indigenous people protested against the exploitation of their customary lands by mining under Freeport Inc. in Timika, Irian Jaya, and by logging in East and West Kalimantan. These incidents, particularly in Timika, have strongly influenced the government to design a resettlement program to relocate these tribal groups from their customary lands.

References

Achmad, Ichlasul. 1984. "West Sumatra and South Sulawesi: Two Regions in Their Relation to Central Government, Indonesia," unpublished Ph.D. thesis, Monash University.

Anderson, Benedict. 1972. *Java in Time of Revolution: Occupation and Resistance, 1944–1946*. Ithaca: Cornell University Press.

———. 1985. "Current Data on the Indonesian Military Elite." *Indonesia* 40: 131–164 (October).

Arndt, Heinz. 1984. "Transmigration in Indonesia." Working Paper No. 146, ILO.

Arsip Nasional Republik Indonesia (National Archive of Republic of Indonesia). 1981. *Laporan-Laporan tentang Gerakan Protes di Jawa pada abad XX* [Reports on Protest Movement in Java at the 20th Century]. Jakarta.

Babcock, T. 1986. "Transmigration: Land Settlement or Regional Development." *Bulletin of Indonesian Economic Studies* 12 (3): 72–90.

Bachtiar, Harsya. 1974. *The Indonesian Nation: Problems of Integration and Disintegration*. Singapore: Institute of Asian Studies.

Beddoes, G. 1976. *Report on Transmigration Budgetary and Accounting Procedures.* Jakarta: Department of Transmigration.

Crouch, Harold. 1986. "Security Concerns Posed by Indonesia's Armed Forces." *Indonesia Issues* No. 3 (November).

Department of Information, Republic of Indonesia. c. 1964. *"Soal Transmigrasi adalah Soal Mati Hidup Bangsa Indonesia"* [Transmigration Is a Matter of Life or Death for Indonesia], President Sukarno, speeches in the General Meeting of National Movement of Transmigration, 28 December, Jakarta.

Dove, Michael. 1985. "The Agroecological Mythology of the Javanese and the Political Economy of Indonesia." *Indonesia* 39: 1–36 (April).

Feith, H., and D. Lev. 1963. "The End of the Indonesian Rebellion." *Pacific Affairs*, 36 (1): 32–46 (Spring).

Glassburner, B. 1978. "Political Economy and the Soeharto [*sic*] Regime." *Bulletin of Indonesian Economic Studies* 14 (3): 24–51 (November).

Guinness, Patrick, ed. 1977. "Transmigrants in South Kalimantan and South Sulawesi: Inter-island Government Sponsored Migration in Indonesia." Report Series No. 15, Yogyakarta: Population Institute, Gajah Mada University.

Hamidy, U. U., and M. Ahmad. 1984. *Masalah Sosial Budaya dan Teknologi Transmigrasi Lokal* [The Socio-Cultural and Technological Problems of Local Transmigration]. Pekanbaru: Bappeda Riau.

Hardjono, J. M. 1986. "Transmigration: Looking to the Future." *Bulletin of Indonesian Economic Studies* 22 (2): 28–53 (August).

Hardjosudarmo, S. 1965. *Kebijaksanaan Transmigrasi dalam rangka Pembangunan Masyarakat Desa di Indonesia* [Transmigration Policy in the Context of Rural Development in Indonesia]. Jakarta: Bhratara.

Hatta, Mohammad. 1954. *Beberapa Fasal Ekonomi: Djalan ke Ekonomi dan Koperasi* [Some Economic Aspects: The Path Toward Economy and Co-operative]. Jakarta: Perpustakaan Perguruan Kementrian P.P. dan K.

Heeren, H. J. 1979. *Transmigrasi di Indonesia* [Transmigration in Indonesia]. Yogyakarta: Gajah Mada University Press.

Hugo, Graeme, et al., eds. 1987. *The Demographic Dimension in Indonesian Development*. Singapore: Oxford University Press.

Hulme, David. 1987. "State-Sponsored Land Settlement Policies: Theory and Practice." *Development and Change* 18: 413–436.

Kahin, George McT. 1965. "Indonesia," in *Major Governments of Asia*, George McT. Kahin, ed. Ithaca, NY: Cornell University Press.

Kartodirdjo, Sartono. 1973. *Protest Movements in Rural Java: A Study of Agrarian Unrest in the Nineteenth and Early Twentieth Centuries*. Singapore: Oxford University Press.

Kompas. 1985a. "Pengiriman transmigran ke Irja akan ditingkatkan" [The Sending of Transmigrants to Irian Jaya Will Be Increased]. 26 February: 1.

———. 1985b. "Program transmigrasi penting bagi ketahanan nasional" [Transmigration Program Is Necessary for National Defense]. 8 March: 12.

————. 1997. "Bentrok massal di Sanggau Ledo: 3.250 orang mengungsi ke Singkawang" [Mass Conflict in Sanggau Ledo: 3,250 People Flee to Singkawang]. 3 January: 1.

Kuntjorojakti, Dorodjatun. 1978. "The Political Economy of Development: The Case Study of Indonesia under the New Order Government." Unpublished Ph.D. thesis, University of California, Berkeley.

Legge, J. D. 1965. *Indonesia*. Englewood Cliffs, NJ: Prentice Hall.

Levang, Patrice. 1995. "Transmigration as a Medley of World's Resettlement Policies." Paper presented at the International Seminar on Population Resettlement for Poverty Alleviation, organized by Ministry of Transmigration and Forest Squatter Resettlement, Jakarta, 27 November–1 December.

MacAndrews, Collin. 1986. *Central Government and Local Development in Indonesia*. Singapore: Oxford University Press.

Mackie, Jamie. 1980. "Integrating and Centrifugal Factors in Indonesia Politics since 1945," in Jamie Mackie, ed., *Indonesia: The Making of a Nation*. Canberra: Research School of Pacific Studies, Australian National Universities.

Mangkusuwondo, S. 1970. "Repelita: The First Six Months," in *Five Papers on Indonesian Economic Development*, pp. 15–31. Jakarta: Yayasan Badan Penerbit Fakultas Ekonomi Universitas Indonesia.

Manning, C., and M. Rumbiak. 1987. "Irian Jaya: Economic Change, Migrant Labor and Indigenous Welfare." Paper presented in the Indonesian Regional Economic Surveys Workshop, 2–6 February, ANU, Canberra.

Mantra, Ida Bagus. 1992. "Pola dan Arah Migrasi Penduduk Antar Propinsi, di Indonesia, Tahun 1990" [The Pattern and Trends of Inter-provincial Migration in Indonesia in 1990], *Populasi* 2 (3): 39–59.

Maryanov, G. S. 1958. *Decentralisation in Indonesia as a Political Problem*. Modern Indonesia Project. Ithaca, NY: Cornell University.

McIntosh, C. Alison, and Jason L. Finkle. 1985. "Demographic Rationalism and Political Systems," in Proceedings of International Population Conference, pp. 319–329. Florence: IUSSP.

McNicoll, Geoffrey. 1966. "Internal Migration in Indonesia: Descriptive Notes." *Indonesia* 5: 29–92.

Nawawi, M. A. 1968. "Regionalism and Regional Conflicts in Indonesia." Unpublished Ph.D. thesis, Princeton University, Princeton NJ.

Multatuli. [1860] 1972. *Max Havelaar, or the Coffee Auctions of the Dutch Trading Company*. Djakarta: Djambatan (in Indonesian). English-language edition 1982. Amherst MA: University of Massachusetts Press.

Nitisastro, Widjojo. 1970. *Population Trends in Indonesia*. Ithaca NY: Cornell University Press.

Pauuw, D. S. 1963. "From Colonial to Guided Economy," in Ruth McVey, ed., *Indonesia*. Southeast Asian Studies. New Haven: Yale University Press.

Pelzer, K. J. 1945. *Pioneer Settlement in the Asiatic Tropics*. New York: Institute of Pacific Relations.

Penders, C. L. M. 1969. "Java's Population Problem during the Colonial Period." *World Review* 8 (1): 24–34 (March).

Ricklefs, M. C. 1981. *A History of Modern Indonesia*. London: MacMillan.

Rudner, Martin. 1976. "The Indonesian Military and Economic Policy: The Goals and Performance of the First Five-Year Development Plan, 1969–1974." *Modern Asian Studies* 10: 244–284.

Sebastian, Leonard C. 1996. "Indonesian National Security and Defense Planning," Unpublished Ph.D. thesis, Australian National University.

Sjamsu, Amral. 1960. *Dari Kolonisasi ke Transmigrasi, 1905–1955* [From Colonization to Transmigration, 1905–1955]. Jakarta: Penerbit Djambatan.

Sugardo, Edi. 1987. "Pengaruh Distribusi Penduduk terhadap Geo-Politik dan Geo-strategi Indonesia" [The Impact of Population Distribution on Geo-Politics and Geo-Strategy in Indonesia]. Paper presented at the Seminar on Population Redistribution Policy in Indonesia, organized by the State Ministry of Population and Environment, Jakarta, 16 July and 14 August.

Tanter, Richard. 1991. "Intelligence Agencies and Third World Militarization: A Case Study of Indonesia, 1969–1989," unpublished Ph.D. thesis, Department of Politics, Monash University, Australia.

Thee, Kian Wie. 1969. "Plantation Agriculture and Export Growth: An Economic History of East Sumatra, 1863–1942," unpublished Ph.D. thesis, University of Wisconsin.

Thompson, V. 1947. *Labor Problems in Southeast Asia*. New Haven: Yale University Press.

Tirtosudarmo, Riwanto. 1990. "Transmigration and Its Center-Regional Contexts: The Case of Riau and South Kalimantan Provinces, Indonesia," unpublished Ph.D. thesis, Research School of Social Sciences, Australian National University, Canberra, Australia.

———. 1993. "Problem Pemukiman Perambah Hutan." [The Problematic of Forest Squatter Resettlement]. *Populasi* 3 (2): 1–12.

———. 1994. "Indonesia: From Transmigration to Human Resource Migration. A Paradigm Shift?" Paper presented at the Human Resource Migration Session, Fourth Convention of the East Asian Economic Association, 25–26 August, Taipei, Taiwan.

———. 1995. "The Political Demography of National Integration and Sustainable Development in Indonesia." Paper presented at a seminar on "Sustainable Development in Asia Pacific," organized by the Institute of Development Studies, Kota Kinibalu, Sabah, Malaysia, 26–28 October.

———. 1996. "The Politics of Population Mobility in Southeast Asia: The Case of Indonesian Migrant Workers in Malaysia." Paper presented at a seminar on "Movements of Peoples within and from East and Southeast Asian Regions: Trends, Causes and Consequences, and Policy Measures," conducted by the Indonesian Institute of Sciences and The Toyota Foundation, Jakarta, 5–6 June.

———. 1997. "From *Emigratie* to *Transmigrasi*: Continuity and Change in Migration Policies in Indonesia." PSTC Working Paper #97-05, Brown University.

van der Kroef, J. 1956. "Population Pressure and Economic Development in Indonesia," in *Demographic Analysis: Selected Readings*, J. J. Spengler and O. D. Duncan, eds., pp. 739–754. Glencoe, IL: The Free Press.

Weiner, Myron. 1975. "Internal Migration Policies: Purposes, Interests, Instruments, Effects," in W. F. Ilchman et al., eds. *Policy Sciences and Population*. Lexington, MA: Lexington Books.

Wertheim, W. F. 1959. "Sociological Aspects of Inter-islands in Indonesia." *Population Studies* 7 (3): 184–201 (March).

World Bank. 1988. *Indonesia: The Transmigration Program in Perspective*. Washington, D.C.: The World Bank.

CHAPTER 8

A Question of Outsiders: Bangladesh, Myanmar, and Bhutan

Sanjoy Hazarika

The eastern edge of the Himalayan Range dips south past India's North East ridge, across the hill tracts of Chittagong and the rugged terrain of Myanmar's Northern and Western Provinces, sweeping down to the Bay of Bengal. This spectacular countryside, watered by some of the greatest rivers running through some of the deepest valleys of the world—the Brahmaputra, the Mekong, the Salween and the Irrawady—is home to some of the most complex and remote communities on earth. Over the course of centuries, conflicts have troubled this region as different ethnic groups and coalitions, moving to their current homes from distant places, have sought to stake their control over the territory, impressing their particular stamps of authority on its peoples. There have been few periods when the area has been under any one ruler or political authority. A British official was led to comment with not a little exasperation nearly a century ago:

> It is safe to assert that in hardly any other part of the world is there such a large variety of languages and dialects as are to be heard in the country which lies between Assam and the Eastern border of Yunnan and in the Indo-Chinese countries to the south of this region. The reason for this is not hard to find. It lies in the physical characteristics of the country. It is the high mountain ranges and the deep, swift, flowing rivers that have brought about the differences in customs and language, and the innumerable tribal distinctions which are so perplexing to the enquirer into Indo-Chinese ethnology.[1]

These differences endure to this day, underlined by the fact that some areas have developed economically while others have stayed backward, often as a result of deliberate Federal government policies. The geography of the region, as much as political factors, has played a critical role in defining not just the growth of peoples but also the extent to which local and national political authority has been both exercised and accepted. The basic economic and social index defining a decent standard of living, whether it is with regard to health and sanitation or education and nutrition, is extremely poor, and all three nations come close to being the least developed countries in the world.

In addition, of the three countries that are the focus of this study—Bangladesh, Myanmar and Bhutan—two (Myanmar and Bhutan) share some characteristics, since they host different ethnic groups that are distributed in different parts of the country. However, Bangladesh is overwhelmingly dominated by Bengali speakers, who are also largely Muslim. There are small pockets of different religious and ethnic groups—Bangladesh does not recognize the concept of "indigenous peoples," saying that all those who live within its borders are indigenous. The largest of these pockets is to be found in the Chittagong Hill Tracts.

For decades, the hills, plains, and jungles of these areas—barring Bhutan, which is a new entrant to the theatre of low-intensity agitation—have surged with conflict and violence. Indeed, Myanmar has had some of the longest-running ethnic insurgencies in the world, some, such as the Karen rebellion, going back almost to the earlier half of the twentieth century. In the cases of Myanmar and Bangladesh, the insurgents have tried to carve out separate homelands partly because of their own sense of history and partly due to their opposition to dominance by a "mainland" Centrist authority. The case of Bhutan is quite different, as we shall see later in this chapter: No organized, armed rebellion as such exists there that could be defined or qualify as an insurgency.

The significance of this region's location is also in that it abuts India's turbulent North East, which has seen innumerable insurgencies rise and fall as well as countless crackdowns against these militant movements in which thousands have perished, tens of thousands more have been injured or crippled for life or made homeless, and property worth millions of dollars destroyed. Indeed, Major Davies's remarks about the bewildering range of ethnic groups is as relevant to that part of the world as it is to Myanmar: There are no fewer than 66 recognized major ethnic groups and another 100 subgroups, speaking almost as many languages. Many of the people of the Indian North East have their ethnic roots in South East Asia, especially Thailand and Myanmar, as well as the areas bordering China's Yunnan Province and Myanmar. They have migrated here over the centuries, fleeing either internecine conflicts or other wars as well as natural calamities.

Thus, the Khasis of the state of Meghalaya, who follow the matrilineal form of inheritance and family structure, come from Kampuchea and speak a form of Mon-Khmer. However, their script is Roman, brought to them by British Church missionaries in the nineteenth century. The Tai-Ahoms, as the name suggests, came from the Shan Province bordering

Myanmar and Thailand. The Khamtis traveled from North East Myanmar in the eighteenth century and settled in the plains of Arunachal Pradesh state. The Mizos of Mizoram are related to the great Kuki-Chin race on the western side of Myanmar and there are Mizos or Lushais in Myanmar, as well as Nagas and Kukis on either side of the border.

There are Chakmas and Hajongs as well as Mogs and Tipperas in Bangladesh and in Tripura on the Indian side; Bhutan has Meches, actually a small sub-group of the Bodo community, the largest plains tribe group in Assam state, where it has a population of above 1.1 million. The state has a population of more than 23 million and the whole of the North East accounts for about 32 million people, less than 3 percent of the entire Indian population. Nowhere in India or South Asia is there such a diverse range of people concentrated in such a small area.

This is the melting pot of Asia, where the brown and yellow races have met and mingled. This cauldron continues to bubble and seethe with unrest and rebellion, drawing brutal responses from the Indian state, although efforts to forge reconciliation are also continuing. Of the insurgencies, the Naga is the oldest and there are vigorous ones in Assam and Manipur states as well as in Tripura, which borders Bangladesh. Assam has a small direct border with Bangladesh, while both Nagaland and Manipur have extensive frontiers with Myanmar; communities span the international border and pro-independence militants there have long had connections with insurgent groups in Myanmar.

The political structures of the three countries under study are extremely dissimilar: Bangladesh has a democracy, which was a crucial factor in settling the Chakma insurgency; Myanmar has been under military rule, apart from two brief brushes with democracy at the time of independence, and then under U Nu before he was toppled by a military coup in 1962. Its most recent manifestation is LORC—the Law and Order Restoration Committee (formerly SLORC, the Socialist Law and Order Restoration Committee), which is as grim as it sounds. Bhutan has been a monarchy since the early twentieth century; it has a National Assembly but no political parties.

It is interesting to note that Bangladesh (then East Pakistan) and Myanmar (then Burma) gained independence from foreign rule at about the same time. In both cases, it was Britain that let go of its imperial dominions. India and Pakistan were formed in 1947 with the partition of the Indian subcontinent. Pakistan's founder, Mohammad Ali Jinnah, was to describe his inheritance as a "moth-eaten" nation, with one section in the West and the other in the East, separated by thousands of miles of Indian territory. One year later, it was Burma's turn to become independent.

Bhutan has had a very different history. Buddhism was brought to this Himalayan kingdom, it is believed, by Guru Rimpoche, who arrived on the back of a great tiger in the ninth century. Still, it was not until the seventeenth century that Ngawang Namgyal, a Tibetan prince who left his homeland to escape internecine conflicts and settled in Bhutan, united the country, instituted a system of law, and organized the fort-monasteries or *dzongs*, which functioned as the religious-administrative and military headquarters of various areas. It was Namgyal who built the foundations for Drugpa power in the political, religious, and administrative arenas. The Drugpa are basically Bhutanese of Tibetan origin. In the latter half of the nineteenth century, the governor of the influential province of Tongsa in Central Bhutan, Jigme Wangchuk, established himself as the strongman of Bhutan. His son, Ugen Wangchuk, was accepted by other chiefs as the country's first king in 1907. Thus began the line of the Wangchuks; the latest in the dynasty is King Jigme Singye Wangchuk.

This chapter is an effort to analyze the role of the state in each of the three nations in creating the conditions of anarchy and violence, of militarization, brutality, intimidation, and political pressure, that have uprooted entire communities and forced them to seek shelter in an alien land. Their own governments have turned against them, giving them little option but to leave. However, there are still grounds for hope, as is most evident from the example of Bangladesh, where the government of Premier Sheik Hasina Wajed decided to give a degree of autonomy to the Chakma hill people. Yet the agreement, which was hailed as an act of statesmanship at the start, has run into significant problems, with divisions between the hill communities and settlers from the plains. There is concern that the agreement is not being implemented and that it did not redress the major grievances of the Chakmas.

Migrants, refugees, and internally displaced people are among the world's most vulnerable communities; the groups studied here are a part of this vulnerable population. Democracy and representative government are the best ways of resolving the festering conflicts that have shattered the peace of the Chittagong Hill Tracts, Myanmar, and Bhutan, but each must proceed without haste, which could force changes that may backfire on those who advocate transparency and dialogue.

It is worth noting here that in all three cases under study in this chapter, a religious minority was seen as a threat to the majority of a different faith. All three cases, interestingly enough, have Buddhists as protagonists on one side or the other. In the case of Myanmar, it was an Islamic minority pitted against a Buddhist majority; in the case of Bangladesh, it was a Buddhist minority facing the pressure of a Muslim majority. And in Bhutan, a large Hindu presence was threatened by a Buddhist majority.

Bangladesh: Chakmas of the Chittagong Hill Tracts— A Bit of Peace

Historical Background

The Chittagong Hill Tracts cover 16 percent of Bangladesh's total land mass and lie along a narrow strip of land that borders the Indian states of Mizoram and Tripura and the Myanmar province of Arakan. The official attitude that ruled policy for many years toward the thinly populated hills, in what is the most densely populated place on earth, was reflected in a document that details failed discussions between Chakma militant leaders and the Government at Dhaka (Government of Bangladesh 1993).

At the outset, the document describes Bangladesh as a densely populated country of 110 million people squeezed into approximately 54,000 square miles of territory. "Its man-land ratio is recognised to be among the highest in the world and ... this demographic factor is a crucial denominator in understanding the problem of the tribal people." It went on to compare the density of 1,844 persons per square kilometer for the country with a bare 140 per square kilometer for the Chittagong Hill Tracts (Government of Bangladesh 1993). Thus, land was seen as the critical factor in determining the political equations that fashioned a tragic set of responses and counter-responses that led to much bloodshed and trouble in the Hill Tracts.

The hills are covered with teak forests, riven by innumerable streams; farmers practice *jhum*, or slash-and-burn cultivation, also known as "shifting farming." This form of farming is prevalent across national frontiers as well, and is widely practiced in the hills of India's North East, showing that cultures and traditions are similar in the belt stretching from the Eastern Himalayas down to the Gulf of Tonkin and the Mekong Delta.

The results of this form of agriculture are particularly obvious in the form of damaged ecosystems, especially the topsoil and forest cover, making erosion by wind and rain easier and leading to land degradation. Yet this system has traditional sanction and has, for centuries, been environmentally friendly: The lack of population pressure earlier meant that the slash-and-burn cycle in one area would not return for 10 or 15 years. These days, because of market competition and population pressures, the *jhum* cycle has been reduced to five years or less, giving the soil little time to rest and regenerate.

The largest ethnic groups of the Chittagong Hill Tracts are the Chakmas and Marmas, comprising 90 percent of the population. Both communities are predominantly Buddhist but other significant tribes (there are 12 in all) include Tipperas (Tripuri), Morangs, and Bawms. The Chakmas migrated from the southeastern plains along the Bay of Bengal to the hills after the seventeenth century, when they were confronted by Bengali settlers who had earlier moved to that area.

When the British took control of the Hill Tracts in 1860, they divided the area into three administrative "sub-divisions" corresponding roughly to the chieftainships of the three main tribes. In 1900 the British announced a regulation outlining the new rules that would govern the administrative setup of the Hill Tracts: the settlement of outsiders was banned, as was the transfer or sale of land to non-indigenous people. In 1935, the area was defined by a new law as a "Totally Excluded Area," meaning that administrators from the plains—who were looked upon with extreme suspicion and dislike by the hill people—could not run its affairs; instead, local chiefs were given powers to tackle local, minor problems, using traditional ways of consultation and governance, an exclusivity that was resented by the politicians from the plains. In 1947, the subcontinent was partitioned into India and two halves of Pakistan (East and West), however, the British award on the Hill Tracts flew in the face of the logic adopted to carved out separate nations on the basis of religion: A religious majority, living in a contiguous area, was placed either in Hindu-majority India or Muslim-majority Pakistan. The Hill Tracts, overwhelmingly dominated at the time by Buddhists, was handed over to East Pakistan. The news of the award surprised the Chakmas, who had already raised the Indian flag on their homes and government offices at the district headquarters of Rangamati.

The decision to award the Hill Tracts to East Pakistan followed the award of Calcutta to India, despite its being a river port for the Bengal hinterland. The Bengal hinterland was dominated by Muslims; Chittagong was given to Pakistan as an alternative port with the Hill Tracts as its hinterland. The Pakistani army took down the Indian flag at Rangamati, but mainland distrust of the people of the Hill Tracts grew, especially their loyalty to Pakistan and later to Bangladesh. The Chakmas were viewed as "showing an intransigence toward the new state in religio-cultural terms" (Phadnis 1989).

Weapons of Displacement

First exodus: After independence from Britain, East Pakistan followed a steady strategy of disbanding the British colonial system of checks and special rights for the Hill Tracts. First the tribal police force was dismissed and replaced by police from the mainland. Then the special "Excluded" status of the region was first amended and finally repealed.

The next step in the process of the Chakma/hill people's alienation came in the form of a hydroelectric project commissioned and completed on the Karnaphuli river in the early 1960s. The lake formed by the dam was so large that it submerged 20,000 hectares of cultivable land (40 percent of the total cultivable land in the Hill Tracts) and displaced not fewer than 18,000 families, or about 100,000 hill people (Elahi 1998).

The East Pakistan Government had rehabilitated only 5,633 families by 1964. Those with land rights (another 4,500 families) were left out of this package, nor were 8,000 families without land titles (the slash-and-burn cultivators) given any land. From an early area of 655 square kilometers, the lake now covers about 1,000 square kilometers in the rainy season. (Elahi 1998).

Left to fend for themselves and driven to desperation, many Chakmas took shelter in other parts of the Hill Tracts, but more than 20,000 fled to Tripura and Assam before the Indian Government transported them further north and placed them in what is now Arunachal Pradesh. They are largely in the Changlang District of the state, then known as the North East Frontier Agency.

More than 34 years later, their numbers have swollen to over 65,000 but they are still not Indian citizens and the basic facilities of free education and access to health care are denied them by local authorities. Indeed, this first group of Chakmas represents one of the more tragic situations of refugees: They neither have access to international agencies such as the United Nations High Commissioner for Refugees, nor are they accepted in their present home, where they are targets of political pressure. There is virtually no chance of their repatriation to their original lands because their existence is not even acknowledged at official meetings between Bangladesh and India.

Rejection, settlement: Soon after Bangladesh had won its liberation war against Pakistan, with massive intervention by the Indian Army, a delegation of representatives of the Hill people called on the Premier, Sheik Mujibur Rahman. Their leader was Manobendra Larma, a member of Parliament. There are different accounts of that meeting, where the delegates presented a set of demands including autonomy for the Hill Tracts.

> In the tradition of a modernist, not to mention suffering somewhat from the glories of Joi Bangla [Victorious Bengal] and 'Bengali Nationalism,' Mujib told the CHT delegation, 'No, we are all Bengalis; we cannot have two systems of government. Forget your ethnic identity, be Bengalis.' (Ahmed 1996)

One of Sheik Mujib's associates at the time, Rehman Sobhan, then chairman of the country's Planning Commission, said that the Prime Minister had sent Larma to him for a discussion on developing the Hill Tracts.[2] A proposed joint visit to the area did not take place. One account says that soon after the Mujib-Larma meeting,

> [u]nits of Mujib's personal fighting force launched attacks in the CHT. The raids were considered retaliation against those tribals who had collaborated with the Karachi regime during the [1971] uprising, even though many had aided the Bengalis. Tens of thousands of Marmas and Tipperas fled into India and Burma—some of their havens were in the same locations as today's camps—and their lands were take over by Bengalis from the plains. (U.S. Committee for Refugees 1988)

Thus, the intent of Bengali nationalism and assimilation was clear from Mujib's personal interaction with the Hill leaders as well as the physical crackdown that followed: to put the Chakmas under pressure, to make them feel not just unwanted but extremely insecure and, in addition, unrepresented.

But although Mujib was in favor of the assimilation of the hill people, he did not live to see the demographic changes that were to come. After his assassination in August 1975, it was his successor, President General Ziaur Rahman (1975–1981) who began placing Muslim settlers in the Hill Tracts. The "success" of this feat of demographic engineering is seen in the startling statistics that map the growth of the Bengali population and the stagnation of the hill people.

In 1951, the hill people made up 261,538 of a total of 287,688, or 90 percent, of the population of the Hill Tracts; in 1974, after the creation of Bangladesh, their number had risen to 449,315 of a total of 508,199 (88.4 percent). In 1981, the respective figures for hill people and Bengali settlers were 439,458 and 268,998, with a total of 708,456. In 1991, the year of the last national census, the figures were 498,595 for the hill people and 468,825 for the Bengalis: The hill peoples' proportion of the total population had fallen to 62 percent in 1981 and to 51.5 percent in 1991. At the natural growth rate set between 1951 to 1974, the total Bengali settler population should not have been more than 83,000 in 1991. The actual figure was 5.6 times this number.

The drop in the percentage of the Chakmas to total population during this period can be attributed to their outflow to India (as many as 58,000, or above 12 percent of the population, were living in refugee camps in Tripura state). On the other hand, there can be no doubt that the increase in the Bengali population is a result of state-sponsored settlement. The Bengali settlers did not come alone: They were accompanied by military and paramilitary forces. According to one estimate, the military presence was as high as 50,000 in over 400 camps. "[I]t was Ziaur Rahman's regime which aggravated the issue by resettling Bengali landless peasants from the coastal areas on land occupied by the CHT hill tribes," says Guha-Thakurta (1998: 812).

The Hill Tracts were looked upon by Dhaka as empty land upon which landless farmers could be settled to relieve some of the intense pressure on land in other parts of the country. As part of this policy, the Government organized "cluster villages" for both the Bengalis and the hill people. (Guha-Thakurta 1998). For the former, the clusters, with security support, were meant to protect them from the Shanti Bahini, the insurgent group, which had formed in 1973. This was a temporary solution but aimed at making patrolling easier for the security forces. The Chakma clusters were intended by the authorities to disrupt the structures of kinship and community living in villages which had sustained them for centuries. An entire way of life was devastated and still remains largely beyond repair.

The Parbatiya Chattagram Jana Sanghati Samiti (PCJSS) was the political representative of the hill groups; the Shanti Bahini (Peace Force) was its military wing. In May 1977 the insurgents conducted their first major raid on Bangladesh security forces, who rushed reinforcements to the area. In the conflict that followed, Chakma villagers became the victims of military violence: organized killings, kidnappings, abductions, torture, illegal detention, and rape. What was significant about these incidents was the involvement of Bengali settlers and their active participation in massacres, including killings in 1980, 1986, and 1992 in which no fewer than 500 are reported to have died, mostly Chakmas and other tribals (Ahmed 1996). There were counter-attacks by the Shanti Bahini, which by this time was being armed, trained, and sheltered by an Indian intelligence agency under instructions from the Indian Government as part of New Delhi's reaction to the assassination of Sheik Mujib. His successor, General Ziaur Rahman, was not particularly friendly toward India.

Thus, New Delhi's policy of assisting the Chakma rebels also played a part in their tragic flight to India. The first exodus of refugees to Tripura followed the start of military assistance to the Shanti Bahini. Indeed, the successive surges of refugees from the Chittagong Hill Tracts followed military operations by Bangladesh forces and counter-attacks by the Shanti Bahini, which worked out of camps on the Indo-Bangladesh border as well as from within the territory of the Hill Tracts. These operations by Bangladesh forces created "fresh waves of refugees into India, most notably in 1978, 1981, 1984 and 1986" (Timm 1991).

Calculated sexual assaults: One of the strategies used to strike fear among the Chakmas and force their departure was the pattern of calculated and extensive sexual assault on their womenfolk by both security forces and settlers. This has been documented by human rights groups and remarked upon by the report of the Chittagong Hill Tracts Commission (1992). There are accounts of forced intermarriage, of hill women being kidnapped by settlers and converted to Islam. There are examples of gang rape and at one point, the Commission remarked that the fear of sexual assault was so widespread that "some young women told the Commission that they are no longer able to wear their traditional dress [long skirts and short blouses, which mark them out as indigenous people]. If they do, they run the risk of being raped. For their own safety they are forced to hide their identity as much as possible. It is also too dangerous to leave their homes at night" (Chittagong Hill Tracts Commission 1992).

It is material here to note that in their campaign against the Chakmas and other hill people, the Bangladesh forces showed little sensitivity. They appeared to have forgotten that they were inflicting the very forms of violence and intimidation that occupying Pakistani troops had unleashed on Bangladeshi women and civilians during the bloody crackdown of 1970 that eventually led to the country's independence and the breakup of Pakistan.

Dispossession: The other weapon used deliberately in the quasi-military campaign in the hills was the possession or dispossession of lands—possession for the settlers and dispossession of the hill people. The rise in the Bengali population is the clearest indication of this policy, with the Government taking shelter behind the defense that a Bangladeshi citizen's freedom of movement could not be restricted.

The Chakma refugees of 1978, 1981, and 1984 were eventually sent back from India after discussions with Bangladeshi officials, but there were no guarantees of their safe repatriation. When the 1986 influx took place, the Indian authorities desisted from refoulement. One of the reasons for the Central Government's decision to allow the refugees to stay was the stiff public opposition to deportation; another was that India received a fresh influx of refugees on the very day of scheduled repatriation, after renewed attacks on Chakmas by Bangladesh forces.

In the midst of these outflows, the Shanti Bahini split, with one group disarmed by India and the other continuing the campaign with Delhi's support. In additional developments, a large group of rebels surrendered in 1985 and, later that year, the first meeting to look at a possible solution to the problem was held between President H. M. Ershad's representatives and members of the PCJSS.

Weapons of Settlement

Talks, cease-fire, delays: There was little movement forward on the ground partly because the Government at Dhaka lacked the credibility and political support to sustain the talks. Although six meetings between the two sides took place between 1985 and 1988, it was not until 1992 that a new government under Premier Khaleda Zia, the widow of President Ziaur Rahman, began the process that was eventually to lead to a settlement. The most significant part of this strategy was the declaration of a cease-fire by the hill groups that was renewed until the December 1997 settlement that finally ended the fighting. Yet, the 1992 cease-fire was preceded by fierce clashes between the hill groups and the settlers, the latter supported by troops; about 300 were reported killed in one incident in April that year.

Despite the cease-fire, the talks stuttered along under Khaleda Zia, for neither side was prepared to compromise on one crucial issue: the formation of a Regional Council which the Chakmas wanted to run the affairs of the three hill districts under one chairman. A majority of the council was to comprise hill nominees. The Government cited a Local Government Act passed in 1989 which had established three local councils in three districts, saying this was an adequate devolution of powers, especially since the Councils had the power to frame rules and regulations, impose taxes and prepare budgets (Prime Minister's Office 1993).

Two large groups of refugees were repatriated during those years—more than 5,000 in all—but there were accusations by hill leaders that Dhaka was not keeping its promises of rehabilitation and compensation. They said that the returnees were being pressured and intimidated by settlers and security forces.

The talks did not move forward in the last years of Begum Khalida's rule because of political instability and opposition agitations that forced the ruling Bangla Nationalist Party to seek a fresh mandate. The Awami League, regarded as pro-India, came to power in the general elections of 1996, pledging to close the chapter of militancy with a negotiated settlement.

The Awami League initiative: Within a few months the new government had appointed a high-level negotiating team led by the Chief Whip of the

238 | Sanjoy Hazarika

Parliament, Abul Hasnat Abdullah, to talk to the militants. Members of other political parties, including the Opposition, were included in the National Committee on the Chittagong Hill Tracts.

Three months after the formation of the National Committee, Abdullah led the first negotiations with Shantu Larma, the head of the Shanti Bahini and the PCJSS. Six more rounds of talks followed—all in the national capital, Dhaka—which finally ended with a peace agreement on 2 December 1997. The Bangladesh Government acceded to the demand for a Regional Council and agreed to an amnesty for the rebels, a time-frame for the surrender of arms, the closing of temporary government army and paramilitary camps, and the setting up of a Land Commission to tackle all land disputes relating to illegal settlement and encroachment.

As the talks went on, about 13,000 refugees began returning to their homeland from Tripura. With the signing of the agreement and the return of peace to the hills, the camps in Tripura were closed. Virtually all refugees have returned to the Hill Tracts, marking one of the most successful repatriation efforts in South Asia, and one that was achieved without the involvement of international agencies such as the United Nations High Commissioner for Refugees.

Crucial to this process was the political support of the Government of India which welcomed a friendly government in Dhaka, particularly after the signing of the 1996 Ganges water-sharing treaty between then Indian Prime Minister H. D. Deve Gowda and Sheik Hasina.

The Chittagong Hill Tracts accord has been widely criticized in Bangladesh, especially by Begum Khaleda's BNP, which denounced it as a sellout of national interests, organizing strikes and work stoppages in protest. Apart from protests by political parties, local settlers too have fiercely opposed the settlement, saying it is discriminatory and ignores their hard work, since the 22-member Regional Council was to be dominated by hill persons while only seven would be Bengali settlers.

One of the problems the Land Commission is reportedly facing relates to the displacement of settlers from land they had previously taken from hill villagers. "In the process, the Government will be creating a fresh group of refugees," said one prominent Bangladeshi editor.[3]

In addition, young Chakmas have openly opposed the accord and have split with Larma, organizing their own Movement for Democracy in February 1999, accusing him of settling for far less than their original demands and of virtually accepting the Khaleda Zia government's proposals of 1993. The Tribal Affairs Ministry at Dhaka has little to do, because of a duplication of tasks that has taken place as a result of the accord. But months after the agreement was signed, the Regional Council had still not been formed, indicating the sharp differences within the Chakmas, between the hill people and the settlers, as well as with the Government at Dhaka.

Conclusions

The long and tortured militancy in the Chittagong Hill Tracts appears to have been resolved as a result of the convergence of a number of factors: A political party emerged in Bangladesh that had the popular mandate as well as the will to push through an acceptable settlement; the militants realized that they were unlikely to extract much more in terms of political concessions from a sympathetic Awami League government than what was contained in the 1997 accord; and the general public wearied of the conflict as the government offered greater transparency on the issue. According to a prominent scholar, the most important factor behind the end of the armed conflict was the Government of India's support of the peace effort and its scaling down of support of the Shanti Bahini. "India was the center of gravity of the movement," said Ameena Mohsin.[4]

None of the settlers has yet been displaced or moved out of the Hill Tracts. The former refugees who have moved back from India have yet to be properly settled. Currently, they are living with relatives and in temporary camps, injecting a new element of uncertainty and suspicion into an already difficult situation.

The lack of general knowledge about the issue stems partially from the lack of dissemination and open debate. The author was at a conference on the Chittagong Hill Tracts in Dhaka in early 1997; organizers said it was perhaps the first such public discussion of the problem in many years.

Despite these drawbacks, as the next two cases will show, Bangladesh tackled state-organized demographic engineering and mapping through the most representative and open system of governance: democracy. However, this is not likely to end all the area's problems: For example, arguments are being made for the tribal people having greater powers over their own affairs without interference from the National Parliament. These are negotiating positions and an indicator of political jousting for space. Open negotiations under a democratically elected government are the only way forward. Peace is both a condition for and a by-product of such negotiations. The accord has given the hill people an opportunity to reshape their future. In addition, it has taken care of the state's interests without threatening the territorial integrity of Bangladesh, thus meeting majoritarian concerns to a large extent.

Still, questions remain about whether the accord will truly help the hill people in the long term. Mohsin remarks that the unitary structure of the Bangladesh Constitution needs change. She says that this essentially supports Bengali majoritarian rule and makes no concessions or allowances for constitutional amendments to give minority groups a share in the state and recognize their separate cultural status. She points out that the Regional Council as currently structured would be dominated—if not by Bengalis, because that is impossible—but by the major hill groups, thus continuing the process of imposing majoritarian rule over smaller groups.

The Baum group, she says, is growing radicalized and opposed to the control of the Chakmas.[5]

> The CHT is inhabited by 13 different ethnic groups whereas only five have got their representatives in the body. In other words, the RC is replicating and reproducing the hegemony that it had been purporting to fight. (Mohsin 1998)

Myanmar and the Rohingyas: Permanent Losers

Historical Background

The old name for Myanmar is Burma, meaning the union of people who comprised the old kingdom, which stretched from the border of Assam to the edge of the Siamese or Thai kingdom. The Myan, also known as the Burman, were the people indigenous to the plains, who dominated other ethnic groups. Explaining this point, the scholar Barun De says that "Myanmar as a name signifies majoritarian control by the plains of the hills" (De 1998). Thus, the name Myanmar (more than Burma) asserted the dominance of the plains people.

Indeed, the Myanmar Government refuses to recognize the people widely named the Rohingya; it says that this group does not belong to the recognized national races or national racial groups, such as the Karens and Kachins. The position is outlined starkly below as part of a communication on 12 November 1992 from Myanmar's Permanent Mission in Geneva to the Special Rapporteur of the United Nations Commission on Human Rights:

> The Rohingyas do not exist in Myanmar either historically, politically or legally. Nor do they represent any segment of the population in Myanmar including those professing the Islamic faith. The so-called 'Rohingyas' is an invention of insurgent terrorist organizations like the Rohingya Solidarity Organisation (RSO) and the Arakan Rohingya Islamic Front (ARIF).

And a senior Myanmar diplomat emphasized that "there is no such ethnic group in our entire history."[6]

With an official attitude as hostile as this, it is hardly any wonder that the "Rohingyas" are permanent losers in Myanmar's political and ethnic mix. The Myanmar Government usually defines them as Rakhine Muslims, a name that is derived from the name of the province. The Muslims who live in the northern part of the Arakan, also called Akyab and the Rakhine state, number about 1.2 million. Overall, Muslims comprise about 4 percent of the national population but they are not defined as Rahine Muslims or Rohingyas; only those who live in the Arakan region are so called, to distinguish them from the others. In fact, in Yangoon, this group is often called "Bangla" because many of them speak Bengali.[7] The other Muslims are known simply as Muslims.

The Arakan has a common border with South East Bangladesh, where Arab merchants and Yemeni traders settled many centuries ago; over time a mixed Muslim-Burman society evolved. The sailors were accompanied by Muslim imams, and Islam won a number of converts. In the fifteenth century, a Muslim governor of Bengal helped reinstate a deposed king of the Arakan, Narmikhila. Thus began an increased Muslim presence in the region as well as Bengali influence. Confrontation between the two communities is said to date to 1785, when a Burman king annexed the Arakan.

The conflicts spilled over into British India and led to the first Anglo-Burmese War of 1824–1826. The British annexed the Arakan and Tesessarim and subsequent wars led to the establishment of British control over all of Myanmar. The Myanmar Government of today traces the illegal presence of Muslims of Bengali stock to their incursion after the First Anglo-Burmese war. Blaming the British for bringing in agricultural labor from India, Myanmar says that such "illegal settlement created problems for the local populace," and in a leap across time, declares that the 1991/1992 exodus of Muslims from Rakhine was "essentially an illegal immigration problem" caused by people who did not want to be checked by immigration officials (United Nations 1993).

The 1911 Census defines an ethnic group called the Arakanese but no Rohingyas or Rakines. The same census notes that there were as many as 178,381 "Mohamedans" in Akyab State. Significantly, in that very year, the number of Bengali speakers was 181,509, barely 3,000 over the figure for Muslims, confirming the description. On the other hand, the number for Buddhists was 302,527 and those who listed their main language as Burmese was 93,480. People who spoke Arakanese numbered 208,527.

Weapons of Displacement

During World War II, the Muslims worked for the British; the Buddhists of the Arakan supported the Japanese, who briefly occupied the country. There are accounts that the British even promised a Muslim National Area to the Arakanese Muslims but did not honor this commitment (United Nations 1993).

In 1948, an armed rebellion aimed at carving out an independent Muslim state exploded but was crushed by the Burmese military. Burman suspicions of the Muslims deepened, and the government began a purge of Muslim officials in the Arakan, replacing them with Buddhist civil servants, policemen, and village headmen (Abrar 1998). Those who had fled during the war had their lands confiscated.

Discrimination continued over the decades, and yet a migration of people from Bangladesh to Myanmar continues, especially to the Arakan (Abrar 1998). As the Bengali-speaking Muslim population grew dramatically (particularly during the British and East Pakistan periods), so did its confrontation with authorities at Yangon.

Burman Policy and Exodus in 1978, 1991

The Muslims had sought autonomy in the 1960s, but the Burmese/Myanmar Government reacted by considering them separatists. In 1970, the Buddhists of the Arakan, also known as the Maghs, joined the Muslims in submitting a memorandum demanding autonomy to the Government at Yangon. While the Arakanese Buddhists got this autonomous status in 1974, the Muslims were denied any special position; indeed, according to Elahi, "Muslim persecution in Arakan reached its climax in February, 1978, when it was perpetrated by the Burmese Army under the code name 'Nagamin Operation'" (Elahi 1998). The operation was aimed at determining the nationality of the Arakan Muslims as a prelude to a forthcoming national census.

"The army determined nationality by identifying smallpox vaccination marks on peoples' arms," according to this account. It was the beginning of a controversy about citizenship that has dogged the Arakan Muslims ever since. Vaccinations had been administered in Arakan at the time of the British and also in what now comprises Bangladesh; those with vaccination marks were thus non-nationals, according to this arbitrary policy. In the following weeks, Muslims were arrested by the thousands and many villages were torched.

As a result, over 167,000 fled to the Chittagong area of Bangladesh. Myanmar claimed that 150,000 left the country. The two countries began talks to facilitate the return of the refugees; a Myanmar diplomat involved in the negotiations says that only 3,000 were "genuine identity card holders," referring to cards issued in 1955.[8] The bilateral talks failed, but under international pressure Myanmar agreed to the intervention of the UNHCR. Finally, in July 1978, it agreed to take back all refugees.

The 1978 exodus and return was the precursor of a greater flight of Muslims in 1991. Over a quarter million refugees took shelter in the Teknaf–Cox's Bazar region of Bangladesh. The repatriation of this group is the second largest UNHCR operation in Asia, after the Cambodian operation. This outflow created an enormous financial and social burden for Bangladesh, one of the poorest countries in the world.

The reasons for the flight in 1991 were different from those behind the 1978 outflow: On 21 December 1991, Myanmar forces attacked a Bangladeshi border post, purportedly in pursuit of Muslim guerrillas. This incident led to the intensification of an army crackdown against the Muslims in the Arakan, triggering the flight. The outflow was aggravated in 1997 by another movement of people who were crossing over to escape economic hardship and forced labor and who lived in villages, rather than camps.

While most of the original refugees identified by the UNHCR and living in camps have returned to their homeland, an estimated 14,000 have stayed in the camps, ignoring Bangladeshi warnings that they were overstaying their welcome. A large proportion are also in villages. Some 7,000 refugees are on the UNHCR's list of people to be repatriated and cleared by Myanmarese authorities.

On 22 October 1998, local police stormed a refugee camp to flush out militants opposing repatriation. Officials said about 100 were injured in the incident, which followed clashes the previous year between refugee militants and police. The latter were attacked with stones, staves, and bows and arrows when they tried to enter a camp to press ahead with unilateral repatriation.

The unilateral process was stopped after protests from UNHCR, and Myanmar was so informed. Before this, Bangladesh had forcibly sent back about 190 persons from 46 families, against the wishes of the refugees and without medical examinations. Both are necessary conditions for voluntary repatriation.

Before these clashes, the refugees had organized fasts, sit-in protests, and demonstrations demanding full citizenship for the Muslims and the restoration of democracy in Myanmar, clearly indicating their political sympathies with the pro-democracy movement. However, things are not as simple as they may appear: Accounts from UNHCR officials indicate that there is an element of coercion among the refugees and they are under pressure from their Islamic fundamentalist leaders.[9]

Ordinary refugees have been held hostage by armed groups to prevent Bangladesh Government forces from moving into camps to remove the militants. News reports of this situation have appeared in the Bangladesh Bengali language press, and the problem has been defined as acute in Nayapara camp.[10] There are reports that women and children are at risk of being used as human shields, and that radicals do not want women to wear traditional Muslim dress and object to girls attending school (*Bhorer Kagoj* [Dhaka], 11 January 1997; *Janakantha* [Dhaka], 8 and 12 January 1997).

Tools of pressure, ousters: As one of its main strategies against the Muslims, Myanmar has effectively used the weapon of non-citizenship, of majority assertions that the Muslims were outsiders who did not belong to Myanmar, an argument used as early as twenty years ago. As far as the Arakanese Muslims were concerned, Myanmar defined nationality on the basis of religion rather than ethnicity and historic links. This was one of four specific weapons of displacement that the Myanmar regime has followed and is perhaps the most discriminatory of these forms of intimidation. Indeed, of these three case studies, Myanmar is the most difficult, displaying arbitrary, violent abuse of the human rights of residents who are its own nationals.

The first weapon of displacement is the denial of citizenship rights. In 1982, Myanmar promulgated a citizenship law that defined three types of citizens: full, associate, and naturalized. A full citizen must be able to prove his birthplace and the nationality of his ancestors prior to the first British annexation (1826), and these must have belonged to an ethnic group settled on the territory before that year. An associate citizen is one whose grandparents were citizens of another country, a form of citizenship reserved for former foreign citizens or stateless persons. However, authorities have made applications under this category virtually impossible because the deadline for submission of applications for associate citizenship ended in 1982. Citizenship by naturalization is granted to persons who can prove they were born in Myanmar and whose parents had entered and lived in the country before 4 January 1948. There are other conditions permitting those who do not fulfil this criterion to apply.

The decision to grant citizenship lies within the discretion of the authorities. Citizenship law also includes a clause that enables the government to revoke citizenship. All nationals are expected to carry citizenship identity cards at all times. These cards are colored differently according to the type of citizenship that the holder enjoys and must be produced to use essential services: to vote and to travel, for medical treatment, or for education. In 1990, the ID cards were changed to include mention of the holder's ethnic origin and religion.

A UN document points out that many members of ethnic minorities in Myanmar have no identity cards, and proving entitlement to citizenship is "made difficult by lack of access to written records and the difficulty of travelling to government-controlled areas for registration. Furthermore, government officials are said to be generally unwilling to register persons belonging to minorities."[11]

Of the 1.2 million inhabitants of the Rakhine (Arakan) state, a total of 845,000 applied for citizenship by December 1992. About one-third of this number were either rejected by the authorities or their cases were undecided. In 1995, the Myanmar Government issued new "temporary registration certificates" which targeted the Muslims of the Arakan, many of whom have not been issued citizenship cards even under the provisions of the naturalization law. In addition, refugees have reported that documents that might have allowed them to apply for citizenship were seized and confiscated during military operations.

The second weapon of displacement, forced labor, has been extensively practiced in Myanmar for decades, especially by the military. Since the 1980s, Muslim village headmen would be summoned by troops and ordered to organize porters to carry heavy loads of food, construction material, and ammunition, as well as to build roads and barracks. There are accounts of abductions of Muslims who were then forced to work at different sites, including the building of military camps and trenches. They were fed poorly and for the most part unpaid. There were other forms of ill-treatment, including being tied up at night, torture, and executions. Women were also abducted, kept at military camps, and repeatedly raped, according to accounts received by human rights monitoring groups (United Nations 1997). There are also credible accounts of Muslims fleeing the country being fired upon, leading to numerous deaths, as well as attacks on boats carrying refugees. Refugees who fled to Bangladesh have listed forced portering and ill-treatment during their work as major reasons for their escape, especially in the Second Exodus of 1991–1992.

Arbitrary taxation and extortion are also calculated to force out the targeted group. Across Myanmar, the practice of taxation in kind has long existed. Under this system, farmers must sell a part of their crop to government agencies at a price fixed by the authorities. In the Arakan, however, the rice tax is determined as a percentage not of the harvest but of the land available to farmers. There are other forms of tax including chili tax, fish tax, and even fees for cutting bamboo.

Religious persecution, forced relocation, and population transfers make up the rest of the tactics used by Myanmar to rid itself of an unwanted population. Refugees say that the Muslims of the Arakan are subject to persecution involving the closing and destruction of mosques, harassment of and attacks on religious leaders and worshippers, and a ban on open religious activity (such as public prayer), and are even denied access to the purchase of Islamic literature. One of the worst incidents occurred on 3 April 1992, when army troops fired indiscriminately at a crowd of worshippers at a mosque in the town of Maungdaw, killing about 300 and wounding 150.

Occasional harassment, refugees have said, included closure of Muslim schools, beatings for praying outside one's home or in fields, and forced labor to build "model" homes and villages for non-Muslims. In many cases, the Muslim laborers were not paid. There are widespread accounts of destruction of mosques, particularly after the Opposition, under Daw Aung Sang Kyu Chi, swept the 1990 elections and then was denied power by the military junta. Refugees speak of Buddhist temples being built in place of mosques; of farm land being seized by the military or distributed to non-Muslims.

The Buddhist settlers, as in the case of the Bengali Muslim settlers in the Chittagong Hill Tracts, were given incentives to settle in the Arakan, including the gift of a cow and land as well as weapons training. This is viewed as part of a larger plan to bring about demographic change in the state. At one point in the 1990s, nearly 20 percent (over 260,000 individuals) of the Muslim population in the Arakan had fled to Bangladesh. Most of the refugees have since returned, after a series of discussions and programs facilitated by the UNHCR. Yet Bangladesh has at times acted unilaterally and forced the eviction of refugees as in 1992, leading to UNHCR's withdrawal from the process. However, the UN agency returned to help resolve the situation within a year and secured the official cooperation of Myanmar in the resettlement of the refugees. There has been criticism of this policy, since UNHCR has been unable adequately to monitor the resettlement of the refugees on the Myanmar side.

Conclusion

Despite the repatriation, the condition of Muslims in the Arakan remains tenuous. This is a people who, despite their ancestry, have been treated as non-citizens by their own government and become permanent losers in a situation in which they have few rights and little protection. Muslims must carry ID cards that identify them as "foreigners" without Burmese nationality, and are not allowed to travel without a special permit.

The role of the UNHCR during the 1978 and 1991 exoduses requires examination, especially during the 1997 refugee outflow. Particularly troubling has been the manner in which the agency withdrew from the repatriation process after differences with Bangladesh arose. The UNHCR later returned to the scene and made a significant step forward in its assertion that Myanmar is finally giving UNHCR field officers access to the resettlement sites and schemes.[12]

However, the later exodus to Bangladesh shows that conditions are far from satisfactory. The question of the resettlement of the Rohingyas raises a larger issue: Is the UNHCR going beyond its original charter on repatriation? That, however, is not the subject of this discussion.

For the "Rohingya," a group that Myanmar says does not exist, as well as for the numerous national racial groups that have been marginalized over the decades by the ruling junta, the only sure route to acceptance and survival lies in the return of democracy to their country, with a transparent and representative government that consults them and guarantees their right to citizenship, life, and liberty.

The Bangladesh approach to the Chittagong Hill Tracts problem, one of consultation, negotiation, and acceptance of basic demands that do not impinge on questions of national sovereignty—or accords that are "saleable" to the ethnic majority—appears to be the way forward.

Bhutan and the Lhotsampas: Migrants and Refugees

Historical Background

Among the various refugee movements of South Asia, the outflow of Nepalese-speaking people from Southern Bhutan, known as the Lhotsampas or residents of Southern Bhutan, is perhaps among the best documented and researched. The Bhutanese of Tibetan origin call their country Druk-yul and themselves Drukpa, followers of the Drukpa Kagyapa sect of Buddhism. The expression "Druk," commonly used to refer to a dragon (in Bhutanese tradition, the dragon represents absolute truth), is the name of a small monastery in Tibet where the Kagyapa Sect originated.

Bhutan became a monarchy in 1907, when the founder of the present Wangchuck dynasty was anointed to the throne. The British ruled in neighboring India and to all intents and purposes, Bhutan was regarded as another princely state, with its ruler drawing a pension from the Imperial Treasury. The British decided to leave the status of the Himalayan kingdom "in convenient ambiguity," and in 1949 the Indo-Bhutan Treaty recognized Bhutan as a sovereign nation but one that would be "guided" by Indian advice in its foreign policy.

Nepali Settlement

Nepali settlement in Bhutan is more than a century old and was first encouraged by Kazi Ugen Dorji, the influential Governor of western Bhutan and grandfather of the only Premier the country has ever had—Jigme Dorji.

The Dorji clan was encouraged by the British in India to take Nepalis to Bhutan. Although the British never directly ruled Bhutan, they had forced a treaty on the country in 1865 that required it to lease, in return for annual payments, the contiguous plains and the areas of many passes, or *Duars*, that had long been its territory. The hardworking and acquisitive Nepalis cleared thick vegetation and established themselves as cultivators in the Duar region. Nepali immigration continued until it was banned in 1959. During the intervening period, they transformed the southern edge of Bhutan into a rich farming region with crops of oranges, rice, cardamom, and pulses. It was Bhutan's "bread basket" (Sinha 1991).

The movement of people from Nepal was facilitated by the traditional, open Indo-Nepal border. Bhutan and Nepal do not share a common border with each other but with India, and the movement of people from either country to the other has to be via India. Thus the districts of Samtse, Gelegphu, Chirang, and Samdruk Jonkhar came to be dominated by Nepali migrants, known as Lhotsampas, or Southern Bhutanese.

Their readiness for physical labor, their Spartan lifestyles, and their vision of Nepal and India "as the founts of their civilisation, their historical achievement and where their places of pilgrimage are" were central to their development as a community in Bhutan (Sinha 1991).

The size of Bhutan's population is a matter of considerable controversy: Until 1988, the figure given was 1.375 million. In 1991, the Bhutan Government declared that enumerators had made major mistakes in the headcount; the actual population, it said, should not be more than 600,000. The Bhutanese had by now, by their account, identified more than 113,000 persons of Nepali origin as illegal immigrants.

Michael Hutt (1994) says that the ethnic structure was probably as follows: 10–28 percent were of the Ngalong group, which is currently wielding political and administrative power; another 30–40 percent were the Sarchops, or inhabitants of the East, who were very underdeveloped and politically marginalized. Hutt estimated the size of the Nepali-origin population at 25–52 percent.

Weapons of Displacement: Citizenship, Marriage, Census, and Demographic Strategy

As far back as 1958, the Bhutan Government began taking measures to check the Nepali inflow and to protect Drupka ethnic and political control. Thus, the 1958 Citizenship Act outlined three basic criteria for the recognition of a citizen: his/her father was a Bhutanese national and a resident of Bhutan; he/she was born within or outside Bhutan after the commencement of the 1958 law, provided the father was a Bhutanese national at the time of the person's birth. A foreigner who was of age and eligible could be granted citizenship provided he/she had been a resident of Bhutan for more than 10 years and owned agricultural land. In addition, a woman married to a Bhutanese citizen could be given citizenship. Foreigners seeking citizenship, who had served in the government for five years and who had resided in the country for 10 years, could be considered for recognition. These provisions were changed in 1977 to 10 years of service and 20 years of residency.

Thus, over the years, the Bhutanese elite clearly foresaw the problems that migration was likely to cause and armed itself, at irregular intervals, with legal weapons to combat the potential threat.

Eight years later the Bhutan Government adopted the 1985 Citizenship Act, which set 1958 as the cutoff year for acquisition of Bhutanese nationality. This effectively meant that those who had settled after that year would be stripped of their citizenship or would be ineligible to seek a Bhutanese identity. The target was clearly the people of Nepali origin, for this was the only group that was mobile, in terms of migration.

In 1980, the Bhutan Marriage Act was promulgated under which Bhutanese married to non-Bhutanese (whether resident in the kingdom or not) were subject to controls in various aspects of life. For example, Bhutanese citizens married to non-nationals were not eligible for promotion, nor could they be employed in defense or foreign affairs departments, and welfare facilities such as loans, agricultural subsidies, health services, and training abroad were to be denied to them.

Citizens were divided into seven categories. The census for 1988 was based on this structure, and the most vulnerable became the group born after 1958. The individual needed to have one Bhutanese parent, with fluency in spoken and written Dzongkha (the main language of the dominant North) and documentary evidence of 20 years' residence in Bhutan. His or her name had to be in a census register maintained by the Home Ministry. However, the Ministry itself did not exist until 1968, and the records generally held by village headmen were regarded as neither comprehensive nor accurate (Lama 1998). In a nation that had only recently begun publishing its basic economic and administrative documents, such a method of identifying its citizens was both subjective and questionable in law.

A second round of the Census was held exclusively for the Southern Districts in 1988 and under this, according to King Jigme Singye Wangchuk, no fewer than 113,000 illegal nationals were located.[13]

"The results of the census revealed exactly what was suspected and which could not be explained by any demographic extrapolations," said the government (Thinley 1993). "Planned and systematic infiltration by the immigrant Nepalese had been taking place." The census was also part of a policy known as Ta-Wa Sum, or King, People, and Country, aimed at imposing a common dress code and language (both of the Northern group) on all of Bhutan. In 1989 the teaching of Nepalese was stopped in all schools of the South and announcements were made asking "illegals" to leave the country.

As the pressure grew during the 1980s, resistance and bitterness built up among the Nepalese-speakers. The Bhutan Government began the forcible eviction of people identified by the census as illegals without giving them access to courts or a proper, unprejudiced hearing. The Lhotsampas began fleeing across the border to India and then to the land of their ancestors, Nepal, arriving with stories of discrimination and violence. One of their main spokesmen was a former advisor to King Jigme, Tek Nath Rizal, who fled the country attacking the failure of his government to "respect individual identity." At the request of the Bhutan Government, Rizal, a former member of the Royal Council, was arrested in 1989 by authorities in Nepal, where he had fled that same year, and extradited to Bhutan. He remains in prison despite international appeals for his release.

The first outflow of refugees came in a small rush to Timai, on the banks of a stream in Nepal's Jhapa district. Once Nepal began accepting the refugees, the flow became a torrent, placing the Nepal Government's capacities under intense pressure. By early 1992, over 1,000 asylum seekers were crossing into Nepal every day. The Bhutanese king was sufficiently disturbed by the exodus to travel personally to the southern districts, meeting with the Nepalis and urging them to stay. Few listened to his requests, concerned as they were by the pressure from local police and authorities. Many sold their lands officially to the district administration, renounced their citizenship, picked up cash compensation, and left. Others fled with only the clothes on their backs and what little money and valuables they could carry.

Katmandu appealed to the United Nations High Commissioner for Refugees for assistance, and the UNHCR stepped into the situation in September 1991. By May 1997, over 92,000 refugees were listed in seven camps in southeastern Nepal, a situation that still exists at this writing. In addition, an estimated 15,000 are living outside the camps and another 20,000–30,000 are said to be sheltering with kin and Nepali villagers in West Bengal and the Assam States of Eastern India.

The camps are administered by the Government of Nepal, while the UNHCR looks after food supplies, shelter, health, and sanitation for the camps. Other major donors of bilateral and multilateral aid to the camps include the World Food Programme, the Lutheran World Service, and Oxfam. Conditions have improved from the first months when the refugees set up their own settlements without outside help; there are schools and medical facilities in the camps, but little work for the refugees, and many slip out to work in farms and as labor outside.

Diplomacy and Negotiations

In 1993, the Governments of Bhutan and Nepal began ministerial-level discussions on a resolution of the refugee crisis. As many as seven rounds of talks were held, first between the Home Ministers of the two countries, then between the Foreign Ministers. In October 1993, they agreed to identify refugees on the basis of four categories: (a) genuine Bhutanese who have been forcibly evicted; (b) Bhutanese who emigrated voluntarily; (c) non-Bhutanese in the camps; and (d) Bhutanese who have committed criminal offences.

Beyond this basic concord, there has been no progress on the actual identification and categorization of the refugees. This is largely because of the failure of the Nepal Government to present a coherent diplomatic strategy: In the space of eight years, as many as six governments of different ideologies and interests have taken office. Political survival took precedence over settling the Lhotsampa question, much to Thimpu's advantage. The lack of progress in the ministerial talks has led to their being held at the official level; three such rounds have been held, with no progress. In the process, the issue has become a bilateral one between Bhutan and Nepal, whereas the real problem is between the Government of Bhutan and those who have left their country. In the camps, rebellious groups have succeeded in leading marches to the Indian border as part of their campaign to demand repatriation. Members of these groups were arrested at the border and dispersed by police authorities in India.

In late 1998, Bhutan showed fresh interest in tackling the issue, partly as a result of international pressure. In June, King Jigme stunned his nation by announcing that he was handing over the daily running of national affairs to a Cabinet of Ministers, handpicked by him but approved by the rubber-stamp National Assembly. The Cabinet was to be led by one of the ministers on the basis of rotation. Its current head is Jigme Thinley, formerly Home Secretary, later Ambassador to the United Nations in Geneva, who also is Foreign Minister and has led his government at several international conferences and discussions.

During these meetings, another drama was played out behind the scenes. This involved the arrest in India of Rongthong Kuenley Dorji, a leader of the Sarchop community, which is akin to the main ruling Drukpa group but more numerous and less developed. Bhutan demanded Dorji's extradition, but the move was stalled following protests from several Indian leaders like George Fernandes in 1997, of the Opposition, and court orders blocking the extradition. Rongthong Dorji is chairman of a fledging pro-democracy party called the United Front for Democracy and is believed to be influential among his community. The significance of this case lies in that Dorji has received strong support from the anti-monarchists among the Nepalese speakers who live in exile and there is deepening concern in Bhutan that the alliance could complicate matters for the ruling elite and create political instability in the future.

In 1998, Fernandes was appointed Defense Minister in the national right-wing Government under Prime Minister Atal Bihari Vajpayee; he continues to take a close interest in the Dorji case as well as in greater transparency and liberalization of the political system in Bhutan.

Government Seizure of Vacant Lands

During these events, the Bhutan Government quietly began a process of turning over to others, lands vacated by the refugees. "People have been resettled from other parts of Bhutan, especially those who have no property—they get priority," said a Bhutanese diplomat.[14] The procedure is simple: apply to the local headman for land. The request is forwarded to the local district administration, which then makes a decision on allotment of vacant land.

The resettlement package was approved in July 1997 by the National Assembly, which also took another controversial decision—the retrenchment of relatives of refugees. These moves were part of an overall strategy of the Bhutan Government to weaken the position of the refugees back "home" and strengthen its own position. It is a signal of resistance to repatriation.

The Lhotsampas sacked from Government service or "compulsorily retired" were ousted after being investigated for their role in the antimonarchy agitation and for any connections with the opposition in Nepal. As many as 219 doctors and engineers were dismissed in the first half of 1998 on these charges.

The policy of settling other Bhutanese on lands vacated by the refugees is similar to what was done in the Chittagong Hill Tracts, as well as in Myanmar with the Rohingyas. Although not many have so far been settled, the strategy is to offer an incentive of the equivalent of about 10,000 Indian rupees (200 U.S. dollars) and then a further amount of 100,000 rupees (2,000 dollars) once the family has completely settled in the area. It is significant that the new settlers are not other Lhotsampas but members of Rongthong Dorji's community, the Sarchops, who are becoming politically restive and need placating. About 400 landless Sarchop families were settled on vacated lands. These have been moved from the Tashigang area, the main town of the Sarchop-dominated eastern belt of Bhutan.

The political aim is three-fold: first, to put the refugees and Nepal on alert again about Bhutan's weariness with discussions that have not been producing results and its ability to go ahead with unilateral decisions that could have long-term effects on the refugee population; second, to diversify the ethnic "spread" of the southern population; and third, to reduce potential Sarchop opposition to the ruling elite. These moves coincide with the new interest that Bhutan and Nepal show in discussing the Lhotsampa problem, but the Bhutanese elite continues to take a tough line on returnees.

The official newspaper of the Bhutan Government, *Kuensel*, said in the summer of 1998 that National Assembly members made "angry calls" opposing any plans to bring back those who had "emigrated." One legislator was quoted as saying, "The return of these people who left of their own accord will seriously undermine Bhutan's citizenship laws."

Another described the refugees as people who had "chosen to bite the hand that fed them" (Kuensel, 18 July 1998 p. 16).

Despite the rhetoric, one basic question yet remains: How many will Bhutan be ready to take back? International agencies met Bhutanese leaders in November 1998, urging that Thimpu send "positive signals" on the refugee issue. Bhutan has consistently declared that only a small number of the refugees are actually Bhutanese and says it is not prepared to take back those who "voluntarily" surrendered their citizenship and their lands. Bhutanese officials rarely speak of numbers but it appears, from several discussions, that they are unlikely to consider a refugee-returnee figure of much more than 10,000. Still, a beginning has to be made; otherwise the refugee camps could well become a breeding-ground for greater confrontations by frustrated younger camp members and anti-monarchy political groups.

Conclusions

The Lhotsampa situation has been allowed to drift and stagnate for years, partly because of India's refusal to get involved in any form of discussions that could lead to a settlement. India has emphasized that the problem is bilateral, involving two friendly neighbors, conveniently forgetting that it is also involved, since its territory is used as the transit route by refugees and it is itself host to a substantial number of Lhotsampas in Assam and West Bengal.

Bhutan is also concerned by the presence of two extremely well-armed and powerful Indian insurgent groups in its southern belt, bordering the Indian state of Assam. These groups, the United Liberation Front of Asom and the National Liberation Democratic Front of the Bodos, have bases that the Bhutanese are unable and unwilling to tackle. Accounts of extortion by the groups, which move around with weapons, and some clashes with local police have been reported. Bhutan says its small army and police force are no match for the heavily armed insurgents.

On 6 October 1998, the King of Bhutan told reporters during an official visit to New Delhi that "We will never allow our land to be used by anyone against the interests of India." However, there has been no action against these groups and there are unsubstantiated allegations that the Bhutan Government is allowing the Indian militants, who have well-organized camps with surveillance systems and radios, to stay on as another unfriendly gesture to the Lhotsampa. The Bhutan Government, too, is troubled by the fact that its southern districts, which have extensive trade links with Assam, have already been disrupted by the Indian army's tightened vigil on the border to control the militants, who slip into Assam to conduct occasional ambushes against Indian troops as well as government offices.

India is reluctant to flush out the extremists, who say they want independence for parts of oil- and tea-rich Assam. It is concerned that such a move could create a full-fledged insurgency in a small country like Bhutan. This could in turn lead to instability on the border; India is also acutely conscious of the close attention that China pays to developments in Bhutan, which abuts on Tibet.

What is needed, as in the case of Myanmar, is greater openness on both sides, a readiness to talk clearly and with flexibility, especially from the Bhutanese, and to set a timeframe for the identification and repatriation of the refugees, who have already been in the camps for more than seven years. A gesture that could generate greater regional goodwill might take the form of inviting a respected interlocutor group like the Eminent Persons Group of South Asia, which includes senior scholars and professionals from all seven countries in the region, to involve itself in the discussions and enable them to move forward on an informal but politically significant track, setting guidelines that could enable officials to break the stalemate and take the process forward.

General Conclusions

These studies of Bangladesh, Myanmar, and Bhutan show commonalities as well as differences in the approaches of the three countries to "inconvenient" minority groups. The biggest difference has been in the way that Bangladesh has sought to cope with the question of the Chakmas, through a process of dialogue, however incomplete and fractured. Yet there are few alternatives to this formulation of steady capacity-building, creating better understanding at the political and social levels, and an open process of democratic discussion and debate.

As noted earlier, although the three cases are extremely different in nature, they share several similarities. These include the reality of a religious and linguistic majoritarian group pitted against a smaller religious and linguistic minority. This minority group, when pushed to the brink, resorts to violent means to assert its identity, as in the cases of Bangladesh and Myanmar, although this is far more subdued in the Bhutanese example.

Demographic engineering tools have been similar—questioning the citizenship of the minority group from whom a purported threat emanates, even to the extent of not recognizing those living on the land as citizens, as in the case of Myanmar. Other forms of pressure have included intimidation and ouster from ancestral lands and the resettlement of "friendly" groups on these lands. All three countries have followed this practice in varying degrees.

Myanmar has a rather unique distinction, that of forced labor, which is seen neither in Bangladesh nor Bhutan. Bhutan has extended its hostility to those opposed to its political system to dismissing the relatives of refugees to Nepal.

International organizations have had a mixed record and a limited role in defusing these confrontations. Only one of the three situations—that of the Muslim refugees from the Arakan—has seen the full involvement of an international agency (UNHCR) with both sides of the problem. But even this, as has been noted, is not a completely successful story.

As far as Bhutan is concerned, it has not yet given UNHCR a mandate to assist in the detection and repatriation of the Lhotsampa refugees, although a UNHCR delegation met with the King and other top leaders. The UNHCR is active only in the Nepali refugee camps. India refuses it access to the sites where the Lhotsampas are living in Eastern India. In the case of Bangladesh, the Chakma problem was resolved domestically after India stopped its support of the rebels.

In each case, an outside actor has been cited as a spur to the problem. In each case, too, this problem has been further identified as a meddling neighbor: India for the Chakmas (Bangladesh), Bangladesh for the Rohingyas (Myanmar), and Nepal for the Lhotsampas (Bhutan).

The case of Bangladesh stands out as the only one that has ended in a settlement, even though this accord is being challenged by various groups in the Hill Tracts as well as nationally. Often solutions are slowed by countries that see domestic problems next door as opportunities to exert pressure on their neighbors. Such interference must cease. In addition, influential, non-partisan groups such as the Eminent Persons Group of South Asia should be persuaded to play an informal role. In these developing circumstances, international organizations like the UNHCR may be called upon by the governments of the area to play a more active role in resettlement and repatriation. They will need to move with sensitivity and steadiness if they are to work effectively.

Yet, eventually, it is the basics of democracy, open governance and transparency in negotiations, that will help defuse and reduce such complex ethnic conflicts and majoritarian-minority confrontations.

Notes

1. Maj. H. R. Davies, quoted in *Census of India* 1911.
2. Interview with author, 8 March 1999.
3. Interview with author, Dhaka, February 1998.
4. Interview with author, Dhaka, 1 March 1999.
5. Interview with author, Dhaka, 1 March 1999.
6. Interview with author, New Delhi, October 1998.
7. Imtiaz Ahmed, discussion at workshop on Ethnicity, Refugees, and the Environment at Hikkedewa, Sri Lanka, March 1998.
8. Myanmar diplomat, interview with author, New Delhi, 1998.
9. UNHCR officer, interview with author, New Delhi, November 1998.
10. UNHCR officer, interview with author, New Delhi, November 1998.
11. Interview with author, New Delhi, November 1998.
12. Interview with author, Thimpu, Bhutan, March 1993.
13. Interview with author, October 1998.
14. Interview with author, October 1998.

References

Abrar, Choudhury R. 1998. "Issues and Constraints in the Repatriation/Rehabilitation of the Rohingya and Chakma Refugees and the Biharis." Paper presented at the Conference of Scholars and Other Professionals Working on Refugees and Displaced Persons in South Asia, Rajendrapur, Bangladesh, 9–11 February.

Ahmed, Imtiaz. 1996. "Refugees and Security: The Experience of Bangladesh." In *Refugees and Regional Security in South Asia*, eds. S. D. Muni and Lok Raj Baral. New Delhi: Konarak Publishers Pvt. Ltd.

Chittagong Hill Tracts Commission. 1992. *Life Is Not Ours: Land and Human Rights in the Chittagong Hill Tracts*. London: Chittagong Hill Tracts Commission.

De, Barun. 1998. "Moving Beyond Boundaries." In *States, Citizens and Outsiders*. Katmandu: South Asia Forum for Human Rights.

Elahi, K. Maudood. 1998. "Population Shifts and Refugees in Bangladesh: An Overview." Paper presented at Conference of Scholars and Other Professionals Working on Refugees and Displaced Persons in South Asia, Rajendrapur, Bangladesh, 9–11 February.

Government of Bangladesh. 1993. "The Problems of the Chittagong Hill Tracts and Bangladesh Responses for their Solution." Dhaka: Prime Minister's Office.

Guha-Thakurta, Meghna. 1998. "Bangladesh, a Land of Shifting Populations." In *States, Citizens and Outsiders*. Katmandu: South Asia Forum for Human Rights.

Hutt, Michael. 1994. "Bhutan's Crisis of Identity." *The World Year Book*. London.

Lama, Mahendra. 1998. "Political Economy of Lhotsampa Refugees: State Behaviour, Aid Intervention and Repatriation Process." Paper presented at the Conference of Scholars and Other Professionals Working on Refugees and Displaced Persons in South Asia, Rajendrapur, Bangladesh, 9–11 February.

Mohsin, Amena. 1998. "The Chittagong Hill Tracts Peace Accord and the Hill People." Unpublished paper.

Phadnis, Urmila. 1989. *Ethnicity and Nation-Building in South Asia*. New Delhi: Sage Publications.

Prime Minister's Office. 1993. "Report on the Problems of the Chittagong Hill Tracts and Bangladesh Responses for their Solution." Dhaka: Government of Bangladesh, Prime Minister's Office.

Sinha, A. C. 1991. *Bhutan: Ethnic Identity and National Dilemma*. New Delhi: Reliance Publishing House.

Thinley, Jigme. 1993. "Bhutan: A Kingdom Besieged." In *Bhutan: A Traditional Order and the Forces of Change. Three Views from Bhutan*. Royal Government of Bhutan, Ministry of Foreign Affairs.

Timm, R. W. 1991. "The Adivasis of Bangladesh." London: Minority Rights Group International (December).

U.S. Committee for Refugees. 1988. "From Isolation to Exile: Refugees from the Chittagong Hill Tracts of Bangladesh." Washington D.C.: U.S. Committee for Refugees (September).

United Nations. 1993. "Rapporteur's Report on Myanmar" (6 January).

———. 1997. "Special Rapporteur's Report on Myanmar" (16 October).

༄

CHAPTER 9

Impacts of Migration to China's Border Regions

Judith Banister

Migration is a demographic variable that strongly affects national security and human security. Spontaneous migration can happen because people flee invading armies or the oppression of their own government. Migrants also move toward places where they expect greater economic, political, and personal security as well as greater happiness. Most of the migration streams in human history were these kinds of unorganized, non-directed population movements.

Another type of migration with major security implications is migration directed by governments, by governmental units such as armed forces, or by other institutions such as companies and international organizations. Governments mandate, sponsor, and direct migration in order to relieve population pressure in their most densely populated areas and simultaneously to make better use of their least inhabited lands. In addition, governments send troops, officials, administrators, cadres, workers, and settlers to frontier and border areas to strengthen government control over border regions and to prevent foreign encroachment. This latter type of government-directed migration in the People's Republic of China (PRC) is the focus of this chapter.

Historical Precedent in China

Migration built China as a geographic and multiethnic entity (Lee 1978). Chinese migration was largely an occupation of sparsely populated land, an expansion of the frontiers of Chinese settlement. While much of this migration was private and unofficial, Chinese governments have frequently played a major role in encouraging, organizing, and aiding internal migration to the frontiers.

For at least three millennia, Chinese historical records have documented government-sponsored migrations linked to control of what were then China's borders (Lee 1978). The state repeatedly used migration as a major tool to further its policies of political and social integration, economic development, disaster relief, and government control of the rich and powerful. From at least the first millennium B.C.E., the Chinese government relied on organized migration to garrison and develop newly won border areas and to facilitate their eventual political and social integration with the rest of China. These frontier regions had been lightly populated by non-Han peoples, and the Chinese government moved Han Chinese military colonists into the frontiers to establish its territorial administrations, often in migrations organized by the army and involving hundreds of thousands of settlers (Lee 1978: 23–24). Most government migrants were placed on farmland, where soldiers worked with their families as agricultural colonists. Throughout much of China, particularly the provinces of China proper now densely populated with the Han Chinese people, the Chinese language of the Han in-migrants displaced the native languages and helped build a relatively homogeneous civilization. The geographical extension of Chinese territory was often a violent process, including wars and forced migrations of indigenous peoples.

China's last two dynasties further expanded its borders. During the early nineteenth century, the Qing (Manchu) dynasty reached its fullest geographical extent. The Chinese empire before the mid-nineteenth century exercised suzerainty over a large part of the Asian continent extending from Siberia to Indochina (Tzou 1990: 1). Thereafter, the empire began to weaken and to disintegrate at its outer reaches. Successive pieces of China were unwillingly ceded or leased to invading colonial powers, for instance Hong Kong to Britain and part of Shandong province to Germany. Russia's drive to the east permanently captured huge pieces of Siberia from China.

After the collapse of the Qing dynasty in 1911, China was ruled by competing warlords under the nominal control of the Kuomintang (Nationalist) government of the Republic of China. Mongolia took advantage of this weakness to achieve its independence from China, backed by the power of Russia and then the Soviet Union.

In 1949, after decades of Japanese invasion and civil war, the People's Republic of China was founded. Its boundaries encompassed the remaining areas that had been controlled by the Qing dynasty, including provinces and cities that had been taken by Japan and Germany and then returned to China after the Second World War. However, PRC territory did not include Mongolia, Siberia, or countries in Indochina that had been taken by other colonial powers such as France and Britain. Areas that had paid nominal allegiance to China or that had been loosely controlled by China, such as Tibet and Xinjiang, were included within PRC boundaries.

Insecure Borders of the People's Republic of China

Given this most recent century of territorial losses, there was no guarantee that the PRC could keep all the border provinces and regions that remained precariously within its 1949 boundaries. Secessionist sentiment was very strong in Tibet and Xinjiang; the Mongols in Inner Mongolia had a natural affinity to their brethren in Mongolia. (See Map 9.1.) China's new Communist government was opposed by most Western governments in the early 1950s, although it was supported by the Soviet Union. A declaration of independence by a border province of China might have received overt or covert international assistance and approval.

Policies toward Minority Peoples

During the Republican period from 1912 to 1949, the basic aim of policy toward the minorities was consistently to preserve China's national unity (Mackerras 1994: 53–57). At first the policy of the Kuomintang government was to assimilate minority groups without much regard for their distinctive characteristics. By 1924, however, the Nationalists had formed a "United Front" with the Chinese Communist Party (CCP), and the Nationalist Manifesto of that year adopted stated policies from the Soviet Union toward its minorities. These principles included the equality of all the nationalities within China's borders, the right of "self-determination" of each nationality, and the right to "autonomy." These terms never meant independence, and under Chiang Kai-shek, the Kuomintang moved back toward an assimilationist policy during 1927–1949 (Dreyer 1976: 40). This had only limited practical consequences for the minorities, because much of China was under warlord control throughout the Republican period (Bockman 1992: 186).

The Chinese Communist Party followed the Marxist-Leninist terminology and ideas about minority nationalities, establishing the first "autonomous region" in 1947 (Inner Mongolia Autonomous Region), followed gradually by four more after 1949. Government policy toward the minorities was relatively benign in the early 1950s, but by the late 1950s PRC policies had hardened against any distinctiveness in the minority groups that could be seen as backward, such as their religions, languages, customs, dress, food restrictions, and beliefs. China's minority nationalities were harassed and suppressed during the anti-Rightist campaign of 1957, the Great Leap Forward of 1958–1960, and the Cultural Revolution period of 1966–1976. As one expert on the minorities put it, they were subjected to "the feverish Great Cultural Revolution's wanton destructions and persecutions," which "aimed at erasing their ethnic and cultural differences" (Lemoine 1989: 2).

After the death of Mao Zedong in 1976, the arrest of his widow and others in the "Gang of Four," and the rise to power of Deng Xiaoping, the PRC government determined that its policies toward the minorities had been too harsh and restrictive. In the early 1980s, China's government began to encourage some expressions of minority cultures. Policy changes were spelled out in the 1982 Constitution for Guiding the Socio-political Structure of the Minority Regions, and in the 1984 Law on Regional

Autonomy for Minority Nationalities. Certain leadership positions and specified proportions of representatives at different levels of autonomous region governments were reserved for members of the minority nationalities (Wu 1989: 13). In addition to economic reform and cultural liberalization seen throughout China in the 1980s, there was "a kind of cultural revival particularly pronounced among the minority nationalities" (Schein 1989: 199). In some places this has included reinstitution of bilingual education, publication of newspapers in the minority language script, some intensification of ritual activity, documentation and preservation of minority folklore, and encouraging performances of minority songs and dances.

For some of the minority groups, this cultural revival has included renewed resistance against the Chinese government, opposition to Han Chinese cultural dominance, and a strong religious resurgence. The Muslim minorities of Xinjiang and the Tibetan Buddhists stand out in this regard. China's government has reacted with alarm to the strongly expressed desires for greater autonomy and, by some, for independence in Tibet and Xinjiang. Some authors argue that the PRC has instituted a re-centralization policy in both provinces in the 1990s, withdrawing some of the limited autonomy that had been tried in the 1980s and cracking down on all forms of dissent and many types of cultural expression (Becquelin 1999; Karmel 1995).

Northern and Western Borders—General Characteristics

When the PRC was founded, the Han Chinese population constituted 94 percent of the total Mainland China population, and the 55 minority nationalities together made up only 6 percent (China 1953 Census 1954). Therefore the Han majority enjoyed overwhelming numerical dominance in the PRC as a whole.

In 1949, most of China's Han population was uneducated or illiterate, poverty-stricken, economically undeveloped, engaged in agriculture or other primary sector production, and socially unsophisticated, with high fertility, morbidity, and mortality. The minority nationalities of China's northern and western border provinces were also poor, uneducated, and disadvantaged. In spite of the many similarities between the Han and most minority groups, Han Chinese saw themselves as more civilized and cultured, more economically and socially advanced, and less superstitious than the minority peoples. This attitude of ethnic superiority is characterized by PRC leaders as "*da Han zhuyi*" which means "Great Han-ism" or "Great Han chauvinism." During its less fanatical periods, the PRC government has tried to minimize Han Chinese attitudes and expressions of intolerance toward the minorities.

Some of the minority groups were located in rugged, inhospitable, non-Han territory on or near China's inexact borders with neighboring countries, where the strategic importance of those particular minority nationalities far outweighed their absolute numbers. In Tibet, Xinjiang, and Inner Mongolia (Map 9.1), there were settled agricultural populations and nomadic herders linked to cross-border populations with the same ethnic identity, culture, language, and religion as their own. For many centuries, the borders of these regions had been fluid and traders, nomads, and herders had customarily crossed them regularly or seasonally.

Inner Mongolia, Xinjiang, and Tibet consist primarily of vast, thinly populated, arid, and often cold grasslands, deserts, plateaus, and mountains, mostly unsuitable for settled intensive agriculture. In past centuries, except when Han Chinese were sent to control and settle the borders, they did not move in and settle Tibet, Xinjiang, or the northern parts of Inner Mongolia in huge numbers. It was also important that during some periods, China's dynastic government policy had been to forbid private, unofficial Han Chinese settlement of some of these regions.

At the beginning of the 1950s, the new government of China developed and implemented a variety of policies toward the border minority areas. One was to send certain categories of Han Chinese migrants to these provinces, apparently in an attempt to consolidate control over the border regions, to pacify the minority nationality peoples living there, to develop the economies of these large territories, and to link their economies and polities with the rest of China.

From the beginning, a top priority of the PRC government has been to hold on to all the territory it conquered when it was established, including lands the government pacified soon thereafter. According to a specialist on China's minorities, the Chinese Communist Party (CCP) "places an extremely high priority on national unity. Its first task was to effectively unify the state it had created. Next to its own overthrow, its greatest fear has always been the secession of nationality regions and the consequent disintegration of the PRC" (Mackerras 1994: 140).

The following sections examine the goals and results of government-directed migration to the three potentially most explosive border regions of the People's Republic of China, provinces known as "Autonomous Regions," consistent with inherited Marxist ideology that minority nationalities had the right to rule themselves autonomously under communism.

Xinjiang

Muslim Peoples of Central Asia

The Qing dynasty consolidated its control over Muslim peoples in the eastern part of Central Asia in the eighteenth century; the region was never regarded as part of the Chinese heartland, however, nor was large-scale colonization by Chinese settlers attempted (Ferdinand 1994: 272). As Russian influence gradually penetrated the region in the nineteenth century, Muslim riots and rebellions were frequent, culminating in a large uprising in the 1860s and the establishment of an anti-China East Turkestan government that was finally defeated by China in 1878. In 1884, the region was declared a province of China and named "Xinjiang," which means "New Frontier." Rebellions continued in the late nineteenth and early twentieth centuries. Xinjiang was ruled by Chinese warlords in the Republican period 1912–1949, despite the Soviet Union's strong economic and military influence there. Muslims in Xinjiang tried to set up an East Turkestan republic in the 1930s and again during 1944–1948.

More than 200,000 Han Chinese, fleeing famine and warfare, migrated to Xinjiang during the Republican period; they came primarily from Shanxi province in north China, and some also moved from Yunnan province in the southwest (China Population, Xinjiang Volume, 1990: 57). In 1949, a communist army entered Xinjiang and negotiated the surrender of an ethnic minority army and of Nationalist forces. The Communist and Nationalist armies were almost all Han Chinese men, and they were directed to settle in Xinjiang as troops and farmers (O'Neill 1998b: 16). By year-end 1949, a Han Chinese population of 291,000 constituted 7 percent of Xinjiang's population (see Table 9.1). The largest population group was the Muslim Uighurs, who were primarily agriculturalists using natural runoff to farm in oases and at the bases of mountains. When the PRC was founded in 1949, Xinjiang had 3.3 million Uighurs, 76 percent of the region's population. The next-largest group was 444,000 Kazaks, nomadic herders whose ancestors came from Kazakhstan, constituting 10 percent of the population. Many smaller Muslim minority groups also inhabited the region.

Directed Migration to Xinjiang

The partially demobilized Han armies in Xinjiang began building irrigation works and opening up new agricultural land. At the same time, they retained the task of military consolidation of Xinjiang under PRC control, including suppressing revolts by the minorities. The government organized women to move from Han areas of China to Xinjiang to become wives of the army men. In 1954, the government established a paramilitary corps called the "Bing Tuan" (Army Corps), or more formally the Xinjiang Production and Construction Corps, staffed by the settler-soldiers. Many of the migrants to Xinjiang were associated with the Bing Tuan. From the beginning, its stated role was "to develop Xinjiang, defend the nation's borders and protect social stability" (Eckholm 1999: A1).

Table 9.2 provides official data on the net migration to Xinjiang by year through 1991. The permanent population registration system was not functional until 1954, so for earlier years the available figures are just residual numbers calculated from population, birth, and death figures or estimates. Beginning in 1954, figures in Table 9.2 are calculated three different ways, from the Public Security System compilations of population

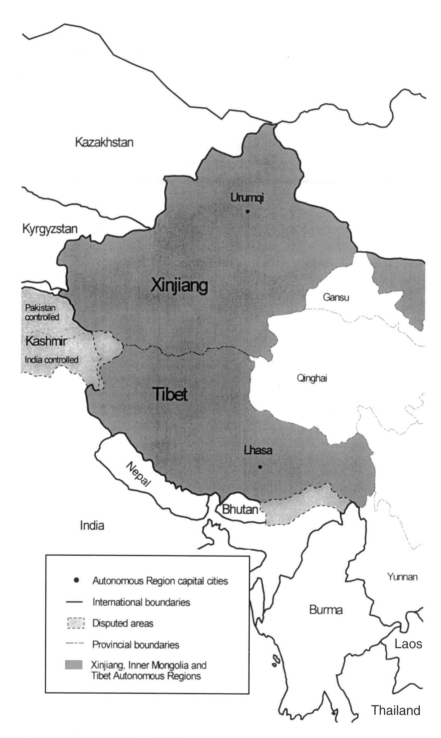

MAP 9.1 Political Divisions of China

TABLE 9.1 Han and Non-Han Population in Xinjiang, Selected Years, 1949–1997

Year	Total Population (Year-end) (1,000)	Han Number (1,000)	%	Non-Han Number (1,000)	%	Uighur Number (1,000)	%	Kazak Number (1,000)	%
1949	4,333.4	291.0	7	4,042.4	93	3,291.1	76	443.7	10
1952	4,651.7	326.0	7	4,325.7	93	3,500.9	75	494.5	11
1953*	4,873.6	346.6	7	4,527.1	93	3,678.3	75	507.1	10
1957	5,580.1	821.5	15	4,758.6	85	3,867.1	69	530.7	10
1962	6,989.7	2,077.2	30	4,912.5	70	4,004.7	57	487.4	7
1964*	7,270.1	2,321.2	32	4,948.9	68	3,991.3	55	489.1	7
1965	7,891.0	2,758.4	35	5,132.6	65	4,115.1	52	524.0	7
1970	9,765.8	3,681.2	38	6,084.6	62	4,673.3	48	616.3	6
1975	11,545.3	4,780.1	41	6,765.2	59	5,266.0	46	751.4	7
1978	12,330.1	5,129.0	42	7,201.1	58	5,555.3	45	821.0	7
1980	12,832.4	5,310.3	41	7,522.1	59	5,764.6	45	876.8	7
1982*	13,081.5	5,284.0	40	7,797.6	60	5,956.0	46	903.3	7
1985	13,611.4	5,349.2	39	8,262.2	61	6,294.4	46	987.2	7
1986	13,836.4	5,386.3	39	8,450.1	61	6,431.0	46	1,010.5	7
1987	14,063.3	5,429.8	39	8,633.5	61	6,562.2	47	1,034.3	7
1988	14,264.2	5,470.1	38	8,794.1	62	6,675.2	47	1,055.9	7
1989	14,541.6	6,531.6	38	9,010.0	62	6,827.3	47	1,087.9	7
1990*	15,156.8	5,695.4	38	9,461.4	62	7,191.8	47	1,106.3	7
1990	15,291.6	5,746.6	38	9,545.0	62	7,249.5	47	1,139.2	7
1991	15,545.7	5,842.1	38	9,703.6	62	7,362.8	47	1,161.3	7
1992	15,806.3	5,940.0	38	9,866.3	62	7,474.1	47	1,182.0	7
1993	16,052.6	6,036.7	38	10,015.9	62	7,589.5	47	1,196.4	7
1994	16,327.0	6,164.8	38	10,162.2	62	7,697.3	47	1,217.0	7
1995	16,613.5	6,318.1	38	10,295.4	62	7,800.0	47	1,237.7	7
1996	16,892.9	6,432.8	38	10,460.1	62	7,916.0	47	1,257.0	7
1997	17,180.8	6,601.3	38	10,579.5	62	8,020.0	47	1,270.8	7

Sources: Data for 1949: *China Population, Xinjiang Volume,* 1990: 283; Data for 1952–1994: *Xinjiang Statistical Yearbook 1995:* 45; Data for 1995–1997: *Xinjiang Statistical Yearbook 1998:* 55, 57.

*From census data in the middle of the year of 1953, 1964, 1982 and 1990.

TABLE 9.2 Migration in Xinjiang, 1950–1991

Year	Average Population (1,000)	Source A		Source B		Source C	
		Net Migration (1,000)	Net Migration Rate (per 1,000)	Net Migration (1,000)	Net Migration Rate (per 1,000)	Net Migration (1,000)	Net Migration Rate (per 1,000)
1950	4,386.2	–	–	–	–	61.0	13.91
1951	4,492.7	–	–	–	–	59.2	13.18
1952	4,599.0	–	–	–	–	53.3	11.59
1953	4,717.6	–	–	–	–	71.3	15.11
1954	4,892.2	168.0	34.34	168.0	34.34	146.2	29.88
1955	5,059.3	63.2	12.49	63.2	12.49	34.7	6.86
1956	5,224.8	58.6	11.22	58.5	11.20	125.6	24.04
1957	5,455.9	108.3	19.85	108.3	19.85	153.1	28.06
1958	5,701.8	138.9	24.36	160.4	28.13	140.6	24.66
1959	6,156.7	293.9	47.74	511.2	83.03	598.4	97.19
1960	6,676.6	288.0	43.14	287.9	43.12	290.3	43.48
1961	6,982.0	155.7	22.30	155.7	22.30	143.5	20.55
1962	7,045.1	-196.1	-27.83	-194.6	-27.62	-268.1	-38.05
1963	7,060.4	30.1	4.26	30.1	4.26	-40.0	-5.67
1964	7,286.5	149.7	20.54	149.6	20.53	121.9	16.73
1965	7,666.4	199.9	26.07	199.9	26.07	214.9	28.03
1966	8,135.5	299.7	36.84	298.8	36.73	255.5	31.41
1967	8,549.2	117.8	13.78	117.8	13.78	99.4	11.63
1968	8,901.3	65.4	7.35	65.4	7.35	85.5	9.61
1969	9,259.9	86.7	9.36	86.7	9.36	72.1	7.79
1970	9,600.7	50.4	5.25	50.4	5.25	57.1	5.95
1971	9,932.4	75.5	7.60	75.5	7.60	62.1	6.25
1972	10,298.0	122.2	11.87	120.8	11.73	84.3	8.19
1973	10,693.8	48.6	4.54	48.0	4.49	71.2	6.66
1974	11,074.5	42.0	3.79	62.0	5.60	66.1	5.97
1975	11,401.8	27.3	2.39	27.3	2.39	9.4	0.82
1976	11,701.7	52.7	4.50	52.7	4.50	62.5	5.34
1977	11,973.9	58.4	4.88	58.4	4.88	18.3	1.53
1978	12,209.9	36.4	2.98	36.4	2.98	58.9	4.82
1979	12,444.9	22.7	1.82	22.7	1.82	52.7	4.23
1980	12,696.1	26.6	2.10	26.6	2.10	99.3	7.82
1981	12,931.5	-43.9	-3.39	-44.0	-3.40	-80.0	-6.19
1982	13,094.8	-6.5	-0.50	-6.5 -	0.50	-61.5	-4.70
1983	13,246.0	-8.6	-0.65	-20.6	-1.56	10.6	0.80
1984	13,386.9	-7.5	-0.56	-18.7	-1.40	-70.4	-5.26
1985	13,526.1	-25.8	-1.91	-56.2	-4.15	-10.7	-0.79
1986	13,723.9	-19.6	-1.43	-42.8	-3.12	27.2	1.98
1987	13,949.8	-5.2	-0.37	-22.0	-1.58	16.6	1.19
1988	14,163.8	6.7	0.47	-17.6	-1.24	7.2	0.51
1989	14,402.9	-8.4	-0.58	-17.3	-1.20	55.5	3.85
1990	14,764.4	78.5	5.32	3.4	0.23	223.5	15.14
1991	15,133.8	47.0	3.11	25.2	1.67	113.4	7.49

(continued)

TABLE 9.2   Migration in Xinjiang, 1950–1991 *(continued)*

Source: *Towards 21st Century, Xinjiang Volume,* 1994: 224–226.

Source A: Data before 1984 come from *Zhonghua Renmin Gongheguo renkou tongji ziliao huibian 1949–1985 (Compilation of Population Statistics of the People's Republic of China from 1949 to 1985),* edited by China, State Statistical Bureau and Ministry of Public Security. Data after 1984 calculated by *Towards 21st Century, Xinjiang Volume,* 1994, based on the formula: net migration = total number of in-migrants in every level of administrative unit – total number of out-migrants in every level of administrative unit.

Source B: Data before 1980 come from *Xinjiang Weiwuer Zizhiqu renkou tongji ziliao 1976–1984 (Population Statistics of the Xinjiang Uighur Autonomous Region from 1976 to 1984).* Data after 1980 calculated by *Towards 21st Century, Xinjiang Volume,* 1994, based on the formula: net migration = total number of in-migrants to Xinjiang – total number of out-migrants from Xinjiang.

Source C: Calculated by *Towards 21st Century, Xinjiang Volume,* 1994, based on the formula: net migration = total registered population at the end of this year – total registered population at the end of last year – natural increase of the population within this year calculated from registered births and deaths.

registration data plus other information. The registration system was likely to include those migrants whose *hukou* (formal place of permanent registration) changed, but it might have excluded (a) some government-directed migrants whose assignment to Xinjiang was meant to be temporary, even if it lasted for many years, and (b) some spontaneous migrants whose move was neither initiated nor approved by the authorities.

Every year during the 1950s there was a net in-migration to Xinjiang of tens of thousands of people from other parts of China, rising to 100,000–300,000 in each of the years 1954 and 1957–1961, and possibly to a much higher peak in 1959 (Table 9.2 and Figure 9.1). The provincial population grew rapidly, from 4 million in 1949 to 7 million at the beginning of the 1960s. Some of the inflow during 1959–1961 was people fleeing from the famine of the Great Leap Forward in nearby provinces, because Xinjiang was much less affected by it. The sudden migration reversal in 1962 reflected, in part, the famine-generated migrants returning to their home provinces (Dong 1988: 20; Wang 1998: 36). Also important was a mass emigration of about 60,000 Kazaks across the border to the Soviet Union in 1962 (Bockman 1992: 189).

There was a strong net in-migration to Xinjiang during 1964–1966, with smaller numbers in subsequent years. For every year from 1950 through 1980, except for 1962 and possibly 1963, Xinjiang received a net in-migration of tens of thousands to hundreds of thousands. Xinjiang's net migration rates were large and positive through 1961 and in the mid-1960s. During the late 1960s and the 1970s, net migration rates, while small, remained positive (see Table 9.2 and Figure 9.2).

Table 9.1 and Figure 9.3 show the rapid increase of the Han Chinese population of Xinjiang. From fewer than 300,000 in 1949, the number of Han reached 2 million by 1962, 30 percent of the Xinjiang population of

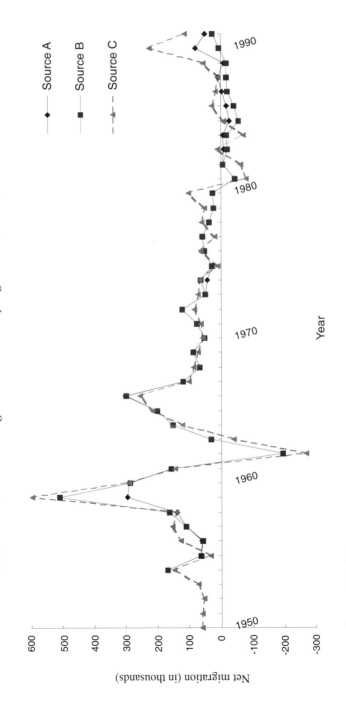

FIGURE 9.1 Civilian Net Migration Data for Xinjiang Province, China, 1950–1991 (*in thousands*)

Source: Table 9.2.

FIGURE 9.2 Civilian Net Migration Rates for Xinjiang Province, China, 1950–1991 *(per thousand population)*

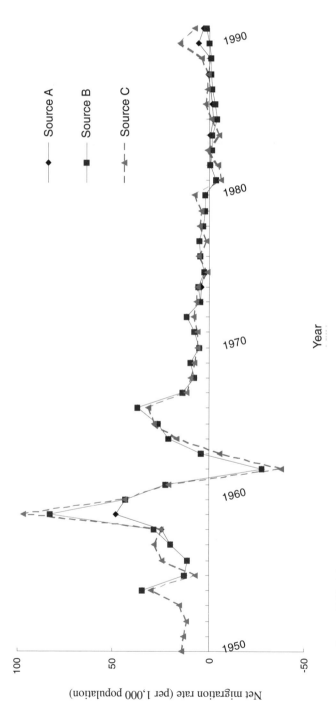

Source: Table 9.2.

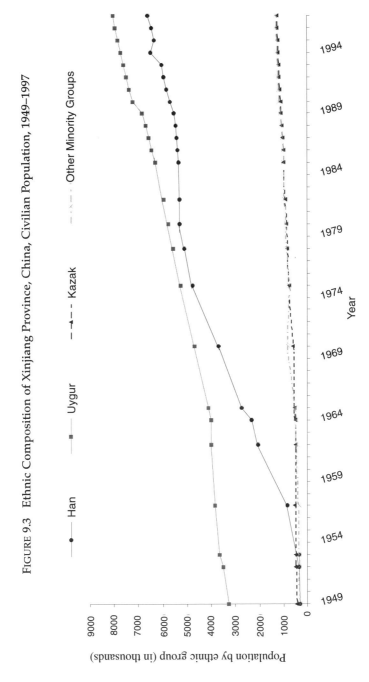

FIGURE 9.3 Ethnic Composition of Xinjiang Province, China, Civilian Population, 1949–1997

Source: Table 9.1.

7 million. Continuing in-migration brought the total Han population to 5 million in 1978, when the Han proportion of Xinjiang's population peaked at 42 percent.

During 1980–1981, violent conflict erupted in Xinjiang, accompanied by Uighur demands for self-rule and for the Han cadres there to leave; the cadres were reportedly eager to do so (Weisskopf 1981; Ma Zheng 1981: 24–25; Banister 1987: 317, 320). There seems to have been a sudden shift in policies toward Xinjiang inter-provincial migration, probably associated with the official reassessment of policies toward the minorities that was already in process during 1980 (Bockman 1992: 190). Every year during 1981–1989, the permanent population registers showed more out-migrants than in-migrants (Tables 9.2 and 9.3, Figures 9.1 and 9.2).

Starting in 1990, and throughout the decade, another apparent shift in migration policy or emphasis brought more migrants into Xinjiang than the numbers leaving, according to Table 9.3. However, this has not increased the Han proportion of Xinjiang's population, since fertility levels are lower among the Han than among the minorities in Xinjiang. The total fertility rates by ethnicity in the early 1990s were: Uighur 4.3 births per woman; Kazak 4.0; Hui 2.5; and Han 1.5 (Anderson and Silver 1995: 215; Toops 1999: 6). Because the natural rate of population increase among the Xinjiang minority populations is so much higher than that of the Han Chinese, the net in-migration of Han is merely keeping Xinjiang's Han population steady at 38 percent. By 1997, as shown in Table 9.1, Xinjiang's Han population comprised 6.6 million of a total population of 17.2 million.

Who Was Sent Where in Xinjiang?

During the decades of strong net in-migration, 1949–1980, the following categories of people were sent to Xinjiang (*Towards 21st Century* 1994, Xinjiang Vol.: 228–253).

Soldier-settlers: The Bing Tuan was set up in 1954 with about 175,000 people, almost all from the army and including very few local Xinjiang people. Since then, military migrants to Xinjiang have not been reported, consistent with PRC policy not to report where its active-duty military personnel are posted. It is very likely, however, that ever since the PRC was established, there has been a large contingent of People's Liberation Army (PLA) soldiers assigned to Xinjiang to guard its long borders with the Soviet Union and successor countries, and its borders with India, Pakistan-held Kashmir, and Afghanistan. Other military personnel may be posted to Xinjiang to put down uprisings, protect oilfields, test nuclear weapons, and for other non-civilian purposes. Except for the original soldier-settlers, active-duty soldiers assigned to Xinjiang are not included in any of the migration data or population data in Tables 9.1, 9.2, and 9.3. Yet the presence of large numbers of Han Chinese soldiers in Xinjiang at all times has a profound effect on the security situation in the province. The

TABLE 9.3   Xinjiang Inter-provincial Migration, 1980–1997

Year	Average Population	Migrants into Xinjiang	Migrants out of Xinjiang	Net Migrants	Net Migration Rate (per 1,000)
1980	12,696,100	131,100	104,500	26,600	2.10
1981	12,931,500	106,600	150,600	-44,000	-3.40
1982	13,094,800	116,200	122,700	-6,500	-0.50
1983	13,246,000	55,700	76,300	-20,600	-1.56
1984	13,386,900	70,500	89,200	-18,700	-1.40
1985	13,526,100	47,900	104,100	-56,200	-4.15
1986	13,723,900	45,300	88,100	-42,800	-3.12
1987	13,949,850	58,000	80,000	-22,000	-1.58
1988	14,163,750	58,500	76,100	-17,600	-1.24
1989	14,402,900	66,600	83,900	-17,300	-1.20
1990	14,916,100	60,400	57,000	3,400	0.23
1991	15,133,800	76,091	50,857	25,234	1.67
1992	15,676,000	76,578	50,299	26,279	1.68
1993	15,929,450	103,077	49,866	53,211	3.34
1994	16,189,800	101,899	43,058	58,841	3.63
1995	16,470,250	107,290	46,785	60,505	3.67
1996	16,753,200	111,973	47,155	64,818	3.87
1997	17,036,850	109,001	52,187	56,814	3.33

Sources: Data through 1990 come from Sun Jingzhi, 1996:1212. Data after 1990 come from *Xinjiang Statistical Yearbook*, 1992:70; 1993:64; 1994:58; 1995:58; 1996:65; 1997:67; 1998:75.

army, police, and paramilitary forces have been sent to put down revolts and demonstrations in Xinjiang for the last half century and are still used for this purpose.

"Young laborers": "Young laborers" in certain periods were sent by the national government from other provinces to Xinjiang. During the Great Leap Forward and its aftermath, 1959–1961, 314,000 such young adult workers were sent to Xinjiang rural communes and the Bing Tuan, and not allowed to return to their provinces of origin. "Because of the policy restrictions, less than 25 percent of them returned inland" (*Towards 21st Century* 1994, Xinjiang Volume: 233). During 1963–1966, 127,000 young adult workers were sent from China's leading and coastal cities to Xinjiang to work in the Bing Tuan.

Volunteer migrants: During the two decades 1958–1978, 1.5 million "volunteers" migrated to Xinjiang from other parts of China, of whom 1.1 million stayed permanently. (It is not clear what proportion of these migrants themselves chose to move to Xinjiang, or what percent were strongly encouraged to migrate as part of a campaign or felt they were given little choice but to migrate there.)

Other categories: Communist Party and government cadres were re-cruited to go to Xinjiang. College graduates were assigned jobs in Xinjiang by the government, and intellectuals were sent there for political reasons. Whole industrial companies were moved to Xinjiang, with their workers. To balance the sex ratio, female migrants were organized by the government, and other family members were also sent.

During the 1980s there was a net out-migration from Xinjiang, but in 1990 and after, in-migration increased, the migrants settling near the borders, on Bing Tuan farms, and in cities along the railway. In addition, newly discovered oilfields were being opened up, and large numbers of oil workers were being sent into Xinjiang.

Inner Mongolia

Pre-1949 Han Migration into Inner Mongolia

In 1771, the Khan of the Mongols submitted to the authority of China's Qing dynasty. At that time, the Chinese government defined two regions, Outer Mongolia and Inner Mongolia, and established the border between them. Outer Mongolia is now the country of Mongolia (see Maps 9.1 and 9.2). At first, Qing frontier policy was to prevent Han migration to Mongol areas, but this was reversed in the mid-nineteenth century, partly in response to Russian intrusion from the north (Khan 1994: 256–261). Beginning in the late nineteenth century, Han Chinese settlers populated southern and eastern parts of Inner Mongolia (Maps 9.1 and 9.2), mixing with the Mongols or pushing them northward (Yahuda 1994: 255). The Han in-migrants took over well-watered areas, particularly in the southeastern parts of the Inner Mongolian grasslands (New Star Publishers 1997: 3–6). Some Mongols feared for their livelihood, as they were pushed farther and farther back into remote, inhospitable areas, at times under military coercion (Khan 1994: 260).

As Outer Mongolia was establishing its independence from China after the 1911 collapse of the Qing dynasty, China's Kuomintang government divided Inner Mongolia into eight pieces that were incorporated into existing provinces or made into new provinces. In 1947, the Red armies and the Communist Party established the Inner Mongolia Autonomous Region (IMAR) with some of the former areas of Inner Mongolia, leaving some Mongol-inhabited areas in the provinces of Heilongjiang, Jilin, Liaoning, and Hebei. Areas incorporated into the IMAR in 1947 included some settled Han Chinese agricultural areas in historical Inner Mongolia where Han penetration had occurred since the late nineteenth century.

In 1954, the PRC government expanded the boundaries of the IMAR to include Suiyuan province, which was historically part of Inner Mongolia and had received large numbers of Han settlers. In 1937, for instance, Suiyuan's population had included 195,000 Mongols and 2,065,000 Han Chinese (China Population, Inner Mongolia Volume, 1990: 52, 54). In 1955 and 1956, other counties from two nearby provinces were added to the IMAR. The outcome of pre-1949 Han Chinese in-migration and the successive boundary decisions was to leave the Inner Mongolia Autonomous Region with over six times as many Han Chinese as Mongols. An official rationale for this situation was given in 1958 as follows:

> On the basis of the historical national relationships in the Inner Mongolia region and its historical conditions, and in order to promote national solidarity and in consideration of the needs of economic and cultural development of the Mongolian and other national minorities in the autonomous region, a large number of Han people, who form the majority of the total population of the autonomous region, is also included in the region. (Cha-leng-ku-ssu 1958; Banister 1987: 313)

Would it have been possible to draw the boundaries of the IMAR to include only a region with Mongols in the majority and Han in the minority? Because of strong Han in-migration into Inner Mongolia before 1949, a policy of strict adherence to historical Inner Mongolia boundaries would have resulted in a large Han majority. On the other hand, drawing truncated boundaries for the IMAR in order to achieve a Mongol majority would have left many more Mongol communities outside the IMAR, because they were located in areas already subject to Han in-migration. The area so delineated as a Mongol province would have included remaining pastoral regions of Inner Mongolia. Though it might have been possible to draw an IMAR with a Mongol majority, the economic viability of such a province would probably have been weak.

Using today's IMAR boundaries (basically those defined in 1956), in 1947, before the founding of the PRC, the provincial population totaled 5.6 million, of whom only 15 percent were Mongol and 84 percent were Han Chinese (Table 9.4). Therefore, historical Han in-migration and successive boundary decisions had the effect of weakening the political power of the Mongols as a group in twentieth-century China.

PRC Inter-provincial Migration to the IMAR

Under the People's Republic of China, the years 1950–1960 saw a strong net in-migration to the Inner Mongolia Autonomous Region (using today's provincial boundaries). As shown in Table 9.5, based on the post-1956 boundaries of the IMAR, Inner Mongolia had a net gain of 150,000–350,000 migrants in most years of the 1950s. Net in-migration escalated rapidly during the Great Leap Forward, peaking at a net gain of 1.1 million migrants in 1960, equivalent to over 9 percent of IMAR's population at the time (Table 9.5 and Figures 9.4 and 9.5). These in-migrants were likely almost exclusively Han Chinese, further increasing Han numerical dominance in the IMAR. After 1960, the government policy of directing migrants into the Inner Mongolia Autonomous Region ceased, judging from the net migration data in Table 9.5. The

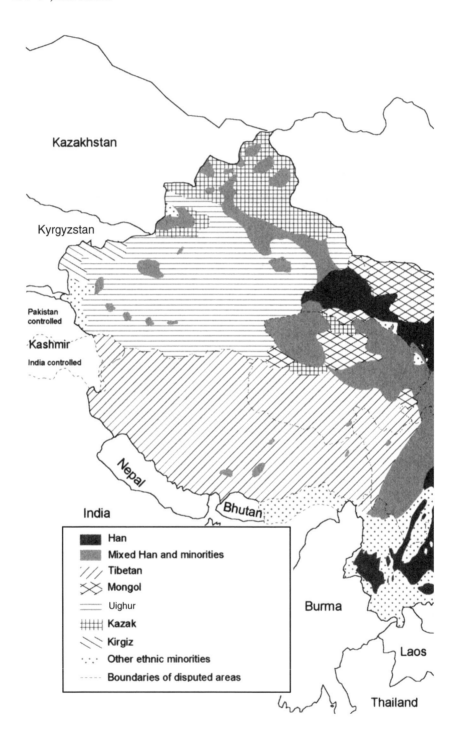

MAP 9.2 China: Nationalities of Three Autonomous Regions and Nearby Areas

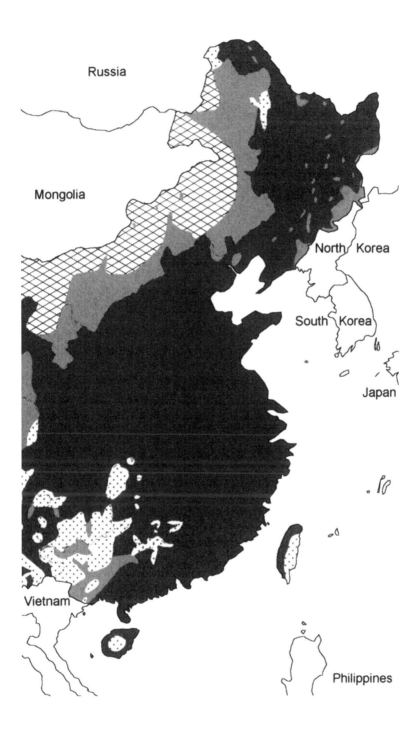

TABLE 9.4 Ethnic Distribution of the Population of the Inner Mongolia Autonomous Region, Today's Boundaries, Selected Years 1947–1996

Year	Population (1,000)				Percent (%)			Time Period	Growth Rate per Year (%)			
	Total	Han	Mongol	Other	Han	Mongol	Other		Total	Han	Mongol	Other
1947	5,617	4,696	832	89	83.6	14.8	1.6	1947–50	5.8	6.8	0.6	1.5
1950	6,599	5,659	847	93	85.8	12.8	1.4	1950–55	5.5	5.6	4.9	5.6
1955	8,430	7,256	1,055	119	86.1	12.5	1.4	1955–60	8.3	8.9	3.0	13.4
1960	11,911	10,498	1,214	199	88.1	10.2	1.7	1960–61	-2.4	-2.7	1.7	-6.5
1961	11,631	10,210	1,235	186	87.8	10.6	1.6	1961–65	2.9	2.7	4.3	5.2
1965	12,964	11,294	1,445	225	87.1	11.1	1.7	1966–71	3.3	3.4	2.9	3.4
1971	15,550	13,582	1,697	271	87.3	10.9	1.7	1971–75	2.9	3.0	2.5	2.3
1975	17,379	15,217	1,866	296	87.6	10.7	1.7	1975–80	1.6	1.5	2.4	3.5
1980	18,765	16,327	2,090	348	87.0	11.1	1.9	1980–85	1.5	0.7	6.3	11.6
1985	20,159	16,862	2,747	550	83.6	13.6	2.7	1985–90	1.5	0.7	3.9	10.9
1990	21,626	17,491	3,285	850	80.9	15.2	3.9	1990–96	0.8	0.7	1.8	-1.5
1996	22,615	18,200	3,642	773	80.5	16.1	3.4					

Sources: *Inner Mongolia Statistical Yearbook*, annual. *Towards 21st Century, Inner Mongolia Volume*, 1994: 19–20. The data were reported from the Public Security Department.

TABLE 9.5 Migration in the Inner Mongolia Autonomous Region, 1950–1990, Based on Today's Boundaries

Year	Average Population (1,000)	Net Migration (1,000)	Net Migration Rate (per 1,000)
1950	6,340.0	329.5	51.97
1951	6,732.5	49.2	7.31
1952	7,012.5	58.0	8.27
1953	7,371.5	202.1	27.42
1954	7,799.5	199.2	25.54
1955	8,222.5	200.4	24.37
1956	8,698.0	348.1	40.02
1957	9,163.0	149.6	16.33
1958	9,610.5	304.3	31.66
1959	10,243.0	561.5	54.82
1960	11,268.0	1,060.8	94.14
1961	11,771.0	-436.7	-37.10
1962	11,674.5	-253.2	-21.69
1963	11,936.0	10.0	0.84
1964	12,345.5	11.0	0.89
1965	12,750.5	35.3	2.77
1966	13,130.0	-36.1	-2.75
1967	13,503.0	47.1	3.49
1968	13,910.0	-31.0	-2.23
1969	14,355.0	33.6	2.34
1970	14,755.0	-173.3	-11.75
1971	15,230.0	160.4	10.53
1972	15,789.5	48.5	3.07
1973	16,270.0	49.0	3.01
1974	16,781.5	143.8	8.57
1975	17,215.5	-25.6	-1.49
1976	17,535.5	3.2	0.18
1977	17,836.5	6.5	0.36
1978	18,107.5	-41.1	-2.27
1979	18,376.0	-28.1	-1.53
1980	18,641.5	-53.7	-2.88
1981	18,897.0	-63.7	-3.37
1982	19,222.5	-15.4	-0.80
1983	19,557.0	-0.8	-0.04
1984	19,814.5	-32.5	-1.64
1985	20,045.0	-3.1	-0.15
1986	20,283.0	-19.5	-0.96
1987	20,535.5	-22.9	-1.12
1988	20,801.5	-0.6	-0.03
1989	21,080.7	-15.0	-0.70
1990	21,423.9	-23.1	-1.08

Sources: *Towards 21st Century, Inner Mongolia Volume*, 1994: 19–20. *China Population, Inner Mongolia Volume*, 1990: 167.

Note: Data from the Inner Mongolia Autonomous Region Public Security Bureau.

FIGURE 9.4 Civilian Net Migration to Inner Mongolia Autonomous Region, China, 1950–1990 *(in thousands)*

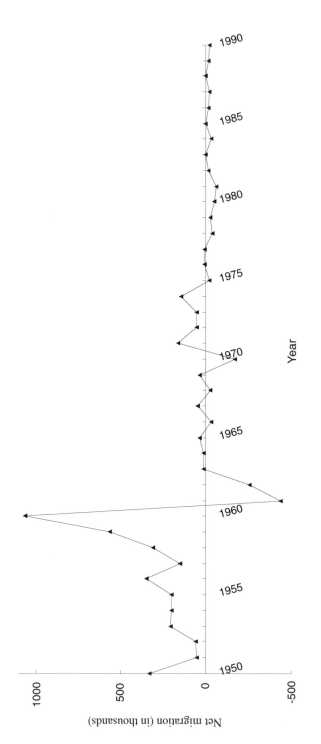

Source: Table 9.5.
Note: Data for the Inner Mongolia Autonomous Region according to today's boundaries.

FIGURE 9.5 Rates of Civilian Net Migration to Inner Mongolia Autonomous Region, China, 1950–1990 *(per thousand population)*

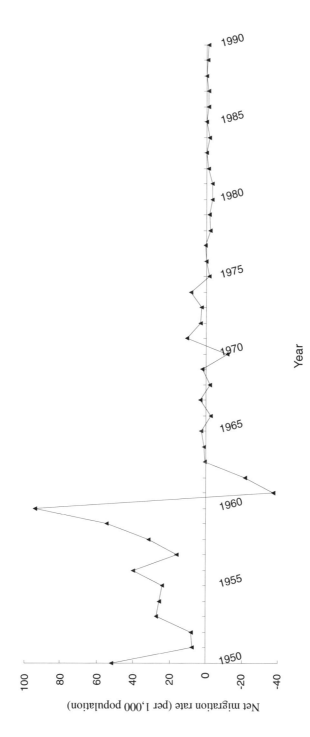

Source: Table 9.5.
Note: Data for the Inner Mongolia Autonomous Region according to today's boundaries.

Han Chinese proportion of the IMAR population peaked in 1960 at 88 percent (Table 9.4 and Figure 9.6).

In most of the years since 1960, the Han Chinese population, in Inner Mongolia as elsewhere, has been subject to much tighter fertility limits than the minority groups, thus in the IMAR the minorities' natural population increase rate has been higher than that of the Han. In addition, in the periods 1980–1985 and 1985–1990, the numbers of Mongols and other minorities in the IMAR grew much faster than a feasible natural population increase rate (see Table 9.4). The most likely reason was that in the 1982 and the 1990 censuses individuals who had previously called themselves Han decided to identify themselves as minority. This presumably indicates that these Mongol and other minority nationality individuals perceived that it had become more favorable to acknowledge their minority heritage than to continue being seen as Han. With fertility levels higher among minorities than Han, with minority self-identification newly taking place, and with net migration no longer playing a significant role in IMAR population growth, the Han proportion of the population declined. As shown in Table 9.4, in 1990 Inner Mongolia had 17.5 million Han Chinese residents, 81 percent of the population, a proportion reduced from 88 percent in 1960 and 1975. By 1990, there were 3.3 million Mongols in Inner Mongolia, 15 percent of the IMAR population. According to China's 1990 census, the other 1.4 million Mongols in China remained outside the IMAR, mostly in the other provinces to which they and their relatives and ancestors had been assigned by the Nationalist and PRC governments (China 1990 Census 1993, Vol. 1: 300–301).

The migrants into the Inner Mongolia Autonomous Region during the 1950s were laborers, cadres, and technicians sent to participate in the construction of the region. During 1950–1957, the government sent workers into Inner Mongolia primarily to a forestry area and to the city of Baotou for industrial jobs. In 1956–1957, young workers were also sent to Inner Mongolia to develop agriculture and stock raising (China Population, Inner Mongolia Volume, 1990: 164–183; *Towards 21st Century*, Inner Mongolia Volume, 1994: 221–239).

During the Great Leap Forward years of 1958–1960, there was a crescendo of government-directed migration into Inner Mongolia (Table 9.5, Figures 9.4 and 9.5). Baotou developed very fast in those three years. One million "volunteers" were "encouraged by the government" to move to Inner Mongolia (China Population, Inner Mongolia Volume, 1990: 174–175). Of these, 873,000 "were settled down" in IMAR to engage in agriculture (47 percent) and household work and other services (45 percent), with small numbers directed to forestry, stock raising, and industry. Four factories were moved to Inner Mongolia from other provinces, with all their workers and family members (China Population, Inner Mongolia Volume, 1990: 164–183; *Towards 21st Century*, Inner Mongolia Volume, 1994: 221–239).

FIGURE 9.6 Civilian Ethnic Composition of Inner Mongolia Autonomous Region, Current Boundaries, Selected Years 1947–1996

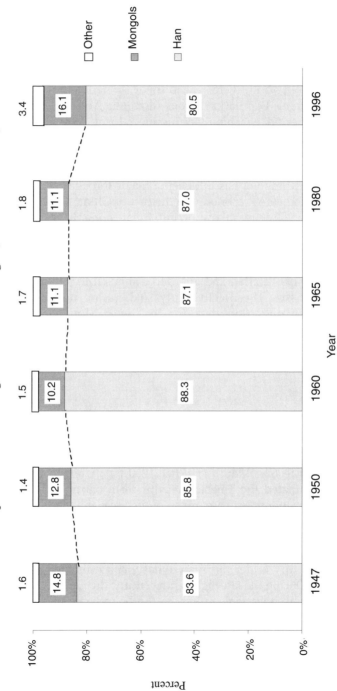

Source: Table 9.4.
Note: Data for the Inner Mongolia Autonomous Region according to today's boundaries.

However, as the Great Leap Forward collapsed, China reversed its policy, sending back home to rural areas some of the migrants it had recently sent into cities. Many workers in Baotou were sent back to their homes in other provinces. In those two years, there was net out-migration of almost 700,000 people from Inner Mongolia.

In subsequent decades, the policy of sending permanent migrants into Inner Mongolia seems largely to have ceased. During 1968–1979, 99,000 educated youth were sent to Inner Mongolia, but 72,000 of them left again (China Population, Inner Mongolia Volume, 1990: 179–180). During the period of China's economic reform, 1978 through at least 1990, Inner Mongolia experienced a net out-migration every year (Table 9.5, Figures 9.4 and 9.5).

Therefore, in contrast to trends in Xinjiang, post-1949 Han in-migration to Inner Mongolia has not been a major force for securing the area and linking the IMAR economy to the rest of China. Given the previous century of Han Chinese migration into Inner Mongolia, plus official decisions about where to draw the IMAR boundaries, the province had plenty of Han Chinese for most civilian economic and political purposes. Of course, it is very likely that a sizable force of China's military personnel has since 1949 staffed and guarded China's IMAR border with Mongolia and Russia. These active-duty soldiers are not included in the population or migration data for the Inner Mongolia Autonomous Region. The data presented here refer only to the civilian population.

Tibet

Boundaries of the Tibet Autonomous Region (TAR)

In the seventh and eighth centuries, the Tibetan Tubo dynasty ruled an area that included the entire Qinghai-Tibet plateau and much of present-day Gansu province (see Map 9.1). After 1260 C.E., China's Yuan (Mongol) dynasty dominated the Tibetan areas under a patron-tributary arrangement. In subsequent centuries, many of the areas that had been under the Tubo dynasty were joined with other provinces of China, including Qinghai, Sichuan, Gansu, and Yunnan provinces. The population of the area that is now the Tibet Autonomous Region of China was surveyed in the late thirteenth century under the Yuan dynasty and estimated at about 1 million people. During the late eighteenth century, the Qing dynasty of China conducted household registrations in the boundaries of what is today's TAR and estimated a population of about 940,000 (Zhang 1997: 1–3).

Political Control over Tibet

After the PRC was established in 1949, negotiations began with the Dalai Lama and other leaders of Tibet. The People's Liberation Army (PLA) entered Tibet in 1950 and 1951, consolidating military control over the region. An uneasy peace prevailed during the 1950s, until the PRC started implementing radical social policies in areas outside the TAR where Tibetans lived. A revolt erupted in 1959 that was quickly suppressed, after which the Dalai Lama and 90,000 Tibetans fled from China, including 74,000 from what is now the TAR (Zhang 1997: 6). The PRC then instituted tighter control over the region and established the TAR in 1965.

During the censuses of 1953 and 1964, part of the population of the TAR was indirectly estimated rather than counted. The estimated total population of the TAR was 1.27 million in 1953 and 1.25 million in 1964. Table 9.6 shows the total population of the TAR from its establishment in 1965 to 1994, during which period the civilian population of the TAR reportedly increased from 1.36 million to 2.30 million.

Directed Migration to the Tibet Autonomous Region

Table 9.6 and Figures 9.7 and 9.8 show reported annual net civilian migration to the Tibet Autonomous Region. During 1965–1979, there was a net in-migration of 4,000 to 20,000 people per year; thereafter, in the early economic reform period and at the insistence of the Tibetans, China's government agreed to pull thousands of cadres out of the TAR. Since then civilian net migration has reportedly been minimal (Table 9.6, Figures 9.7 and 9.8). There was a shift in national policy toward migration into Tibet beginning in 1980; since then, Han cadres and specialists going to work in Tibet have followed a rotation system (Huang 1995; Zhang 1997: 38).

In a 1980 report to the PRC Communist Party Center and the State Council, the Tibetan Party Committee and government requested more doctors, more teachers, and technicians for new investment projects. During the 1980s and 1990s, PRC central government policy was that those transferred into Tibet should be "few in number but high in quality." Political functionaries were to be limited to a number that was "absolutely necessary." Furthermore, ordinary workers were not encouraged to move to Tibet. The apparent goals of these policies were to reduce the Chinese political presence in the TAR in reaction to large anti-Chinese protests there, to raise the proportion of ethnic Tibetans in the leadership of the TAR, "to further stabilize the situation in Tibet," and to promote the economic development of Tibet by sending in selected educational and technical specialists (Huang 1995; Zhang 1997: 8–9). It should not be assumed that all in-migrants were Han Chinese. According to Chinese demographer Ma Rong, of the net intake of 98,500 migrants into Tibet during 1964–1994, 70 percent were ethnic Tibetans from neighboring provinces (Ma Rong 1996: 65; Wang 1998: 56).

Civilian Han Chinese people who have moved to the TAR have gone primarily to Lhasa prefecture, where Tibet's capital city of Lhasa is located, and to Nyingchi prefecture, where most members of the Monba

TABLE 9.6   Migration in the Tibet Autonomous Region of China, 1965–1994

Year	Average Population (1,000)	Net Migration (1,000)	Net Migration Rate (per 1,000)
1965	1359.0	12.3	9.05
1966	1384.0	13.6	9.83
1967	1410.4	20.0	14.18
1968	1437.9	16.4	11.41
1969	1466.1	14.3	9.75
1970	1496.3	8.9	5.95
1971	1532.9	18.4	12.00
1972	1573.3	14.3	9.09
1973	1611.0	10.9	6.77
1974	1645.2	6.6	4.01
1975	1676.2	4.4	2.63
1976	1707.6	8.6	5.04
1977	1740.1	5.7	3.28
1978	1772.2	7.2	4.06
1979	1808.2	15.7	8.68
1980	1840.5	-0.8	-0.43
1981	1856.2	-30.6	-16.49
1982	1876.1	-19.1	-10.18
1983	1912.0	-3.4	-1.78
1984	1949.1	-7.4	-3.80
1985	1980.8	-1.8	-0.91
1986	2009.9	-3.7	-1.84
1987	2052.2	5.3	2.58
1988	2101.3	0.1	0.05
1989	2141.1	-5.3	-2.48
1990	2169.8	-8.6	-3.96
1991	2199.2	-2.3	-1.05
1992	2235.3	-2.1	-0.94
1993	2270.8	0.2	0.09
1994	2304.3	2.0	0.87

Source: Ma Rong, 1996: 37, 65, derived from the Tibet Autonomous Region Statistical Bureau, *Socio-economic Statistical Yearbook of Tibet*, 1989: 61, 140; *Socio-economic Statistical Yearbook of Tibet*, 1993: 67–68; *Tibet Statistical Yearbook*, 1995: 39–40.

FIGURE 9.7 Civilian Net Migration to Tibet Autonomous Region, 1965–1994, as Reported (*in thousands*)

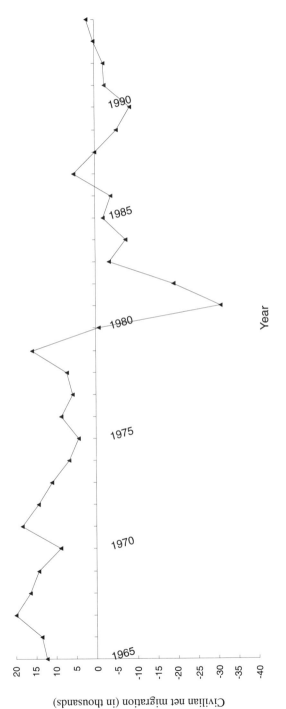

Source: Table 9.6.

FIGURE 9.8 Rates of Civilian Net Migration to Tibet Autonomous Region, 1965–1994, as Reported *(per thousand population of the TAR)*

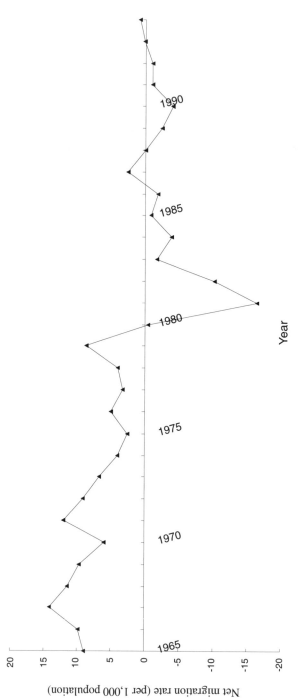

Source: Table 9.6.

and Lhoba minority nationalities live. The population of Lhasa prefecture was 14 percent Han Chinese in the 1982 census; this proportion dropped to 12 percent in 1990. The Han in Lhasa are, however, highly concentrated in the city itself, not in the largely Tibetan rural prefectural counties. In the 1990 census, Han Chinese constituted 29 percent of the total population who had lived in Lhasa City for one year or more (Zhang 1997: 17). In Nyingchi prefecture, the Han proportion of the population was 13 percent in 1982 and 10 percent in 1990. In the TAR's other five prefectures, 1–3 percent in 1982 and 1–2 percent in 1990 were Han Chinese. Tibetans made up 98–99 percent of the populations of these five prefectures in the 1990 census, 87 percent of the Lhasa prefecture population, and 82 percent of the population in Nyingchi prefecture.

It is important to note, as with the other border provinces, that these data refer only to civilians. China maintains a strong military presence in the TAR, as in Xinjiang and Inner Mongolia. It is likely that the active-duty military personnel in Tibet are very largely Han Chinese.

After slow Han civilian migration to Tibet during 1965–1979, their number peaked at 122,000 in 1980, constituting 7 percent of the TAR population (Ma Rong 1996: 66). Subsequently, with the migration policy decision to remove some Han Chinese cadres from Tibet, the Han civilians declined in number. The civilian population of the TAR was 94 percent Tibetan in 1982 and only 5 percent Han Chinese; in the 1990 census 95 percent were Tibetan and 4 percent Han. According to census guidelines, these figures are supposed to include anyone who had been living in the TAR for one year or longer, whether his stay was intended to be temporary or permanent. Many cadres and skilled personnel are sent from other provinces on several-year assignments to the TAR. The terms of service are fixed: five years for Communist Party and government cadres, and three years for technical cadres (Huang 1995: 189).

As of 1990, there were three times as many men as women among the Han civilian residents of Tibet. Few of them had children living in Tibet; most were on three-year or five-year contracts, working away from their families. The personnel sent into Tibet were young cadres, doctors and other medical personnel, engineers and technicians, and teachers. Most were in their twenties, with some in their thirties and some in their late teens (Ma Rong 1996: 43, 73).

The above data and analysis show that Han Chinese residents of the Tibet Autonomous Region constitute a small minority of the civilian population of Tibet. Yet foreign supporters of the Dalai Lama and the Tibetan exile community commonly report that the PRC government has been transferring huge numbers of Han Chinese migrants into Tibet, numerically swamping the Tibetans there, claims that are widely believed internationally. For example, one such analysis reports that Han Chinese have become the "New Majority" in Tibet through in-migration, which the Dalai Lama has referred to as "demographic aggression" (Tibet Support Group UK 1995: 1).

How is this claim supported? First, these observers define "Tibet" as "historic Tibet," that is, the vast area ruled by the Tibetan Tubo dynasty in the eighth century C.E., or "ethnographic Tibet," meaning all those areas where there are concentrations of Tibetans in villages, towns, or cities. However, using such a definition of Tibet ignores the fact that for centuries, Tibetans in China outside of what is now the Tibet Autonomous Region (TAR) have been living as part of Qinghai, Gansu, Sichuan, and Yunnan provinces. Han Chinese were moving into these areas for centuries or at least decades before the founding of the PRC in 1949, by then constituting over 50 percent of the population in some Sichuan and Qinghai counties where Tibetans live. This process of Han in-migration has indeed continued in Qinghai and some other Tibetan-inhabited areas outside the TAR, but the "Tibet" that was ruled from Lhasa during China's Nationalist period 1912–1949 is the TAR only, and this Tibet is far from being swamped with Han in-migrants.

Those who report massive Han in-migration to Tibet are also referring to the assignment of large numbers of Han military personnel to Tibet. The PRC government suppresses information on how many People's Liberation Army soldiers are stationed in the TAR. In the late 1980s, the Tibetan exile community used an estimate of 200,000 PLA troops, while the PRC government and China specialist June Teufel Dreyer estimated the number at about 30,000 (Dumbaugh 1988: 23–24).

Finally, since the early 1980s, the TAR has been opened to the voluntary movement of workers, traders, and visitors from other provinces. This floating population, mostly Han and Hui, may be largely seasonal and temporary, but to some Tibetans these floaters seem to take the good jobs and dominate the economy of Lhasa and wherever else they congregate. Moreover, some of the shops, restaurants, taxi services, and construction businesses established by the "temporary" Han and Hui residents of the TAR have begun to take on a long-term character (Sautman and Eng 2000).

PRC Border Migration Policies

This overview of data on civilian migration to the three border provinces of Xinjiang, Inner Mongolia, and Tibet leads to some interesting conclusions. First, migration policy has not been the same for these three border areas. In Xinjiang, the policy appears to have been to increase the Han Chinese proportion of the population from 7 percent in 1949 to 38 percent, and then to maintain that powerful Han civilian presence in the province. Because the natural population increase rate of the minorities in Xinjiang is much higher than that of the Han Chinese there, the Han proportion of the population would decline steadily without positive net Han migration into Xinjiang. Such migration occurred in the 1990s. However, in Inner Mongolia, Han Chinese control was assured by pre-1949

Han in-migration into what became the "Inner Mongolia Autonomous Region." The directed migration to the province after 1949 was not needed for political and economic control of the IMAR. In Tibet, there has been no policy promoting massive permanent migration of Han Chinese people to the TAR. Rather, control over this small, scattered, poor population of Tibetans has been exercised through a strong military and police presence and small numbers of cadres sent in to exert political control and to set policies in the province.

The directed migration policies in these three provinces not only have had different purposes, but also have varied over time. The decade of the 1950s saw massive net migration into Xinjiang and Inner Mongolia, as the PRC took decisive control and tied these provinces securely to China. In Tibet, the PRC government moved in a more gingerly manner during most of the 1950s. The 1959 rebellion among China's Tibetan minority population happened despite this, and once it was suppressed, the PRC government decided to move more energetically to control Tibet.

In the 1960s, after the disastrous famine caused by China's Great Leap Forward, directed migration to Inner Mongolia abruptly ceased, and subsequent inter-provincial migrants were comparatively small in number. In contrast, migration into Xinjiang resumed in the early 1960s, peaking again in 1966, at the beginning of the Cultural Revolution. Thereafter, net migration to Xinjiang remained positive but smaller in numbers for the subsequent decade and a half. In Tibet, the late 1960s and the 1970s saw positive net in-migration every year from other parts of China, but the numbers of civilians moving in remained small and so did the net migration rate. As shown in Table 9.7, civilian net migration rates into the Tibet Autonomous Region remained in the low range of 3–14 annual net in-migrants per thousand TAR civilian population in the peak in-migration period of 1965–1979. In contrast, the peak period of in-migration to Xinjiang and Inner Mongolia during the 1950s witnessed civilian net migration rates as high as 97 and 94, respectively (see Table 9.7). The modulated rates of net migration to Xinjiang during the 1964–1969 period still amounted to 7–37 annual net in-migrants per thousand population, much higher than rates of civilian net in-migration to the Tibet Autonomous Region (Table 9.7).

In both Tibet and Xinjiang, there was another important policy shift away from directed in-migration, effective in 1980 in Tibet and in 1981 in Xinjiang (Figures 9.1, 9.2, 9.3, 9.7, and 9.8, and Tables 9.1, 9.2, 9.3, 9.6, and 9.7). Mao Zedong died in late 1976, and after some reshuffling of leadership, Deng Xiaoping introduced the economic reform period in 1978, accompanied by some rethinking of political policies as well. In 1980, the national leadership began promoting policies of greater real autonomy for and recognition of the rights of minority nationalities, at the same time rejecting the policies of "coercive assimilation" that had been practiced during the Cultural Revolution (Mackerras 1994: 153–155). This led to a new Law on Regional Autonomy for Minority Nationalities, which

TABLE 9.7   Civilian Net Migration Rates, 1950–1997, into Xinjiang,
Inner Mongolia, and Tibet *(per thousand population)*

Year	Xinjiang	Inner Mongolia	Tibet	Year	Xinjiang	Inner Mongolia	Tibet
1950	14	52		1974	4 to 6	9	4
1951	13	7		1975	1 to 2	-1	3
1952	12	8		1976	5	0	5
1953	15	27		1977	2 to 5	0	3
1954	30 to 34	26		1978	3 to 5	-2	4
1955	7 to 12	24		1979	2 to 4	-2	9
1956	11 to 24	40		1980	2 to 8	-3	0
1957	20 to 28	16		1981	-6 to -3	-3	-16
1958	24 to 28	32		1982	-5 to -1	-1	-10
1959	48 to 97	55		1983	-2 to 1	0	-2
1960	43	94		1984	-5 to -1	-2	-4
1961	21 to 22	-37		1985	-4 to -1	0	-1
1962	-38 to -28	-22		1986	-3 to 2	-1	-2
1963	-6 to 4	1		1987	-2 to 1	-1	3
1964	17 to 21	1		1988	-1 to 1	0	0
1965	26 to 28	3	9	1989	-1 to 4	-1	-2
1966	31 to 37	-3	10	1990	0 to 15	-1	-4
1967	12 to 14	3	14	1991	2 to 7		-1
1968	7 to 10	-2	11	1992	2		-1
1969	8 to 9	2	10	1993	3		0
1970	5 to 6	-12	6	1994	4		1
1971	6 to 8	11	12	1995	4		
1972	8 to 12	3	9	1996	4		
1973	4 to 7	3	7	1997	3		

Sources: Tables 9.2, 9.3, 9.5, and 9.6.

was adopted in 1984. During the 1980s in all three of these border provinces, net inter-provincial migration hovered around zero or was negative; only at the end of the 1980s were there signs of renewed in-migration into Xinjiang.

The fragmentary information available also leads to the conclusion that the government-directed Han migrants into these three Autonomous Regions have gone to targeted areas. The goal has apparently not been to send Han into every part of these provinces to establish direct dominance over the minorities in each locality. Rather, Han Chinese migrants have been sent to:

- the capital cities of Tibet (Lhasa) and of Xinjiang (Urumqi), seats of the provincial governments;
- certain cities targeted for industrial development, such as Baotou in Inner Mongolia and cities along the new railroads in Xinjiang;

- arid areas that could be irrigated to open agricultural lands, such as the vast farms developed by the Bing Tuan in Xinjiang;
- newly discovered but undeveloped oilfields;
- border areas, to block or regulate cross-border traffic and to secure the borders against foreign incursion.

The intent was not necessarily to mix the Han and minority nationalities in these border provinces, nor was it apparently to displace the minorities from their lands or homes. Rather, in the PRC period, Han Chinese moved into previously undeveloped or partly developed areas in order to promote the economic development of the regions and their economic and political integration with the rest of China. For example, before 1949, most of the Uighurs, and most of Xinjiang's population, lived in oases in southwestern Xinjiang; Han Chinese who have moved into Xinjiang have gone primarily to new or expanded cities in northern Xinjiang, particularly the central part of the northern foot of the Tianshan mountains (the Urumqi-Changji-Shihezi-Karamay area). Han migrants have also concentrated in newly developed agricultural lands, recently discovered oil-producing areas, and along new railway lines into and within Xinjiang; in general, the Han in-migration areas were sparsely populated. The Uighurs, meanwhile, remain primarily in their ancestral districts on their historical lands (Wang 1998: 40–43; Toops 1999: 5–9; Becquelin 1999: 8). In the Tibet Autonomous Region, Han in-migrants have gone to urban areas and places served by roads. "Han and Tibetan groups are largely spatially and socially separate, and there has not been a 'melting pot' with a mixing bowl of ideas and peoples in Tibet." (Ma Rong 1998; Clarke 1998: 24)

Spontaneous Migration

From 1949 to the present, some of the migration into Xinjiang and Inner Mongolia was not government-sponsored but was instead voluntary migration in response to perceived opportunity. Indeed, in the century before the PRC was founded, millions of Han Chinese workers and families had migrated from crowded Han provinces in central and north China into China's northeast (Manchuria), and into southern and eastern areas of Inner Mongolia (see Maps 9.1 and 9.2). As the PRC built railways and roads into Xinjiang and Inner Mongolia and established cities and state farms in these regions, some young adult Han Chinese workers and peasants went there for jobs. In the 1950s, domestic Chinese migration was still not strongly controlled or limited by the PRC government, so a large proportion of the huge numbers of migrants to Inner Mongolia and Xinjiang could have been voluntary and self-selected. After the Great Leap Forward economic crisis, China's government tied rural and urban populations to their places of birth by means of a permanent population

registration system linked to food rations. Spontaneous migration, especially from rural to urban areas in the populous Han provinces, was for
the most part successfully blocked, because would-be migrants could not
get food if they tried to move to a city, and they were also subjected to
police harassment.

In spite of these restrictions, the PRC government was apparently
willing to allow spontaneous migration to the frontier province of Xinjiang. In the early 1950s, Xinjiang had no railroad and few roads, so most
voluntary migration was impractical. The opening of the new railway
from Gansu province into Xinjiang in the late 1950s greatly facilitated the
movement of people, and from 1957 to 1984 more than half the migrants
into Xinjiang were unorganized settlers, primarily peasants from Gansu
and other poor Han Chinese provinces (China Population, 1990, Xinjiang
Volume: 140–142; Wang 1998: 38). A 1982 Chinese source stated: "According to data from Xinjiang, the influx of migrants from other provinces (or
regions) through automatic [spontaneous] population flow accounted for
two-thirds of the net population influx for the entire autonomous
region." (Chou Weizhi 1982: 56; Banister 1987: 309).

During the economic reform period following 1978, China's government abandoned most ration coupons, permitted open markets in urban
and rural areas, and loosened restrictions on geographical movement
(Goldstein and Goldstein 1990). Therefore, there has been an increase in
the "floating population," including traders and laborers going into Xinjiang and Tibet to work. Because large numbers of these workers are seasonal, short-term, or mobile (such as inter-provincial truck drivers), they
might not be in the border province long enough to be counted as
migrants (Toops 1999: 7).

Since the 1980s, when previous tight restrictions on temporary
movement into Tibet were cancelled, each summer Han workers come
into Tibet, many of them to Lhasa, for several months, and then return to
their home provinces. They set up small shops and stalls on the streets,
do repair work, sell handicrafts, and run small restaurants, and in the
suburbs they work for Tibetans growing vegetables for the city market.
Large numbers of mobile Han workers are brought into Lhasa for construction projects. During the summer of 1988, for instance, there was a
Han Chinese floating, temporary population of 50,000 in the city, equivalent to 40 percent of the permanent resident population of Lhasa (Ma
Rong 1996: 81–82). Many of the workers who come into Tibet during the
summer months go back to their home provinces or elsewhere for the rest
of the year, while others extend their "temporary" residence in the TAR.
These outsiders are contributing to the provision of services, construction
work, and agricultural production in Tibet.

Xinjiang has experienced vigorous economic growth since 1990, and
this has drawn a large floating population, whose estimated total rose
from 179,000 in 1983 to 350,000 in 1991; by 1996 there were 1.4 million
people with temporary registration status in Xinjiang (Wang 1998: 51–52).

Government-Minority Relations in Border Provinces

Of China's 55 minority groups throughout the PRC, most had already experienced centuries of mixing with Han settlers in their native territories. Most groups remained tiny in number, compared to the Chinese in their midst, and had adopted Chinese dress, or Chinese language, or Chinese customs, or all of these. The highly Sinicized minority groups have given PRC authorities very little trouble, as far as can be discerned.

One could argue that the Mongols of Inner Mongolia fit this description. Outer Mongolia successfully achieved independence from China, partly because it was essentially occupied and protected from China by the Soviet Union for almost seven decades. Mongolia achieved international recognition as a country well before the Soviet collapse, and the PRC would have had great difficulty re-establishing Chinese hegemony in the 1990s. In contrast, the Mongols in Inner Mongolia became outnumbered by Han Chinese migrants in their own lands during the late Qing and the Nationalist periods. Inner Mongolia was subdivided and ruled by Han provinces under the Nationalist government. In the late 1960s during the Cultural Revolution, the Inner Mongolia Autonomous Region came under blistering political attack. Mongols were persecuted and subjected to "full-scale violence" (Bulag 1998: 4).

There have been signs of growing Mongolian nationalism in the IMAR since the mid-1980s (Yahuda 1994: 260). Some Mongol nationalists express "a sense of loss and a refusal to identify with a Chinese state that is largely perceived to be alien" (Bulag 1998: 2). They are not trying to establish a nation-state of their own, rather they support pan-Mongolism, which means unity with Mongolia and the Mongols in Russia. This goal is frustrated by the attitude of Mongols in Mongolia, who look down upon the Mongols of Inner Mongolia as Chinese-Mongol, impure "half-breeds," or "hybrids." The government of Mongolia, fearing the wrath of the PRC government now that Mongolia's former protector, the Soviet Union, is no more, opposes pan-Mongolism (Bulag 1998: 1–7, 18) and is careful to avoid provoking the PRC (Yahuda 1994: 260–261). Mongols in China have nowhere to turn. They are surrounded and outnumbered by Han Chinese, and are highly assimilated. In general, the Mongols of the IMAR have been a docile minority group during most decades since 1949.

The Muslim minorities of China are another matter. Most but not all of China's Muslim minority nationalities are in Xinjiang, but the Muslim Hui are scattered across China, as well as concentrated in the Ningxia Hui Autonomous Region south of Inner Mongolia. Even though the Hui were highly Sinicized before 1949, they have engaged in periodic revolts, a group of them even proclaiming in 1953 an "independent Islamic kingdom" in Henan province, in the middle of Han China (Pillsbury 1981: 113; Banister 1987: 316–317).

The Muslim minorities of Xinjiang province have resisted Chinese control periodically both before and after 1949. They staged demonstrations and armed rebellions during 1957–1962 in reaction to the excesses of the Chinese government, including the Great Leap Forward, and again in 1967 during the Cultural Revolution. Violent protests in 1980–1981 centered on the army's treatment of the minorities. Sporadic ethnic and religious unrest has continued. In 1990, there were protests against newly imposed restrictions on religious activities, culminating in an outbreak of violence near Kashgar that resulted in between 22 and 50 deaths as security forces responded (Ferdinand 1994: 276). Terrorist bombs, assumed to have been planted by Muslim separatists, killed several people in Urumqi in 1992 and again in Kashgar, 1993. There were bus bombings in Urumqi in 1997 (Wang 1998: 59).

In recent decades, demands for Muslim self-rule have reflected both Muslim consciousness and events around the world, especially across the borders in the former Soviet Union. Now that Kazakhstan and Kyrgyzstan are independent countries, some Uighurs in Xinjiang are complaining that they are the only Central Asian Muslim nationality without a country of their own (O'Neill 1998a: 15). To some extent, these are forces beyond the control of the PRC, and China can hardly be blamed for the ongoing dissatisfaction of the Muslims in China. On the other hand, China's leaders in the early 1980s readily admitted that they had been unduly insensitive toward the Muslim minorities, triggering much of the protest.

The Tibetans also had a long history of fending off or fighting Chinese control. Attempts to integrate Tibet into the PRC were bound to meet resistance, but the heavy-handed insensitivity of the Han Chinese, especially during the Great Leap and the Cultural Revolution, worsened an already tense situation. During the 1980s, a lessening of Chinese government authoritarianism in the TAR was met with renewed Tibetan demands for religious freedom and real autonomy. Protests took place during 1987–1989 (twenty-one demonstrations, by government count), followed by the imposition of martial law from March 1989 to April 1990 (Schwartz 1994; Karmel 1995). Now those who hope for autonomy or independence for Tibet have been heartened by international changes in the post–Cold War era, including the breakup of the Soviet Union, the new independence of Eastern and Central European countries and the Central Asian republics, democratization in dozens of countries, and rising ethnic nationalism worldwide. There has been strong international support for Tibetan separatists and demonstrators and for the Dalai Lama. In response, China's government has maintained a continuing crackdown on protests and on political, religious, and educational institutions in the TAR (Karmel 1995).

The PRC government has not succeeded in pacifying the minorities and bringing about general acceptance of its rule in either Tibet or Xinjiang. Nevertheless, it is clear that the PRC has so far succeeded in its overriding goal of firmly attaching Xinjiang, Inner Mongolia, and Tibet to China. For half a century, the PRC has used military and police force to suppress struggles for independence in the border provinces. These

"Autonomous Regions" have little realistic hope of being able to secede from China.

Has the influx of Han civilians into Xinjiang, and the imposition of PRC military control in all border provinces, generated conflict and secessionist movements, or solidified political control? The answer is both. However, it could fairly be argued that the secessionist movements were a pre-existing condition inherited by the PRC, not created since 1949.

What were the consequences of Han in-migration for an extension of state control? The PRC has successfully consolidated its control over these three border provinces, partly through Han in-migration and partly through a powerful and visible Han military presence. The PRC military population as of the 1990 census was 98.6 percent Han Chinese, while the country's total population was 91.9 percent Han. The People's Liberation Army is basically a Han Chinese force, as is the People's Armed Police, which is also used to control dissent in these border provinces.

What were the consequences of Han in-migration for the Sinification of the minority nationalities? In all three of these border provinces, people of the minority nationalities have more opportunities to get ahead in the economic, social, political, and educational spheres if they can speak, read, and write Mandarin Chinese and if they relate smoothly to the Han Chinese with whom they come in contact. The best jobs require working side-by-side with Han Chinese workers (Ji 1990: 253–262). China's policies have promoted the training of cadres from the minority nationalities, acceptance of minority leaders into the Communist Party, and the promotion of higher educational opportunities for minority students on a preferential basis, resulting in acquiescence and cooperation among many people from minority nationalities.

On the other hand, Han in-migration has also brought resentment and cultural clashes between Han and Muslim, as well as Han and Tibetan. The strong religious, spiritual feelings and beliefs of many Muslims and Tibetan Buddhists are alien to many Han Chinese, and this creates bad feelings on both sides. Also, most Han in-migrants to the minority provinces are hard-working and successful. Many minority individuals resent the fact that these intruders are doing a lot better than they are in their own native province (Ji 1990: 250–252, 256–268).

Han In-Migration and Security of the Border Regions

In general, Han in-migration to the border provinces has added to the security of these regions and kept restive minority groups under control, although it has on occasion had the opposite effect, as when radical Red Guards invaded the border provinces during the Cultural Revolution, attacking all things traditional or different in the campaign against the "four olds." In Tibet, Han Red Guards helped organize Tibetan Red Guard groups, who desecrated or destroyed thousands of monasteries and attacked household shrines in their anti-religious fervor. In Xinjiang the Red Guards wrought special havoc, destroying mosques and religious works and savagely repressing minority languages, customs, and religion. Muslims were forced to raise pigs and eat pork (Ferdinand 1994: 274). These brutal, violent, and anti-religious policies during China's most radical periods infuriated the border minority nationalities and generated abiding hatred for Han Chinese people and for PRC control, adversely affecting the security of the border provinces.

The primarily Han Chinese military presence has not always enhanced security; for example, the PRC and India engaged in skirmishes and a war on the Tibet-India border in the Himalayas during the late 1950s and early 1960s. These hostilities, as well as the flight of the Tibetan resistance fighters to India in 1959, poisoned China-India relations for decades.

What were the consequences, intended and unintended, of Han inmigration for relations with neighboring countries? Before the founding of the PRC, the huge territories of Tibet, Xinjiang, and the Inner Mongolian grasslands acted as buffer zones between China and nearby countries. Once the PRC opened up communications and transport into these border provinces, and sent in military and civilians to the border areas, there was no buffer. Han Chinese border guards and settlers found themselves next to Soviet and Indian border guards, which resulted in occasional outbreaks of border violence. International relations with border countries were also harmed by the occasional flight of large groups of Tibetans and Muslims.

Relations between the PRC and India have been tense for much of the time since the PRC was founded; the seeds of this hostility were planted even before 1949 (Tzou 1990: 2–3, 60–68, 140). During 1947–1950, India continued the former British policy of encouraging separatism or de facto independence for Tibet, and China reacted angrily to India's initiatives (Liu 1994: 88–89; Maxwell 1972: 57–64). After a period of apparent calm in China-India relations during the 1950s, an inherited boundary dispute exploded into active warfare on the Tibet-India border. These boundary areas are still disputed, as shown in Map 9.1.

Han Chinese migration into Tibet has had little to do with the strained India-China relations of the last half century. Historical differences over boundaries and establishment of PRC military control over Tibet could have contributed to bad feeling between the governments of India and China, with or without government-sponsored Han Chinese migration into Tibet. The Tibetan revolt of 1959, followed by the establishment of a Tibetan government-in-exile in India, has been an irritant in China-India relations for more than four decades. Continuing anti-China demonstrations in the TAR, and PRC suppression of Tibetan resistance, make it difficult for China and India to have a strong positive relationship. Yet differences over Tibet are a small piece of India-China relations, which have been dominated by much bigger considerations, such as the

India-Pakistan conflict, Chinese support of Pakistan, and India's siding with the Soviet Union during the Sino-Soviet split after 1960.

Tsarist Russia, and then the Soviet Union, had a strong interest in dominating Central Asia, including Xinjiang. China could easily have lost control of Xinjiang to the Soviet Union during the twentieth century. The policy of securing firm control of the territory and economy of Xinjiang through Han Chinese in-migration and military deployment was successful, viewed from the PRC government perspective.

After the breakup of the Soviet Union, the emergence of Central Asian countries such as Kazakhstan and Kyrgyzstan on the borders of Xinjiang fueled the hope among some Xinjiang minority groups that they could become independent of Chinese control. Kazakhstan allows the existence of a non-violent Kazak nationalist party, whose program includes reunification with the Kazak nation in Xinjiang. Uighur Liberation Committees have been set up in Kazakhstan, Kyrgyzstan, and Tajikistan (Ferdinand 1994: 278). Restive minorities in Xinjiang have received covert support, including some weapons, from groups in the new Central Asian republics, although these countries, landlocked and with serious economic problems, need trade and cooperation with China. The PRC government has insisted that the Central Asian republics cease their support of Muslim ethnic separatism in Xinjiang if they want China's support. In their continuing anti-China activities, radical separatists in Xinjiang may be becoming more isolated as China asserts its diplomatic power in the region. In the 1990s, China cultivated strong cooperative diplomatic relationships with the new Central Asian states and elicited their support for suppressing Xinjiang independence movements on their soil (Becquelin 1999). Kazakhstan responded by closing some offices of the Xinjiang separatist groups. In sum, there is no firm evidence that the emergence of the independent Central Asian states has led to a rise in violence or greater support for separatism in Xinjiang; separatist efforts to internationalize the Xinjiang question have failed (Sautman 2000: 246).

Economic Development in the Border Provinces

The three border provinces of our study vary enormously in their basic resources. It is not economically viable to extract the few resources that have been discovered in Tibet. The economy is dependent on agriculture, animal husbandry, and a small amount of industry. In 1994 there were 23 million livestock and herding animals in Tibet, the same number as in 1980 and not many more than the 17 million estimated when the TAR was established in 1965 (Ma Rong 1996: 187). The herds are in a steady state, in balance with the natural fodder in the grasslands of Tibet. While grain production is only double what it was in 1965, the monetary value of agricultural production has increased enormously since the 1970s. Industrial production is still modest in amount. To a great extent, the TAR's lack of economic development can be attributed to its harsh natural conditions, particularly its inhospitable topography and climate, fragile environment, and remote, high-altitude location, which combine to produce prohibitively high transport costs (Clarke 1998). One author also blames some of Tibet's economic problems in the 1980s and 1990s on Chinese government restrictions and rigidity: "Tibet suffers from China's lowest economic growth rates, and the comparatively limited *results* of reform in Tibet appear to be due at least in part to the comparative *restrictions* on reform." He argues that "China seems willing to sacrifice development for stability and order on the Tibetan plateau" (Karmel 1995: 507–508). Urban Tibet did begin to experience some rapid economic growth in the late 1990s, but rural Tibet was barely affected (Sautman and Eng 2000).

Xinjiang offers a stark contrast with Tibet. Xinjiang was extremely underdeveloped in 1949. Since then oil and natural gas have been discovered and exploited there; now Xinjiang is among the top-producing Chinese provinces for over 30 different minerals. Vast arid lands have been opened up to crop production by the Bing Tuan, who are still exploiting only a small fraction of the water in glaciers and underground. Xinjiang grows one-quarter of China's cotton (O'Neill 1998a: 15).

Still, the minority people of Xinjiang, as well as those in Tibet and Inner Mongolia, remain comparatively poor. Xinjiang oil and gas development and cotton production are largely in the hands of Han workers of the state-owned oil company and the Bing Tuan, and many of these products go to the rest of China. While the economic development in Xinjiang has benefited both Han and minority, for example in terms of a better food supply, consumer goods, and education, comparatively speaking the minorities are falling behind. For instance, rural southwestern Xinjiang, with an annual per capita income of less than $120, is one of the most impoverished areas of China; the population is mostly Uighur (Toops 1999: 8). One expert argues that the vast majority of the population of southern Xinjiang has not felt the economic benefits of China's post-1978 economic reform period (Becquelin 1999: 8). The Han-minority income disparities in Xinjiang are associated with the following conditions (Sautman 2000):

- minorities are more rural while Han predominate in the large cities;
- many rural Xinjiang communities are remote and naturally disadvantaged;
- the ability to speak Mandarin Chinese is important for modern-sector jobs and higher education;
- fertility levels and child dependency ratios are far higher among the Xinjiang minorities than among Xinjiang Han.

Although much wealth is extracted from Xinjiang, money also flows into Xinjiang from China's central government, which increased its investments in Xinjiang in the 1990s to build infrastructure (roads, railways, power stations, airports). In 1994, the central government provided over two-thirds of the Xinjiang government budget (Sautman 2000: 261). China's government has also invested in Tibet, transferring RMB 2.9 billion to Tibet in 1994, or RMB 1,240 per capita—equivalent to about U.S. $340 million, or U.S. $150 per capita (Sautman and Eng 2000: 5).

The economy of the Inner Mongolia Autonomous Region depends heavily on its natural resources. Major products are livestock products such as cashmere, agricultural products, timber, coal, iron, and many minerals, including rare-earth elements. Much of its industry is built upon these resources. Tourism is also a source of income. The economy of the IMAR has grown greatly since its founding (New Star Publishers 1997; Hong 1999).

In attempting to improve the economic situation of the minorities of these border provinces, during the economic reform period China's government has reversed its three-decades-long policy of blocking cross-border trade. Now the minorities can once again trade with their compatriots across the border in Mongolia, Russia, the Central Asian Muslim countries, Nepal, and India. These provinces have also been encouraged to develop their tourist trade (Dreyer 1997). Xinjiang cross-border trade, investments, and travel mushroomed in the 1990s, greatly benefiting its economy (Ferdinand 1994: 280–281).

An unintended consequence of this economic opening to the outside world has been increased ethnic consciousness and ethnic identity among the Muslims, Tibetans, and Mongols, as well as global publicity for the minorities' complaints of human rights violations by the Chinese government. The last two decades have seen demonstrations by Mongol, Uighur, and Tibetan separatists, frequent clashes with Chinese authorities, and renewed intransigence on the part of the Chinese government. The leadership's options are limited (Dreyer 1997). Cracking down on the border minority nationalities leads to more protests, but so does loosening controls on them, as the reform decades have demonstrated.

Although the minority peoples of the border provinces remain comparatively poor, they have experienced real social and demographic development since 1949. Death rates have plummeted and health conditions have improved greatly in all three of these Autonomous Regions. The minority nationalities, permitted to have more children than the Han Chinese, also have access to birth control; their birth rates have declined.

Literacy and educational attainment have also greatly improved among the minorities in two of these three border provinces. In Inner Mongolia, illiteracy rates are lower for Mongols than Han, and educational attainment is greater, an impressive achievement (China Population, Inner Mongolia Volume, 1990: 363; Poston and Shu 1992: 583–595; *Towards 21st Century*, Inner Mongolia Volume, 1994: 282; Wang 1998: 58; Bass 1998: 11). There was dramatic improvement in the educational attainment of both Han and minority workers in Xinjiang during the 1980s (Hannum and Yu 1998: 329). As of 1990, 52 percent of the entire Xinjiang minority population had received a primary education, while 16 percent had attained a junior secondary level and 8 percent a higher level. For Xinjiang in 1992, 96 percent of all children, and 95 percent of minority children, entered primary school (Mackerras 1995: 136). Throughout Xinjiang, completion of primary education is now commonplace (Wang 1998: 47).

As of 1989 in the Tibet Autonomous Region, about half of the children ages 7–11 were enrolled in primary school, but in the most rural and pastoral areas only 17 percent of children were in school (Bass 1998: 76–78). According to 1990 census data, the Tibet Autonomous Region still measured "dismally low" in educational experience (Mackerras 1995: 135), with 73 percent of the minority population still illiterate (reduced from "more than 90 percent" before 1949). Only 22 percent of TAR minorities had received a primary education, and only 5 percent of the minorities had attained higher than a primary education (Bass 1998: 11; Chen 1991: 81). By 1998, some improvement was reported, though the TAR's adult illiteracy rate of 54 percent is still high (China Statistical Yearbook 1998: 36). Tibet officials claimed that 81 percent of children entered school as of 1998, although a large proportion continued to drop out (Sautman and Eng 2000).

The quality of life of the border minority peoples in these three provinces has risen enormously since the founding of the PRC. They have longer and healthier lives, fewer and better-educated children, more and better food, and higher real incomes. Much of this improvement has been brought about by the Han Chinese medical personnel, teachers, skilled workers, and cadres who have been sent by China's government to the border provinces. Our study suggests that much of the government-directed Han in-migration has brought direct, tangible benefits to the minority peoples.

Conclusions

The People's Republic of China has used government-directed Han Chinese migration to secure the province of Xinjiang and link its economy and politics tightly with those of the rest of China. The Han presence in Xinjiang is now sufficient to control the economy and the resources of this mineral-rich and energy-rich territory. The minority peoples of Xinjiang have benefited from the development of their province, although it could be argued that the Han in-migrants have benefited more. The PRC has successfully secured the province of Xinjiang as a piece of China and the wealth of Xinjiang as a resource for all China.

However, in the other border regions of our study, Inner Mongolia and Tibet, government-directed migration has been a half-hearted and short-term policy, with uncertain results for China's national security attributable to government-sponsored civilian Han in-migration in the post-1949 period. In Inner Mongolia, historical Han Chinese in-migration had already produced an overwhelming Han numerical dominance before the PRC was founded; in Tibet and Inner Mongolia, Chinese government control of the political system, police, military, and courts, and the pervasive Han military presence, ensure its dominance of both provinces.

Government-directed migration to Xinjiang and Inner Mongolia was a highly politicized Maoist policy during the 1950s. Since then, this form of demographic engineering has ceased in the Inner Mongolia Autonomous Region and has been gradually reduced in Xinjiang. Directed migration to Tibet was very moderate in the 1960s and 1970s. In the 1980s, the PRC government stopped or reversed its policy of promoting Han migration to these three border provinces. In the 1980s and 1990s, spontaneous migration and temporary or circular migration have superseded politically motivated and government-sponsored migration. No matter what the motives and causes for Han Chinese migration and movement toward the border regions, the Tibetans, Muslims, and Mongols continue to be concerned about the effects on their cultures of such a migration. If the minorities receive greater benefits from the future development of their provinces, perhaps they will become less concerned about Han population movement as a threat to their identities and livelihoods.

Acknowledgments

The author would like to thank Wang Jianping, Tommy Chin Man Chui, Cong Ning, and Eilo W. Y. Yu for their valuable research assistance. Sharon Stanton Russell, Myron Weiner, Jack Goldstone, and Barry Sautman provided helpful comments on an earlier version of the manuscript.

References

Anderson, Barbara A., and Brian D. Silver. 1995. "Ethnic Differences in Fertility and Sex Ratios at Birth in China: Evidence from Xinjiang." *Population Studies* 49: 211–226.

Banister, Judith. 1987. *China's Changing Population.* Stanford, CA: Stanford University Press.

Bass, Catriona. 1998. *Education in Tibet: Policy and Practice since 1950.* London: Zed Books.

Becquelin, Nicolas. 1999. "New Mediums of Xinjiang's Integration by the Centre since the Emergence of Post-Soviet Central Asia." Paper presented at the annual meeting of the Association of Asian Studies, Boston (March).

Bockman, Harald. 1992. "The Brewing Ethnic Conflicts in China and Their Historical Background." In *Ethnicity and Conflict in a Post-Communist World: The Soviet Union, Eastern Europe, and China.* Kumar Rupesinghe, Peter King, and Olga Vorkunova, eds. New York: St. Martin's Press.

Bulag, Uradyn E. 1998. *Nationalism and Hybridity in Mongolia.* Oxford: Clarendon Press.

Cha-leng-ku-ssu. 1958. "A Large Han Population Is an Important Condition for Rapid Development of Inner Mongolia Autonomous Region." *Survey of China Mainland Press* 1725, 6 March: 14–19.

Chen Ran, ed. 1991. *Tibet: From 1951 to 1991.* Compiled by *China's Tibet* and *Beijing Review.* Beijing: New Star Publisher.

China 1953 Census. 1954. China State Statistical Bureau. "Communique of Results of Census and Registration of China's Population." New China News Agency, Beijing, 1 November 1954 broadcast. Translated by American Consulate General Hong Kong. *Current Background* 301, 1 November: 1–2.

China 1990 Census. 1993. China State Council Population Census Office and State Statistical Bureau Department of Population Statistics. *Tabulation of the 1990 Population Census of the People's Republic of China.* Beijing: China Statistical Publishing House (4 volumes).

China Population, Volumes on Inner Mongolia, Xinjiang. 1990. Zhou Chongjing, ed. *Zhongguo renkou* [Nei Menggu fence, Xinjiang fence] (China Population, Inner Mongolia Volume, Xinjiang Volume). Beijing: Zhongguo caizheng jingji chubanshe [China Financial and Economic Publishing House].

China Statistical Yearbook. 1998. China, State Statistical Bureau. Beijing: China Statistical Publishing House.

Chou Weizhi. 1982. "Past, Likely Future Trends in Migration Discussed." *Joint Publications Research Service* 79882, 18 January: 51–60.

Clarke, Graham E. 1998. "Development, Society, and Environment in Tibet." In *Development, Society, and Environment in Tibet*, Graham E. Clarke, ed. Vienna: Verlag der Osterreichischen Akademie der Wissenschaften. Pp. 1–45.

Dong Yongmao. 1988. "Migration and Economic Development in Xinjiang." *Xinjiang caijing* [Xinjiang Finance and Economy], No. 4.

Dreyer, June Teufel. 1976. *China's Forty Millions; Minority Nationalities and National Integration in the People's Republic of China.* Cambridge, MA: Harvard University Press.

Dreyer, June. 1997. "Assimilation and Accommodation in China." In *Government Policies and Ethnic Relations in Asia and the Pacific.* Michael E. Brown and Sumit Ganguly, eds. Cambridge, MA: MIT Press.

Dumbaugh, Kerry B. 1988. *Tibet: Disputed Facts about the Situation in Tibet.* Washington, D.C.: Library of Congress, Congressional Research Service.

Eckholm, Erik. 1999. "Remaking a Vast Frontier in China's image." *New York Times.* 17 July: A1, A6.

Ferdinand, Peter. 1994. "Xinjiang, Relations with China and Abroad." In *China Deconstructs: Politics, Trade, and Regionalism.* David S. G. Goodman and Gerald Segal, eds. London: Routledge.

Goldstein, Sidney, and Alice Goldstein. 1990. *Permanent and Temporary Migration Differentials in China.* Honolulu: East-West Population Institute, East-West Center.

Hannum, Emily, and Yu Xie. 1998. "Ethnic Stratification in Northwest China: Occupational Differences between Han Chinese and National Minorities in Xinjiang, 1982–1990." *Demography* 35 (3): 323–333.

Hong Lei. 1999. "The New Face of Inner Mongolia." *China Today* (January): 46–49.

Huang Yasheng. 1995. "China's Cadre Transfer Policy toward Tibet in the 1980s." *Modern China* 21 (2): 184–204.

Inner Mongolia Statistical Yearbook. Annual. *Nei Menggu tongji nianjian* [Statistical Yearbook of Inner Mongolia]. Beijing: Zhongguo tongji chubanshe.

Ji Ping. 1990. *Frontier Migration and Ethnic Assimilation: A Case of Xinjiang Uighur Autonomous Region of China.* Ph.D. thesis, Brown University.

Karmel, Solomon M. 1995. "Ethnic Tension and the Struggle for Order: China's Policies in Tibet." *Pacific Affairs* 68 (4): 485–508.

Khan, Almaz. 1994. "Chinggis Khan, from Imperial Ancestor to Ethnic Hero." In *Cultural Encounters on China's Ethnic Frontiers.* Stevan Harrell, ed. Seattle: University of Washington Press.

Lee, James. 1978. "Migration and Expansion in Chinese History." In *Human Migration, Patterns and Policies.* William H. McNeill and Ruth S. Adams, eds. Bloomington, IN: Indiana University Press.

Lemoine, Jacques. 1989. "Ethnicity, Culture, and Development among Some Minorities of the People's Republic of China." In *Ethnicity and Ethnic Groups in China.* Chien Chiao and Nicholas Tapp, eds. Hong Kong: New Asia College. Special issue. *New Asia Academic Bulletin* 8: 1–9.

Liu Xuecheng. 1994. *The Sino-Indian Border Dispute and Sino-Indian Relations.* Lanham, MD: University Press of America.

Ma Rong. 1996. *Xizang de renkou yu shehui* [Population and Society in Tibet]. Beijing: Tongxin chubanshe.

———. 1998. "Economic Patterns of the Tibet Autonomous Region." In *Development, Society, and Environment in Tibet.* Graham E. Clarke, ed. Vienna: Verlag der Osterreichischen Akademie der Wissenschaften. Pp. 167–188.

Ma Zheng. 1981. "Trouble between Han, Uighur Minority Reported in Xinjiang," *Joint Publications Research Service* 78873, 1 September: 22–25.

Mackerras, Colin. 1994. *China's Minorities, Integration and Modernization in the Twentieth Century.* Hong Kong: Oxford University Press.

———. 1995. *China's Minority Cultures: Identities and Integration since 1912.* Melbourne: Longman.

Maxwell, Neville. 1972. *India's China War.* Garden City, NY: Doubleday.

New Star Publishers. 1997. *Fifty Years of the Inner Mongolia Autonomous Region.* Beijing.

O'Neill, Mark. 1998a. "Pressure Rises in Xinjiang's Melting Pot." *South China Morning Post*, 23 May: 15.

———. 1998b. "Staking Out a Home in a Divided Land." *South China Morning Post*, 30 May: 16.

Pillsbury, Barbara L. K. 1981. "Islam: 'Even Unto China.'" In *Change and the Muslim World.* Philip H. Stoddard, David C. Cuthell, and Margaret W. Sullivan, eds. Syracuse, N.Y.: Syracuse University Press.

Poston, Dudley L., Jr., and Shu Jing. 1992. "The Demographic and Socioeconomic Composition of China's Ethnic Minorities." In *The Population of Modern China.* Dudley L. Poston, Jr., and David Yaukey, eds. New York: Plenum Press.

Sautman, Barry. 2000. "Is Xinjiang an Internal Colony?" *Inner Asia* 2 (2): 239–271.

Sautman, Barry, and Irene Eng. 2000. "Tibet: Development for Whom?" Presented at the 17th Triennial Conference of the International Political Science Association, Quebec City (August).

Schein, Louisa. 1989. "The Dynamics of Cultural Revival among the Miao in Guizhou." In *Ethnicity and Ethnic Groups in China.* Chien Chiao and Nicholas Tapp, eds. Hong Kong: New Asia College. Special issue. *New Asia Academic Bulletin* 8: 199–212.

Schwartz, Ronald D. 1994. "Resistance in Tibet 1987–1990: The Anti-Splittist Campaign and Tibetan Political Consciousness." In *Resistance and Reform in Tibet*. Robert Barnett, ed. Bloomington: Indiana University Press.

Sun Jingzhi, ed. 1996. *Bashi niandai Zhongguo renkou biandong fenxi* [Analysis of China's Population Change in the 1980s]. Beijing: Zhongguo caizheng jingji chubanshe.

Tibet Support Group UK. 1995. *New Majority: Chinese Population Transfer into Tibet*. London: Tibet Support Group UK.

Toops, Stanley. 1999. "The Population Landscape of Xinjiang/East Turkestan." Paper presented at the annual meeting of the Association of Asian Studies, Boston (March).

Towards 21st Century, Volumes on Xinjiang, Inner Mongolia, Tibet. 1994. Kua shiji de Zhongguo renkou (Xinjiang juan, Nei Menggu juan, Xizang juan) bian weihui bianzhu [Compiled by the Editorial Committee for the Xinjiang volume, the Inner Mongolia volume, and the Tibet volume of *The Population of China Towards the 21st Century*], *Kua shiji de Zhongguo renkou, Xinjiang juan, Nei Menggu juan, Xizang juan* [The Population of China Towards the 21st Century, Xinjiang Volume, Inner Mongolia Volume, Tibet Volume]. Beijing: Zhongguo tongji chubanshe [China Statistical Publishing House].

Tzou, Byron N. 1990. *China and International Law: The Boundary Disputes*. New York: Praeger.

Wang, David. 1998. "Han Migration and Social Changes in Xinjiang." *Issues and Studies* 34 (7): 33–61 (July).

Weisskopf, Michael. 1981. "Ethnic Conflict in Strategic Western Province Alarms Peking." *Washington Post*, 12 September: 1, 25.

Wu, David Y.H. 1989. "Culture Change and Ethnic Identity among Minorities in China." In *Ethnicity and Ethnic Groups in China*. Chien Chiao and Nicholas Tapp, eds. Hong Kong: New Asia College. Special issue. *New Asia Academic Bulletin* 8: 11–22.

Xinjiang Statistical Yearbook. Annual. *Xinjiang tongji nianjian* [Xinjiang Statistical Yearbook]. Beijing: Zhongguo tongji chubanshe.

Yahuda, Michael B. 1994. "North China and Russia." In *China Deconstructs: Politics, Trade, and Regionalism*. David S. G. Goodman and Gerald Segal, eds. London: Routledge.

Zhang Tianlu. 1997. *Population Development in Tibet and Related Issues*. Beijing: Foreign Languages Press. Translated from Chinese by Chen Guansheng and Li Peizhu.

CHAPTER 10

Stalinist Forced Relocation Policies: Patterns, Causes, Consequences

Terry Martin

While other states have forcibly relocated more people than the Soviet Union under Stalin,[1] the Stalinist state was unique in the extraordinary complexity of its forced relocation policies, in the variety of political goals pursued through deportation, in the diversity of population categories deported, and in the frequency of mass deportations. Several million Soviet citizens were deported due to their ethnic identity alone; these were, however, only about half the total number of those deported. Mass deportations were also carried out on the basis of "class" identity (kulaks), former occupation (Tsarist or Polish policeman), present occupation (prostitute), former political affiliation (a non-Bolshevik party), political opposition (Trotsky and his followers), criminal potential (former criminals, "suspicious types"), religion (Jehovah's Witnesses), former estate status (nobility, Cossack), wartime behavior ("Vlasovites"), citizenship (Iranians), and family ties (spouses, children).

Mass deportations occurred with great frequency. If we define a mass deportation as the forcible relocation of over a thousand individuals in a single action, then it would appear that at least one mass deportation occurred every year in the period from 1928 to 1952.[2] Peak years such as 1944 witnessed up to a dozen mass deportations. Contemporaries found the pattern and causes of these deportations bewildering. When in 1937 a visitor asked a local peasant why a few thousand Azerbaijanis were being deported to Central Asia, the peasant replied that this action "merely formed part of the deliberate policy of the Soviet government, who believed in transplanting portions of the population from place to place as and when it suited them. The place of those now being deported would probably be taken by other peasants from Central Asia" (Maclean 1949: 34).

This chapter tries to make sense of the bewildering pattern of Stalinist forced relocation policies by addressing three main issues: patterns, causes, and consequences. First, what population categories were being forcibly relocated at different times? From what regions were they being removed, where were they being sent, and who was being resettled in their place? Second, what goals was the state pursuing through the practice of mass deportation? In answering this question, this chapter formulates a typology of Stalinist forced relocation and places exile within the overall repertoire of Stalinist coercion. Third, what were the consequences of Stalinist forced relocation policies, in the short term (to the death of Stalin in 1953), medium term (to Gorbachev's reforms in the late 1980s), and long term (post-Soviet)? In particular, the chapter focuses on the impact of these policies on the evolution of the multiethnic Soviet state. What role did forced relocation play in the transformation of the Soviet Union's ethnic demography? What was the relationship between mass deportations and voluntary or semi-coercive migration and resettlement policies? Did these policies contribute to or undermine the long-term stability of the Soviet state? What impact has the legacy of forced relocation had on the current ethnic conflicts in the former Soviet Union?

Before turning to these questions, a few preliminary remarks about terminology, sources, and statistics should be made. In international law, "deportation" typically refers to the expulsion of non-citizens, either individually or *en masse*, beyond the borders of the deporting state; in Soviet historiography, "deportation" instead refers to the forcible relocation of Soviet citizens and non-citizens both within and (less frequently) beyond the boundaries of the Soviet state. "Deportation" is used here in this latter sense.

Serious scholarly study of Stalinist forced relocation began only a decade ago with the opening of the Soviet archives. While the topic has attracted considerable attention, that attention has been thematically quite uneven: exceptionally strong on the process of deportation and the experience of internal exile, but very weak on the resettlement of the regions from which the deportations occurred, and almost non-existent on the important topic of voluntary and semi-coercive migration and resettlement. This chapter will of necessity reflect that unevenness. Finally, the statistics on the size of the various mass deportations are all based on the reports of the Soviet political police (OGPU-NKVD-MGB-MVD) who carried out the deportations and supervised the places of resettlement. These numbers are absurdly precise: for instance, Zemskov (1990b: 4) reports 1,803,392 "kulaks" deported in 1930–1931. When examined closely, these numbers do prove relatively accurate, but only within a few percentage points (Gur'ianov 1997a, 1997b). Therefore, to avoid a false sense of precision, all deportation figures have been rounded off.

A Typology of Stalinist Mass Deportation

Since the details of Stalinist forced relocation policies are not yet generally well known, a considerable part of this chapter is devoted to a narrative account of what population categories were being deported to and from what regions at different points in time. In order to give order and meaning to this historical narrative, an analytical typology of Stalinist mass deportation is sketched out, one that focuses on the Soviet state's goals in carrying out these massive transfers of their own population. In addition, the role of mass deportation is placed within the overall repertoire of Stalinist coercion.

While there is a relatively large literature that attempts to analyze the phenomenon of Soviet terror (referred to here as coercion, since it involved other goals than terrorizing the population), those works have focused overwhelmingly on arrest and execution (Moore 1954; Brzezinski 1956; Conquest 1990; Getty 1985; Rittersporn 1991; Khlevniuk 1996). Specific deportations, in particular those of the kulaks during collectivization and the "punished peoples" during the Second World War, have been analyzed as individual events, but not as part of the larger phenomenon of Stalinist coercion (Conquest 1977; Nekrich 1978; Ivnitskii 1996; Viola 2000). Leaving aside forms of coercion that stopped short of physically seizing the individual (such as Party purges), there were three major forms of Stalinist coercion: execution, incarceration, and exile. Execution was extremely widespread during the "Red Terror" of the Civil War (Mel'gunov 1989). After this initial period, while there were a few extraordinary waves of mass execution—the 1937–1938 Great Terror (c. 680,000 executions), the execution of 25,700 former Polish officers in 1940, the mass execution of prisoners in the western border regions after the June 1941 German invasion (at least several thousand)—execution typically represented a relatively small percentage of Stalinist coercion (Khlevniuk 1996: 192; Gorlanov and Roginskii 1997: 84; Bilas 1994b: 224–271). Excluding these three events, according to their own statistics the political police issued 120,000 execution sentences from 1921 to 1953, or around 4,000 a year (Popov 1992: 28). A recent survey of archival publications, on the other hand, estimated (and it is surely only a very rough estimate) that approximately 11.8 million individuals were arrested between 1930 and 1953 (a figure that includes a large number of "common criminals"), and 7.0 million were deported (almost all being "politicals") between 1930 and 1948 (Pohl 1996: chap. 1). In terms of political coercion, then, arrest and deportation were about equally common.

Stalinist mass deportation had two typical characteristics. It was categoric and it was prophylactic: categoric in that it focused less on what an individual actually had done than on whether that individual belonged to a stigmatized population category; prophylactic in that exile was used not so much to remove or punish an individual for committing an offense, as to remove individuals who would presumably commit an offense if given the proper opportunity. In other words, the question asked of an individual was "Who are you?", not "What have you done?" The deported were typically only approached individually in order to answer the question: is this person a "kulak"? a Chechen? a Polish "colonist"? a Jehovah's

Witness? There were some exceptions to this generalization. After the Second World War, "Vlasovites" (those who fought alongside the Germans in Vlasov's Russia Liberation Army and other non-Russian legions) were all exiled for six years for a clear individual act (fighting against the Red Army), although those whose actions were deemed particularly egregious were singled out for incarceration in a concentration camp (Polian 1996).

Soviet mass arrest campaigns were partially individual and partially categoric. The campaigns typically targeted a population category—priests and engineers in 1928–1931, for instance—but far from all those in the category were arrested. Instead, those who were already registered (*na uchet*) with the security police for some putatively anti-Soviet or simply suspicious (*podozritel'no*) behavior would be arrested, along with those on whom "compromising materials" (*kompromat*) could be found in the course of the terror campaign. Arrests were still largely prophylactic in that the "compromising materials" most often served only to raise suspicions of anti-Soviet behavior or intent; in contrast to the case of those deported, however, the suspicions were stronger and they were individually anchored. Thus both questions ("Who are you?" and "What have you done?") were asked of those incarcerated. Again, there were exceptions. In particular, the Great Terror was so extensive that significant percentages of entire population categories (in particular, diaspora nationalities) were being arrested and executed, and the individualized aspect of arrest thus became almost entirely superficial (Petrov and Roginskii 1997; Okhotin and Roginskii 1999).

Deportation and incarceration, then, served differing but complementary purposes. Deportation served primarily to remove a suspect population category from a given territory, and to do so without the effort of distinguishing between more or less guilty individuals; incarceration served both to remove and punish suspect individuals as well as to intimidate those not arrested (the terror function). Deportation and arrest were, in fact, typically carried out simultaneously. In almost every deportation we will encounter, a portion of the deported category considered most anti-Soviet (often those already *na uchet* with the security police) would be arrested prior to or during the mass deportations. The practice of mass deportation emerged to serve the state's perceived need to remove large categories of individuals who were considered generically suspect, but whom the regime did not feel the need or desire to process and incarcerate on an individual basis.

This establishes the general function of deportation, but not the reason for targeting specific population categories. To help make sense of the complex pattern of Stalinist deportation, a typology is proposed that consists of two major and four minor types of deportation. These are ideal-types; of course most deportations were, to varying degrees, composites. The typology is meant to be explanatory rather than descriptive: rather than catalogue the various groups being deported at different times, it identifies the principal goals the Soviet state pursued through deportation. The two major types were Sovietization and Security deportations. Sovietization deportations were undertaken, along with mass arrests, as part of a general campaign to establish the fundamental features of Soviet society: hegemonic rule by the Communist Party, rapid industrialization, collectivization of agriculture, abolition of the market, political control of cultural and intellectual life. If we exclude the 1919–1920 Cossack deportations, Sovietization deportations took place in two major waves: in the original USSR from 1930 to 1933 (continuing through the mid-1930s in peripheral regions); then again in the newly acquired western territories from 1939 to 1941 and 1944 to 1952. The kulaks were the primary target of the Sovietization deportations in both these regions.

Security (or xenophobic) deportations were driven by external security fears and focused on the potential disloyalty (indeed treason) of various population categories. The paradigmatic Security deportation was the removal of suspect ethnic groups from the Soviet border regions. Some Security deportations had occurred during dekulakization in 1930, but they only emerged fully with the 1935–1938 "cleansings" of the Soviet border regions. Security deportations flourished through the Second World War and remained a component of post-war deportations from the newly acquired territories.

The four minor deportation types were for Social Disorder, Ethnic Consolidation, Russification, and Retribution. The latter two categories were more contributing factors than the primary cause of any particular mass deportation. Social Disorder deportations began after Sovietization and targeted population categories that the state felt were disrupting the newly established social order; their paradigm was the periodic removal of "socially harmful elements" from the major cities of the USSR. Ethnic Consolidation deportations involved the exchange of ethnic minorities in order to further ethnic homogeneity, and consisted only of the postwar international population "exchanges" that sent Soviet Poles and Czechs to their respective "homelands" and Polish Ukrainians (and some Czechoslovak Ukrainians) to Soviet Ukraine. Russificatory deportations involved the removal of ethnic minorities from the peripheral regions of the Russian Federated Republic (RSFSR) in order to further "the russification of the RSFSR" (Martin 1998b). This goal played a role in the 1944 deportations from Crimea and the North Caucasus. Finally, several of the World War II-era deportations would appear to have had a retributive or punitive component as well.

Dekulakization, 1930–1933: Sovietization

The campaign "to liquidate the kulak as a class," launched in February 1930, marked the onset of the era of Stalinist mass deportations. This was not, however, the first instance of Soviet, or for that matter Tsarist (Lohr

1999), mass deportation. During the Russian Civil War (1918–1921), the primary forms of Soviet coercion were mass arrest and execution, as well as open military action by the Red Army against an array of opposing armies (White, Polish, Ukrainian) and guerilla forces (Makhno's, Antonov's, the Basmachi). Mass deportation appears to have been used relatively infrequently during this first Sovietization campaign, presumably since the population categories then being targeted by the Bolsheviks (landowners, industrialists, the Tsarist elite) were comparatively small, physically scattered, and already being driven away from their homes by mass popular revolutionary violence. The major exception to this rule were the Cossacks, a pre-revolutionary military estate group that formed the backbone of the White army. When the Bolsheviks reconquered the Don Cossack region in 1919, they launched an aggressive "decossackization" campaign that included the mass deportation of the Don Cossack elite (Holquist 1997). In 1920, nine entire Terek Cossack towns in the North Caucasus were deported (Bugai 1993; Tsutsiev 1998: 50, 180–181).

During the era of the New Economic Policy (1921–1928), a less violent period when the Bolsheviks temporarily deferred revolutionary change, a series of small-scale mass deportations were carried out. In 1922, on Lenin's personal initiative, fifty prominent anti-Bolshevik intellectuals were forcibly deported from the USSR. From 1924 to 1928, in an extended series of small actions, most of the remaining former landowners were deported from their home regions, in a kind of state "mop-up" operation where popular revolutionary action had proven inadequate.[3] In 1928, the Kazakh *bai* (traditional feudal leaders, whom the Bolsheviks categorized as the Kazakh equivalent of landlords) were likewise deported (Martin 1996: 547–548). In 1927–1928, the unrepentant membership of the Trotsky-led opposition were deported to remote cities. There also appear to have been small-scale "cleansings" of the capital, Moscow, of "undesirable elements," a practice that would become endemic in the 1930s (Sevost'ianov, Sakharov, and Pogonii N.d.). Not only is this list of mass deportations certainly incomplete, it also excludes the routine exile of individuals by the political police, who were empowered to exile individuals administratively without trial and did so throughout the Stalinist period. These mass deportations were all quite small, never exceeding a few hundred individuals, but at a time of greatly reduced repression, they marked the emergence of mass deportation as a major component of Soviet coercion.

From late 1927 to mid-1933, Stalin launched and carried through a massive Sovietization campaign that involved the nationalization of private enterprise, forced industrialization, the abolition of most free market trade, the collectivization of agriculture, the complete political domination of society by the Communist Party, and the solidification of Stalin's personal dictatorship. This campaign targeted a variety of population categories: priests, "bourgeois specialists" (in particular engineers, academics, non-Russian intellectuals), "former people" (nobles, landowners,

Tsarist officials), former members of non-Bolshevik parties (Mensheviks, various non-Russian parties), "Nepmen" (traders, small businessmen), but above all the kulaks, well-to-do peasants who were said to exploit their poorer neighbors, a massive category estimated by the Bolsheviks as 2 to 3 percent of the entire Soviet population. While priests, engineers, traders, and academics could be intimidated by incarcerating a portion of their number (often with an accompanying show trial), the kulaks were simply too large a category for this strategy. Moreover, the removal of the kulaks was designed to terrorize the entire peasant population, since anyone who opposed collectivization could be categorized as a kulak and arrested or deported. The collectivization of agriculture was by far the most difficult challenge facing Stalin's Sovietization campaign and dekulakization was the key, though far from the only, coercive measure undertaken to achieve this goal. Ultimately 2.1 million peasants would be deported from February 1930 to May 1933 (1.8 million in 1930–1931), and over one hundred thousand would be arrested (Ivnitskii 1996: 115; Zemskov 1990b: 4). Dekulakization would remain the single largest campaign of mass deportation of the entire Stalinist period.

As the largest and the first major Stalinist mass deportation, dekulakization would in many ways become the paradigmatic act of Stalinist forced relocation. It is therefore important to note that it was in many ways quite atypical. First, in comparison to later deportations, there was relatively little advance planning and an enormous amount of chaotic improvisation as the operation unfolded (Viola 2000). Second, while the OGPU carried out the deportation and resettlement of the deported kulaks, as well as the process of selecting which kulaks were to be arrested, they did not control the local process of selecting kulaks for deportation (Viola 2000). In all future deportations, this function would belong exclusively to the political police. Third, dekulakization was carried out simultaneously across the entire Soviet Union; all subsequent mass deportations would be localized, which would allow the political police to concentrate overwhelming resources on a limited area. Fourth, dekulakization was the only major mass deportation to take place prior to the Sovietization of the majority of the country. As a consequence of these four factors, dekulakization would be the only mass deportation campaign to encounter widespread, violent resistance. According to the political police's own statistics, there were in 1930 alone 13,754 mass disturbances and 13,794 acts of terror (including 1,198 murders) tied to the general assault on the villages (Danilov and Berelowitch 1994: 671–676).

Dekulakization provided at least three crucial precedents for future mass deportations. First, deportation and incarceration were used in tandem. The 30 January 1930 decree authorizing dekulakization divided the kulaks into three categories: first, "the counter-revolutionary activists, organizers of terrorist acts and uprisings—incarcerate in concentration camps, and in some individual cases, do not hesitate to execute"; second, "the remaining part of the counter-revolutionary activists from among the richest kulaks and half-landowners—exile to distant parts of the USSR or distant parts of their own provinces"; and third, "the majority of kulak households—resettle within their home districts on land prepared for them outside the collective farms." The decree established a quota of 60,000 households in the first category (head of household to be incarcerated and family members deported) and 150,000 households in the second category (Ivnitskii 1996: 68–69). No numbers were specified for the third category and within a year it had largely disappeared from the dekulakization campaign; such local resettlement would not figure in future campaigns. However, the division of the deported population into two categories—those to be arrested ("Who are you?" and "What have you done?") and those to be deported ("Who are you?")—would endure throughout the Soviet period.[4]

The dekulakization campaign also established an administrative structure for governing the exiled kulaks that would absorb the vast majority of future deported contingents (Viola 2000; Brul' 1999: 102–109; Krasil'nikov 1992, 1993, 1994, 1996; Bugai 1992a). The deported kulaks were formally classified as "special settlers." They were placed in small separate villages under the command of an OGPU *komendant*, who was in charge of maintaining order in the "special settlements," in particular preventing escapes. The primary constraints on the special settlers were that they could not leave their district of exile, even for a brief period of time, without formal permission from the *komendant*; and that they had to engage in whatever work was assigned to them; their status was thus analogous to state serfdom. Unlike prisoners, families lived together. After initially catastrophic fatality rates (ranging as high as 25 percent of the deported populations), within about five to eight years of their deportation the special settler contingents were typically experiencing real population growth (Zemskov 1990a, 1990b, 1993, 1994; Bugai 1994a: 63; Gur'ianov 1997a: 121–127; Brul' 1999: 109–110). Informally, special settlers could suffer from arbitrary behavior by their OGPU overseers, and from close OGPU supervision that included maintaining a dense network of informers (Belkovets 1999). Special settlers were to be paid the same wage for their work as free citizens, but they had to return a percentage to the OGPU (initially 25 percent, declining gradually to a final level of 5 percent in 1937) in payment for their upkeep (Zemskov 1990a; Krasil'nikov 1992). The major tasks assigned to special settlers in separate villages were agriculture, fishing, and felling timber; however the OGPU also increasingly loaned them out to various industrial bureaucracies for work in construction, mining, and other heavy labor. Security in the special settlements was initially quite haphazard: the political police reported an extraordinary 629,000 escapes from 1932 to 1940 (Zemskov 1990b: 6). In the postwar period, extraordinary efforts would be undertaken to increase security, and escapes would as a result become much less common.

The special settlements can best be seen as occupying a mid-point on a hierarchy of confinement in the Soviet Union. Above them lay the "hard regime" concentration camps (for "especially dangerous" prisoners), ordinary concentration camps, and various "corrective labor colonies" (for less serious crimes) (Getty, Rittersporn, and Zemskov 1993: 1019–1020).[5] In these institutions, prisoners lived without their families in heavily guarded camps; they were typically forced to engage in much more severe work, and they received no wages. Below the special settler in this hierarchy there were three less onerous forms of exile: exiled settler, exiled, and deported (Zemskov 1991b). "Exiled settler" (*ssyl'nopose-lenets*) was a rare category, applied only to the contingents deported from the newly acquired western territories in May–June 1941, and not substantially different from special settler. Exiled settlers were settled as families in separate work villages, which they were forbidden to leave, but they were not under formal NKVD supervision and did not pay the NKVD for their upkeep. They were eventually re-categorized as special settlers. The more important category for mass deportations was "administratively exiled" (*administrativno-vyslannye*). This category was further subdivided into "the deported" (*vyslannye*) and "the exiled" (*ssyl'nye*). The latter was used for all mass deportations prior to dekulakization, as well as for the mass deportations from the border regions (1935–1938), for the urban deportations of the Great Terror, and for the April 1940 deportation from western Ukraine and Belarus (Martin 1998a; Gur'ianov 1997a). The sole constraint on such exiles was that they could live only within their place of exile (which could be defined quite broadly, even as an entire republic) and they had to report periodically (ranging from weekly to monthly) to the political police. The category of "deported" was not typically used in mass deportations, with the exception of routine "cleansings" of major cities. Such exiles were free citizens with the sole exception that they could not reside in the large number of "regime cities" as defined by the passport laws.[6]

Finally, dekulakization established a standard set of dumping grounds for the various deported contingents of the next twenty years. The major dumping grounds for the kulak deportations were the European Far North, the Urals, Western Siberia, and Kazakhstan. Over time, Kazakhstan would emerge as the major dumping ground. From the perspective of the Soviet authorities, the principal virtue of these locations was, as the 30 January dekulakization decree put it, precisely their remoteness. The primary motivation of Stalinist forced relocation was overwhelmingly to *remove* population categories *from* a given location, rather than to *send* them *to* a desired location. Special settlers were used to colonize distant and unpleasant regions that could not easily attract or hold voluntary settlers, as well as to provide labor for unpleasant work assignments; however, this motivation appears to have been overwhelmingly secondary. For instance, in 1933 the OGPU proposed a plan that would involve settling a million special settlers (to be acquired through further dekulakization and cleansing of the major cities) in both Kazakhstan and Western Siberia (Krasil'nikov 1994: 263). This appears to be the only case where a proposal for mass deportation was motivated by economic factors and the desire to settle a given region. Significantly, it was rejected. Indeed, minimal efforts were devoted to keeping the existing special settlers from escaping their places of exile.

James Harris (1997: 265–280) has argued that in 1931 an overwhelming need for labor to fell timber in the Urals was a major factor in continuing dekulakization (see also Krasil'nikov 1992: 188), though Viola (2000) did not find a similar pattern in the Far North. In this specific case, given the rapid pace of forced industrialization and the open-ended nature of the kulak deportation, the economic "pull" factor may have been unusually influential. However, the impression received from reading the thousands of pages of published documentation concerning the dozens of mass deportations carried out over the next twenty years is quite the opposite. There can be found not even a minimal preoccupation with providing labor to needed industrial and agricultural sectors, but instead a series of abrupt political decisions to remove vast populations from their home territory, followed by a mad bureaucratic scramble to find somewhere to dump the population, the chaotic process in turn typically leading to a massive loss of labor through death by disease and exposure (Alieva 1993; Bilas 1994a, 1994b; Bugai 1992a, 1994a; Eisfeld and Herdt 1996; Khe and Un 1992; Krasil'nikov et al. 1992, 1993, 1994, 1996; Maksheev 1997; Milova 1992, 1995; Passat 1994; Slyvka 1996).

"Cleansing" the Cities, 1933: Social Disorder

In May 1933, dekulakization was formally halted in the central regions of the Soviet Union, although it continued in remote non-Russian peripheries such as the mountainous regions of the North Caucasus, Transcaucasus, and Central Asia. From 1934 to 1940, several tens of thousands of "kulaks" were apparently deported from these regions (Zemskov 1990a: 124–125; Bugai 1994a: 27). Stalin's successful Sovietization campaign had, however, created an enormous amount of social disorder. Over a million former kulaks either fled their home regions or escaped from exile, and settled illegally in the Soviet Union's major cities and industrial work sites. The massive 1932–1933 famine, itself a direct consequence of Stalin's assault on the villages, led to an enormous increase in homeless children, which in turn exacerbated the Soviet Union's crime and "hooliganism" problem. Rural "banditry" was also a persistent concern. These factors all combined to create the perception of unacceptably high levels of social disorder (Shearer 1998).

As noted earlier, even during the relatively non-coercive 1920s, the OGPU had deported "undesirable elements" from the capital city. However, social disorder deportations only became routine following a December 1932 decree requiring internal passports for all urban residents (Moins 1997; Hagenloh 1999). Issuance of these passports was intended to identify and remove all "socially dangerous elements" from the Soviet Union's major cities, beginning with Moscow, Leningrad, and Kharkov. The major targets were kulaks, various "former people" (nobles, landowners, Tsarist officials), and former White army officers, as well as parasites and anyone convicted of an extensive list of crimes. The list combined traditional "class" categories (representing a continuation of Sovietization) and new "social disorder" categories (criminals and parasites). Among the latter were also the Roma (Gypsies), who were removed from Moscow in 1933, although they were not at this time categorized as an enemy nation; in fact, there was a plan to form an autonomous territory for them. (Martin 1998a: 825–826). Since the 1933 deportations were still part of Stalin's aggressive Sovietization campaign, many of the deported were classified as special settlers. In the routine urban deportations that continued throughout the Stalin period, the deported would typically be categorized as "administratively exiled" (Hagenloh 2000). Social disorder categories would also figure in many other mass deportations, for instance, prostitutes were included alongside other class categories in the deportations from the newly acquired Western territories in 1940–1941 (Gur'ianov 1997a: 120; 1997b: 139).

Security Deportations and Soviet Ethnic Cleansing, 1930–1938

The Soviet Union was founded on an ideology of extreme class hostility. It is not surprising, then, that the state would execute, incarcerate, and exile large numbers of putative "class enemies," just as the Nazi racial state would do with its putative racial enemies. Nor perhaps is it surprising that after having achieved Sovietization, the regime would treat criminals and putative sources of social disorder as being anti-Soviet and so warranting "class" punishment. However, the emergence in the late 1930s of mass deportation based on ethnic identity alone—or as we now call it, ethnic cleansing—was indeed a surprising development (Martin 1998a). Ethnic cleansing is typically understood as resulting from an extreme pursuit of the otherwise orthodox modern goal of forming ethnically homogenous nation-states (Gellner 1983). Soviet ethnic cleansing, however, does not fit this model at all. Since ethnic deportations would have the greatest long-term consequences for the Soviet Union, a brief account here of their relationship to the Soviet nationalities policy and the patterns of ethnic migration is appropriate.

The Soviet Nationalities Policy

The Soviet Union was, in fact, a world pioneer in the practice of minority nation-building. In the early Soviet period, the state aggressively promoted non-Russian national identities through the formation of national territories, the creation of national elites, the promotion of national languages, and the support of various forms of symbolic national cultural expression. The goal of this policy was to prevent the emergence—or where it had already emerged, the exacerbation—of separatist nationalism, so that the Soviet state could pursue its primary goal of transforming the former Russian empire into a highly centralized socialist state. This inventive response to the problem of governing a modern multiethnic state has been termed an Affirmative Action Empire: affirmative action since the policy involved the systematic promotion of non-Russian individuals and non-Russian national identity; empire since the goal was to preserve the territorial integrity of the former Russian empire while dramatically increasing the power of the central state; empire also since the distinction between the "former great power" (Russian) and "former colonial" (non-Russian) nations was preserved but inverted, with Russians now being required to downplay their national self-expression in order to help preserve the unitary, multiethnic state (Martin 1996: 15–62).

Soviet nationalities policy was not static. In the period from 1933 to 1938, it underwent a fundamental revision (Martin 1996: 563–982). In response both to growing Russian resentment and to exaggerated fears of centrifugal "national communism" among its own non-Russian elites, the Soviet leadership determined that its Affirmative Action Empire strategy was not adequately serving the goal of promoting state unity. As a result, not only was traditional Russian national culture rehabilitated, but the Russians were now celebrated as the "first among equals" within the Soviet "family of nations." This status shift did not lead to a policy of russification, but it was accompanied by a marked reduction in the commitment to non-Russian nation-building. While central support for the creation of non-Russian national elites and non-Russian cultural expression continued, it was now accepted that the non-Russian republics would be bilingual and, in most cases, that Russian would be the working government language. Also, instead of the former policy of ethnic proliferation, in which even the smallest ethnic groups were granted full national privileges, a policy of ethnic consolidation was pursued, which aimed at the reduction of the number of officially recognized nationalities and accepted the eventual assimilation of territorially dispersed national minorities. Most significant for our purposes, there was an increased emphasis on the "Russianness" of the multinational RSFSR, which was now conceived of as a national home for the Russians (Martin 1998b). These revisions were symbolically codified in the new and ubiquitous trope of the Friendship of the Peoples, a metaphor which accommodated both the central role of the Russians (as elder brothers) and the continuing separate national identities of the non-Russians. This new paradigm would govern Soviet nationalities policy through the death of Stalin in 1953.

In order to understand Soviet ethnic deportations, which after 1933 became the major form of Stalinist forced relocation, one must also examine the linkage between domestic nationalities policy and Soviet foreign policy goals (Martin 1998a). Given the Soviet belief in the political salience of ethnicity, and the fact that the Soviet Union's borders cut through a number of ethnic groups (on both sides of the politically sensitive western border, there were Finns/Karelians, Belarusians, Ukrainians, Romanians/Moldovans), nationalities policy became intertwined with foreign policy. The Soviet leadership hoped that a generous policy toward these (and other) nationalities within the Soviet Union would attract their ethnic brethren in Poland, Finland, Romania, and elsewhere, which would in turn help undermine those states and so enable Soviet territorial expansion. Ukrainian Communists were particularly avid supporters of this strategy and often referred to Soviet Ukraine as a "Piedmont," which would serve as the center for the eventual unification of all Ukrainian lands. Borrowing this favorite Ukrainian metaphor, the Soviet endeavor to exploit cross-border ethnic ties to project influence abroad is here referred to as the Piedmont Principle. Of course, the Piedmont Principle could work in both directions. Soviet leaders recognized and worried that foreign states could also exploit cross-border ethnic ties to undermine Soviet authority.

Soviet Ethnic Migration Policy

Soviet nationalities policy naturally also intersected with the regulation of internal migration (Martin 1996: 463–562). In the early Soviet period, this linkage was expressed in a tendency—though never an overwhelmingly strong one—to support the consolidation of ethnic groups within their newly formed national territories. This could involve two processes: the "positive" movement of dispersed nationalities to their designated national territories; and the "negative" removal of non-titular nationalities from those same territories. The former process was much more common. For instance, territorially dispersed Jews, Roma (Gypsies), and Assyrians were resettled in compact groups so that they too could form their own national territories. Dispersed Germans, Poles, Karelians, and others were resettled into pre-existing national territories (Martin 1998a: 824–826). While these migrations were largely voluntary and in service of a positive, non-punitive goal, they did establish the important principle of using ethnicity as a criterion for resettlement.

The Soviet leadership was much less willing to sanction "negative" removal measures, since such forcible deportations violated its commitment to the formal equality (excluding affirmative action measures) of national minorities within both Russian and non-Russian national territories. Nevertheless, in the aftermath of the Civil War, two forcible expulsions were sanctioned as one-time decolonization measures. As noted earlier, the inhabitants of nine Terek Cossack towns were deported, partially as a negative Sovietization measure, but also partially as a positive measure to provide land for the indigenous mountain peoples (*gortsy*), who had been progressively driven out of the more fertile Caucasian foothills into the mountains under the Tsars (Bugai 1992b; Bugai and Gonev 1998: 81–100; Tsutsiev 1998: 47–50). A second, much more significant, decolonizing action involved the expulsion of Slavic settlers from southern Kazakhstan. In the last decades of Tsarist rule, as part of an intentionally russificatory colonization strategy, a large number of Slavic peasants had been settled on land traditionally utilized by Kazakh nomads (Demko 1969). These colonization measures created enormous ethnic tension, which exploded in the 1916 Kazakh uprising and again during the post-revolutionary Civil War. These conflicts resulted in a mass flight of Kazakhs and a further influx of Slavic settlers. In September 1920 the Soviet government decreed a set of reparations aimed at reconciling the local population, including the removal of illegal post-1916 Slavic settlers, the equalization of native and European landholdings, and the prohibition of future settlement. Carried out in 1921–1922 in an atmosphere of fierce ethnic hostility, in which the local Kazakh government took a strong anti-settler line, this "land reform" took on the character of a pogrom and resulted in the mass expulsion of an estimated 19.5 percent of Kazakhstan's Slavic population. Central authorities rebuked the local leadership for allowing this to occur and officially halted land reform and all expulsions in 1922. Nevertheless, despite stringent efforts, Slavic settlers continued to be driven off their land in Kazakhstan as late as 1927 (Martin 1996: 529–549; Genis 1998).

Initial Soviet ethnic migration policy, then, appeared to support the principle that control over the ethnic composition of national territories (and hence of ethnic migration flows) was a constituent part of the Soviet nationalities policy. After all, Soviet nationalities policy was explicitly conceived of, and advertised as, an anti-imperial decolonizing measure. Moreover, to the local population in regions of recent, heavy Slavic settlement—Kazakhstan, Kyrgyzstan, Bashkortostan, the North Caucasus, Buriat-Mongolia—decolonization did not mean promotion of the local language or culture, it meant control of agricultural land and the end of Russian colonization, if not the outright removal of the colonists themselves. After the initial chaos of the Civil War had ended, central authorities refused to sanction further expulsions and instead promoted the integration and equal rights of national minorities. This still left a crucial and highly contentious issue: Did non-Russian territories have a right to control internal Soviet migration into their regions? This issue would be fought out and decided in Kazakhstan, which had the largest and most attractive fund of land for colonization, the most severely aggravated ethnic relations in the Soviet Union, and a relatively strong Kazakh national communist leadership fiercely committed to a policy of decolonization. Central economic authorities insisted that agricultural settlement was a purely economic issue, and therefore should be determined by central authorities in keeping with the needs of the Soviet Union as a whole which, they argued, called for settlement. This dispute was hotly contested from 1922 to 1927, with local Kazakh authorities openly contesting colonization and covertly sabotaging it. Ultimately, in 1927, the recalcitrant Kazakh authorities were removed, and the republic was officially opened to centrally planned colonization (Martin 1996: 529–549). Kazakhstan would eventually become the most important dumping ground for Stalinist deportees.

This is a crucial and still largely unrecognized moment in the history of the Soviet Union as a multiethnic state. There has been an extensive scholarly debate over the ethnic pattern of internal Soviet migration, in particular the mass outflow of Russians into the non-Russian republics under Stalin, a debate which has centered on only two options: Either this migration was part of an intentional policy of russification, or it was the consequence of voluntary internal migration and the russificatory outcome can be explained by the size of the Russian population and its relatively high level of social mobilization (Lewis, Rowland, and Clem 1977; Kolstoe 1995; Saar and Titma 1992; Titma and Tuma 1992; Sakkeus 1993). If the debate is limited to these two options, the latter is much more convincing. Despite strong popular beliefs to the contrary, with the probable partial exception of Estonia and Latvia (Saar and Titma 1992; Titma and Tuma 1992), little evidence has emerged of a planned policy of russification through directed migration.

However, this debate is not particularly satisfactory, as already in the 1920s both central authorities and non-Russian elites recognized that an ethnically neutral internal migration policy would inevitably promote russification. The crucial question was whether Soviet "affirmative action" would be extended to migration policy. Once the decision had been made in 1927 to decouple migration and nationalities policy, the mass influx of Russians (and quickly russified Slavs) was inevitable. As Table 10.1 illustrates, the crucial increase of Russian representation took place during the forced industrialization of the 1930s, with a much more gradual increase in the 1940s and 1950s.

This development had very little to do with forced relocation policies, although it was certainly welcomed by the authorities and fostered in modest ways, for instance by guaranteeing that Russian-speakers could function perfectly well in most non-Russian republics without learning the native language (Simon 1991: 114–127). It was, rather, the combined result of comparatively greater Russian social mobilization (greater urbanization, education levels, social uprootedness), a vastly greater Russian population, the tendency of many non-Russians to russify when removed from their home republics, and the political decision not to allow the union republics to defend their ethnic majorities through control of migration. This decision created far more long-term ethnic problems for the former Soviet Union than the more dramatic and reprehensible acts of Stalinist forced relocation.

On the other hand, as Table 10.1 also indicates, as Russians underwent a demographic shift to low fertility and the Soviet Union's "eastern"

TABLE 10.1   Percentage of Russians in Non-Russian Republics, 1926–1989

Republic	1926	1939	1959	1970	1979	1989
Ukraine	8.6	10.4	16.9	19.4	21.1	22.1
Belarus	4.9	4.3	8.2	10.4	11.9	13.2
Estonia	3.5	4.5	20.1	24.7	27.9	30.3
Latvia	8.0	9.0	26.6	29.8	32.8	34.0
Lithuania	2.6	2.6	8.5	8.6	8.9	9.4
Moldova	8.2	7.7	10.1	11.6	12.8	13.0
Georgia	3.6	8.7	10.1	8.5	7.4	6.3
Armenia	2.3	4.0	3.2	2.7	2.3	1.6
Azerbaijan	9.6	16.5	13.6	10.0	7.9	5.6
Kazakhstan	21.2	40.3	42.7	42.4	40.8	37.8
Uzbekistan	5.2	11.5	13.5	12.5	10.8	8.3
Turkmenistan	7.4	18.6	17.3	14.5	12.6	9.5
Tajikistan	0.6	9.1	13.3	11.9	10.4	7.6
Kyrgyzstan	11.6	20.8	30.2	29.2	25.9	21.5

Source: Kaiser 1994: 118, 174.

nationalities entered a period of high fertility, the percentage of Russians began to decline quite rapidly in the three Transcaucasian republics (Georgia, Armenia, Azerbaijan) and the five Central Asian republics (Kazakhstan, Kyrgyzstan, Uzbekistan, Turkmenistan, Tajikistan), while it continued to grow in the six other western republics. This decline in the eastern republics was only partly explained by comparative fertility. It also reflected an actual absolute outflow of Russians that began in the 1970s in Transcaucasia and in the 1980s in Central Asia. This development quite strongly suggests that in the Brezhnev period the regime did not have control of migration patterns, since this outcome was from their perspective quite undesirable.

Ethnic Cleansing

Even if forced relocation was not the major factor driving the transformation of the Soviet Union's ethnic geography, Soviet ethnic cleansing would gradually shape subjective perceptions of the Soviet state, despite its minority nation-building policies, as fundamentally anti-national and imperial in essence, which would in turn have an important long-term impact in lessening the viability of the multi-national state (Beissinger 1995). Soviet ethnic deportations had their origin in the class-based dekulakization operation. Many Soviet diaspora nationalities—Germans, Finns, Poles, Latvians, Czechs, Greeks, and others—responded to Soviet collectivization with emigration movements aimed at leaving the Soviet Union for their "home" countries, despite the fact that most were Soviet citizens whose forebears had resided in the Russian empire for a century or more (Martin 1998a: 836–842). This action raised Soviet concerns that the Piedmont Principle was now working against them, and that their diaspora nationalities were potentially disloyal and so a security risk. The result was the first Soviet deportation specifically targeting an ethnic group. In March 1930, in the aftermath of a mass uprising along the Ukrainian-Polish border involving over a hundred thousand peasants, the Soviet Politburo ordered the deportation of 65,000 to 100,000 kulaks from the border regions of Belarus and Ukraine with the stipulation, "in the first line, those of Polish nationality."[7] This action can legitimately be considered the first Soviet Security deportation, since the decree specifically expressed fear of Polish intervention and singled out the Soviet Union's border regions, even though it was obviously also part of the larger Sovietization campaign. A second Security deportation, involving the removal of some Koreans from the Soviet border with Japanese-occupied Korea, was authorized in 1930, but later abandoned (Martin 1998a: 841–842). Nevertheless, the transition from Sovietization to Security deportations had begun.

The year 1933 marked a pivotal moment in this transition. In addition to the passportization deportations of that year, there was a renewed deportation of "kulaks" tied to the famine and grain requisitions crisis of that year. Among the deported "kulaks" were three entire Kuban Cossack towns and an estimated sixty thousand individual Cossacks (Martin 1996: 627–632). As with the passportization deportations, this action was partially the tail end of the "class-based" Sovietization campaign. However, the Kuban Cossacks were also considered ethnic Ukrainians by the regime, and their deportation was one of the first blows struck in a 1933 terror campaign against "Ukrainian nationalists" that was associated explicitly with fear of Ukrainian separatism and potential German efforts to exploit it. The year 1933, then, marked a transition from Sovietization to Security and Social Disorder deportations.

By 1935 Security deportations had emerged as the major category of Stalinist forced relocation. In the spring of 1935, as part of a series of measures to strengthen the Soviet Union's western border regions, "unreliable elements" were deported from the entire stretch of the Soviet western border, from the Baltic to the Black Sea. Of the fifty to sixty thousand individuals deported, over half were the now stigmatized diaspora nationalities: Poles, Germans, Finns, Estonians, Latvians. A second wave of deportations in the fall of 1935 and spring of 1936, amounting to perhaps seventy thousand individuals, now exclusively targeted these diaspora nationalities, who were exiled to Siberia and Kazakhstan. These were still, however, partial deportations. Approximately half of Ukraine's Poles and Germans, and 30 percent of Leningrad's Finns, were deported in 1935–1936 (Martin 1998a; Gelb 1996; Matley 1979). In 1937, the "cleansing" of the Soviet Union's border regions continued. Along the Transcaucasian border with Iran, Kurds and Iranians were deported (Bugai 1995: 17, 26). Finally, in the Far East, Chinese and Koreans were targeted, beginning in

August 1937 as another partial ethnic deportation, but within a month expanding into a total removal of all 172,000 Koreans in the Far East to Kazakhstan and Uzbekistan (Khe and Un 1992). With the Korean deportation, the concept of the enemy nation had fully emerged. During the Great Terror of 1937–1938, not only were the enemy diaspora nations subjected to deportation from the Soviet border regions, they were also targeted for arrest and execution throughout the entire Soviet Union (Petrov and Roginskii 1997; Martin 1998a; Okhotin and Roginskii 1999).

The Newly Acquired Territories, 1939–1941, 1944–1952: Sovietization and Security

As a result of the August 1939 Nazi-Soviet pact and subsequent military actions by Nazi and Soviet troops, in 1939–1940 the Soviet Union suddenly acquired a large swath of territory along its entire western border populated by over fifteen million non-Russians: the majority Ukrainian and Belarusian regions of Poland; the three Baltic states of Estonia, Latvia, and Lithuania; the Romanian provinces of Moldova (with a Romanian majority) and Bukovina (with a Ukrainian majority); and a small portion of Finland. This confronted the Soviet leadership with two major and apparently conflicting problems, security and Sovietization. Sovietization measures would inevitably lead to massive popular discontent in the short term (even the regime accepted this as a fact) which, given the immediacy of the security threat from Germany, might have seemed intolerable to the Soviet leadership. In fact, it did not. Instead, the Soviets went forward with an extraordinarily rapid Sovietization drive, which appears to have reflected their belief that Sovietization and security were inseparable.

The focus here will be on the pre-war Soviet occupation of western Ukraine and Belarus, since these regions were occupied a year earlier and therefore experienced a more severe Sovietization process.[8] As usual, arrest and deportation were employed in tandem. Arrests began immediately upon the arrival of Soviet troops in September 1939 and continued up until the German invasion in June 1941. In total, approximately 108,000 individuals were arrested, or just under 1 percent of the entire population. These arrests targeted exactly those population categories that had been the principal focus of Soviet terror during the Russian Civil War, the "former people": nobles and other privileged estates, large property holders, officials, officers, police, and so forth (Gorlanov and Roginskii 1997). Ethnic Poles were disproportionately affected by these arrests, but this is probably only marginally due to Soviet hostility to ethnic Poles (although this did exist), and instead can best be explained by the fact that the inter-war Polish regime was a nationalizing state which systematically gave preferences to ethnic Poles, who therefore represented a disproportionate number of Poland's "former people."

Deportation affected approximately three times as many individuals as did incarceration.[9] In a series of four deportations carried out in February, April, and June–July 1940, as well as May–June 1941, approximately 320,000 individuals were deported (Gur'ianov 1997a, 1997b). These deportations differed radically from the 1930–1933 dekulakization. They were well-planned; the NKVD controlled all details; those to be deported were identified by the NKVD in advance; the operations took place with great rapidity (typically in a single day); and resistance was minimal and ineffective. All of this would be true of all future Soviet mass deportations. The February 1940 deportation targeted *osadniki* (veterans of Pilsudski's legions granted land allotments in Poland's eastern regions as a colonization measure) and *lesniki* (members of the local forest watch), both being politically identified with the old regime. These were less dangerous second-order "former people," who could be removed prophylactically through deportation to the special settlements without any special individualizing attention. They were, again, almost all ethnic Poles.

The April 1940 deportation targeted the family members of those arrested so far, mostly Poland's "former people," who were likewise disproportionately ethnic Poles, but included some Ukrainians, Belarusians, and Jews. Prostitutes were also included in this deportation as a Social Disorder category. This contingent was considered less socially dangerous and so placed in the "administratively exiled" category. The June 1940 deportation targeted illegal refugees from Germany's occupation zone, here clearly a Security rather than Sovietization measure. Naturally the majority of these refugees were Jews, and were sent to the special settlements. Finally, the May–June 1941 deportations again targeted family members, this time those of active, arrested, or executed underground nationalists, predominately members of the Organization of Ukrainian Nationalists. This contingent, along with those deported from the Baltics and Moldova at the same time, were for some reason categorized as exiled settlers. In total, about 438,000 individuals (over 3 percent of the total population) were arrested or deported in nineteen months, an extraordinarily high rate of repression, explained by the fact that Sovietization and Security measures which took much longer in the Soviet Union proper were here telescoped into nineteen months.

The end of the Second World War left the Soviet leadership facing a perhaps even more severe Sovietization problem than they had faced in 1939–1941, given the development of full-scale partisan nationalist armies in Ukraine and Lithuania, although obviously the Soviet Union now enjoyed a vastly improved international security position. In discussing post-war Sovietization, the focus will be on forced relocation policies in the three Baltic states (Zemskov 1993; Vitovskii and Iampol'skii 1990; Bugai 1995: 221–250). There were two main deportation categories in the period from 1944 to 1952. First, beginning with the arrival of Soviet troops, there were deportations of active members of the Lithuanian partisan army ("bandits") and their families, as well as the families of active, arrested, or executed nationalist fighters. From 1945 to 1948, in four separate operations, 49,000 Lithuanians in this category were deported. In 1949, during the larger dekulakization operation, there were further deportations of family members (they are included in the general "kulak" total). Finally, in late 1951 and early 1952, another 18,000 Lithuanians were deported (Zemskov 1993: 4–5). These deportations were not only unambiguously a part of the post-war Sovietization campaign in the Baltic states, but also a direct component of the fierce military action against, in particular, the tenacious Lithuanian underground army. An even fiercer struggle was waged in Ukraine (Burds 1997), where from 1944 to 1948, 114,000 members of the Organization of Ukrainian Nationalists and their families were deported (Bilas 1994b: 545–546).

The second major category was "kulaks." In 1949, collectivization began in earnest in the newly acquired territories and was again accompanied by dekulakization. A total of 93,000 "kulaks" (Estonia 20,000; Latvia 40,000; Lithuania 33,000) were deported from the Baltic states, almost 2.5 percent of the total population in a matter of days, as opposed to 1.5 percent of the population over three years in the 1930–1933 dekulakization campaign (Zemskov 1993: 5). In Moldova, 36,000 "kulaks" were likewise deported over a two-day period (Passat 1994: 341–557). Oddly, there do not appear to have been major mass dekulakization deportations in western Ukraine and Belarus (unless the anti-banditry deportations effectively served this purpose). Bugai reports only 1,100 "kulaks" deported from Izmail'skaia Oblast of western Ukraine in 1948, 5,600 from western Ukraine and Belarus in 1951, and another 5,600 from western Belarus in 1952 (Bugai 1992a: 186–187; 1995: 234, 249). This would represent just over a tenth of 1 percent of the population, whereas the "banditry" deportations involved almost 2 percent of the total population.

In total, then, approximately 160,000 individuals were deported from the three Baltic republics, a region with a population of about four million. If we add an estimated 96,000 prisoners (Zemskov 1993: 9–10), the post-war Sovietization operation incarcerated or exiled over 6 percent of the population. Although these deportations targeted class, religious, and political categories, not explicitly national ones, they were nevertheless perceived in national terms by the local populations. As we shall see, the categorization of the Baltic deportees in exile gives some reason to believe this assessment was not without merit.

International Population "Exchange," 1944–1947: Security and Ethnic Consolidation

Germany's defeat in the Second World War led to the expulsion of over ten million Germans from Czechoslovakia, Poland, and from German territory that was to be transferred to Poland and the Soviet Union. The expulsion of the Germans began spontaneously and then was ratified by international convention at the Potsdam Conference (Ziemer 1973; Schechtman 1962). In the East, the Soviet Union likewise sponsored a large-scale population "exchange" between its Republic of Ukraine and the new communist Polish state. In September 1944 the Communist-dominated Polish Lublin Committee and the Ukrainian government signed an agreement authorizing a putatively voluntary exchange (in practice, there was much coercion) of the Polish population lying to the east of the Curzon Line (the new border) and the Ukrainian population (as well as a small Belarusian and Russian population) lying to the west. Ultimately 490,000 Ukrainians were resettled from Poland into Ukraine, and 810,000 Poles from the Soviet Union into Poland (Kordan 1997; Slyvka 1996: 294–647). The 139,000 Polish Ukrainians who had not been relocated by 1947 were then rounded up and deported to north-west Poland (Kordan 1997: 712–717; Misilo 1993). There was also a much smaller exchange of Soviet Czechs and Slovaks for Czechoslovakia's Ukrainians, largely voluntary, as Czechoslovakia was not yet communist. The majority of Soviet Czechs and Slovaks emigrated, while only 4,500 of Czechoslovakia's 91,000 Ukrainians moved (Schechtman 1962: 43–49). These exchanges are particularly interesting, as while they clearly served the goal of ethnic consolidation (as well as security by removing OUN's cross-border Ukrainian base in eastern Poland), none of them involved Russians. The Soviet Union was acting as a kind of internationalist ethnic cleanser, furthering the ethnic homogeneity of its own republics and of its new communist neighbors.

Wartime Deportations and After, 1941–1953: Security? Social Disorder? Russification? Retribution?

The largest Soviet ethnic deportations all took place during the Second World War and in its immediate aftermath. These deportations can be divided into two categories. First, seven entire Soviet nations, each with its own official national territory, were deported during the war for alleged widespread collaboration with the enemy: the Soviet Germans (1941–1942: 1,200,000), the Kalmyks (1943: 90,000), the Karachai (1943: 70,000), the Chechens (1944: 390,000), the Ingush (1944: 90,000), the Balkars (1944: 40,000), and the Crimean Tatars (1944: 180,000). Second, there were a number of small, scattered minority populations who were likewise subjected to deportation: in 1942 the Leningrad Ingrian Finnish community (9,000) was deported; in July 1944, 47,000 individuals comprising three small populations (the Meskhetian Turks, Kurds and Khemshils—Islamicized Armenians) were deported from the Georgian-Turkish border; shortly after the deportation of the Crimean Tatars the entire Greek, Bulgarian, and Armenian populations of the Crimea (4,000) were likewise exiled. Similarly, Greeks were also deported from the Black Sea region of Krasnodar and from the Transcaucasus. In addition, there were a number of deportations of foreign citizens (Bugai 1995).[10]

There are four potential explanations for this wave of deportations: Security, Social Disorder, Russification and Retribution. Several of these deportations quite closely resemble the pre-war Security deportations of ethnic groups from the border regions (Nekrich 1978: 104). This was particularly true of the removal of diaspora minorities (Bulgarians, Greeks, Armenians) from Crimea, the Black Sea region, and the Transcaucasus. Likewise, given the looming possibility of conflict with Turkey in the aftermath of the Second World War, it is not surprising that the Meskhetian Turks and other Islamic peoples would be removed from the Turkish border. Indeed, in justifying this deportation, Lavrentii Beria specifically cited "the cross-border family ties with residents of Turkey, the appearance of a desire to emigrate [to Turkey], participation in guerilla uprisings and espionage" (Bugai 1995: 176). The formal decree authorizing the deportation of the Crimean Tatars likewise spoke of the "undesirability of the further residence of the Crimean Tatars in a border region of the USSR"(Bugai 1995: 150). The deportation of the Volga Germans has also been widely interpreted as a Security deportation motivated by Soviet fears that they would side with the invading German armies. However, when we turn to the five North Caucasus peoples, who resided quite far from the Turkish border and who were all unambiguously "indigenous" Soviet nationalities, the security explanation becomes altogether tenuous.[11]

When one examines the deportation of the Ingush and, above all, Chechens, social disorder appears as a likely contributing factor. While the official decrees explaining these deportations emphasized treason during the war, internal discussion of the Chechen deportation placed a great deal of emphasis on the intractable problem of "banditism" in the Chechen mountains (Bugai 1994a: 28–29, 37, 45–46). In fact, one Chechen band and its leader, according to an NKVD report, was active for the entire period from 1920 to 1939 (Bugai 1994a: 28). The mountainous regions of Chechnya had still not been collectivized on the eve of the war; there had been major anti-Soviet uprisings in Chechnya and Ingushetia in 1930, and again in Chechnya in 1932 and even 1938 (Ivnitskii 1996: 156–158; Martin 1996: 607–608).

Leaving aside these more dramatic forms of social disorder, it is also the case that Soviet indigenization policies, the attempt to form a Sovietized native elite to run the national republics, failed impressively in the North Caucasus, with the striking exceptions of North Ossetia and, to a lesser degree, Dagestan (Martin 1996: 287–302; Tsutsiev 1998: 50–63). These were the two main republics not subjected to deportation. In short, social disorder, and to a degree even the failure of Sovietization, can legitimately be seen as a contributing factor in the North Caucasus deportations.

Third, there is a sense in which several of these deportations, and these alone, might have been intended to serve a russificatory purpose. Beginning in the mid-1930s, with the rehabilitation of Russian culture, there was also a pronounced policy shift aimed at raising the status and

"Russianness" of the Russian Federal Republic and establishing it as more of a Russian homeland than it previously had been (Martin 1998b). To that end, national minorities living in Russian regions (that is, not in the RSFSR's autonomous republics and oblasts) had their small national territories abolished and their national schools closed, and were expected eventually to assimilate with the Russian majority. At the time of the abolition of these small national territories in 1938, the leadership of the Crimean Republic even suggested that Crimean Tatar national districts in their republic should be abolished as well, an astounding suggestion at a time when the Crimean Tatars were the official indigenous nationality justifying the Crimean Republic's existence (Martin 1996: 788). It was, in effect, a proposal to abolish the Crimean Republic. While this proposal was rejected at the time as too radical (even the Volga German Republic was not abolished until 1941), it was taken up again in 1944 with a vengeance not only in Crimea, but in the North Caucasus as well. These regions were all resettled primarily, though not exclusively, with Russians, and to that extent they extended the Russification of the RSFSR southward.

Finally, there is the problematic category of retribution or simply punishment. The official explanation was that the deported peoples had behaved treasonously during the German advance into the North Caucasus in 1942 and during the occupation of Crimea, and were being punished accordingly (Bugai 1995). Nekrich (1978: 108) has examined this argument most thoroughly, and while he vehemently denies the charge of treason, he likewise presents compelling evidence that the charge may well have been convincing to many contemporaries, partially because it confirmed pre-existing historical stereotypes stemming from the long Tsarist campaigns to conquer the Crimea and North Caucasus. After all, these were not the first deportations from the Crimea and North Caucasus: the conquest of those regions in the eighteenth and nineteenth centuries had been followed by mass coerced migration to the Ottoman Empire (Fisher 1987).

Resettlement

Deportation is only one half of forced relocation. In order for such relocation to be permanent, it must typically be complemented by a successful resettlement policy. Ideally, we would now examine Stalinist resettlement policies as intensively as Stalinist deportation. Unfortunately, this is not possible, as there simply has not been enough scholarship or published documentation devoted to this issue. Two available case studies do, however, illustrate both the differing resettlement strategies that accompanied different types of deportation, and the great difficulty not only of finding settlers but of getting them to stay, once settled (Martin 1996; Bugai 1994a). From 1929 to 1938, the Soviet regime's preferred strategy for settling its most sensitive border regions, whose populations were being thinned by repeated deportations of "unreliable elements," was the formation of "Red Army collective farms" (Martin 1996: 740–744). With the exception of a failed attempt to form a "Special Collective Farm Corpus" in the Far East, these collective farms were composed, not of active members of the Soviet armed forces, but rather of recently demobilized Red Army soldiers.

Earlier we noted that the removal of suspect ethnic groups from the Soviet border regions stemmed not from a russificatory impulse but rather from a more general security concern. The same was true of the Red Army resettlement strategy. There is no evidence that ethnic Russians were preferred settlers; indeed, the only evident screening by nationality was the insistence on ethnic Karelian and Jewish soldiers for the Red Army settlements in the Karelian ASSR and the Birobidzhan Jewish region (Martin 1996: 742). The Red Army collective farm strategy appears to have been adopted for two main reasons: first, for security reasons, the regime wanted trained soldiers near the borders in case of a need for rapid mobilization; second, after collectivization, it became extremely difficult to recruit agricultural settlers, since land had become worthless to individuals and therefore the risk associated with resettlement pointless. It was much easier to recruit settlers out of the Red Army, where they had been trained to obey orders; in fact, Red Army settlement was at best semi-voluntary. As a result of this coercion, however, Red Army settlement was also vulnerable to very high rates of desertion, which again and again led to the failure to fulfil resettlement quotas (Martin 1996: 740–744).

The situation in Chechno-Ingushetia was quite different. There, as argued earlier, a russificatory impulse was indeed present, although it was by no means the only factor in play. After the mass deportation of the Chechens and Ingush, the republic was divided into five parts, presumably to help eliminate the memory of the former republic (Bugai 1994a: 76–77; Tsutsiev 1998: 63–80). Three small portions went to the three neighboring non-Russian republics of North Ossetia, Dagestan, and Georgia. These sections were resettled quite quickly with natives from those republics, as the respective republican elites were eager to claim and nationalize the new territory (Bugai 1994a: 112–113). The northern part of the republic went to a neighboring Russian region and the center was renamed Grozny Province, after the capital city. This part was resettled with Russians, initially with surprising speed. Within four months of the deportation, the 32,110 families that had been deported from what now made up Grozny Province had been replaced by 12,692 families (Bugai 1994a: 84). However, by 1952 that total had increased to only 14,000, or 42 percent of the pre-deportation total. Again, it proved difficult to keep settlers in place. Of 6,151 families settled in Grozny Province from 1945 to 1950, only 66.2 percent remained in 1952 (Bugai 1994a: 112–113). A similar pattern characterized the resettlement of the Volga German Republic (Bugai 1999). Settlement from the adjacent national republics proved much more successful and durable. Indeed, its durability would prove to be one of the most important unintended consequences of the Stalinist forced relocation project.

The Ethnicization of Exile

As the preceding historical narrative of Stalinist forced relocation has demonstrated, ethnic deportations represented only a part, albeit a growing part, of the practice of Stalinist deportation. In fact, well over half of the individuals deported, including the majority from the newly acquired western territories, were resettled as part of class-based Sovietization deportations. Nevertheless, the regime's attitude toward its ethnic deportees was strikingly different from that toward the earlier group. Indeed, there was not only a trend toward ethnic deportations, but also an increasing ethnicization of the existing special settler population. From the moment of their initial exile, deported kulaks were able to flee their settlements without great difficulty. Although 2.1 million kulaks had been deported by 1933, only 1.1 million remained in the special settlements. Between 1932 and 1940, there were 629,000 successful instances of kulak flight from the special settlements, slightly over half the total population. Obviously, the regime was not wholeheartedly committed to keeping the kulaks in the special settlements. In 1938, children reaching 16 years of age, "if they had no marks against them," were freed; by 1940, this already represented 77,000 individuals (Zemskov 1994: 129). In April 1942, special settlers began to be drafted into the army en masse, so that by the end of the war only 600,000 remained in the settlements (Zemskov 1994: 131–132). After the war, the regions were given permission to free their kulak contingents; by 1949 only 130,000 remained in the special settlements. Two months before Stalin's death that number was just under 25,000 (Zemskov 1994: 129–142).

This number, it is important to note, did not include those former "kulaks" who began to be deported from the newly acquired western territories in 1949. They were treated completely differently, since they were categorized as ethnic rather than class deportees. From the beginning, escape by ethnically defined special settlers was treated much more seriously. While many attempted to escape, most were eventually caught and returned. Those who did escape were of sufficient concern to the regime to prompt the draconian decree of 26 November 1948, which stated, first, that for deportees exiled according to ethnicity or those from the western territories, exile was eternal; second, for those consigned to eternal exile, the punishment for attempted escape would henceforth be twenty years' hard labor in a "hard regime" concentration camp, and that free citizens helping a runaway were to get five years in a camp (Zemskov 1990b: 9). Nothing remotely similar had been applied to the original kulak contingent. Strikingly, all of the deportees from the newly acquired western territories, regardless of why they had been originally deported, were included in the eternally exiled category. In this way, the Sovietization deportees were ethnicized, and by the time of Stalin's death, the special settler population was almost entirely ethnic.

It is quite striking to compare the fate of the ethnic contingents with another that emerged at the same time. Approximately 130,000 "Vlasovites" (a category that included not only those who served in General Vlasov's Russian Liberation Army and fought alongside the Nazis, but also members of the many Nazi-formed non-Russian legions and the Nazi local police forces in occupied Soviet territory) were given a six-year sentence as special settlers, to be served in heavy industry (Bugai 1995: 221–224; Polian 1996). Although the Vlasovites were all, in the regime's eyes, individually guilty of serving alongside the Nazis and fighting against the Red Army, and therefore might have been expected to receive particularly harsh treatment, they were regularly released after serving a six-year term, unless they were also from a stigmatized ethnic category, in which case they were exiled to the special settlements "for eternity." This pattern points to the instrumental fashion in which deportation could be deployed. Vlasovites, like kulaks, were not a long-term threat, as they were not territorially based and after they had been isolated and intimidated they could be freed on the assumption they would be quickly assimilated into whatever environment they entered (although this is not to suggest that they were not viewed with great suspicion and often kept under surveillance). The ethnic deportees, on the other hand, would inevitably return to their home region, where their presence would create an awkward political fact, given the abolition of their national territories; in the case of the western territories, they might exacerbate a dangerous nationalist threat. Once an entire national category was deported, the prophylactic measure became eternal.

The Consequences of Stalinist Forced Relocation

The major short-term consequence of Stalinist forced relocation, the complications created by ethnic deportations, has already been noted. As a policy, deportation provided the Stalinist state with a certain flexibility. A population category deemed threatening at one point could be prophylactically neutralized and later set free without immense complication. This was done with the former kulaks and Vlasovites. However, when an entire ethnic group had been deported, its national territory abolished and resettled, this was no longer possible without restoring the abolished national territory, a step Stalin would surely have been unwilling to consider. Otherwise, the freeing of a given nationality would almost certainly lead to their return to their homeland and political conflict with the new settlers. This meant the creation of a permanent population of several million state "serfs." The Stalinist system was apparently capable of bearing this burden, but it nevertheless did cause considerable strain, both in the pressure on the political police to prevent escape and to hunt down fugitives, and in the rather high level of ethnic conflict between deportees and locals in the places of exile (Kozlov 1999: 99–104).

In looking at the medium-term consequences (from the death of Stalin to Gorbachev's reforms), it becomes evident that the Stalinist system of forced relocation was unviable. Within a year of Stalin's death, before any contender for the succession had concentrated power in his hands, the system of forced exile was already collapsing (Zemskov 1991a). Three years after Stalin's death, Khrushchev denounced his ethnic deportations, and within another few years the majority of deportees had returned home to their re-established republics. Given that almost all communist systems witness a moderate reform period after the death of the leader who engineered the country's transformation, this strongly suggests that the Stalinist system of mass deportation and exile was not robust (in contrast to, say, the system of collectivization or state ownership of industry). As to the return of the exiles, this proved surprisingly smooth. There were some serious ethnic incidents in Chechnya and the formerly Ingushetian regions of North Ossetia (where the boundary change in favor of North Ossetia was not amended), but considering the massive population flows involved and the potential for settler-deportee conflict, these were surprisingly limited (Kozlov 1999: 99–154; Tsutsiev 1998: 80–81).

Khrushchev's error, one that he bequeathed to Brezhnev, was his failure fully to rehabilitate all the "punished peoples." Four deported nations—the Crimean Tatars, Meskhetian Turks, Germans, and Koreans—were not allowed to return to their historic homelands. The Crimean Tatars responded to this felt injustice with a mass campaign that involved almost the entire Tatar population. They produced petitions with over a hundred thousand signatures, held mass demonstrations, and made connections with Moscow human rights activists and through them with western journalists, a disaster from the Soviet perspective. In a society in which open political dissent was exceptionally rare, the Crimean Tatars represented its largest single reservoir (Kreindler 1985; Fisher 1978). The Meskhetian Turks were less active, but nevertheless also managed to keep a consistent public profile (Kreindler 1985; Bugai 1994b). Despite being an exceptionally large population, the Germans were much more passive, largely abandoning the cause of restoring their Volga German Republic, their activists eventually settling on emigration to Germany as the most popular cause (Kreindler 1985). The Koreans were utterly quiescent, so that foreigners regularly failed to list them as one of the punished peoples. Here one sees a striking example of the institutionalization of the principle that diaspora nationalities lack the same status as indigenous nationalities. Germans and Koreans received this message through foreigners (especially from West Germany, which granted Germans the right of return), from their own government (which refused to restore their national territories), and from their fellow citizens. They responded accordingly and did not demand as insistently the restoration of their national territories.

The long-term consequences of Stalinist forced relocation for the current crisis in the former Soviet Union are not negligible, but they are likewise not as significant as often asserted. With the notable exception of Chechnya, most of the major conflicts do not involve the punished peoples, and the non-ethnic forced relocations are scarcely remembered. The 1989 attacks on the Meskhetian Turks in the Fergana Valley and their subsequent dispersion throughout Russia clearly would not have occurred without the deportations, but the Meskhetian issue is now a minor one (Bugai 1994b); on the contrary, the first Chechen war (1994–1996) and its sequel beginning in 1999 are clearly not minor. It would be easy to attribute this conflict to the deportation, but this assertion is quite problematic. The Chechens are the only "punished people" to develop a serious separatist movement. They have also historically been by far the most rebellious of Russia's current national minorities (Lieven 1998; Dunlop 1998). An equally strong argument could be made that Chechen resistance would be stronger if they had not suffered the demographic losses associated with the deportation. It is probably best to withhold judgement on this issue.

A much more plausible candidate for a serious long-term consequences was the violent 1992 clash between Ossetians and Ingush in North Ossetia's Prigorodnyi District, the territory abutting Vladikavkaz that had belonged to Ingushetia prior to the Ingush deportation. These clashes led to a second expulsion of most of the region's Ingush population, and this issue remains unresolved (Human Rights Watch 1996; Tsutsiev 1998). If we take a longer perspective, however, the 1944 deportations are not the origin, but the mid-point, of this territorial conflict. Prior to the Russian conquest, it appears that the territory was primarily settled by Ingush tribes with a small Ossetine minority, but their identities were completely prenational. After the Russian conquest, the inhabitants of this region were expelled to make room for the settlements of the Sunzha line of Terek Cossacks. In 1920, as we noted earlier, these Cossacks were deported and the territory granted to the Ingush, who were in turn deported in 1944 and the territory given to North Ossetia. With the return of the Ingush in 1957–1958, the territory remained with North Ossetia but Ingush were allowed, with some difficulty, to settle there, where they remained as a minority until the latest round of ethnic cleansing (Tsutsiev 1998). The 1944 deportation, then, clearly played a role in the current conflict, but hardly an exclusive one.

Perhaps the most important single long-term consequence of the Stalinist ethnic deportations was perceptual. Beissinger (1995) argues persuasively that the question of whether the Soviet Union was an empire or not is a vain one, but the fact that it was increasingly perceived to be an empire by outsiders and its own population was crucial; in the modern world, it is assumed that empires will collapse. The Stalinist "punished peoples" were small nationalities, and they did not decide the fate of the Soviet Union in 1991. However, their plight was widely publicized during the Gorbachev period (and abroad during the Brezhnev period), and perhaps nothing the Soviet Union ever did made it look more imperial than the deportation of the entire population of numerous small nations and the subsequent failure to allow the return of several of them. This was certainly not the cause of the collapse of the Soviet Union, but it undoubtedly ought to be considered a contributing factor.

Conclusions

The history of Stalinist forced relocation policies suggests the following tentative conclusions. First, internal forced relocation (that is, within the boundaries of a state) is not particularly robust in the long term. Within several years of Stalin's death, the majority of exiles had been freed and allowed to return to their homes. Others have returned in the past decade. Indeed, one of the main current obstacles to return is the formation of international boundaries between the exiles and their home territories (Crimean Tatars, Meskhetian Turks). Second, diaspora nationalities form an exception to this rule. The pervasiveness and depth of the nation-state ideal worldwide (even when it is superficially denied) gives an emotional priority to the claims of "indigenous" nationalities to "their" territory and a secondary priority to diaspora nations, who have another "home" territory. Soviet Germans were told this by the international community (which promoted their emigration to West Germany), by their home country (which refused to rehabilitate them), and by their fellow citizens. Third, international forced relocation (that is, beyond the boundaries of the state) is very robust. The return of Poles to Ukraine and Ukrainians to Poland is not on anyone's agenda; indeed, the formation of a clear ethnic boundary has apparently resolved a century-old ethnic conflict (Kordan 1997). Fourth, voluntary migration in a multiethnic state is more consequential than forced migration. The central fact in the former Soviet Union is the Russian diaspora, which was not the consequence of forced migration. Fifth, perceptions matter. The Stalinist ethnic deportations were an important factor contributing to the subjective perception of the Soviet Union as an empire, and that subjective perception was crucial to the collapse of the Soviet Union.

Notes

1. If one includes its actions in occupied territory, Nazi Germany forcibly relocated more people than the Soviet Union did under Stalin. It would be surprising if Maoist China did not do the same, given China's larger population and similar policies. There were, in fact, more Germans (eleven to twelve million) expelled from eastern Europe after the Second World War than there were people deported within the Soviet Union under Stalin.

2. The only year in which I have been unable to document such a mass deportation is 1934, but I strongly suspect that mass deportations of kulaks from national regions such as the North Caucasus, Transcaucasus, and Central Asia took place in that year. Official OGPU/NKVD statistics registered the arrival of 24,196 "former kulaks," a category which then included both those exiled as kulaks and those exiled as part of the passportization campaigns in the cities and border regions. (Zemskov 1994: 124).

3. GARF (Gosudarstvennyi arkhiv rossiiskoi federatsii) fond 374, opis' 27, delo107, 1119.

4. The two mass operations of the Great Terror—the operation targeting "former kulaks and other anti-Soviet elements" (NKVD *prikaz* 00447) and the national operations targeting diaspora nationalities (NKVD *prikaz* 00485 and subsequent decrees modeled on it)—also involved dividing the targeted population into two categories: the first, to be executed; the second, to be incarcerated in concentration camps. This clearly resembled dekulakization and was presumably modeled on it. It is certainly true that the Great Terror was so massive and arrests so categoric that it resembled Soviet mass deportations more than any other Soviet arrest campaign. This was particularly true of the national operations that were carried out by the *"albom* method" (lists of victims compiled locally and sent to the central NKVD authorities for approval), which did not even require the assembly of compromising materials on an individual. However, I am aware of no case in which an attempt was made to arrest all members of a targeted category, nor is it at all clear that the division into first- and second-category was anything but quite random. In the national operations, the NKVD asked not only "Who are you?" and "What have you done?", but also "Where do you live and work?" (Petrov and Roginskii 1997; Okhotin and Roginskii 1999).

5. There was also often a very large prison population, but these individuals were typically awaiting sentencing or being held until they could be tried and sent off to serve their time in a camp or colony. There was also a system of non-custodial "corrective work," which was in many ways a less severe form of confinement than the "special settlements" (Getty, Rittersporn, and Zemskov 1993: 1020).

6. GARF fond 9401, opis' 12, delo249 (01.06.39): 394–409.

7. RTsKhIDNI (Rossiiskii tsentr khraneniia i izucheniia dokumentov noveishei istorii) fond 17, opis' 162, delo8 (05.03.30): protokol 119, punkt 5.

8. In Moldova and the Baltic states, the first deportations took place only on the brink of war in May–June 1941. For the Moldovan deportations see Passat, 1994; Gur'ianov 1997b; for the Baltic deportations see Gur'ianov 1997b; Zemskov 1993; Vitkovskii and Iampol'skii 1990. According to Gur'ianov (1997b), whose analysis is impressively scrupulous, the total numbers deported were:

Estonia 6,300, Latvia 10,400, Lithuania 12,800, Moldova 25,700. The total number arrested as part of these operations was: Estonia 3,700, Latvia 5,300, Lithuania 4,700, Moldova 4,700.

9. This ratio would appear to be roughly similar to the epoch of dekulakization in the USSR proper, although reliable statistics are not available. From 1930 to 1933, 2.1 million were deported to special settlements, and presumably a small number were administratively exiled as well. According to Popov (1992), the OGPU arrested and convicted 770,000 in the same time period, the majority of whom were not charged as kulaks. A similar ratio prevailed during the May–June 1941 deportations from the Baltics and Moldova, with about 55,200 deported and 18,400 incarcerated in concentration camps, an exact 3:1 ratio.

10. This chapter does not deal with several small deportations in the post-war period. Several thousand Jehovah's Witnesses were deported from the western borderlands (Zemskov 1993: 5; Passat 1994: 591–637) as well as over a thousand members of the "True Orthodox Church" from central regions of the USSR (Zemskov 1991a: 155). As far as I am aware, these were the first exclusively religion-based mass deportations, although it would not be surprising to find some small pre-war examples. Both were seen as dangerous "sects" and these can be best categorized as Social Disorder deportations. In 1951, there was an enigmatic deportation of 3,000 "Basmachi" from Tajikistan to Kazakhstan (Bugai 1995: 244–245). Bugai does not provide a description of this category. The "Basmachi" were a Central Asian anti-Bolshevik guerilla movement, most active during the Civil War but not entirely suppressed until 1934 (Hayit 1992). It is not clear if these were former Basmachi, or part of some revived guerilla movement. If the former, their deportation at this late date is striking evidence of the great Soviet concern over peripheral guerilla nationalist movements, as they faced difficult guerilla warfare in western Ukraine and Lithuania. A final, larger deportation category only awkwardly fits the mass deportation category. Throughout 1948, 38,485 individuals (counting family members) were deported from collective farms for "parasitism" or more formally for failing to work a sufficient number of work-days on the collective farm (Bugai 1995: 235). On the one hand, these were all individual deportations and so functioned more like the routine removal of former criminals from major cities. On the other hand, this was a concerted large-scale campaign and the individuals were not simply administratively exiled, but were classified as special settlers and treated as a distinct contingent. In any case, this would clearly fit the Social Disorder deportation category.

11. Although it is true that the Balkars and the Karachai are the only two Turkic peoples of that region with their own national territories (Conquest 1977: 11).

References

Alieva, S. U., ed. 1993. *Tak eto bylo. Natsional'nye repressii v SSSR, 1919–1952 gody.* 3 vols. Moscow: Insan.

Beissinger, Mark. 1995. "The Persisting Ambiguity of Empire." *Post-Soviet Affairs* 11: 149–184.

Belkovets, L. 1999. "Spetsposelenie nemtsev v Zapadnoi Sibiri (1941–1955 gg.)." In *Nakazannyi narod. Repressii protiv rossiiskikh nemtsev.* Moscow: Zven'ia.

Bilas, Ivan. 1994a. *Represyvno-karal'na systema v Ukraini, 1917–1953. Suspil'no-politychnyi ta istoryko-pravovyi analiz.* Vol. 1. Kiev: Lybid'—Viis'ko Ukrainy.

———. 1994b. *Represyvno-karal'na systema v Ukraini, 1917–1953. Suspil'no-politychnyi ta istoryko-pravovyi analiz.* Vol. 2. Kiev: Lybid'—Viis'ko Ukrainy.

Brul', V. 1999. "Deportirovannye narody v Sibiri (1935–1965 gg.). Sravnitel'nyi analiz." In *Nakazannyi narod. Repressii protiv rossiiskikh nemtsev.* Moscow: Zven'ia.

Brzezinski, Zbigniew. 1956. *The Permanent Purge: Politics in Soviet Totalitarianism.* Cambridge, MA: Harvard University Press.

Bugai, N. F., ed. 1992a. *Iosif Stalin – Lavrentiiu Beriia. "Ikh nado deportirovat'…" Dokumenty, fakty, kommentarii.* Moscow: Druzhba Narodov.

Bugai, N. F. 1992b. "20-40-e gody. Deportatsiia naseleniia s territorii Evropeiskoi Rossii." *Otechestvennaia istoriia* 4: 37–49.

———. 1993. "Kazaki." *Shpion* 1: 40–55.

———, ed. 1994a. *Repressirovannye narody Rossii. Chechentsy i Ingushi.* Moscow: Kap'.

———. 1994b. *Turki iz Meskhetii. Dolgii put' k reabilitatsii (1944–1994).* Moscow: Izd. Dom Ross.

———. 1995. *L. Beriia – I. Stalinu. "Soglasno Vashemu ukazaniiu …"* Moscow: AIRO XX.

———. 1999. "Avtonomiia nemtsev Povolzh'ia: problemy destrukturirovaniia i sotsial'noi naturalizatsii." In *Nakazannyi narod. Repressii protiv rossiiskikh nemtsev.* Moscow: Zven'ia.

Bugai, N. F., and A. M. Gonov. 1998. *Kavkaz. Narody v eshelonakh (20-60-e gody).* Moscow: Insan.

Burds, Jeffrey. 1997. "AGENTURA: Soviet Informants' Networks and the Ukrainian Underground in Galicia, 1944–48." *East European Politics and Societies* 11: 89–130.

Conquest, Robert. 1977. *The Nation Killers: The Soviet Deportation of Nationalities.* London: Macmillan.

———. 1990. *The Great Terror: A Reassessment.* New York: Oxford University Press.

Danilov, Viktor, and Alexis Berelowitch. 1994. "Les documents de la VCK-OGPU-NKVD sur la campagne sovietique, 1918–1937." *Cahiers du monde russe* 35: 633–682.

Demko, George. 1969. *The Russian Colonization of Kazakhstan, 1896–1916.* Bloomington: Indiana University Press.

Dunlop, John. 1998. *Russia Confronts Chechnya: Roots of a Separatist Conflict.* Cambridge: Cambridge University Press.

Eisfeld, A., and V. Herdt, eds. 1996. *Deportation, Sondersiedlung, Arbeitsarmee. Deutsche in der Sowjetunion, 1941 bis 1956.* Cologne: Verlag Wissenschaft und Politik.

Fisher, Alan. 1978. *The Crimean Tatars*. Stanford: Stanford University Press.
———. 1987. "Emigration of Muslims from the Russian Empire in the Years after the Crimean War." *Jahrbuecher fuer Geschichte Osteuropas* 35: 356–371.
Gelb, Michael. 1996. "The Western Finnic Minorities and the Origins of the Stalinist Nationalities Deportations." *Nationalities Papers* 24: 237–268.
Gellner, Ernest. 1983. *Nations and Nationalism*. Ithaca, NY: Cornell University Press.
Genis, V. L. 1998. "Deportatsiia russkikh iz Turkestana v 1921 godu ('Delo Safarova')." *Voprosy istorii* 1: 44–58.
Getty, J. Arch. 1985. *The Origins of the Great Purges*. Cambridge: Cambridge University Press.
Getty, J. Arch, Gabor Rittersporn, and Viktor Zemskov. 1993. "Victims of the Soviet Penal System in the Pre-war Years: A First Approach on the Basis of Archival Evidence." *American Historical Review* 98: 1017–1049.
Gorlanov, O. A., and A. B. Roginskii. 1997. "Ob arestakh v zapadnykh oblastiakh Belorussii i Ukrainy v 1939–1941 gg." In *Repressii protiv poliakov i pol'skikh grazhdan*. Moscow: Zven'ia.
Gur'ianov, A. E. 1997a. "Pol'skie spetspereselentsy v SSSR v 1940–1941 gg." In *Repressii protiv poliakov i pol'skikh grazhdan*. Moscow: Zven'ia.
———. 1997b. "Masshtaby deportatsii naseleniia v glub' SSSR v mae-iiune 1941 g." In *Repressii protiv poliakov i pol'skikh grazhdan*. Moscow: Zven'ia.
Hagenloh, Paul. 1999. "Police, Crime, and Public Order in Stalin's Russia, 1930–1941." Ph.D. diss., University of Texas, Austin.
———. 2000. "'Socially Harmful Elements' and the Great Terror." In Sheila Fitzpatrick, ed. *Stalinism: New Directions*. New York: Routledge.
Harris, James. 1997. "The Growth of the Gulag: Forced Labor in the Urals Region, 1929–31." *Russian Review* 56: 265–280.
Hayit, Baymirza. 1992. *"Basmatschi." Nationaler Kampf Turkestans in den Jahren 1917 bis 1934*. Cologne: Dreisam Verlag.
Holquist, Peter. 1997. "'Conduct Merciless Mass Terror': Decossackization on the Don, 1919." *Cahiers du monde russe* 38: 127–162.
Human Rights Watch, Russia. 1996. *The Ingush-Ossetian Conflict in the Prigorodnyi Region*. New York: Human Rights Watch.
Ivnitskii, N. A. 1996. *Kollektivizatsiia i raskulachivanie, nachalo 30-kh gg.* Moscow: Izd-vo Magistr.
Kaiser, Robert. 1994. *The Geography of Nationalism in Russia and the USSR*. Princeton: Princeton University Press.
Khe, Li U, and Dim En Un. 1992. *Belaia Kniga o deportatsii koreiskogo naseleniia Rossii v 30-40-kh godakh*. Moscow: Interpraks.
Khlevniuk, O. V. 1996. *Politbiuro. Mekhanizmy politicheskoi vlasti v 1930-e gody*. Moscow: Rosspen.
Kolstoe, Paul. 1995. *Russians in the Former Soviet Republics*. Bloomington: Indiana University Press.
Kordan, Bohdan. 1997. "Making Borders Stick: Population Transfer and Resettlement in the Trans-Curzon Territories, 1944–1949." *International Migration Review* 31: 704–720.
Kozlov, V. A. 1999. *Massovye besporiadki v SSSR pri Khrushcheve i Brezhneve (1953 – nach. 1980-kh gg.)*. Novosibirsk: Sibirskii khronograf.
Krasil'nikov, S. A., et al., eds. 1992. *Spetspereselentsy v Zapadnoi Sibiri, 1930 – vesna 1931 goda*. Novosibirsk: Nauka.

———. 1993. *Spetspereselentsy v Zapadnoi Sibiri, vesna 1931 goda – nachalo 1933 goda*. Novosibirsk: Ekor.

———. 1994. *Spetspereselentsy v Zapadnoi Sibiri, 1933 – 1938*. Novosibirsk: Ekor.

———. 1996. *Spetspereselentsy v Zapadnoi Sibiri, 1939 – 1945*. Novosibirsk: Ekor.

Kreindler, Isabelle. 1985. *The Soviet Deported Nationalities: A Summary and an Update*. Jerusalem: Hebrew University of Jerusalem, Soviet and East European Research Centre.

Lewis, Robert, Richard Rowland, and Ralph Clem. 1977. *Nationality and Population Change in Russia and the USSR: An Evaluation of Census Data, 1897–1970*. New York: Praeger.

Lieven, Anatol. 1998. *Chechnya: Tombstone of Russian Power*. New Haven: Yale University Press.

Lohr, Eric. 1999. "Enemy Alien Policies within the Russian Empire During World War I." Ph.D. diss., Harvard University.

Maclean, Fitzroy. 1949. *Eastern Approaches*. New York: J. Cape.

Maksheev, V. N., ed. 1997. *Narymskaia khronika*. Moscow: Russkii put'.

Martin, Terry. 1996. "An Affirmative Action Empire: Ethnicity and the Soviet State, 1923–1938" Ph.D. diss., University of Chicago.

———. 1998a. "The Origins of Soviet Ethnic Cleansing." *The Journal of Modern History* 70: 813–861.

———. 1998b. "The Russification of the RSFSR." *Cahiers du monde russe* 39: 99–118.

Matley, Ian. 1979. "The Dispersal of the Ingrian Finns." *Slavic Review* 38: 1–16.

Mel'gunov, S. P. 1989. *Krasnyi Terror v Rossii, 1918–1923*. New York: Izd-vo Brandy.

Milova, O. L., ed. 1992. *Deportatsii narodov SSSR (1930-e – 1950-e gody)*. Vol. 1. Moscow: Institut etnologii i etnicheskoi antropologii RAN.

———. 1995. *Deportatsii narodov SSSR (1930-e – 1950-e gody). Deportatsiia nemtsev (sentiabr' 1941 – fevral' 1942 gg.)* Vol. 2. Moscow: Institut etnologii i etnicheskoi antropologii RAN.

Misilo, Eugeniusz. 1993. *Akcja "Wisla". Dokumenty*. Warsaw: Archiwum Ukrainskie.

Moins, Nathalie. 1997. "Passeportisation, statistique des migrations et controle de l'identite sociale," *Cahiers du monde russe* 38: 587–600.

Moore, Barrington. 1954. *Terror and Progress USSR: Some Sources of Change and Stability in the Soviet Dictatorship*. Cambridge, MA: Harvard University Press.

Nekrich, Aleksandr. 1978. *The Punished Peoples: The Deportation and Fate of Soviet Minorities at the End of the Second World War*. New York: Norton.

Okhotin, N., and A. Roginskii. 1999. "Iz istorii 'nemetskoi operatsii' NKVD 1937–1938 gg." In *Nakazannyi narod. Repressii protiv rossiiskikh nemtsev*. Moscow: Zven'ia.

Passat, V. I., ed. 1994. *Trudnye stranitsy istorii Moldovy, 1940–1950*. Moscow: Terra-Terra.

Petrov, N. V., and A. B. Roginskii. 1997. "'Pol'skaia operatsiia' NKVD 1937–1938 gg." In *Repressii protiv poliakov i pol'skikh grazhdan*. Moscow: Zven'ia.

Pohl, J. Otto. 1996. *The Stalinist Penal System: A Statistical History of Soviet Repression and Terror*. Jefferson, NC: McFarland.

Polian, P. M. 1996. *Zhertvy dvukh diktatur. Voennoplennye i ostarbaitery v Tret'em Reikhe i ikh repatriatsiia*. Moscow: Vash vybor TSIRZ.

Popov, V. P. 1992. "Gosudarstvennyi terror v sovetskoi Rossii, 1923–1953 gg. Istochniki i ikh interpretatsiia." *Otechestvennye arkhivy* 2: 20–31.

Rittersporn, Gabor. 1991. *Stalinist Simplifications and Soviet Complications: Social Tensions and Political Conflicts in the USSR, 1935–1953.* New York: Harwood Academic Publishers.

Saar, Ellu, and Mark Titma. 1992. *Migrationsstroeme im sowjetisierten Baltikum und ihre Nachwirkung auf die baltischen Staaten nach Widerherstelung der Selbstaendigkeit.* Cologne: Bundesinstitut für Ostwissenschaftliche und Internationale Studien.

Sakkeus, Luule. 1993. *Post-War Migration Trends in the Baltic States.* Tallinn: Estonian Interuniversity Population Research Centre.

Schectman, Joseph. 1962. *Postwar Population Transfers in Europe, 1945–1955.* Philadelphia: University of Pennsylvania Press.

Sevost'ianov, G. N., A. N. Sakharov, and Ia. F. Pogonii, eds. N.d. *"Sovershenno Sekretno:" Lubianka. Stalinu o polozhenii v strane. 1924 god.* Moscow (forthcoming).

Shearer, David. 1998. "Crime and Social Disorder in Stalin's Russia: A Reassessment of the Great Retreat and the Origins of Mass Repression." *Cahiers du monde russe* 39: 119–148.

Simon, Gerhard. 1991. *Nationalism and Policy Toward the Nationalities in the Soviet Union.* Boulder, CO: Westview Press.

Slyvka, Iu., ed. 1996. *Deportatsii zakhidni zemli Ukrainy kintsa 30-kh—pochatku 50-kh rr. Dokumenty, Materialy, Spohady. Vol. 1, 1939–1945.* Lvov: In-t ukrainoznavstva NAN Ukrainy.

Titma, Mark, and Nancy Tuma. 1992. *Migration in the Former Soviet Union.* Cologne: Bundesinstitut für Ostwissenschaftliche und Internationale Studien.

Tsutsiev, A. A. 1998. *Osetino-ingushskii konflikt (1992–…). Ego predystoriia i faktory razvitiia.* Moscow: Rosspen.

Viola, Lynne. 2000. "The Role of the OGPU in Dekulakization, Mass Deportations, and Special Resettlement in 1930." Pittsburgh: Center for Russian and East European Studies, University of Pittsburgh.

Vitkovskii, A and V. Iampol'skii. 1990. "Vchera eto bylo sekretom. Dokumenty o Litovskikh sobytiiakh 40-50-kh gg." *Izvestiia TsK KPSS* 10: 129–319.

Zemskov, V. N. 1990a. "'Kulatskaia ssylka' v 30-e gody." *Sotsiologicheskie issledovaniia* 10: 3–21.

———. 1990b. "Spetsposelentsy (po dokumentam NKVD-MVD SSSR)." *Sotsiologicheskie issledovaniia* 11: 3–17.

———. 1991a. "Massovoe osvobozhdenie spetsposelentsev i ssylnykh (1954–1960)." *Sotsiologicheskie issledovaniia* 1: 5–26.

———. 1991b. "Zakliuchennye, spetsposelentsy, ssyl'noposelentsy, ssylnye i vyslannye (statistiko-geograficheskii aspekt)." *Sotsiologicheskie issledovaniia* 5: 151–165.

———. 1993. "Prinuditel'nye migratsii iz Pribaltiki v 1940–1950-kh godakh." *Otechestvennaia istoriia* 1: 4–19.

———. 1994. "Sud'ba 'kulatskoi ssylki' (1930–1954 gg.)." *Otechestvennaia istoriia* 1: 118–147.

Ziemer, Gerhard. 1973. *Deutscher Exodus. Vertreibung und Eingliederung von 15 Millionen Ostdeutschen.* Stuttgart: Seewald.

INDEX

Studies in Forced Migration
General Editors: **Dawn Chatty** and **Chaloka Beyani**

Volume 8

FEAR IN BONGOLAND
Burundi Refugees in Urban Tanzania

Marc Sommers, Boston University

This volume, the first full-length study of urban refugees in hiding, tells the story of Burundi refugee youth who escaped from remote camps in central Tanzania to work in one of Africa's fastest-growing cities, Dar es Salaam. This steamy, rundown capital would seem uninviting to many, particularly for second generation survivors of genocide whose lives are ridden with fear. But these young men nonetheless join migrants in "Bongoland" (meaning "Brainland") where, as the nickname suggests, only the shrewdest and most cunning can survive.

Mixing lyrics from church hymns and street vernacular, descriptions of city living in cartoons and popular novels and original photographs, this book creates an ethnographic portrait of urban refugee life, where survival strategies spring from street smarts and pastors' warnings of urban sin, and mastery of popular youth culture is highly valued. Written in accessible prose, this book offers an intimate picture of how Africa is changing and how refugee youth are helping to drive that change.

"...skillfully weaves the tapestry of fear and resourcefulness, religion and politics, survival and loss, that make up the lives of Burundi refugees in urban Tanzania... In showing some of the divisions within the Burundi refugee community... provides a welcome corrective to the totalizing ethnic categories that dominate so much of the writing on the Great Lakes region." —Peter Uvin, author of the 1999 Herskovits Award Winner *Aiding Violence: The Development Enterprise in Rwanda*

"This finely-crafted ethnography gives us a powerful sense of what it must be like to be caught in the net of political control and social obligation, and yet through hard work, luck or concentration, to open a hole in the net and wriggle free... Highly recommended." —Paul Richards, author of *Fighting for the Rain Forest*

"...innovative and pioneering research [that] contributes immensely to our understanding of African refugees and...to our knowledge about self-settled urban African refugees." —Art Hansen, from the Foreword

Summer 2001, 240 pages, 7 photos, 4 ills., 3 maps, bibliog., index
ISBN 1-57181-263-6 hardback ca. **$59.95/£40.00**
ISBN 1-57181-331-4 paperback ca. **$22.50/£15.00**

www.berghahnbooks.com

Studies in Forced Migration

General Editors: **Dawn Chatty** and **Chaloka Beyani**

Volume 9

WHATEVER HAPPENED TO ASYLUM IN BRITAIN?

A Tale of Two Walls

Louise Pirouet

Refugees and asylum-seekers are high up on many people's political agenda. Even so, there is a remarkable lack of information. Who are these asylum-seekers? Aren't they almost all "bogus"? How do Western immigration authorities decide whether or not they are genuine? Is the UN convention on Refugees out of date and in need of renegotiation?

This book brings insider knowledge to the study of asylum in Britain today. It is based on visits to places where asylum-seekers are detained, on working with lawyers representing asylum-seekers, and on a close knowledge of many of the refugee organizations. It argues passionately that Britain shall not throw away, through ignorance and misunderstanding, a reputation for providing a place of safety for the persecuted, and the chance of welcoming people who have much to contribute to national life and culture.

Louis Pirouet has been involved with refugee concerns for many years both in Africa and Britain. She is a trustee of Asylum Aid, helps to run a group in Cambridge that works for safeguards for asylum-seekers held at a detention center near Cambridge, and assists Kenyans and Ugandans appealing against refusal of asylum.

Spring 2001, ca. 208 pages, bibliog., index
ISBN 1-57181-991-6 hardback ca. **$59.95/£40.00**
ISBN 1-57181-468-X paperback ca. **$19.95/£13.50**

www.berghahnbooks.com

Studies in Forced Migration

General Editors: **Dawn Chatty** and **Chaloka Beyani**

Volume 10

DISPLACEMENT, FORCED SETTLEMENT, AND CONSERVATION

Edited by **Dawn Chatty** and **Marcus Colchester**

Wildlife conservation and other environmental protection projects can have tremendous impact on the lives and livelihoods of the often mobile, difficult-to-reach, and marginal peoples who inhabit the same territory. The contributors to this collection of case studies—social scientists as well as natural scientists—are concerned with this human element in biodiversity. They examine the interface between conservation and indigenous communities forced to move or to settle elsewhere in order to accommodate environmental policies and biodiversity concerns.

The case studies investigate successful and not so successful community-managed, as well as local participatory, conservation projects in Africa, the Middle East, South and Southeast Asia, Australia, and Latin America. There are lessons to be learned from recent efforts in community-managed conservation, and this volume significantly contributes to that discussion.

Dawn Chatty is General Editor of Studies in Forced Migration and teaches at the Center for Refugee Studies of the University of Oxford. **Marcus Colchester** works for the Forest Peoples Programme.

Winter 2001/02, ca. 304 pages, bibliog., index
ISBN 1-57181-841-3 hardback ca. **$69.96/47.00**
ISBN 1-57181-842-1 paperback ca. **$25.00/£17.00**

www.berghahnbooks.com